# MUSLIM FAMILIES IN NORTH AMERICA

# MUSLIM FAMILIES
# IN NORTH AMERICA

Edited by

*Earle H. Waugh*
*Sharon McIrvin Abu-Laban*
*Regula Burckhardt Qureshi*

THE UNIVERSITY OF ALBERTA PRESS

First published by
The University of Alberta Press
141 Athabasca Hall
Edmonton, Alberta
Canada T6G 2E8
1991

ISBN 0-88864-225-3

**Canadian Cataloguing in Publication Data**

Main entry under title:
Muslim families in North America

Includes bibliographical references and index.
ISBN 0-88864-225-3

1. Muslims—Canada. 2. Muslims—United States.
3. Family—Canada—Religious life. I. Waugh, Earle
H., 1936–      II. Abu-Laban, Sharon McIrvin.
III. Qureshi, Regula Burckhardt.
E29.M87M88 1991      305.6'971'071      C90-091727-X

Typeset by The Typeworks, Vancouver, B.C., Canada

Printed by John Deyell Company, Lindsay, Ontario, Canada

◆ The publisher acknowledges with gratitude the financial assistance received from the Alberta Foundation for the Literary Arts towards production costs and from Alberta Culture and Multiculturalism for the cost of editing.

# Contents

# Preface

On 21 August 1982, the new al-Rashid Mosque and Education Centre was officially opened in Edmonton, Alberta. A tense but revealing confrontation took place at the opening ceremony between two influential leaders, the provincial premier Peter Lougheed and Dr. Ismail al-Faruqi, an internationally renowned Temple University Islamic scholar. Each speaker focused on issues relating to the state of the family in North America; each gave a different assessment.

Dr. al-Faruqi characterized the North American family as deficient, typified by shallow values, decay, divorce, and child neglect. In his view, the solution to the plight of the North American family could be found in the dynamic role of the mosque, vigorously promoting revitalized Islamic values. An irate Premier Lougheed took exception to Dr. al-Faruqi's characterization of the North American family and its possible demise, by energetically defending the strength, morality, and viability of contemporary family life, particularly as demonstrated in the province of Alberta.

This confrontation between political leader and religious scholar echoed a familiar theme, both historically and cross-culturally. The status of entire civilizations has often been linked to foundations in the family, in the conviction that strong families produce superior citizens and societies. The dispute between the two men was revealing in several ways: it reflected the new importance of the Muslim family in North America; it also showed that the Muslim presence as outlined by al-Faruqi may not be one of traditional minority accommodation but a challenge to *change* North America; and it suggested that the impact and implications of Islam in North America might be better understood by examining Muslim family life. In this way, it provided a partial catalyst for this book.

There is a tragic irony in this book. Although some of its inspiration was derived from the work of both Ismail and Lois Lamiya Ibsen al-Faruqi (also an academician) and the al-Faruqi's had indicated their personal interest in contributing to this book, their lives were brutally cut short in 1986 by an assassin who invaded their Philadelphia home.

vii

Their survivors include five children. This tragedy has touched many people, both specialists in the study of Islam and Muslims generally, who mourn the loss of these fine people and honour their work among us. Those of us who knew the al-Faruqi's personally knew the sincerity and depth of their conviction that the Islamic tradition could improve the lives of North American families and bring them closer to the ways of God. It is our hope that the work of the scholars represented in this collection will contribute to a broader understanding of Islam, its role in the lives of its practitioners, its significance for Muslim family life and its impact on North American society.

# Contributors

SHARON MCIRVIN ABU-LABAN, Ph.D. is a professor of Sociology at the University of Alberta, Edmonton, specializing in Social Differentiation, Comparative Family, International Development, and Religion and Belief Systems.

NA'IM AKBAR, Ph.D. is a professor of Psychology at Florida State University, Tallahassee, Florida and Director of Mind Productions and Associates, Inc.; Dr. Akbar is a member of the African-American Muslim community.

BARBARA C. ASWAD, Ph.D. is a professor of Anthropology at Wayne State University, Detroit, Michigan and specializes in research on Arab village life, Arab-American communities, and Arab women in both the Middle East and the United States.

NIMAT HAFEZ BARAZANGI, Ph.D. specializes in the education of cultural minorities and Arab Muslim cultural adaptation. Currently she is designing an action plan for Islamic education in North America based on findings from her Ph.D. dissertation.

ILYAS BA-YUNUS, Ph.D. is a professor of Sociology and Anthropology at the State University College at Cortland, New York and specializes in Immigrant Groups and Anthropology of Religion.

LOUISE CAINKAR, Ph.D. is a sociologist and Director of the Chicago-based Palestine Human Rights Information Centre-International. Her specializations include Immigrant Communities and Sociology of Gender.

W. MURRAY HOGBEN, Ph.D. is a historian, teaches at the college militaire royal de Saint-Jean in Saint-Jean, Quebec, and is a journalist with *The Whig-Standard*, Kingston, Ontario. A convert to Islam, Dr. Hogben has been active in Muslim organizations for over thirty years.

Azim Nanji, Ph.D. is a professor of Religious Studies at Oklahoma State University, Stillwater, Oklahoma, and specializes in Islam, Ismaili Tradition and History of Religion.

Regula Burckhardt Qureshi, Ph.D. received her doctorate in Anthropology and is a professor of Music at the University of Alberta. Professor Qureshi's specializations include Ethnomusicology, Cultural Anthropology and Islamic Studies.

Saleem M.M. Qureshi, Ph.D. is a professor of Political Science at the University of Alberta, Edmonton and specializes in Pakistan Political History, Islamic Governments, and Islamic Political Theory.

Fariyal Ross-Sheriff, Ph.D. is a professor of Religion at Oklahoma State University, Stillwater, Oklahoma and specializes in Islamic Groups, North American Islam, and Women and Islam.

Vernon James Schubel, Ph.D. is a professor in the Department of Religion at Kenyan College, Gambier, Ohio and specializes in Islam, Shi'a Religious History, and Religion and Culture.

Marilyn Robinson Waldman, Ph.D. is a professor of Religion and past Dean of Humanities at Ohio State University and specializes in Islamic History, Religion and Methodology, and Tradition and Culture.

Earle H. Waugh, Ph.D. is a professor of Religious Studies and Chair of the Canadian Studies Program at the University of Alberta. He specializes in Islam, Religion in Canada, and Contemporary Religious Issues.

# Introduction

◆  ◆  ◆  ◆

Islam is now the third largest world religion in North America; the number of its adherents has grown phenomenally as a result of fertility, immigration, intermarriage and proselytization. This increased presence of Islam has contributed to important changes in both the religious and family climate in North American society. Across cultures, family and religion reinforce one another, serving as centers for personal identity and a sense of belonging (Hargrove, 1983). To understand Islam and Canadian and American Muslims better and to explain Islamic traditions and the family lives of believers, it is necessary to examine their interactive relationship. This is the rationale for this collection.

Many long-standing difficulties militate against an adequate understanding of Muslim families. For example, the North American media and often, Western scholarship describe and interpret Islam and Muslims as "other," "non-us," or "them." Islam is held up as an "alien" religion against an idealized, ahistorical Judeo-Christian mirror. In this distorted view the relationship between religious codes and family life may be particularly suspect. Family practices are associated with images of gender oppression, multiple marriage, seclusion, and subordination; and thus they are judged but not understood. Such views, informed by established preconceptions, give a distorted view of "the" Muslim family —a story told at a slant.

Anwar Abdel-Malek (1963) and Edward Said (1978), among others, have observed that there is a discernible "orientalist" bias in much of the research on Eastern peoples and Islam that assumes not only a stagnant orient but also a dramatic hierarchical demarcation between East and West—with Western values always on the top. One result of this perspective is that Islam and Muslims are

...stamped with an otherness—as all that is different, whether it be "subject" or "object"—but of a constitutive otherness, of an essentialist character.... This "object" of study will be, as is customary, passive, non-participating, endowed with a "historical" subjectivity, above all, non-active, non-autonomous, non-sovereign with regard to itself. (Abdel-Malek, 1963:107-8)

Nor can we factor out the sense of difference that Muslims encounter every time a news report identifies a crisis *as Muslim* somewhere in the world. Given the largely negative connotation of much media reportage, North American Muslims may feel defensive *just because they are Muslim*. We have tried to avoid these conceptual traps by including in this volume the inside views of committed believers, as well as more conventional academic analyses.

The religious domain inheres in a complex, apparently seamless world. Those who are Muslims are sometimes immigrants and they may hold important ethnic identifications. But analyses that focused only on immigrants, would ignore the reality of African-American Islam, the Islam of the convert to the tradition from among the population at large, and the Islam of the younger generation that knows nothing of a foreign country and the immigrant experience. Similarly, while ethnicity might highlight a critical element in immigrant identity, alone it would be insufficient.

The strongly community-oriented nature of Islam gives a singular character to the interface of ethnicity and religion. A starting point is Levy's *The Social Structure of Islam* (1962) which switches from an attempt to isolate general Islamic principles to particulars of local Muslim communities; today, Muslim academics are adding new dimensions to scholarship and providing the beginnings of a growing discourse across the disciplines among students of contemporary Islam. Some of these are represented here.

Muslim families in North America operate in a socio-cultural environment with three primary domains that relate to each other through both commonalities and contradictions. The first domain is the universal ideology of Islam as presented in texts and interpretations, the second is the particular Muslim ethno-cultural identities, and the third is the larger North American society. Many of the key issues in these domains are canvassed in Section I: Muslim Normative Traditions and the North American Environment, particularly in the article by Saleem Qureshi. But throughout this book, the interrelationship of these domains remains an underlying theme. It seems evident that the three domains are of varying importance for different Muslim groups, even though there appears to be a shared tendency among them for ethnocultural content to diminish as a component of Muslim identity and for there to be related shifts in degree of social cohesion. The study of this complex interactional whole is made more difficult because each domain has its own historically-shaped character, by which its study has become linked to particular disciplinary orientations (Waugh). Furthermore, all of these are not equally conducive to family analyses (Abu-Laban).

Second, Muslim families, like all other families, are situated in their respective ethno-cultural matrices, whether they are recent immigrants or North-American converts. How such families operate in their particular cultural matrix has much to do with their adaptation in the North American environment; thus, families that are highly integrated into the endogamous, kinship-based units of a stratified society make it a social priority to proceed to build analogous social units in North America. Muslims from South Asia are examples of this tendency as the contributions by Ross-Sheriff and Nanji and by Regula Qureshi show in a variety of ways. They also reach out extensively to the homeland for many kinds of social and cultural reinforcements. Their very pervasive social control over the individual is a powerful defense mechanism against the potentially destructuring effects of their exposure to the non-Muslim host society.

Religious ritual has an important role in strengthening this socio-cultural identity; conversely, shared social identity is a nurturing soil for the cultivation of religious observances. Both facets of this relationship become clear in the chapter by Schubel. In addition, the particularly strong identification between socio-cultural background and religion that exists among Muslims of Arab origin is strengthened by the increased economic power and political importance of Arab nations. Morever, the recent rise of an international Islamic movement has regenerated the conception of Islam as a portable way of life, abstracted from any specific socio-cultural matrix. This latter aspect, along with the organizational strength of the movement in North America, has generated a strong sense of the force of Islam which holds up to North

American Muslim families a model based on traditional religious ideals. In particular, this movement enables Muslims socialized in the United States and Canada to follow Islam as members of the North American commonality, rather than only as members of a particular minority group. But the movement affects Muslim ethno-cultural groups as well, leading them to greater confidence in the use of religious practices and symbols affecting the family. This new consciousness is especially significant for Muslim families of North American origin, as is shown by Akbar, but affects other groups as well, as is seen in the studies of Abu-Laban and Barazangi. While the Islamic movement gives Muslims a broader perspective on their place within the North American whole it also tends to create a sense of opposition to that social universe. The role of women is often a flash-point for this sense of opposition; indeed, conflict and ambiguity are continuing themes as the studies of Aswad, Cainkar, and Waldman show.

The growing literature situating ethnic families within the North American host society helps establish a common basis for the family experience of the culturally different (Harrison et al., 1984). But Muslims have yet to find a place within that literature, and their parallels to and divergences from the pattern have not yet been identified. That the dynamic of interfacing with that society is many-faceted and not unproblematic is shown by this entire collection, particularly the chapters by Hogben, Akbar, and Ba-Yunus.

This work reflects the multidisciplinary nature of contemporary research. Sociologists, anthropologists, historians of religion, political scientists, psychologists, and others are represented in this collection. In a number of important ways, the contributors are breaking new ground. We hope this work will encourage and stimulate others to initiate research into the lacunae revealed.

We have also been concerned that voices *inside* the tradition be heard since a conventional framework may mute the voice of the people studied. It is our hope that the complementary perspectives adopted in this volume on Muslim families in North America will provide insight into the family as a religious and social institution and the nature of the encounter between Muslim family forms and the larger North American society.

# Part One

## Muslim Normative Traditions and the North American Environment

◆　◆　◆　◆

◆　◆　◆　◆

Like all great religious traditions, Islam has manifested itself in a diversity of forms. Social, cultural, and intellectual dimensions relate to the norms and standards of the religion both historically and structurally, developing a rich tapestry of achievement. In this section, three studies articulate the primary boundary markers with which the Muslim family in North America must operate: first, Abu-Laban describes the link forged between the sacred tradition and the various Muslim populations during their immigration to North America; then Saleem Qureshi examines the ideals established by Sacred Writ and its interpretation in the so-called orthodox literate tradition; and finally, Earle Waugh deals with the complex relationship of religion and ethnicity as it has been experienced by Muslim families in the process of adaptation to the North American situation.

A number of themes are explored by these articles that join them at important points. A primary focus is the way religion is mediated to the believer. Because of its nature, Islam has not developed uniformly. But it has, at all times, insisted on the essential superiority of the religious vision it provided for humanity. This is not a naive self-confidence derived from Islam's success in building major empires, although it certainly has done that. Rather, Islam contends that humans cannot be left on their own to develop social systems, that God is a key ingredient in instituting and maintaining an acceptable political structure, and that the model drawn from scripture and put into play from the time of the Prophet has been immensely successful in promoting excellent human values. Thus, whatever formulation is given for the human situation, Muslim experience has always been judged to be under the beneficent hand of deity. Relatedness to God not only involves participation in the great Muslim community, the *umma*, but also God's presence is mediated in some sense to the believer through its forms and directives. Examples of these truths are replete in the articles: Abu-Laban's differentiated cohort of immigrants, facing prejudice and social alienation, have responded by reaching into their religion for sustenance and community, so that the family becomes the focal point for increasing Islamic awareness and strengthening self-identity. Waugh, on the other hand, points out that there are strong social and cultural pressures for maintaining an ethnic orientation to Islam. Especially in Canada, with its official policy of multiculturalism, ethnic identity becomes an acceptable means of maintaining distinctiveness, and thus ethnicity may be retained as a vehicle for strengthening religious convictions in a culturally acceptable manner.

The abidingness of the Muslim life derives from the forms instituted. Of prime place in any list of essential Muslim contributions to the world must be the law. Islamic law has been hegemonic from the beginning; responsibilities and ethical requirements seem to have been introduced almost from the first sura of the Qur'an. Saleem Qureshi stresses the traditional codes that made up this ethical package. The emphasis on action, the orientation to doing God's will, propelled the early Muslim community towards law. Immigrants must deal with this thrust in adapting to North America. What if the ethical code violates laws in North America? Qureshi shows that interpretation has also played a role in the law, so that Muslim families who try to live according to rules from this hemisphere have a solid tradition of moderating the rules to the Muslim situation. Part of the agenda of reformers is to establish what they think is the proper interpretation of the traditional code for Muslims in today's world, and Muslims in Canada and the United States must adjust their vision of when and where the law should apply. This process of adaptation is sometimes dependent upon the host culture and its priorities, as Abu-Laban shows. And since it cannot be applied fully to the social environment in which Muslim families live, what should be applied, and how strictly? Waugh indicates that some of these issues have not been resolved.

Another cardinal area of concern is the relationship between religion and culture. Muslim families are diverse in their forms and cultural origins. They do not react to the dynamics of North American culture in any monolithic style. For some, the essence of their faith is religion, not culture. Qureshi's contribution focuses on this aspect. For others, the only way to retain their identity is to continue practices derived from the homeland. Waugh's paper surveys some of those reactions, as does Abu-Laban's. The important point is that culture is taken as a positive element in Muslim family life, even if some aspects of the host culture challenge traditional Muslim values. Thus, there are traditions within both Canada and the United States that mesh with the dominant Muslim concern for culture and allow Muslims to relate creatively to their environment. All of the contributions provide different perspectives on the tensions and reactions between the expectations and ideals of the Muslim family as it works out its meaning in an indifferent social setting.

Finally, all of the papers highlight the immense resources which can be drawn upon to establish acceptable Muslim family life. The strategies and assimilative techniques rest upon the Muslim confidence that the tradition can be successful in any environment and Abu-Laban underlines how these methods have shifted, formed, and reformulated under pressures of their environment. Muslim families in North America are still in the process of evolving, just as the larger North American setting is undergoing change. What is evident is that Islam will continue to provide a blueprint for a significant minority in Canada and the United States for the foreseeable future.

# Family and Religion among Muslim Immigrants and Their Descendants

## Sharon McIrvin Abu-Laban

◆　◆　◆　◆

For a growing number of Americans and Canadians, family orientations and practices are interwoven with Islamic traditions and
beliefs. The presence of Muslim families on the North American continent is relatively recent and includes new immigrants from diverse
cultural and linguistic backgrounds who are coping with a strange language, strange customs, and separation from their ancestral lands and
traditions; North American born converts; and, as well, second-,
third-, or fourth-generation descendants who have never ventured beyond North American shores. These families thus represent a diverse
span of generations, experiences and backgrounds, yet they all share a
socio-cultural milieu where English is the dominant language, Christianity the dominant religion, and Islam, the religion of their ancestors,
is frequently misunderstood and sometimes maligned (Said, 1978;
1981). Although Muslim families have been growing in number and
importance on this continent, they continue to be understudied
(Ghayur, 1981; Rashid, 1985).

Traditionally, both religion and family tend to be central to personal
identity and sense of social support (Hargrove, 1983). Both can be
guardians of heritage and elicit strong feelings of belongingness. Em-
pirically, this intermesh between religion and family appears to be

qualitatively important. Recent North American research attempting to identify the characteristics of "strong families" found two factors consistently present—religious orientation and family commitment (Stinnett et al., 1982). Religion can provide an ideological framework and a codified assurance of kinship reliability and empowerment. Larsen and Goltz (1988:80) state that a religious orientation gives family members "a sense of commitment and values oriented to the needs and welfare of others."

For immigrants to a new culture, the convergence of family and religion can ease adaptation or, conversely, strengthen resistance to assimilation. In times of major crisis, while family ties can be principal sources of support, religious faith seems to provide even further strength (McCubbin 1979). Thus where family and religion are in tandem, they mutually reinforce one another, not only facilitating the socialization of the young but also fortifying the continuing resocialization of adult family members. Religious belief can help maintain separate codes of honor, if necessary, codes that are distinct from those of the dominant culture. The power of divine justification can be used to sanction the interpersonal relations, rights, obligations, and ethics of families; kinship itself is placed in a framework of ultimate meaning.

Neither religion nor family operates in a vacuum, however. It will be argued that socio-historical factors affect the family-religion link and those that affect the first generation of Muslim immigrants can reverberate to subsequent generations. This study is based on census data; a re-examination of several scattered, sometimes conflicting studies done on Muslims in North America over the past twenty or so years; interviews; and extensive contact with this community over almost three decades. The chapter proposes an alternative way of looking at aberrations in data by using as an analytic device family types based on immigration cohort. It focuses on some of the commonalities and diversities among Muslim families by looking at three cohorts of Muslim immigrants in North America; their descendants; and the distinctive family patterns resulting from the dynamic interaction between social conditions and group characteristics. It will be argued that typically the dynamic between religion and family has been different for each group and its descendants, thereby affecting the forms of Muslim family in contemporary North America.

## ISLAMIC TEACHINGS ON THE FAMILY

Islam, as a major world religion, encompasses a range of socio-cultural manifestations and cultural identities. Some general understanding of broad family codes is necessary to an understanding of Muslim families in North America. The generalizations which follow are presented with a caveat; they are not intended to mask the reality of variation among the over one billion adherents of world-wide Islam, with their distinctive societies, laws, histories, experiences with foreign domination, ethnic, tribal, economic, geographical and educational differences. For Muslims, as for others, life is lived in context.

For Muslims religious teachings prescribe a number of family behaviors. These admonitions are based on sacred texts, the Qur'an (the holy book of Islam) and the Hadith (a collection of the sayings and teachings of Prophet Mohammad) and juridical opinions. Both the Qur'an and the Hadith deal with issues relating to the regulation of mate selection, marriage, children, divorce, authority, inheritance and family rights and responsibilities. Of the legal injunctions of the Qur'an, some one-third relate to marriage and the family (Islam, 1984). The tradition of juridical interpretation of the Qur'an and Hadith is highly developed. The *Sharicᵃ* (Islamic) courts rely on an all-embracing code of moral, ethical, criminal, and civil law developed by scholars and jurists and they have served a unique role in defining rights and responsibilities of family members. However, because there are different legal schools in Islam (Rahman, 1980), interpretations and theological positions can differ. Consequently variation in practice and legal reform can be found across Muslim societies.

Islamic teachings often emphasize the equality of all people; however there has been considerable variation in interpretations regarding the role of women. Women tend to be viewed as complementary to men, finding their fulfillment through association with their husbands, fathers, and children (Smith 1984). The family system, itself, is embedded in patriarchy. Interpretations that support male authority are common. However, from the beginning, the teachings of Prophet Mohammad, originating in early Arabia in 610 A.D., specified protections and rights for women which were radical departures from the existing culture. These included, for example, inheritance rights, property rights, marriage contracts, divorce, dowry, child custody, and *limitations* on polygyny (which was a practice without limits in pre-Islamic Arabia).

A recent study of Egyptian court records documents historic examples of women's rights under Islam. Tucker (1985) argues that nineteenth century Egyptian peasant women were empowered by their access to the *Shari'a* courts which guaranteed the implementation of Islamic principles spelling out the rights of women to inheritance, property, and the Mahr (bride price). Tucker's evidence suggests, in fact, that Egyptian Muslim women had more power *before* Europeanization and colonization than after.

With respect to contemporary Islam, El-Amin (1981:93) has observed:

> . . . a woman in Islam has her own individuality within the family. She does not bear the name of her husband or his family and can run her own financial matters without reference to him. However rich she may be, she can keep her wealth to herself and do with it whatever she likes. On the other hand, however poor her husband may be, he is obliged to provide her with all the necessities of life she was used to . . . (when she lived with her parents).

In practice the lives of contemporary Muslim women are variable and complex. They both have rights and are denied rights.

Marriage legitimates sexual relations. However, demands for chastity in the unmarried and fidelity in the married are more stringent for women than for men. The personal conduct of women tends to be seen as reflecting the honor and good name of their family as well as the status of their men. Fathers, husbands, and sons are often placed in protector/guardian roles, monitoring the conduct of daughters, wives, and sisters. Sex segregation, the physical separation of women from unrelated men is common, although to a varying degree. Both men and women are expected to be modest and dress in socially acceptable ways but the definitions of modesty differ by culture and are more exacting for women than for men. Dress codes for women often require concealing skirts or trousers, long sleeves, and sometimes complete or partial covering of the head and face. Until a few years ago, "veiling" practices were on the decline. More recently, starting in the 1970s, there has been a significant return to some kind of head covering for women, sometimes this has been a voluntary adoption, sometimes it has been imposed.

Given the tradition of sex segregation, women have tended not to participate in formal religious observances in mosques. However, evidence suggests that they play an important role in private religiosity in the family, and in the transmission of Islamic belief, ritual, history, and morality to younger family members, and reinforcing the behavior of older family members. Further, evidence suggests that women are active in informal religious activities associated with prayer, charity, life cycle rituals such as those associated with birth and death, and healing and health care of various kinds (Beck, 1980).

Generally marriages are arranged, but theoretically, consent of both husband and wife is necessary. Although the prospective bride and groom may meet one another before the marriage, the formal contracts are usually completed by males or male guardians; at the informal level, kinswomen influence the selection process. Marriage between cousins is allowed and in some areas has been encouraged.

Endogamous marriage is demanded of women and desirable for men. In practice men (only) can marry outside Islam as long as the prospective wife is either Christian or Jewish, since these religions are seen as standing in a special relationship to Islam. The greater freedom given to males appears to be linked to the assumption that children will follow the religion of their father.

According to Islamic teachings, men are allowed to marry up to four wives at one time, under the condition that they treat each wife "equally." In practice, given the usual ratio of men to women in a society, this can, at best, be practiced by a small (if visible) *minority* of the population; most Muslim marriages are monogamous. Some writers have challenged the feasibility of "equal" treatment for four wives. In practice there have been both governmental and interest group attempts to further control or eliminate polygyny; however it remains as a theoretical option. While men and women both have access to divorce it has been more easily obtained by husbands, with fewer sanctions. In cases of divorce, both parents have child custody rights, however these vary by jurisdiction. Among the qualifiers, the age of the child is an important consideration. Mothers (or the maternal line) tend to get custody of very young children, while the custody of older children tends to be given to the father or paternal line.

Children are highly valued, particularly sons. Most Muslim countries tend to be strongly pronatalist. There are no Qur'anic restrictions placed on birth control, although, over time, there have been variations in the interpretation given to the absence of such injunctions.

There is wide-spread folk knowledge regarding contraceptive techniques and, in this century, particularly for the educationally advantaged, there has been some access to birth control (Goode, 1963).

Filial ties and expectations tend to be strong. Just as parents are expected to provide for their children so adults are expected to care for their aging parents. There are specific Qur'anic injunctions regarding respect and care for aged parents. In practice, the proportion of elders actually surviving into chronological old age has been small, given life-expectancy rates in the Third-World. Those elders who survive into old age tend to be from advantaged groups. There are institutions for dependent elders but very few; most elders live with relatives.

Recent research suggests the tentative nature of current understandings about religious practices and patterns of interpersonal influence in Muslim families. Evidence suggests, for example, not only the need to examine the power of Muslim women in the domestic sector, but also to re-examine their (perhaps underestimated) influence in the public sector (Altorki 1977; Nelson, 1974). Further, evidence suggests that some Islamic teachings may be understood and implemented in different ways by female in contrast to male members of the family (Dwyer, 1978). As with other religions, ideals, as expressed through sacred writings, teaching, or scholarly interpretations are subject to the practicalities of both individual and sub-group understanding and implementation.

To sum up, in Islamic teachings, family rights and obligations encompass a range of relationships; strongly differentiate between men and women; identify specific female rights but exercise heavier controls over women and girls; advocate marriage (in practice monogamy but controlled polygyny is an option); maintain sexual conservatism; place a high value on childbearing and childrearing; and emphasize responsibilities to elder members of the family.

### DEFINITIONS AND ESTIMATES

For the purpose of this discussion, Muslim will refer to people who self-identify as Muslim or are so identified by others. There are problems with designations of religion, including the important consideration that labels alone do not address degree of belief, measures of religiosity, or the relation between belief and practice.[1]

It is difficult to gauge the number of Muslims in North America. Estimates vary widely and are drawn from a range of sources. In Canada, census questions can request personal religious affiliation. In the 1981 census, 98,165 Canadians identified themselves as Muslim. In the United States, however, given the constitutional distinction between church and state, questions regarding personal religious preference are proscribed in U.S. census surveys.[2] Consequently, U.S. figures are derived indirectly or are dependent on sometimes erratic organizational statistics. In the early 1980s these statistics estimated over two million Muslims, with the numbers increasing significantly.[3] Estimates are that there are now more Muslim-Americans than Japanese-Americans or Chinese-Americans (Ghayur 1981:150), and in Canada, Muslims outnumber Mormons, Hindus, Sikhs, and Buddhists (Statistics Canada 1981c). Although Muslim Immigration began in the nineteenth century, most people arrived in North America only within the last twenty years (Ghayur 1981; Rashid, 1985). The majority of North American Muslims, then, are foreign-born and relatively recent immigrants. In addition, in the United States, there is a significant group of indigenous Muslims—an estimated 100,000 African-American Muslims (*World Almanac*, 1984). The focus of this chapter, however, will be confined to immigrant groups and their descendants.[4]

The ethnic composition of the Muslim population varies somewhat between the two countries. In the United States most Muslims are Arab-American in background; Iranian-Americans make up the second largest group (Ghayur, 1981). In Canada, the most common ethnic designation of Muslims is Indo-Pakistani (some 40 percent of the total) while about one-fifth of Muslims are of Asian Arab origin (Statistics Canada, 1981c).

## A TYPOLOGY OF MUSLIM IMMIGRANT FAMILIES

To paint a monolithic picture of "the" Muslim family in North America would deny the important variations within and between types of families. North American Muslim families are similar but they are also different. It will be argued that an important factor in understanding this variability is the immigration cohort. By using cohort as an analytical devise, a *dynamic* of socio-cultural-temporal factors which influence the links between family and Islam in North America can be illustrated. The resultant typology of immigrant cohorts is tentative because it reflects an on-going process; as conditions change and new research evidence appears, earlier understandings may be modified. The typology is intended to draw together the current evidence, provide a framework for understanding the dynamic and point to areas in need of research. This paper examines three major phases in Muslim immigration, the broad patterns characterizing family life for each cohort and variations in the links with religion.

If we examine families by designating all foreign-born members, regardless of era of immigration, as "first generation" (which technically they are), we lose the relevance of major cohort-historical differences *within* this first-generation group which spans some one hundred years of immigration. The first year of relocation in North America was very different for those arriving in 1907 than for those who came in 1957 or in 1987. Awareness of these differences is important for understanding the variation in Muslim family forms today. In this analysis three first generation groups, three second generation descendant groups and one third generation group will be examined. The groups will be designated as (1) the *Pioneer*, dating from the latter part of the last century up to and including World War II; (2) the *Transitional*, dating from Post-World War II to about 1967, and (3) the *Differentiated*, dating from around 1968 to the present. Each will be discussed in turn.

## Pioneer Families (Nineteenth Century to World War II)

ENTRY CHARACTERISTICS. There is evidence that the first Muslims in North America may have been seafarers who made the hazardous voyage across the Atlantic Ocean before Christopher Columbus (Van Sertima, 1976; Weiner, 1922). Later, an undetermined number (possibly thousands) of African Muslims were forced to the Americas by pre-nineteenth century Atlantic slave traders (Muhammad, 1984). These men and women were severed from their faith, their traditions and their friends and families. The adoption of Islam by some twentieth century African-Americans has been linked, in part, to this early historical connection.

The earliest Muslim immigrants began to trickle to North America in the late 1800s. Most of these early pioneers were from the area of Greater Syria (today including Lebanon, Syria, Palestine and Jordan) which was under the rule of the Ottoman Empire. In immigrating to Christian-dominant North America they were confronted with the prospect of being a religious minority. There was a great deal of apprehension about the implications of this (Elkholy 1966). During this period immigrants sometimes crossed back and forth across the Canada-U.S. border, more often south than north (McVey 1983). Thus the 1871 Canadian census reports thirteen Muslims while ten years later the 1881 census does not report any. Both Canada and the United States were less than enthusiastic in their receptivity toward non-Christian, non-European immigrants (Barron, 1967; Davie, 1957). Immigration policies in both countries worked against immigrants from Asia. By 1908 immigration of Muslims to Canada was effectively curtailed while the U.S. immigration laws of 1921 and 1924, which imposed nation-specific quota systems, greatly limited the number of new Muslim immigrants. There was minimal immigration during this period until after the end of World War Two.

FIRST GENERATION PIONEERS. The earliest Muslim immigrants were mostly male, young and unskilled. These early immigrants were often unilingual, with little formal education and no specialized job training and most were single or if they were married they travelled without wives and children. They tended to see their North American experience as a temporary one which would give economic advantage and ensure them financial security when they returned to their homelands. There was apprehension about moving from a hegemonic setting, under Islamic even if Ottoman rule, to a setting where they would live among non-Muslims. Initially, given the presumed duration of their stay and the few Muslim children, there was less concern about the absence of religious institutions or formalized systems of religious socialization. While the first generation Pioneer Muslims were similar in some ways to the more prevalent European immigrants of the time, in other ways Muslim immigrants were markedly different. They were few in number making it more difficult to set up communities; they tended to immigrate without wives and children; few North Americans could speak their language (Arabic); their religion was misunderstood and marked them as distant outsiders during an era when strangers and non-Christian religions were regarded with suspicion and often hostility. At the same time distance imposed barriers between the immigrants and their families back home. It was difficult to maintain contact with the old country. Ocean travel was expensive, arduous, and time consuming and letters took a very long time. Even after the advent of trans-Atlantic telephone, communication remained expensive and difficult to arrange. For the extended family, both traditional social support and social controls were difficult to effect across such an expanse of distance.

In North America, age-peers and co-villagers tried to support one another. It was difficult to establish new families. There were few Muslim women available for marriage and an undetermined number of young men married non-Muslims and reportedly drifted away from Islam (Naff 1980). Many young men arranged marriages with cousins or co-villagers in the old country. Increasingly, young Muslim women began coming to North America (although rarely independent of male kin). As a new generation was born, the difficulties of living in a non-Muslim setting became apparent.

Early communities were found in several cities in the United States and in Canada. The first Canadian mosque, built in 1938 by twenty Edmonton families, attests to the role women often played in those early mosques. The incorporation papers list both men's and women's names as founders. Women tended to be active in the first mosques, organizing community activities and participating to a far greater degree than would have been possible in their ancestral lands at that time. The early mosques, themselves, served as community centres, bringing people together for prayer, religious instruction, marriages, and funerals and for general activities such as dinners and bake sales. The presence of such activities helped to facilitate endogamous marriage. Yet Islamic institutions tended to be few in number, scattered, and sometimes vulnerable. Both Haddad (1978) and Naff (1985) cite the small community of Ross, North Dakota as an example of the difficulties of trying to maintain religious distinctiveness with few supports. In Ross, Muslims held group prayers in the early 1900s; by 1920 they had constructed a mosque; but by 1948, the mosque had been abandoned. With institutional supports minimal and precarious, there tended to be an emphasis on acculturation and adaptation.

SECOND AND THIRD GENERATION PIONEERS. The first generation Pioneers were distinguished by their dedication to thrift, hard work and industriousness. The second generation shared many of the early sacrifices resulting from their parents' economic and linguistic struggles and their isolation from the homeland. Their parents were at a status, language, and occupational disadvantage. In consequence, ties with the ancestral homeland weakened; while ties within the local community grew stronger. Sometimes the community substituted for the homeland, reproducing the family relationships which would have been available in the country of origin. Independent of biological or legal relatedness, kinship labels were often used for intimate acquaintances.

The muting of ancestral language skills is significant for the Pioneer group. At one level, the names and nicknames selected for their children began to reflect the common names of the new community rather than the names common to their ancestral history. A far more significant reflection of the way families adapted is found in the gradual loss of Arabic, their ancestral and, in a sense, liturgical language. This is a pointed loss. Classical Arabic is the language of the Qur'an; even non-Arabic speaking Muslims place a high value on knowledge of the Arabic language. Its incremental loss to the children and then the children's children of the first generation pioneers has both ethnic and religious significance.

The second-generation descendants, growing up as a religious minority, did not have access to the formal religious instruction common in predominantly Muslim countries. Their school system denied religious diversity and assumed Christianity. Muslim holidays were not recognized nor was prayer five times a day; fasting during the month of Ramadan; or the Arabic language. Grandparents were not likely to be available to reinforce religious teachings; food and beverage prohibitions were regularly challenged by the larger society, there were few trips to the ancestral homeland to reinforce religious values. Instead the second generation in Pioneer families were part of a society which assumed uniformity and rewarded the (apparent) absence of difference.

Elkholy (1966:148) noted that where the second generation was religious it was likely to have learned about religion from a mosque rather than a parent. Under such conditions, knowledge of religious teachings sometimes faltered. Similarly Barclay (1969) argued that one way the Muslims he studied adapted to North America was to stress the similarities between Islam and Christianity, sometimes to the point of denying differences. Young people growing up with minimal access to formal religious training combined with extensive exposure to the sometimes contradictory norms of the larger society, may be confused. The consequences of this can reverberate through descendant generations. This is illustrated by the perhaps surprising but genuine confusion of one Muslim student (third generation Pioneer) when informed of Islamic prohibitions against alcohol:

> Beer? What's wrong with beer? What do you mean we aren't supposed to drink beer?

Intermarriage is often viewed as a hallmark of loss of religion. For the Pioneer cohort and its descendants, intermarriage rates appear to increase with each generation. Contemporary youth face a possibly limited field of eligibles, particularly if their focus is only on native-born Muslims. This is particularly salient for women. Compromises may be created as reflected by one young career woman (third-generation Pioneer):

> I feel my chances for marriage improve if I can consider two kinds of men, not only good Muslims but also good non-Muslims who don't care very much about religion.

While this is contrary to Islamic injunctions against women marrying non-Muslims, the range of eligible men expands by adding the personal condition that a man may be suitable if good and religiously malleable. The descendants of the early Pioneer families are now in the third and fourth generations and the evidence suggests the strong likelihood that they will be in a religious intermarriage. The 1981 Canadian Census indicates that of third-generation Muslims who were married sixty percent were intermarried, that is, at the time of the census, their spouse was not a Muslim (Rashid, 1985). Evidence suggests even further movement away from active involvement with Islam, given that couples with mixed religious traditions tend to reduce their involvement in religious activities (Besanceney, 1970; Nye and Berardo, 1973). While this may appear to be an equitable way for couples to balance their religious differences, doing so may severely jeopardize Muslim traditions given that the larger society is not equally balanced.

The early Pioneer families and their descendants had few formal reli-

gious supports; it was not easy to practice Islam in a Christian dominated environment. Nevertheless the adaptations and accomodative
changes of the Pioneers and their descendants have generated the particular disdain of the newest Muslim immigrants, those who arrived after 1967.

### Transitional Families (Post World War II—1967)

ENTRY CHARACTERISTICS. Muslim immigration after World War II
up until approximately 1967 took on a different character. While there
was some continuation of the chain migration of Arab-Muslims supported by friends and relatives already in North America, there was a
new and significant addition: foreign students and professionals. During this period large numbers of Egyptians, Palestinians, Syrians, Jor-
danians, Iraqis, Indians, Pakistanis, and others came to North America
to study and to advance professionally. Most of these newcomers were
young, unmarried men from well-established families, potential elites
in their countries of origin. They were educated, multilingual, and often westernized. They had been advantaged in their homelands and
they came to the United States and Canada in order to advance further.
Furthermore, these Muslims met an exceptionally favorable economic
climate. Even those immigrants in the Transitional cohort who came
from less advantaged backgrounds were likely to thrive in the receptive
socio-economic climate of the time. There were abundant job and career opportunities, given the demands of an expanding economy and
the huge post-war baby boom population which had yet to hit the job
market. The Transitional Muslims who settled in North America were
disproportionately likely to move into higher status occupations and
they linked well with the larger society. The Transitional cohort helped
to introduce a significant twist in North America's exposure to and understanding of Muslims; members of this cohort were among the first
to be highly placed leaders and professionals.

The contribution of the Transitional cohort to North America is associated with a loss to their homelands. As part of a feared "brain
drain" from east to west, fueled by the opportunity structure in North
America at that time, these young people were in ambivalent positions:
often drawn to the West, democracy, and socio-economic advancement yet also drawn back to their origins (Abu-Laban and Abu-Laban,

1972; 1986). They tended to down-play religion and see nationalism and development as keys to social change and the eradication of Third-World social inequities. It has been suggested that many in this group were "Eid-Muslims" (Haddad, 1979; 1983), in effect "Holiday Muslims". That is, their religious interests were activated on a calendaric basis for major Islamic holidays: *Eid al-Adha* (occurring at the end of the annual pilgrimage to Mecca) and *Eid al Fitr* (occurring at the end of *Ramadan*, the month of prescribed fasting from sunrise to sunset).

FIRST GENERATION TRANSITIONALS. The class, linguistic, educational, and career advantages of these young Muslims, together with their North American training and the need for their expertise, created a welcoming climate in the host culture. In contrast to the Pioneer cohort, the Transitional Cohort could fit in easier and sooner than earlier immigrants. But they were often dispersed geographically; separate from regular contact with significant numbers of fellow Muslims; isolated from established Islamic institutions; and, at the same time, embraced by work-related professional and academic settings. This combination often functioned to cut them off from co-religionists with similar interests.

Further, these new immigrants were young and mostly single. The likelihood of a mixed-marriage is related to the density of co-religionists in the community and hence the availability of potential mates. The pre-existing Muslim communities in North America were small and often isolated from university and professional groups. Hence, the marriage-eligible young men who immigrated at this time did not have many opportunities to meet Muslim women either in the local community, on campus, or on the job. Muslim families attempt to control the addition of new members by designating categories of eligibility; controlling the interaction of marriageable young people; and using elders as matchmakers. All of these strategies work to channel young people toward particular partners but these processes were sharply compromised in the post-war North American setting.

A high proportion (an estimated two-thirds) of these young Muslim students and professionals married native-born North Americans (Elkholy, 1969; Suleiman, 1969). In most cases these marriages were both cultural and religious inter-marriages. Since Islamic teachings allow men to marry not only Muslim women but respectable women "of the book" (i.e., Christians and Jews), this did not pose a particular challenge to religious tradition. Notably, however, these marriages were unlikely to have been arranged by parents back in the home country and some indeterminate number were likely contracted in spite of parental objections (from one or both sides). Religious intermarriage, particularly when it is marriage between two sharply different traditions, poses interpersonal challenges and some typical adaptations. Existing research evidence on family processes in such settings suggests that religion is likely to have been de-emphasized during the courtship phase (Nye and Berardo 1973:153-154) as well as during the marriage itself. The high incidence of inter-religious/inter-cultural marriage not only increased the Transitionals familiarity with the North American culture but may have further eased their integration into the majority group, a kind of assimilation by marriage.

SECOND GENERATION TRANSITIONALS. The second generation of the Transitional cohort are most likely to have grown up in a relatively secure socio-economic environment. As a consequence of family (parental) adaptation to mixed traditions as well as their own exposure to the North American religious environment, this descent group is likely to be distinctive compared to other second generation groups. The occupational advantage of their parents suggests that extra-kin contacts and choice of residential neighborhood, may have been mediated more by class than religion. Consequently, this group is less likely to have grown up with Muslim peers, or with Muslim relatives. Where the extended family has had influence, North American evidence would suggest that it is more likely to have been from the maternal (generally non-Muslim) side.

In addition, this second generation has grown up not only without many supportive Muslim institutions but in an increasingly vehement anti-Muslim environment. The 1967 Arab-Israeli War; the oil embargo of 1973; aircraft hijackings; the Iranian crisis of the late 1970s; the 1982 Israeli Invasion of Lebanon; the Palestinian *Intifadah* of the late 1980's; Ayatollah Khumeini's threats to British author Salman Rushdie, the 1990 Iraqi occupation of Kuwait — all of these have been covered by an often openly hostile media which often puts complex multi-leveled historical, social, political, and economic issues into simplistic frameworks grounded in religious ethnocentrism. Radio, film, television, video casettes, school curricula, and church school materials have been found to carry profound anti-Muslim messages (S. Abu-Laban, 1975; Kenny, 1975; Said, 1981). In childhood and in adolescence, the Transitional second generation, together with the third generation Pioneer descendants, has perhaps born the brunt of the anti-Muslim fervor in the North American media. To the extent that open racism is even more difficult for children than for adults, it is these descendant generations which seem most vulnerable because they have had fewer familial and institutional supports. In contrast, for reasons to be discussed, the children of Differentiated families may fare quite differently.

The likely de-emphasis of religion in combination with growing up in a predominantly Christian environment with non-Muslim peers, few Muslim institutions or age peers; less contact with Muslim grandparents; in essence the lack of an Islamic support network, has tended to produce a second generation more loosely identified as Muslim and likely to intermarry as well. People of mixed backgrounds are comparatively less likely to take spouses of the same or similar ancestry (Alba and Golden, 1986). When parents defy rules of religious endogamy, their descendants are even less likely to observe such rules (Besanceney, 1970).

### Differentiated Families (1968 to the present)

ENTRY CHARACTERISTICS. The largest and most recent wave of Muslim immigrants has arrived since the 1967 Arab-Israeli War. The societies from which they have come have quite different geopolitical social characteristics from those of the previous immigrant eras. The receiving societies have altered too and these changes have implications for family functioning. In some areas, the newest cohort of Muslims is more likely to *differentiate* itself, disdaining an assimilationist—accommodationist stance toward the larger society and giving preference to pluralistic integration.

The dramatic nature of this change is found in the diverse origins of the Differentiated cohort which reflect the cosmopolitan nature of world Islam. These newest families are from over one hundred different countries, including North America, colonialized Africa, the Fertile Crescent, Pakistan, Bangladesh, Turkey, the Gulf States, Indonesia, and the Caribbean. These new immigrants have often seen a resurgence of Islamic pride coupled with the global socio-economic power of Muslim oil producing countries; a power which has had impact on both Canada and the United States. They are more likely to have witnessed the rise of normative (reform) Islam within their ancestral countries, a move which re-emphasizes visible behavioral codes and dismisses claims that current Western technology exemplifies the superiority of the West over the East.

Some implications of this greater sensitivity to normative Islam can be found in the personal lives of the most recent Muslim immigrants. Compared to the preceding cohorts, they are more likely to emphasize the public demonstration of religious beliefs. For example, distinctive clothing is much more prevalent among North American Muslim women than previously. Such clothing can send a signal to outsiders while reminding its wearer of normative expectations; it can contribute to an interactive pressure toward conformity to Muslim precepts. For some women, covering the head with a scarf (*hijab*) is a badge of proud difference that may cue observers into expecting conservative behavior to follow conservative appearance. Some see this identification as bene ficial. In the words of one woman,

> It [the *hijab*] improves your chances of getting a husband. Many men wouldn't consider a girl [for a wife] who doesn't cover herself [dress Islamically]. [First Generation Differentiated]

In contrast, those able to forego identifiable clothing (including most North American Muslim males) are in less structured normative situations when away from the home. Expectations regarding food, alcohol, fasting, prayer, or modesty can be more quickly compromised when a Muslim is unrecognized and/or among non-Muslims, who know little about Islamic practices and obligations. It is the absence of support from the larger society, as well as its temptations, which rule-conscious Muslims can see as potentially jeopardizing.

There has also been a re-emphasis on dietary rules. For some North American Muslims eating in non-Muslim restaurants or with non-Muslim families is too risky. Food may not be *hallal* (obtained according to prescribed rituals), or it may contain pork or pork by-products such as the enzymes recently found in a seemingly innocuous product used by a popular fast food chain. Further, in line with the increased tendency to adhere to rules and stand apart from the ways of the larger society, sex segregation may be emphasized not only by conservative clothing on women but also by prohibitions against contact between unrelated women and men (such as in co-educational classes) or, at an extreme, even against men and women shaking hands with one another.

It is the Differentiated families who are more willing to stand out as different, live their lives as different, take pride in their differences and teach their children to do the same. Interestingly, they are also more likely to differentiate themselves from other Muslims (particularly those from Transitional or Pioneer families).

FIRST GENERATION DIFFERENTIATED   The most recent immigrants more often came to North America as couples with children. They represent the largest proportion of Muslims in Canada and the United States. Their motivations for immigration include economic gain, educational advancement, civic freedom, sanctuary from war and political repression, family reunification, and a spirit of adventure. Thus they represent a diversity of educational backgrounds and occupations but they immigrated at a distinctive point in history. They have access to greater numbers of co-religionists and they can find support in the extensive network of religious institutions that now exists. Many of these institutions have developed and flourished in the past twenty years through the financial aid of Muslim oil-producing countries. The ability and willingness of wealthier Muslim nations to assist North American Muslims has had not only a practical outcome in terms of institution-building but also a psychological outcome in terms of enhanced pride and identification.

As never before for any first-generation group, the newest Muslim immigrant bestrides two worlds. Technology facilitates physical and psychological proximity to origins. It can create a strong network that fortifies Differentiated families in their attempt to live a code of ethics and faith different from the North American majority. Telephone contact is far easier than in the past; trans-atlantic trips are within regular reach; audio tapes and video cassettes, and sometimes computers and fax machines can be used to exchange information, bring home distant family events and sometimes move Third World problems into the living rooms of North American Muslims.

He listened to the tape of his family and in the background he could hear gunfire. [First Generation Differentiated]

We called again and again after the bombing. But it took a while to get through [First Generation Differentiated]

War, turmoil and other political and social problems, as well as the personal lives of distant family members are no longer so far away. Return trips are taken more frequently, sometimes coinciding with weddings, illnesses, and births; family ceremonies and milestones are more readily shared. Frequent travel is associated with the exchange of messages and gossip between the old and new countries which can create a kind of shared international knowing, while strengthening the network of social control. Technology has decreased the opportunities for anonymity; it has lengthened and strengthened the reach of the extended family.

While, in principle, contemporary Pioneer and Transitional families now share the same access to technological advances, the critical difference is in the timing of their accessibility. The intensive two-world grounding facilitated by technology *did not* accompany the early North American adaptation of other Muslim immigrant groups. Only the most recent Muslim immigrants have had, from the point of arrival, access to a kin network so elaborated by technology.

SECOND GENERATION DIFFERENTIATED    Differentiated parents have what some view as worrisome models of the North American child as found in the descendant Pioneer and Transitional generations. Sometimes they are shocked by Muslims they meet. For the first time, a first generation group can have an anticipatory view of what their child could become. No longer are parental worries about phantom children who will someday be born, grow up and become North American. The descendants of the Pioneer and Transitional families are sometimes seen as clear embodiments of how far Muslim children in North America may stray from children in the old world. Irrespective of the fact that the Pioneer and Transitional second generations, had very different experiences as children than the on-going experiences of today's second generation differentiated; the most recent immigrant parents tend to sometimes view these young people with alarm. Such observations can further strengthen traditional ways. The successful adaptations of earlier groups may be held up as an illustration of the dangers in the North American environment.

In fact, the second generation Differentiated is exposed to a world very different from the childhood of other second generations. For the first time a network of mosques, Muslim institutions and Islamic instructional materials are in place for the religious training of children. Few second generation Pioneers or Transitionals had this in the past.

Further, the second generation Differentiated shares in the two-world life of its parents. Ancestral religion, customs, and language are more likely to receive community and extended family reinforcement. Muslim friends are more readily obtainable for children and for adults. The ancestral country is linked by feeling, by travel, and by technology. The regular reinforcement of Islamic conduct codes abroad can give further credence to parental teachings, since the restrictions over teenagers in the old country, which may be looked back upon with nostalgia (S. Abu-Laban, 1979) can make North American parents look moderate, by comparison. In adolescence, trips back to the homeland may be even more stressed for daughters than for sons. Nevertheless, in North America family controls over young unmarried females can still be so pervasive that marriage may be seen as a step toward freedom rather than as the relinquishment of it.

As expressed by one young woman:

My parents won't let me go anywhere without my brother. Now my brother has a girlfriend and doesn't want me tagging along! I'm so bored. It would be nice to be married. [Second Generation Differentiated]

The two-world grounding of children is also reflected in teachers' reports about children's keen awareness of major international crises that affect Muslim leaders or Muslim countries. Their concerns sometimes find outlets in both their classroom drawings and playground games. Compared to earlier second generation children, Differentiated children are less likely to find themselves relegated to ethno-religious silence and they are more likely to find others who share similar (minority) world views. Should they experience discrimination or unfairness because of their religion, they are more likely to find Muslim peers to affirm their feelings and give them support. Concomitantly, the experience of shared discrimination can be associated with strengthened Islamic identification and, when need be, with greater resistance to majority (non-Muslim) group definitions.

## CONTEMPORARY FAMILY DIVERSITY

These three cohorts, Pioneer, Transitional, and Differentiated, and their descendants, co-exist in contemporary North America. All three have experienced the shifts in worldwide Islam and shifts in geopolitical power. The Pioneer and Transitional groups have responded differently to this new religious reality.

Muslim immigrants, generally, have come from areas characterized by a broad sense of familialism structured by rights, reciprocities, commitments, and obligations. They come from world regions which are less dependent on governmental aid and assistance; more reliance is placed on kin reciprocities and responsibilities. Families generally, and particularly in times of crisis such as immigration to a new country, turn to one another in the expectation of reciprocal support. In North America, new Muslim families not only face a religious mosaic but also fear the loss of their own family life.[5]

The general North American public may decry the "state" of the family and the uncertainties of relations between men and women and between generations but for North American Muslims there is not only the pressure to retain religious ideals in an unsupportive religious climate but their new environment appears to work directly against the traditional Islamic family. Further, there have been significant family related changes in both Canada and the United States, that fuel the apprehensions of new immigrants. Both countries have experienced marked increases in the incidence of divorce, out-of-wedlock births, reported child abuse, and residential isolation of elders (Elkin, 1985; Sussman, 1987).[6] All of these combine to create an image of the North American family at risk. At its extreme, North American women are seen as too powerful and their husbands as too weak; children as out of control; the aged as abandoned; promiscuity as rampant. Irrespective of evidence or experience which might temper such assessments, these are often believed. As well, immigrants are susceptible to selective recall about the virtues of family life "back home" (see for example, Elkholy, 1980; Islam, 1984). Moreover, Differentiated families are often acutely aware that relatives and friends in the old country are monitoring and assessing their family's adaptations in non-Muslim North America. They are aware they are being judged.

All North American Muslim families face the reality of living, almost daily, with negative media portrayals of Islam, Muslim countries, and Muslim leaders. At times the Western press seems to mock Islam, singling Muslims out for persecution, strengthening the xenophobia of non-Muslim readers; for some, the media barrage creates almost a state of siege. Many major world events, implicitly if not explicitly, are "explained" by "Islam," "fundamentalist" Islam and "militant" Islam. Unexamined preconceptions are applied to decontextualized "facts" which increase the risk that anti-Muslim feelings will be exacerbated still further. Muslim parents live with the knowledge that they have little control over the images that represent them. These images have implications for passing on traditions to the young; for the retention and transmission of religion; the development of family identification and family esteem; and the nature of the evolving paradigm of values and world views transmitted from one generation to the next, which make for the distinctiveness of a family to its own. These distorted images contributed to the difficulties of descendant Pioneer parents and Transitional parents in relation to their children. Differentiated families, however, have been empowered in many ways; they are more likely to respond to such images, not by inconspicuous "adjustments" but by open, even organized outrage. Their two-world orientation and the links between ancestral and adopted countries facilitate their active identification with Muslim homelands and Muslim issues.

The nexus between family and religion can be important and interactive, mutually empowering or weakening for both institutions. The resultant differences between the three first generation immigrant groups and their second and third generations, can have an impact on the religion-family link in several areas including personal meaning and identity, social control, social support, and integration into the North American society.

The new waves of Muslim immigrants who entered North America from about 1970 to the present have deeply affected established Pioneer and Transitional Muslims. They now find themselves outnumbered by immigrants who have brought a new vision of Islam to North America. Many emphasize normative (reform) Islam, the public demonstration of Islamic piety, segregation of the sexes, and Islamic dress for women. The conflicting practices surrounding the covering of women's heads are painful for many. While the wearing of the hijab is not a practice of the majority, its presence is conspicuous and laden with symbolism. This can be particularly difficult for Pioneer and Transitional women. Some see it as furthering North American hostility by reinforcing negative stereotypes of underdevelopment and repression in Muslim countries.

I hate it when I see those scarves. They make people look so ignorant [Young woman, Second Generation Transitional]

There they were attending our meeting with that thing [*sic*] tied around their heads. [Older woman, Second Generation Pioneer]

While, in and of itself, neither the veil nor any other head covering is inherently repressive it should be noted that most contemporary women's movements in Muslim countries have focused attention on eradicating the veil. Further, historically, mandatory dress codes have not been associated with the empowerment of women, quite the contrary.

Tension often exists between the three immigrant descent groups as one attempts to impose its views on the other. The tension is felt between families and within institutional settings, as people find themselves in disagreement over appropriate personal conduct and religious practices.

The newest immigrants have often been empowered by their two-world contacts and the foreign support given in aid of developing institutions in North America. They represent a new first generation leadership, that has challenged many of the established ways of accommodation.

"*Why* don't we see you at Friday prayers?" [First Generation Differentiated man]

[Angrily] "I do what I do. Nobody comes between me and my Islam." [First Generation Transitional man]

Both Pioneer and Transitional groups feel the pressure toward the public display of religious belief. It has had a particular impact on Transitional and Pioneer women. It introduces uncertainty into some social settings where they may not be sure how much public conservatism is to be required.

> He stopped the wedding and shouted at the teenager. "Cover your arms!" Something like that would never have happened back home. [Transitional, First Generation Caribbean-born woman]

Sometimes women have tried to challenge the dominance of male leadership in mosques by seeking the vote when disenfranchized or by refusing to cover their heads.

> He told us, "[Women] cover your heads, you're in the mosque." We said, "We're in the meeting room not the mosque, just as you are. If we should cover our heads, then you should remove your shoes!" [as is required within prayer areas]. [A Pioneer, Second Generation woman and Transitional, First Generation woman]

It is not easy to mount challenges however. The communities are still small; the gossip networks are strong; and women worry about their reputations. Since there tends to be some belief that North American husbands are subordinate to their wives, a Muslim woman who challenges male edicts risks being viewed as overassimilated. While married women may be able to endure this, it can be anathema for the unmarried woman. The threat of unmarriageability is a potent form of social control over young women, whether they are Pioneer, Transitional, or Differentiated descendants.

Mate selection is basic to the family processes of all groups. The greater freedom given to young men and their greater leeway to marry outside the group, means that young women may find themselves dependent on a dwindling pool of available mates. Parents, most particularly the parents of young women, recognize the compromised marital opportunity structure which their daughters face.

> My sister *has* to marry a Muslim. My mother says I have to marry a Muslim too. But I know every Muslim girl in town and none of them interest me. I want to make up my own mind. [Male student—Third Generation Pioneer]

> My daughters are all good girls, thank God. Who knows they may *never* find Muslim husbands but they will have each other. [Mother, Second Generation Pioneer]

Mixed marriages present major threats to identity and the perpetuation of tradition. Mixed ancestry is one potential marker of identity loss in descendant generations. The evidence is predictive of a high rate of eventual intermarriage on the part of third-generation Pioneer descendants and second-generation Transitional descendants. It is the Differentiated families, however, which are more likely to have the community strength and support, the numeric base, and the extended family contacts which would strengthen the effectiveness of parental pressures toward endogamy. However, a more sensitive test of the strength of the Differentiated cohort may be the extent to which they are successful in encouraging males, as well as females, to marry only a Muslim or Muslim convert.

There is evidence that the patterns of family and religion among Pioneer, Transitional, and Differentiated groups are linked to differential integration into North American society. The rate of out-marriage, sex differences in marital opportunities, discordance between traditional practices regarding male rights and the realities of life in North America, and the impact of mixed ancestry on children's religious development suggest vulnerable areas, in need of further research. For some Muslims the authenticity of their religious identity and practices has been challenged; there are difficulties in passing on the tradition to subsequent generations; and estrangement from the formal institutional supports which would help in the socialization of children. All of these are areas of family concern.

Questions and challenges concerning the meaning and purpose of life and death and commitments and obligations to others arise in the day to day intensity of family life. Generation after generation, children are born, life is lived and then ends; ultimately individual family members are ephemeral. Religious exegesis on life's meaning can provide a transcendent interpretive framework for families. Family and faith, in tandem, can provide shared meanings and mutually reinforce the socialization of members. The distinctive variability in Muslim family forms in North America and particularly cohort differences in response to this variability, have probable implications for the perpetuation of Muslim identity. To the extent that Pioneer, Transitional, and Differentiated groups and their descendants move further away from tolerance and accomodative adjustments with one another, community divisions may deepen and Muslim families may become more vulnerable as they attempt to live their beliefs and transmit their traditions in the North American environment.

### Notes

* Some parts of this paper were presented as "West Meets East: Retention and Transmission of Islamic Tradition among Immigrants to North America," at the Annual Meetings of the Canadian Sociology and Anthropology Association, Windsor, Ontario, June 1988.

The author would like to thank Valerie Irwin and Shirley Stawnychy for their help with manuscript preparation, Sheridan. Anderson for her work as a research assistant, and Baha Abu-Laban, Charles W. Hobart, and Michael Suleiman for comments on an earlier draft of this paper.

1. See Lenski (1963:17-23) for discussion regarding the measurement of religiosity.
2. The U.S. Bureau of the Census has not collected information on religion or on religious intermarriage since 1957 (Broderick, 1988:134).
3. The 1983 *Encyclopedia Britannica Book of the Year* indicates 1,326,200 Muslims in North America (*Encyclopedia Britannica*, 1983, as cited in *World Almanac*.
4. African-American Muslims have a unique history and experience with racism which makes them quite different from immigrant and immigrant descent groups; for this reason, African-American Muslims are not included in the discussion.
5. Religion generally may be less salient in North America than in the old country. A comparison of international Gallup Poll data examined cross-national differences in three areas of religious belief (1) belief in God; (2) belief in life after death and (3) feeling that personal religious beliefs are "very important." Countries of the Third World tended to report highest religiosity on these factors, western European countries the least, while North America was in between (Sigelman, 1977:290).
6. On several traditional indicators of family distress, including divorce and illegitimacy, U.S. rates are higher than Canadian rates (Elkin, 1985). In addition Canada does not have *to the same degree* the social problems which plague many U.S. African-American and Hispanic families (although Canadian Native families have severe problems). Given that the bulk of the Muslim population has appeared only recently in both countries, and that research in this area is just beginning, it is still early to assess possible national differences in family organization and assimilation.

# The Muslim Family: The Scriptural Framework

## Saleem Qureshi

◆   ◆   ◆   ◆

For Muslims the source of all guidance for correct Islamic living is the Qur'an which they believe to be the directly revealed word of God, sent down to the Prophet Muhammad—the last prophet in a line that includes Abraham, Moses, and Jesus. As a revelation the Qur'an was completed in the life time of Muhammad. It was compiled in written form during the reign of the third caliph Uthman (644-656), and in that form it has remained the scripture of all Muslims. Regardless of the many sectarian and political differences among Muslims over the past fourteen centuries, the Qur'an has remained undisputed and no sect or group has either challenged its authenticity or produced another version.

Muslims believe that the Qur'anic regulations deal with every aspect of life be it *ibadat* (obligations to God, more specifically, devotional and religious rituals and observances) or *muamalat* (affairs among people including contracts and agreements as well as social etiquette, penal laws, economics and commerce).

Since the Qur'an is not a book of laws and specific legislation constitutes a very small portion of it (Coulson, 1978: 12), Muslims have looked to the practices and pronouncements of the Prophet Muhammad for elaboration. These practices and pronouncements are referred to as *sunna*—literally, the traditions of Prophet Muhammad. The compiled form of the sunna is called *hadith*, which is the record of what the prophet said about the various matters or how he acted in specific situations. Thus, the hadith is next to the Qur'an in authority. The development of hadith, however, was a lengthy process (Robson, 1971: 23-28). The most authoritative collections of the hadith are considered to be two, the Sahihs of al-Bukhari and Muslim (d. 875), both dating from the later part of the ninth century.

As Muslims believe that all aspects of life should be regulated by laws based on religion, the earliest theological and intellectual activity among them pertained to the elaboration of laws; the science of these laws is *fikh* (Schacht, 1964: 886-91). In fact, detailed elaboration of the laws preceded the collection of the hadith. During the initial stages of the development of fikh no distinction was made between law and tradition. Thus, the collection of the hadith by Imam Malik (d. 795), called the *Muwatta*, could have been used as the law of the land if Imam Malik had acceded to the request of the Abbasid caliphs Abu Jaffer al-Mansur (754-775) and Haroon al-Rashid (786-809). On the other side, Imam Abu Hanifa (d. 767), predecessor of Imam Malik, made no use of hadith in the elaboration of his fikh.

Two other schools of fikh in addition to those of Abu Hanifa and Malik bin Anas came to be recognized as equally acceptable, those of Shafi'i (d. 820) and Hanbal (d. 855). All four of these are regarded as equally authentic and authoritative, and any Muslim can choose to be governed by the rites of any of the schools. There seems to have been no overt animosity among the founders of these schools or among their early disciples; they accepted the legitimacy of each other's views, which is understandable since the basic sources and motivations as well as the people for whom the fikh was developed were more or less the same. Thus, there are no differences among the schools on fundamental doctrinal matters; since all accept the Qur'an—in exactly one common form—as the directly revealed word of God and Muhammad his last prophet. The differences pertain only to interpretation, emphasis, and acceptance or rejection of certain traditions on the basis of chains of narrators and on the liberal or literal construction put on the Qur'an and the sunna.

All four schools of fikh as well as the hadith in the two Sahihs are accepted by the Sunnis, who constitute about 90 percent of the population of Muslims. The Shi'i have their own fikh, the most widespread being that of Imam Jaffar. Regarding hadith, the primary difference between Shi'i and Sunni pertains to the narrators. The Shi'i accept only those that have come down through 'Ali's descendants whereas the Sunni accord equal validity to all companions of the Prophet. Thus, even between the Shi'i and the Sunni the difference is neither fundamental nor doctrinal but only of emphasis or detail.

Regulations governing the family, that is, marriage, divorce, inheritance, care of the children etc., are based on the Qur'an, the hadith and the fikh. In family matters, the Qur'an itself is very detailed; it lays down the fundamental structure of the family and admonishes men and women on how to behave and treat each other. Where the Qur'an does not go into detail, Muslims seek guidance from the traditions of the Prophet, that is, from what he said and how he himself behaved as a family man. The fikh incorporates both these sources and provides further details where necessary. From the beginning of Islam, Muslims have observed these rules. Guidance has been provided by theologian-jurists and learned interpreters called the *muftis*, whose interpretations have been designated as *fatwa* (pl. *fatawa*). In addition, religious leaders or scholars called *alim* (pl. *ulama*) and prayer leaders called *imam* have been a source of information.

The scriptural framework for the family discussed in this chapter is based on the Qur'an and the collections of hadith by Imams Bukhari and Muslim as well as the *Mishkat al-Masabih*, a widely accepted selection of hadith. The main explanations for fikh are collected in the fatawa of Imam Fakhruddin Hassan Bin Mansur al-Uzjandi al-Farghani, known as Kazee Khan, who was a famous Hanafi mufti and scholar and compiler of juristic works and commentaries on Hanafi fikh.

### THE FAMILY IN ISLAM:
### THE SCRIPTURAL FRAMEWORK
*Family and Marriage*

According to the Islamic scripture, the family is established by marriage. Marriage is a social contract; it is not a sacrament. It is legally established when one party makes an offer and the other accepts it. No religious rite or ceremony is required to make a marriage valid. Freedom is a necessary condition since a person who is not free cannot enter into a valid contract. A slave needs the permission of his or her master to marry and without it cannot contract a valid marriage. The importance of marriage is emphasized in the Qur'an:

> Marry off those who are single among you, and those of your male and female servants who are righteous. If they are poor, God will enrich them of his grace, for God is bounteous and all-knowing. (XXIV:32)

And

> Those who cannot afford to marry should abstain from what is unlawful until God enriches them by his grace. (XXIV:33)

Fornication, on the contrary, is emphatically condemned: "And do not go near fornication, as it is immoral and an evil way" (XVII:32, also XXIV:2,3, XXV:68, LX:12). The Prophet is said to have admonished fathers of marriageable sons and daughters to arrange for their marriages. According to Baihaqi, as transmitted in *Shuab al-Iman*, Abu Said and Ibn Abbas reported God's messenger as saying

> He who has a son born to him should give him a good name and a good education and marry him when he reaches puberty. If he does not marry him when he reaches puberty and he commits sin, its guilt rests upon his father. (Cited in *Mishkat*, 1981:666-67)

And Umar bin al-Khattab and Anas bin Malik reported God's messenger as saying that it is written in the Torah that

> If anyone does not give his daughter in marriage when she reaches twelve and she commits sin, the guilt of that rests on him. (Mishkat, 1981: 666-67)

The legal term for marriage is *nikah*, which is the act of completing a marriage contract in which the consent of the two parties in the presence of two witnesses is all that is required (Thanwi, 1981:278-88). Literally, nikah means carnal union; legally, according to Islamic jurists, it is an agreement for the lawful enjoyment of woman. Nikah confers *mulk al-muta*, i.e., the right or power of enjoyment. According to Muhammad Essad, mulk al-muta means:

> Ownership of the right of enjoyment of the woman; not ownership of the person of the wife, or of anything not connected

with the marital rights of the husband. This right of enjoyment is mutual. The reason why reference is commonly made only to the husband's right of enjoyment is because it belongs especially and preeminently to him. The wife is restricted to the enjoyment of her husband alone; the husband may legally marry other wives. The wife cannot claim intercourse with her husband as a matter of right, at least not more than once after marriage, while the husband is entitled to intercourse with his wife at his pleasure.[1]

## REQUIREMENTS FOR A VALID MARRIAGE

Technically any free Muslim woman or man who possesses discretion (*akl*) and has reached the age of puberty (*bulugh*) can contract a valid marriage provided neither party is legally prohibited, i.e., the woman is already married or the man already has the prescribed number of wives. According to Islamic law the parties to marriage are not only permitted to see each other before marriage but it is recommended that they should do so (Shukri, 1966:43). Underage or insane persons can be married by their guardians (*wali*). The prophet is said to have declared that "marriage is committed to the parental kindred" (ibid.:52). Thus, the father is the guardian and in his absence his father or some other male. The right to give a ward in marriage belongs to the father or another male guardian. Marriage can also be contracted by proxy either through a particular or a general agency, and the agent can be either a man or a woman (ibid.:53-54). However, according to tradition, as transmitted by Ibn Majah, a woman can neither give herself nor another woman in marriage, and according to another, transmitted by Ahmad, Tirmidhi, Abu Dawud, Ibn Majah, and Darimi:

> Aisha reported God's messenger as saying, "If any woman marries without the consent of her guardian her marriage is void." If there is cohabitation she gets her dower for the intercourse her husband has had. (Mishkat, 1981:666)

In addition to the offer and acceptance, for a valid marriage contract to exist, witnesses and the constitution of dower are also essential. A marriage is valid only if contracted in the presence of two sane, free, male witnesses. Hanafi and Shafiʿi schools of jurisprudence also accept one male and two female witnesses. The witnesses not only testify to the fact of the marriage contract but also their presence is essential to the validity of the contract, and in their absence the marriage is void (Shukri, 1966:47-48).

### Dower

Payment of a dower by the husband to the wife is necessary for a valid marriage contract and is required by the Qur'an.

> Give to women their dowries of your free will; but if they forego part of it themselves, and that too willingly, then use it to your advantage. (IV:4)

The dower can be money or some other property that vests entirely in the wife (Bellefonds, 1971: 1078-81). Whether a sum of money or property is specified or not and whether a man is rich or poor—even an iron ring or half his cloak or if the husband is so poor that he cannot afford these, the teaching of the Qur'an to the wife (*Fatawa*, 1977:111, and *Sahih al-Bukhari*, 1984:15-16)—and even if it be expressly stipulated that there shall be no dower, a reasonable dower is the right of the wife, and it vests in her immediately upon marriage. However, dower may be deferred by agreement, and the husband can stipulate for the consummation of marriage before the payment of the dower (Shukri, 1966:71) provided the wife agrees to such stipulation.

Islamic jurisprudence rejects the notion of the dower being the bride price. "Dower is a result of marriage imposed by law" and according to the *Hidaya*, it is "merely a token of respect for its object, the woman" (Quoted in Shukri, 1966:57). Dower or *mehr*, according to anthropological research in the society of Arabia before Islam, was the purchase price of the woman, right down to the time of the Prophet, and was paid to the father of the bride while *sadac* was the gift given by the husband to the wife. As Robertson-Smith says:

> Before Islam a custom had established itself by which the husband ordinarily made a gift—under the name of *sadac*—to his wife upon marriage, or by which part of the *mahr* was customarily set aside for her use, and that thus the new law of Islam which made the dower a settlement on the wife was more easily established.

There are old traditions of such a practice . . . though the persistancy with which the prophet insists on a present from the husband . . . seems to show that there was no absolute rule on the matter before his time. What does appear to be possible is that the alleviations which the prophet introduced in the hard condition of married women were partly based on the more advanced laws of his own city of Mecca. (Robertson-Smith 1903:119-20)[2]

## EQUALITY OF MARRIAGE PARTIES

In addition to the legal requirements of eligibility for marriage, marriage contract, witness to marriage, and the payment of dower, the Prophet also insisted that marriage should be contracted between equal parties. The concept of *kafah* or equality in marriage between the man and the woman technically relates to six points: tribe or family, religion, character, occupation, fortune, and freedom. Some writers have entertained doubt whether in addition to these six qualifications such factors as equality in age, beauty, and understanding should also be taken into account; however, it appears that the enumerated six appear essential (Shukri, 1966:34-41). The emphasis on equality in marriage, so that the marriage has the character of being a suitable union in law, is attributed to the Prophet, who is said to have declared:

Take ye care that none contract women in marriage but their proper guardians and that they be so contracted only with their equals.

also that

Cohabitation, society and friendship cannot be completely enjoyed excepting by persons who are each other's equals. (Cited in Shukri, 1966:35)

That man and woman are the equal of each other, especially in marriage, is clear from the Qur'anic injunctions:

O men, fear your lord who created you from a single cell, and from it created its mate, and from the two of them dispersed men and women [male and female] in multitudes. So fear God in whose name you ask of one another [the bond] of relationship. (IV:1)

And

He it is who created you from a single soul, and of the same he did make his spouse, that he might find comfort in her. (VII:189)

Imam Muslim interprets this verse as saying that both

Man and woman are the joint heirs of the grace of life, and unless there is a very close and intimate form of companionship in them, they cannot enjoy the true grace of life. (*Sahih Muslim*, 1984:701)

The Qur'an further says:

And of his sign is that he has created wives for you from your-selves that you might find quiet of mind in them, and he put be-tween you love and affection. (XXX:21)

According to Imam Muslim this verse means:

the female is not inferior to the male in the sense that the former is created out of a superior stuff while the latter comes of a base origin. Both man and woman are the progeny of Adam and thus both have the same soul. The purpose of marriage, according to the holy Qur'an, is therefore, the union of the two souls which are one in essence. Their separate existence is an unnatural state of their being which changes into the natural state when they are united by marriage and thus brought close to each other physi-cally, mentally and emotionally. (*Sahih Muslim*, 1984:701)

### MUTA

*Muta* refers to temporary marriage, which, according to Bukhari, was permitted in the early days of Islam but was cancelled later (*Sahih al-Bukhari*, 1984:36-37). Muslim, on the other hand, says that a muta marriage was permitted during the time of Muhammad and Abu Bakr, the first caliph, and was abolished by the second caliph, Umar (*Sahih Muslim*, 1984:706, hadith 3249). Muslim also reports several other hadith that say that muta marriage was abolished by Muhammad himself.[3] Ibn Abbas, according to Tirmidhi in *Kitab al-Nikah*, said:

> The temporary marriage relates to the early days of Islam. A man would come to a settlement where he had no acquaintance and marry a woman for the period he thought he would stay there, and she would look after his belongings and cook for him. However, when this verse was revealed "Except for their wives or the captives their right hand possesses" (XXIII:5-6) intercourse with anyone else became unlawful. (*Sahih Muslim*, 1984:709)

It thus appears that muta as marriage has been considered unlawful almost from the very beginning of Islam even if at some earlier time it may have been considered permissible.[4]

## PRIVACY AND MODESTY IN FAMILY LIFE

The act of marriage lays the foundation of a family, but a family needs privacy for procreation and for the proper socialization of the children. In a desert society with tents as general dwellings and with a relaxed social style, the concept of privacy and the sanctity of the family may not have been taken seriously. The family in Islam, however, is a domestic and private institution and its preservation as such is not left to chance but sanctified by the Qur'anic commands themselves:

> O you who believe, do not enter other houses except yours without first asking permission and saluting the inmates. This is better for you: you may haply take heed. (XXIV:28)

and further

> If you find that no one is in, then do not enter unless you have received permission. If you are asked to go away, turn back. That is proper for you. God is aware of what you do. (XXIV:28)

Privacy and the house is sanctified by the Qur'an by requirements of decency and modesty in the interfamilial and general social behavior. The Qur'anic commands provide for the establishment of a moral pattern of behavior on the part of various members of the family within the house as well as without. The Qur'an particularly abhors lewdness, exposure, and display of the body. Both men and women are admonished "to lower their eyes and guard their private parts" (XXIV:30).

Women are especially ordered to

not display their charms except when it is apparent outwardly, and cover their bosoms with their veils and not show their finery . . . They should not walk stamping their feet lest they should make known what they hide of their ornaments. (XXIV:31)

However, within the family and in the presence of close relatives such as husbands, fathers, fathers-in-law, sons, step-sons, brothers' and sisters' sons, young boys before they reach the age of puberty, women attendants and those men attendants "who do not have any need [for women]" life is more relaxed and no particular guarding is required (XXIV:31 and XXXIII:55). But even within this very close family circle the Qur'an commands that permission be asked for entering on three occasions:

Before the early morning prayer; when you disrobe for the midday siesta; and after prayer at night. These are the three occasions of dishabille for you. There is no harm if you or they visit one another at other times [without permission]. God thus explains things to you clearly, for God is all-knowing and all wise. (XXIV:58)

And these rules also apply to one's children when they have reached the age of puberty; that is, they should ask permission to enter (XXIV:59).

Requirements of modesty, while somewhat relaxed for older women and women beyond the child-bearing age (XXIV:60), are more strict for the wives and daughters of the Prophet (XXXIII:55,59), who are treated differently:

O wives of the Prophet, you are not like other women. If you are mindful of God, do not be too obliging in your speech, lest someone who is diseased of mind should covet your person; so say only customary things (XXXIII:32). Stay at home and do not deck yourselves with ostentation as in the days of Paganism. (XXXII:32)

## WHOM CAN A MUSLIM MARRY?

Whom a Muslim male may or may not marry is very clearly laid down in the Qur'an. A Muslim is forbidden to marry the wives of his father; his own mother, daughters, or sisters; foster mothers and foster sisters; mothers of wives; daughters of wives with whom marriage has been consummated; wives of sons; two sisters at the same time; or married women, unless they have been captured in war (IV:22). For purposes of marriage, Islam does not treat blood and foster relationships as basically different; thus foster mothers and foster sisters are included in the prohibition along with real mothers and sisters (*Fatawa*, 1977:104-5).

A Muslim male is permitted to marry any chaste Muslim woman or any chaste Christian or Jewish woman (people of the Book)[5] but he must pay their dowers. By especially emphasizing cousins as marriage partners the Qur'an appears to indicate a preferential marriage relationship, though permission to marry beyond the cousin range is general with only the qualification of chastity being emphasized, which corresponds with the general tone of the Qur'an regarding all relationships between the sexes and the emphasis on modesty and decency. The permission or prohibition regarding marriage partners that is addressed to males equally applies in reverse to females. However, it does not apply with regard to marriage with the people of the Book. Thus, permission is given for a Muslim woman to marry a Christian or a Jewish man provided he pays her dower.

## MONOGAMY VERSUS POLYGAMY

No other Qur'anic provision has aroused as much global controversy as the one relating to the number of wives a Muslim male may marry. Is it a permission or a prohibition? Is it the epitome of morality or of lechery? And in light of it, is Islam an ethical religion or a license for male chauvinism and lasciviousness? The Qur'an talks about marriages and wives in the plural not only because it is an address to Muslims in general but, indeed, even if the addressee were a single male Muslim, the Qur'anic exhortation would still be in the plural. The rather brief regulation dealing with the number of wives is to be found in the chapter entitled "women" (IV:3) and it says:

And if you fear you cannot be fair to orphan girls [in your charge], then marry women who like you, up to two three or four; but if you think you cannot treat so many with equity marry only one, or the captives under you. This is more suitable than acting unjustly [with many]. (Ahmed Ali, 1984)

That same verse has been translated slightly differently by Pickthall:

And if ye fear that ye will not deal fairly by the orphans, marry of the women, who seem good to you, two or three or four; and if ye fear that ye cannot do justice [to so many] then one [only] or [the captives] that your right hand possesses. Thus it is more likely that ye will not do injustice. (1983:76)

Maulana Muhammad Ali (1951:187) translates this verse with very slight variations, as does Muhammad Husayn Haykal (1976:293), but the sense remains the same. All four translators, two Pakistani but from two different traditions or sects, one British, and one Egyptian, give the same essential rendering. Pickthall tells us that this verse was revealed in the fourth year of the *hijra* in the months following the battle of Uhud or as Noldeke puts it, "between the end of the third year and the end of the fifth year" (quoted in Pickthall, 1983:75) after Muhammad's migration to Madina. Haykal, on the other hand, says that this verse was revealed toward the end of the eighth year of the hijra. Both °Ali and Haykal interpret this verse as indicating a commandment to take only one wife. Haykal says "that Muhammad stood for monogamy and counselled its observance" (1976:292)[6] which should be obvious from Muhammad's married life with Khadijah, whom he married at age twenty-five when she was forty; he remained monogamous throughout the twenty-seven years of their married life until Khadijah's death. With reference to the further Qur'anic commandment, which does emphasize the difficulty of doing justice to several wives:

Howsoever you may try you will never be able to treat your wives equally. But do not incline [to one] exclusively and leave [the other] suspended [as it were]. Yet if you do the right thing and are just, God is verily forgiving and kind. (IV:129)

Haykal asserts that:

> these verses were revealed in order to stress the superiority of monogamy over polygamy. The Qur'an commanded the limiting of one's self to one wife out of fear of the possibility of injustice and conviction that justice to more than one wife is not within the limits of men's capability. The revelation, however, realized that in the exceptional circumstances of a people, it is quite possible that there might be a need for more than one wife; but it has limited polygamy to four and conditioned its practice to capacity for fairness and justice on the part of the husband. (1976:293)

Muhammad ʿAli also argues the same point, saying that the verse IV:3

> *Permits polygamy under certain circumstances: it does not enjoin it, nor even permit unconditionally.* (1951:187, emphasis in original)

He further argues that this verse is directly related to the consequences of the battle of Uhud in which seventy out of 700 Muslims were killed, depriving a number of Muslim families of breadwinners and guardians and the number of the males was to dwindle further as a result of the battles yet to be fought:

> It would thus be clear that the permission to have more wives than one was given under the peculiar circumstances of the Muslim society then existing, and the Prophet's action in marrying widows, as well as the example of many of his companions, corroborates this statement. (Ibid.:187)

Using more practical social and functional reasons, ʿAli goes on to assert:

> It may be added here that polygamy in Islam is both in theory and practice an exception, not a rule, and as an exception it is a remedy for many of the evils especially prevalent in European society. (Ibid. :187-8)

To Western observers, however, this verse contains permission to marry four wives. Maxime Rodinson considers the Muslim arguments to be rationalizations based on defensiveness:

> What we see here is a typical childish example of apologetical reasoning which, as usual, runs completely counter to the historical

spirit. It is hard to see how an encouragement to take concubines if one is afraid of not acting fairly towards a number of wives can be a move in the direction of the supposedly more moral idea of monogamy. Moreover the Quranic text is clearly not a restriction but an exhortation, somewhat vaguely [for us] connected with fairness to orphans. (1983:232)[7]

On the question of how Muslims in general have interpreted this verse when they have taken more than one wife, Rodinson may be nearer the truth than either ʿAli or Haykal. The permission is explicit in the Qur'an, and any Muslim determined to make use of it is not going to be, and has not in the past been, deterred from doing so. Economic or social pressure or peer disapproval may act as a brake, but it is not arguable that Muslims have considered this permission to be bound to a particular time in their history or that fear of behaving unjustly[8] toward other wives has prevented any Muslim from utilizing what he sees as divine sanction. Since the Qur'an is the direct word of God, it is immune from human improvement and amendment; and Sunni Islam does not recognize any authority after Muhammad to amend the Qu'ran or to delete or add anything to it. Also, since Islam has no organization like the Roman Catholic church, there is no institutional authority that can make binding pronouncements or interpretations on religious or doctrinal matters. Muslims have historically observed religious rituals and commands in accordance with what they have believed to be correct as approved by their local community. Thus, polygamy has been practiced in every Muslim society and in every age; it has been restricted by a variety of considerations but not necessarily by justice. One attempt to restrict polygamy by positive law without appearing to tinker with God's command was made in Pakistan in 1962 by the martial law government of Field Marshal Ayub Khan when it issued the Family Laws Ordinance. According to this regulation, Muslims could still marry several wives, but for each additional wife, the written permission of the previous wife or wives was required as well as a fee that increased astronomically. The ordinance was vehemently opposed by the conservative religious males when the national assembly met. Only the absence of real democracy helped women for the president rejected the demand of the elected legislators. However, even that limited concession has been nullified by the current wave of Islamization.

The Prophet's own example during the last few years of his life—he took ten wives in all after the death of Khadija—set a pattern that does not strengthen the arguments of Haykal and ʿAli.[9] Even Muhammad's wives became jealous, some believing he was paying excessive attention to one at the expense of the others, and they ganged up on him, disgusting him so much that he vowed to keep himself aloof from all his wives for one month (*Sahih al-Bukhari*, 1984:87-91, hadith 119). Nevertheless, on the basis of logic and reasonable interpretation of the Qur'anic commands (IV:3, 129), Haykal and ʿAli and those who agree with them appear more sound than Rodinson. Permission to marry *"up to* two, three or four" appears to indicate an upper limit rather than command a specific number; the language of this verse is not legislative but concessional; it immediately goes on to say, "but if you cannot treat so many with equity *marry only one.*" This concern for equity is reinforced by the later verse: "However you may try you will never be able to treat your wives equally." Therefore, the emphasis on justice is far greater, not only in the case of plurality of wives but as the general theme in the Qur'an, which requires all human relations to be governed by fairness, equity, and justice. The overwhelming majority of Muslims, whether contemporaneously or historically, have confined themselves to monogamy: cases of polygamy are rare and therefore must be treated as deviations rather than the general rule. Consequently, those Muslim writers and theologians who do not treat the concession for up to four wives as a general rule, are expressing a logical and reasonable interpretation of the Qur'anic verses, and indicating the general marriage practice among Muslims. This same view is also affirmed by Robert Roberts who says that the enactment of the verse IV:3

> shows, that no man should marry more wives than he could adequately provide for. And this command is generally observed, since one wife is the rule among the poorer classes, nor is it by any means confined to these alone. (1971:9-10)[10]

Along with an upper limit of four wives the Qur'an also talks of "those which their right hands possess" (LXX:33, also IV:3). This verse refers to female slaves, and the Qur'an appears to indicate that cohabitation was permitted. Such slaves were acquired in war or through purchase or a gift. Roberts sees in these verses a great motivation for the early wars of Islam:

The permission naturally furnished a strong inducement to his [Muhammad's] followers to fight the battles of Islam, since the women taken captive in battle would become lawful concubines to their captors. (1971:10)

There is no legal limit to the number and they are permitted in addition to four legally married wives. Muhammad Ali, however, sees these commandments somewhat differently:

If the reference here is to sexual relations, the permission regarding those *whom their right hands possess* must be read subject to the conditions of IV:25. It may be added that slave girls, when taken as wives, did not acquire the full status of full wife, and hence they are spoken of distinctly. (1951:1714-5)[11]

The Qur'an IV:25 says:

And whoever among you cannot afford to marry free believing women, [let him marry] such of your believing maidens as your right hands possess. And Allah knows best your faith—you are [sprung] the one from the other. So marry them with the permission of their masters, and give them their dowries justly, they being chaste, not fornicating, nor receiving paramours: then if they are guilty of adultery when they are taken in marriage, they shall suffer half the punishment for free married women. This is for him among you who fears falling into evil. And that you abstain is better for you.

On the basis of this verse, ʿAli disagrees with the view that unlimited concubinage is permitted. Sexual relations with slave girls, he says, are allowed only within the context of marriage; and they are conditional upon the slave girl being Muslim, and they are only permitted where a Muslim male cannot afford marriage and is afraid of commiting fornication. ʿAli is quite emphatic that this verse cannot be taken to mean sexual license (1951:197-98; 561). The *Mishkat* (1984:677), however, refers to sexual intercourse with slave girls, and the language indicates that the slave girl is not a wife: "I have a slave girl who is our servant and I have intercourse with her, but do not want her to conceive."[12] and

we went out with God's messenger on the expedition to the B. al-

Mustaliq and took some Arab women captive, and we desired the women, for we were suffering from the absence of our wives.[13]

In both of these narrations the question was whether the man could withdraw the penis in order to avoid conception, not whether or not sexual intercourse was permitted. The Prophet's reply was that they could, which would imply that he found nothing wrong in having sexual intercourse with slave girls and did not demand marriage as a condition of cohabitation.

### Rights and Duties of Husbands and Wives

The Qur'an bestows clear and mutual obligation on both husband and wife:

> women ought to behave toward their husbands in manner as their husbands behave towards them, according to what is just. (II:228, also II:187)

And this command is further confirmed and strengthened by the Prophet in his last address from *Jabal Arafat*:

> verily you have got certain rights over your women and your women have certain rights over you (Akbar, 1981:86)

The obligations are mutual but not identical. Thus, the husband's responsibilities pertain to providing for the wife and treating her kindly, while the wife is required to be submissive and obedient. The Prophet is reported to have admonished husbands about their wives:

> That you give them to eat when you eat yourself, and clothe them when you clothe yourself, and do not slap them, nor separate them in displeasure, except in your own house. (*Fatawa*, 1977:119, hadith 784)

And, according to Aisha and Abu Huriarah, the Prophet said:

> He is of the most perfect Muslemans, whose disposition is most liked by his family. (*Fatawa*, 1977:120, hadith 788)

> This is the most perfect Musleman whose disposition is best; and the best of you is he who behaves best to his wives. (*Fatawa*, 1977:120, hadith 789)

The best wife, as the Prophet admonished, is

> The one who pleases [her husband] when he looks at her, obeys him when he gives her a command, and does not go against his wishes regarding his person or property by doing anything of which he disapproves.[14]

Support for the wife is obligatory on the husband whether the marriage is consummated or not, provided consummation is physically possible. According to Shafiʿi, the right of maintenance of a wife "is the consequence of submission and restraint" (Shukri, 1966:71).[15] The husband's responsibility to maintain the wife is neither eliminated nor suspended if he is imprisoned, even if the imprisonment is the result of nonpayment of a debt incurred by his wife, while, if the wife is imprisoned or abducted, the husband is not responsible for her maintenance unless he has caused her imprisonment for a debt incurred by him (Ibid.:74). The wife's entitlement includes clothing, proper housing where she does not feel lonely, and household and toilet articles (Ibid.:78-80).

The wife must maintain her husband's property, keep the house in good order, and in general obey him in what is lawful. She is, however, not obliged to bake, cook, or clean, or to spin or weave; but the husband has to provide for these services only if "she is the daughter of respectable persons and did not herself work in her own family" (quoted in Ibid:81). She must also yield her person to her husband within reasonable bounds of time, place, health, and decency; if she does not, she becomes rebellious, and the husband has the right to punish her. A wife must live with her husband wherever he chooses to reside and remain in the house, not quitting it without his permission. However, the husband has no right to prevent a wife from going out to acquire religious knowledge which is enjoined on both males and females, and he cannot prevent his wife from going out to care for her parents even if they are infidel because caring for her parents takes precedence over the rights of the husband (Fatawa, 1977:117-19).[16] In spite of the general requirement of submission on the part of the wife she is not required to contribute toward household expenses not even for her own personal needs, since a Muslim woman, whether married or maiden, has absolute right to her own property including the dower and does not need her husband's consent to dispose of it. The power of the husband over his wife is only disciplinary and proprietary, and as part of that disciplinary power, a husband can inflict corporal chastisement for the following reasons:

(a)  if she fails to beautify or adorn herself when her husband desires her to do so,
(b)  if she refuses to have intercourse with him,
(c)  if she does not offer prayers, and
(d)  if she goes out of the house without his permission—apart from the exceptions already mentioned—after she has received her full dower. (Shukri, 1966:83-89)

Does this framework of the family create a relationship of equality between the husband and the wife? There are several verses in the Qur'an that emphasize mutuality and, by implication, the equality of the sexes and thus, by extension, the equality of relationship between husband and wife. The following would indicate an intention toward equality:

O men, fear your lord who created you from a single cell, and from it created its mate, and from the two of you dispersed men and women. (IV:1)

We shall invest whosoever works for good, whether man or woman, with a pleasant life, and reward them in accordance with the best of what they have done. (XVI:97)

Verily men and women who have come to submission,

men and women who are believers, men and women who are devout, truthful men and truthful women, men and women with endurance, men and women who are modest, men and women who give alms, men and women who observe fasting, men and women who guard their private parts, and those men and women who remember God a great deal, for them God has forgiveness and a great reward. (XXXIII:35)

As for the thief, whether man or woman, amputate his arm as requittal for what he has done. (V:38)

However, the Qur'an also very categorically affirms the superiority of men and husbands over women and wives:

Men are the guardians of women as God has favoured some with

more than others, and because they spend of their wealth [to provide for them]. So women who are virtuous are obedient to God
and guard the hidden for God has guarded it. (IV:34)

And the same verse goes on to give men power to chastise women:

As for women you feel are unyielding, talk to them suasively;
then leave them alone in bed (until they are willing); and then
have intercourse with them. If they open out to you, do not seek
an excuse for blaming them. (IV:34)

No complementary or parallel power is given to women over men. The
superiority of men over women is further confirmed by giving men
double the share of women (IV:11, 12), by substituting two female
witnesses for one man (II:282), and, finally, by giving the absolute and
almost unlimited power of divorce to husbands (Shukri, 1966:87-88).

How has the Muslim society interpreted these various verses of the
Qur'an? In spite of the many verses that put man and woman at the
same footing it appears that Muslims have shown preference for those
that establish male superiority in structuring the family. Both historically and spatially Muslim societies and families are male-dominated.
Since the Qur'anic commands and laws depend upon interpretation for
implementation, the consistent pattern of male domination that can be
observed throughout the Muslim world, clearly indicates that this is to
be the Divine intent as Muslims see it. In short, in a Muslim family, the
female has a subordinate role, and it remains arguable whether that
role is inferior or not.

### Chastity, Adultery, and False Accusation

The Qur'an permits the enjoyment of sex within the limits of marriage
only and lays down clear and stiff penalties against fornication and
adultery as well as against false accusation of extramarital sex. It appears that the early Qur'anic commands dealing with adultery were less
specific about the acts involved as well as about the punishment and
that the specificity and severity of the crime and punishment came
later. Thus, the verses under the chapter "The Women" say:

If any of your women is guilty of an immoral act, bring four of
your men to give evidence; if they testify against them, retain

them in the house until death, or until God provide some other way for them. (IV:15) If two among you are guilty of such acts then punish both of them. But if they repent and reform, let them be for God accepts repentance and is merciful. (IV:16)

Elaborating the meaning of these verses, Muhammad ʿAli says that the Arabic word used is *al-fahishah*, which refers to acts that are lewd, obscene, immodest, and gross; and that here it does not indicate fornication. Since the act is not as extreme as fornication, the punishment is also moderate, for example, curtailment of liberty (1951:193-94, 551-2). However, according to another Muslim writer, these two verses were abrogated when later and more specific verses were revealed (El-Awa, 1982:14-15). The Arabic word for illict sexual intercourse, *zina* includes both adultery [between two married individuals] and fornication [between an unmarried man and woman], and the last verse to be revealed dealing with zina is very specific:

The committers of *zina*, male and female flog each of them with a hundred stripes, and do not let pity for the two withhold you from obedience to God, if you believe in God and the day of Judgement. And let a party of believers witness their punishment. (XXIV:2)

The expression "committers of zina" has also been translated as "the whore and the whoremonger" and "the adulterer and the adulteress". El-Awa says that flogging is the punishment for fornication and stoning to death for adultery (1982:14-15). However, if the punishment for adultery was death, the following verses of the Qur'an would be redundant :

The adulterer can marry no one but an adulteress or idolatress, and the adulteress cannot marry anyone but an adulterer or an idolater. (XXIV:3)

Bad women deserve bad men, and bad men are for bad women; but good women are for good men, and good men for good women. (XXIV:26)

Just as the Qur'an is very unambiguous and severe with illicit sexual relations, so it is with false accusations of unchastity:

those who defame chaste women and do not not bring four witnesses should be punished with eighty lashes, and their testimony
should not be accepted afterwards, for they are profligates.
(XXIV:4, also 23 and 58).

Five verses (XXIV:6-10) deal with accusations of unchastity by the
husband against the wife where the husband is the only witness. The
husband has to swear four times to his accusation and the fifth time to
the curse of God if he is false. The wife can avert punishment by swear-
ing four times that her husband is a liar, and the fifth time she swears
invoking the curse of God if she is a liar.

All accusations of zina require four male eyewitnesses, who have to
testify that they saw the actual sexual intercourse with their own eyes
for the Qur'anic punishment to become obligatory. And these four
witnesses have to meet the other conditions of being reliable and trust-
worthy. If the accuser cannot produce four such witnesses, then the accuser himself stands accused of false accusation for which the Qur'an
specifies clear punishment. Taking the Qur'anic verses dealing with
zina in their entirety, it appears obvious that for a hundred lashes to be
inflicted, sexual intercourse has to take place in a place open to the public so that four eye witnesses could be assembled. On the other hand,
only a husband has the right to go into his house without permission
and unannounced and he might apprehend his wife committing zina
without having witnesses. The Qur'an, therefore, deals with such a situation differently and relies upon the oaths of the two, and the wife becomes liable to punishment only if she accepts her guilt; otherwise, she
cannot be punished.

### Children

The Qur'an shows great concern for the well-being and care of children in respect to their well being, care, just treatment of orphans,
proper care of the orphans' property, and the duties of the children toward their parents. The Qur'anic commands clearly indicate, and filial
relationships among Muslims all over the world confirm, that children
are not only loved but greatly indulged and that in turn children show
great love and respect for their parents. A Muslim family not only the-

oretically and scripturally but also in reality, by and large, is a model of love, care, and support. The family bond is so strong that it overshadows all other social relationships and in many ways the focus is so exclusively on the obligations to the family, that it makes other social relationships weak.

The Qur'an says that children are a blessing from God, who in His pleasure bestows sons or daughters as He pleases and some he chooses to leave childless (VII:198). Thus, sons and daughters are equal blessings, with neither superior to the other. The father is responsible for caring for the family and the Qur'an commands men to provide for their families according to their means without hardship being imposed (*Sahih Muslim*, 1984:701). Even when a man divorces his wife, he is required to house and feed her according to his means and if she is pregnant, then the husband is responsible for maintaining her while she is suckling the child (XXX:21). The responsibility of the mother to suckle the child and of the father to maintain and provide for them is general:

> The mothers shall suckle their babies for a period of two years for those fathers who wish that they should complete the suckling, in which case they should feed and clothe them in a befitting way; but no soul shall be compelled beyond capacity, neither the mother made to suffer for the child nor the father for his offspring. The same holds good for the heir of the father [if he dies]. If they wish to wean the child by mutual consent there is no harm. And if you wish to engage a wet nurse you may do so if you pay her an agreed amount as is customary. (II:233)

Not only is it incumbent upon men to support their families, but also when they see death approaching; they are required to arrange for and leave behind provision for one year's maintenance and lodging for their families (II:240).[17] There are numerous hadith which confirm and reinforce these Qur'anic commands through the words of the Prophet (Mishkat, 1984:714). The Prophet preferred that property be left first to one's family rather than to Allah's cause (*Sahih al-Bukhari*, 1984:202). According to Abu Huraira, Muhammad said: "The best alms is that you give when you are rich, and you should start first to support your dependants" (ibid.). Also, in case of a niggardly or irresponsible father, the wife can take of the husband's property for herself and her children without his knowledge "and the amount should be just and reasonable" (XXIV:32). The care of the children and their welfare has thus been made paramount. The Qur'an continually admonishes the guardians of children, especially orphans, to be punctilious in the care of their wards' property. Abusing and squandering such property is a cardinal sin in Islam; a guardian can use his ward's property only to improve it or when it is absolutely necessary but then also only reasonably and justly. A guardian must give account of the property of a minor when the latter comes of age in the presence of witnesses (XXIV:33).

The father is the first and the natural guardian of a child. And fatherhood is established according to a hadith: the child belongs to the marriage bed, that is, the child is attributed to the man on whose bed it is born (XVII:32, also XXIV:2, 3, XXV:68, LX:12). After the father comes the executor of the father, and, in the case where no executor has been appointed and the father's father is still alive, then he becomes the guardian. In short the Qur'an, the hadith, and Islamic jurisprudence have considered the care and welfare of the children important enough to spell out detailed provisions dealing with these subjects.

The Qur'an and the hadith emphasize children's responsibility to their parents. "We have enjoined on man to be good to his parents" (XXIX:8, XXXI:4), and:

> that ye do good unto your parents, whether the one of them, or both of them attain to old age with thee. And say not unto them "uphi"[18] and reproach them not, but speak kindly to them, and submit to act humbly towards them, out of tender affection, and say, "O Lord, have mercy on them both, as they nursed me when I was a child." (VI:152-54)

Between the parents, in case of separation or divorce, the mother has superior right to custody. According to Tirmidhi and Darimi, Abu Ayub told of hearing God's messenger say:

> If anyone separates a mother from her child, God will separate him from his friends on the day of resurrection. (*Mishkat*, 1984:716)

According to another hadith transmitted by Ahmad and Abu Dawud, a woman said:

Messenger of God, my womb was a vessel to this son of mine, my breasts a water skin for him, and my lap a guardian for him, yet his father has divorced me and wants to take him away from me.

God's messenger replied,"you have more right to him as long as you do not marry." (Ibid.:719-20)

Adoption is not generally recognized in Islamic jurisprudence, and it seems that the purpose of this negative position is to reject the traditional and pre-Islamic Arabian tradition of creating by fiction a blood relationship that did not exist

> the fiction of adoption by which a new tribesman was feigned to be the veritable son of a member of the tribe is evidence of the highest value that the Arabs were incapable of conceiving any absolute social obligation or social unity which was not based on kinship; for a legal fiction is always adopted to reconcile an act with a principle too firmly established to be simply ignored. (Robertson-Smith, 1903:62, also 27, 36-37)

Since adoption created a blood relationship, it would also create the same impediments to marriage as a natural relationship. This was seen as contrary to Islam and it is clear in the Qur'an: "nor has he made your adopted sons your real sons" (XXXIII:4), even if one calls another his son. Every person should be called by the name of his father, "and if ye know not their fathers, let them be as your brethren in religion" (XXXIII:5). Some Western writers attribute this rejection of adoption to Muhammad's desire to marry Zainab, who was the wife of Muhammad's adopted son and freed slave Zaid, but Muslim writers reject Roberts's imputations of lust to the Prophet (1971:50-51).[19] However, while adoption is rejected, acknowledgment or *ikrar* by a man of a son creates paternity and confers on the son the same legal rights as are conferred by the rule *al-walad li'l-firash*, i.e., "the child belongs to the marriage bed." A man can so acknowledge a son without reference to or permission from his wife or wives so long as the mother of the acknowledged son does not stand in a prohibited relationship to the man (*Encyclopedia of Islam*:1078-81).

*Inheritance*

The important element regarding property and holding of property in Islam is individual possession and control. As we have seen in the case of dower, it is the wife herself and in her own right who possesses her dower as well as other property, and she can dispose of it as she pleases without reference to or interference from her husband or any other male relative. The Qur'an also puts an individualistic stamp on the inheritance of property by allocating distinct and specific shares to both men and women:

> Men have a share in what the parents and relatives leave behind at death; and women have a share in what the parents and relatives leave behind. Be it large or small a legal share is fixed. (IV:7)

However, the Qur'an does not altogether abolish old Arabian customs, and inheritance principles accommodate some of them, such as "the principle that the dead do not inherit and the living cannot represent the dead" (Watt, 1951:290). The general principles of inheritance lay down that relatives toward whom a man has natural obligations cannot be deprived of their share. There is no distinction between the first born and others, and they all share equally, except that the daughters' share is half that of their brothers, but regarding parents, brothers and sisters, while their share is small, all have equal shares without distinction of sex (Roberts, 1971:61). There is also no distinction between the child of a lawful wife and that of a concubine if acknowledged by the father. An illegitimate child cannot inherit from his father, but inherits from his mother as she does from him. Also, non-Muslim relatives of a Muslim do not inherit property of a Muslim (ibid. :66). There are two categories of inheritors: normal heirs such as sons, father, and brothers, who share the main part of the estate, and the Qur'anic heirs such as the widower or the widow(s), parents, daughters, sisters, and brothers (Watt, 1951:291).

The Qur'an lays down that

> As for the children, God decrees that the share of the male is equivalent to that of the two females. If they consist of women only, and of them more than two, they will get two-thirds of the inheritance; but in case there is one, she will inherit one-half. The par-

ents will inherit one-sixth of the estate if it happens that the deceased has left a child; but if he has left no children, and his parents are his heirs, then the mother will inherit one-sixth after payment of legacies and debts.

Your share in the property the wives leave behind is one-half if they die without an issue, but in case they have left children, then your share is one-fourth after the payment of legacies and debts; and your wife shall inherit one-fourth of what you leave at death if you die childless, if not she will get one-eighth of what you leave behind after payment of legacies and debts. If a man or woman should die without leaving either children or parents behind but have brother and sister, they shall each inherit one-sixth. In case there are more, they will share one-third of the estate after payment of legacies and debts without prejudice to others. (IV:11-12)

To give an idea of what these shares would look like, Montgomery Watt has prepared some examples of the distribution of shares:

Wife, son: receive respectively 1/8, 7/8.
Wife, son, daughter: 1/8, 7/12, 7/24.
Wife, two sons, two daughters: 1/8,7/24 (2), 7/48 (2).
Husband, two sons, two daughters: 1/4, 1/4 (2), 1/8 (2).
Two daughters, father or distant agnates: 1/3 (2), 1/3.
Two daughters, father, mother: 1/3 (2), 1/6, 1/6.
Father, mother: 2/3, 1/3.
Father, mother, brother: 5/6, 1/6, nil.
Father, mother, wife, two sons, two daughters: 1/6, 1/6, 1/8, 13/72 (2), 13/144 (2).
Husband, son: 1/4, 3/4.
Husband, father: 1/2, 1/2.
Father's father, two brothers: 2/3, 1/6 (2).
Sister, no children: 1/2.
Brother, sister, no children: 1/3, 1/6 (1951:291-92)[20]

### Divorce

Divorce is the termination of marriage. The Arabic word for divorce is *talaq* which means untying a knot, i.e., bringing apart something that was held together. While talaq is permitted in Islam, according to a saying attributed to the Prophet, it is the most reprehensible of all things permitted in the sight of God (Fyzee, 1974:146). ʿAli, the Prophet's cousin and son-in-law, is said not only to have refused to divorce one of his own wives in order to marry another but also to have advised the Kufans not to marry their daughters to his own son Hasan since he was in the habit of marrying and divorcing many wives (ibid.).

The subject of divorce is treated in detail in the Qur'an[21] and the hadith. There are numerous sayings attributed to the Prophet (*Sahih Muslim*, 1984:754-55) on this subject. The Qur'anic verses dealing with interpersonal interactions, emphasize justice, compassion and charity, which men are exhorted to show to their wives, and it is men who are addressed especially because the Qur'an places the power of divorce in the hands of men.

> There is no sin in divorcing your wives before the consummation of marriage or settling the dowry; but then provide adequately for them, the affluent according to their means the poor in accordance with theirs as befitting. (II:236)

And

> When you have divorced your wives, and they have reached the end of the period of waiting, then keep them honourably [by revoking the divorce], or let them go with honour, and do not detain them with the intent of harassing them lest you should transgress. (II:231)

Further,

> And if you divorce them before the consummation of marriage, but after settling the dowry, then half the settled dowry must be paid, unless the woman forgoes it, or the person who holds the bond of marriage pays the full amount. And if the man pays the whole, it is nearer to piety. (II:237)

As a marriage is a social contract, so is its termination. A divorce can be effected by death, by the parties to the marriage, and by judicial decree. A husband can divorce his wife by repudiating her, i.e, by pronouncing talaq; he can also take a vow to abstain from having marital relations for four months, i.e., *ila*; or he may compare her to one of his female relatives within the prohibited degrees, i.e., *zihar* (Shukri,

1966:111).[22] All that the husband need do is pronounce the talaq without assigning any cause and without the wife being present and, among the majority of Muslims (i.e., Hanafis), without following any particular form (*Sahih Muslim*, 1981:172, hadith 3257). According to the same hadith, a husband may delegate his power of divorce to anyone, including the wife. This is called *tafwiz*.

Where tafwiz has been made over to the wife, according to Islamic jurists, it may take one of three forms: *ikhtiyar, amr bil-yad, or mashiah* (Shukri, 1966:104). Under ikhtiyar the wife is given the authority to divorce herself, amr bil-yad leaves the matter in the wife's hands, and under mashiah the wife has the option to do as she pleases (ibid.). The distinctions between these Arabic terms are not significant in countries where Arabic is not spoken; according to Fyzee, the main element in tafwiz is that the husband delegates the power and the wife acquires the right to initiate divorce upon herself; however, the delegation is not absolute and unconditional, and it can be used only on reasonable grounds (1974:159), though once exercised tafwiz by the wife would be one in which the husband makes a promise to the wife and fails to keep it, such as a promise by the husband to provide certain maintenance or not to take another wife, would enable the wife to divorce herself, and such a divorce would be both valid and irrevocable. For a Muslim wife tafwiz is perhaps the most powerful weapon for securing her freedom from an undesirable marriage.

A marriage can also be terminated by mutual consent by *khul* or *mubara'a*. Kuhl literally means to strip off or to put off. Legally, khul leads to separation in which the wife redeems herself by surrendering or returning to the husband some financial consideration, such as a portion of her mahr or some other property, in return for which the husband agrees to release her from the marriage bond (Shukri, 1966:106-10). However, Fyzee says that a khul divorce is not dependent either upon consummation of marriage or upon the payment of compensation by the wife and there is no general presumption that the husband has been released of the obligation to pay mahr so long as mutual consent is established (1974:165). The difference between khul and ordinary talaq is that khul establishes a single irreversible divorce independent of *idda* (waiting period) whereas a husband may revoke ordinary talaq before the expiry of the waiting period (Shukri,

1966:106-7). In mubara'a the wife releases the husband from the payment of mahr where that has not yet been paid. Mubara'a also terminates all other rights of both parties that result from marriage.

A marriage may also be dissolved at the request either of the husband or the wife. If the decree is granted as a result of the husband's initiation, it is in effect talaq; if on the wife's initiative, it is tantamount to an annulment or recision (*faskh*). The wife can sue for divorce on the grounds of impotence, or the husband charging the wife with adultery (*hain*), his abstaining from marital relations for at least four months (*ila*), his comparing her to his female relatives in the prohibited degrees (*zihar*), apostacy or his failure to discharge his general marital obligations. The last includes the following grounds: failing to provide subsistance or clothing to the wife, forcing the wife to be without habitation or leaving her without providing for her or refusing to visit her, and treating the wife cruelly or beating her without cause (Shukri, 1966:111-23, also Fyzee, 1974:168-77).

According to Islamic law, there are three kinds of divorce: *talaq ahsan, talaq hasan or talaq bida*, i.e., most laudable, laudable, or irregular. Talaq ahsan occurs when the husband pronounces divorce in the wife's period of purity (i.e., not during menstruation) during which time he has not had intercourse with her and she is allowed to observe her idda or waiting period. Talaq hasan takes place when a husband divorces an enjoyed wife by pronouncing three talaqs during three periods of purity. In talaq bida the husband pronounces three divorces at once. It is accepted as binding but it contravenes the spirit of the Shari'a and is considered offensive though legal (*Sahih Muslim*, 1984:754-59). The Qur'anic verses on this subject lay down that:

> divorce is [revocable] two times [after pronouncement], after which [there are two ways open for husbands], either [to] keep [the wives] honourably, or part with them in a decent way. (II:29)

and

> "If a man divorces her again [a third time], she becomes unlawful for him." (II:230)

Remarriage is permitted in Islam, especially for divorced or wid-

owed women and it is considered commendable and preferable in view
of the very strict and prohibitive attitude of the Qur'an regarding zina.
The Qur'an clearly says:

> When you have divorced your wives, and they have reached the
> end of the period of waiting, then keep them honourably [by re-
> voking the divorce], or let them go with honour, and do not de-
> tain them with the intent of harassing lest they should transgress.
> (II:231)

> When you have divorced your wives and they have completed the
> fixed term [of waiting], do not stop them from marrying other
> men if it is agreed between them honourably. (II:234)

Remarriage of the same partners after they have been divorced is not
easy. A woman divorced by her husband can remarry him, but only after she has married another husband, that marriage has been consummated, the new husband has then willingly divorced her, and she has
observed the full period of idda. The Qur'an says:

> If a man divorces her again [a third time], she becomes unlawful
> for him [and he cannot remarry her] until she has married an-
> other man. Then if he divorces her there is no harm if the two
> unite again if they think they will keep within the bounds set by
> God and made clear for those who understand. (II:230)

Some Western writers consider this to be a humiliating imposition
on the wife, whereas most Muslim writers hold the view that the imposition of this hardship has been intended to prevent men from treating
women as playthings and to compel them to consider seriously and
coolly the consequences of divorce before pronouncing it, since once it
is formally effective, talaq becomes irrevocable, and sexual relations between divorced husband and wife become zina and are subject to the
very severe punishment prescribed in the Qur'an.

Idda is prescribed by the Qur'an for both widows and divorcees.

> Women who are divorcees have to wait for three monthly peri-
> ods, and if they believe in God and the last day they must not hide
> unlawfully what God has formed within their wombs. (II:228)

> As for your women who have lost hope of menstruation, and in
> case you have a doubt, the prescribed period of waiting for them

is three months, as also for them who have not menstruated yet.

As for those who are pregnant, their prescribed period is until the delivery of the child. (LXV:4)

The Qur'an thus leaves no ambiguity regarding the length of the idda and the purpose for which it is prescribed. The paternity of the child and the responsibility of the father must be clearly established and they become all the more important in case of divorce. Also, no person other than the father is to be held accountable for maintaining and providing for the child and the child's mother during the time the child is dependent on her. In three hadith, discussing the period of idda, Muslim says that it comes to an end with the birth of the child and that the woman can marry thereafter as soon as she pleases. However, if the woman is not pregnant then she must wait four months and ten days before remarrying (*Sahih Muslim*, 1984:775, hadith 3536-38). The same duration is also prescribed for mourning for the husband, though for other relatives the mourning period is only three days (ibid.:776-78, hadith 3539-52).

Maintenance of the divorced women during the idda remains the responsibility of the husband.

House the (divorced) women where you live, according to your means; but do not harass them so as to reduce them to straightened circumstances.

If they are pregnant, then spend on them until they give birth to the child. And if they suckle the child for you, then make the due payment to them, and consult each other appropriately. But if you find this difficult, let some other woman suckle (the child) for her. Let the man of means spend according to his means, and he whose means are limited, should spend of what God has given him. (LXV:6,7)

There are numerous hadith dealing with maintenance and its exact duration; however, *Sahih Muslim* essentially repeats the story of Fatima bint Qais through many narratives and chains of transmission. The confusion pertains to whether a woman divorced by three pronouncements of talaq is entitled to maintenance or not. According to Muslim, it would appear that such a woman is not entitled to any lodging or maintenance allowance (ibid.:769-77).[23] A pregnant woman, on the other hand, is entitled to these privileges, since she carries the burden of her husband in her womb, and while she is in that state, her husband owes the responsibility of her board and lodging. Caliph Umar and the Hanafi school took the stand that the case of Fatima bint Qais was particular and that the general rule of idda is the same for pregnant and non-pregnant women, i.e., entitlement of board and lodging for the duration of three monthly periods, extended to the delivery of the child for pregnant women, but Hafiz Ibn Qayyim, in his *Zad al-Ma'ad* referring to this hadith, says that divorced women are not entitled to maintenance during idda (ibid.:774).

### How Valid Is the Scriptural Framework for Muslim Families in North America?

For the enforcement of any religious regulations Muslims have always recognized the ultimate authority of the Qur'an. Of all the matters on which the Qur'an has provided legislation, the most detailed, specific and unambiguous are those that relate to the family. The Qur'an is not exclusively a book of laws; as a matter of fact, specific legislation constitutes a very small portion of its verses. As a result, the detail pertaining to the family structure has to be seen as indicating the very high priority that Islam accords to the family. Further, the Prophet himself was very particular about the family. His own marriages and household, his treatment of his wives, daughters, and grandchildren, all recorded in considerable detail, provide a full and comprehensive picture of what Muslims consider the ideal behaviour of members of a family towards each other, the relations between husband and wife/wives, and the care of children. By the time the Prophet and his companions had departed this world the Islamic family was an established institution, its features clarified and a consensus determined regarding its correct form and procedures.

Since there are no fundamental disagreements among Muslims on the Qur'an, hadith and fikh, the structure of the family as established and approved by the Prophet and his companions, has been reinforced and affirmed. The preachers and later the mystics accompanying the Islamic armies carried the original structure of the Islamic family from Arabia to the outposts of the Islamic world.

The basic form of the Islamic family survived, but it did not remain totally unchanged as it came into contact with many local populations and traditions. Thus the value of the dower and the dowry has undergone a substantive change though its outward form has not. In the same way, while no one disputes the inheritance scheme as laid down in the Qur'an, its actual implementation has changed. For instance, there is often a reluctance to leave property to distant male relatives even if there are no sons. However, the inner core of the family structure has not deviated from the original because the Qur'anic instructions are both clear and exceedingly detailed and no Muslim wants to be seen as defying the Qur'an.

The religious functionary class, especially the imam or prayer leader who usually performs the nikah ceremony and participates in other life-cycle rituals and celebrations, makes sure that inadvertent deviations are rectified without delay. It is therefore not necessary for a Muslim to discover the exact scriptural instructions for himself in order for him to establish a correct Islamic family. His social environment and his own socialization are sufficiently strong mechanisms to produce conformity. Thus, a Muslim can travel in any part of the Islamic world, settle down, marry, and establish a family without feeling that he is compromising his tradition.

### Notes

1. Quoted in Shukri, 1966:21. Both Watt (1956:277-278) and Fyzee (1949:90) also give the same interpretation.
2. Robertson Smith, *Kinship and Marriage in Early Arabia*, Boston: Beacon Press, first pub. A.& C. Black, 1903), pp. 119-20. Maulana Muhammad ʿAli, in his commentary on the Qur'an confirms Robertson Smith's interpretation. ʿAli says "The word used here is *saduqat*, pl. of *saduqah* (from *sidq*, meaning truth), which means dowry or nuptial gift. Other words used for dowry are *mahr* and *suduq*. It is necessary that a "dowry" should be given to every woman taken in marriage, whether she is a free woman, an orphan, or a prisoner of war. So every woman begins her married life as the owner of some property, and thus marriage is the means of raising her status, in many respects elevating her to a plane of equality with her husband. The dowry must be paid at the time of marriage, and it is the bride's property. To show that she is full owner of it, it is laid down that she can give it to anyone that she likes, and can give a portion of it even to

her husband. The practice has, however, become more or less general to recognize dowry as a debt which the husband owes to the wife and which she can claim when she likes." (1951:188)

3. See hadith, nos. 3251, 3253, 3255, 3257, 3259, 3261 and 3263, in *Sahih Muslim* (1984:707-8).

4. *Fatawa-i-Kazee Khan* also mentions three hadith which indicate that muta was permitted only in the very beginning of Islam and was then forbidden when the Quranic revelation prohibited sexual intercourse with anyone "except their wives, or the captives which their right hand possesses" (*Fatawa*, 1977:103). Watt says that muta was prohibited by the Caliph Umar and it may have continued later too (1956:279).

5. People of the book refers to Jews and Christians, i.e., people to whom God sent his revelation—the Book.

6. Watt, however, says that the Quranic command IV;3 is not a restriction but an encouragement to marry four wives for men who had only one wife, but this was a reform nonetheless. (1956:279)

7. The same point is made by Watt (1956:274, 277) upon whose work Rodinson has based his to a large extent.

8. The kind of justice that Haykal and Ali and, indeed, the Qur'an, IV:129 insist upon may not be humanly possible, since even in the case of the Prophet himself there is evidence that all wives may not necessarily be treated with perfect equality and thus arouse jealousy among other wives. It is reported by Aisha, the Prophet's favourite wife:

    I felt jealous of the women who offered themselves to Allah's messenger and said: Then when Allah the exalted and glorious revealed this: you may defer anyone you wish, and take to yourself any you wish; and if you desire any you have set aside [no sin is chargeable to you]. (XXXIII:51)
    I (Aisha) said: "It seems to me that your lord hastens to satisfy your desire." (*Sahih Muslim*, 1984:478-9, hadith 3453). For Aisha being the favourite wife see *Sahih al-Bukhari*, hadith no. 119 (1984:87-91).

9. Watt tends to put a slightly different interpretation on this argument by saying that Muhammad's multiple marriages as well as those of his closest companions were essentially political and based on alliance formation (1951:284-89), thus implying that jealousy should not enter into the matter since such marriages did not mean a personal preference; however, to women who were so married it could have made a great difference because for them this was their married life.

10. Also, with reference to Syed Ameer ʿAli, the famous Indian Muslim jurist, Roberts confirms monogamy as the preferred pattern of family for about 95% of Muslims in India (1971:11).

11. Watt considers concubinage so insignificant that he dismisses the subject in one line (1951:283).

12. This is narrated by Jabir and transmitted by Muslim.

13. Ibid. This is narrated by Abu Said al-Khurdi and transmitted by Bukhari

and Muslim. *Mishkat* also reports hadith dealing with intercourse with slave girls (1984:713), but here, too, the emphasis is on waiting to determine whether the girl was pregnant, not on marrying.

14. According to Abu Hurairah as transmitted by Nasai and Baihaqi in *Shuab al-Iman*, quoted in *Mishkat* (1977:694).

15. This places the maintenance of a wife on the same footing as an indebted prisoner who must be maintained.

16. Hadith no.s 772, 780, 781-83.

17. See also *Sahih al-Bukhari* (1984:204).

18. A term of derogation or exasperation.

19. This interpretation is also rejected by Watt (1951:282-83).

20. This would be according to the Hanafi law.

21. See verses II:226-32, 236-37, IV:128, 130.

22. For legal details, see Fyzee, 1974:148-51.

23. See hadith no.s 3512-34 and especially, 3527.

# North America and the Adaptation of the Muslim Tradition: Religion, Ethnicity and the Family

## Earle H. Waugh

◆  ◆  ◆  ◆

### ISLAM AND THE ISSUE OF WESTERN INTELLECTUAL BIAS

Islam integrates all aspects of life into one comprehensive system. Consequently, it concerns itself with codes of life as much as philosophy, and with politics as much as theology. As a result, scholars in the Western social science and humanities traditions have difficulty analyzing Muslim phenomena, for their training assumes that religion is but one of several elements in the cultural matrix. Since the Renaissance in the West, the study of religion has retreated from the center of knowledge, and religious presuppositions have been eliminated from all but the most faith-oriented of disciplines. In effect, knowledge and belief can be safely distinguished from each other.

The Muslim academy fundamentally rejects this viewpoint. It holds that all knowledge, including science, must be properly grounded and hence it cannot operate as if it is neutral and beyond bias. Thus, to be properly oriented, knowledge must begin with religious belief. Such a perception raises significant questions about Western human sciences; for the Muslim scholar, even the most detached disciplines give evidence of hidden agendae, which are held to derive from the "religious" presuppositions of the West. Thus, the vaunted objectivity of much

Western scholarship is regarded with suspicion.[1] Any attempt to analyze the current position of Islam in the world or to investigate Muslims in any cultural context requires an awareness of this basic Muslim critique.

At the same time, modern scholars of all persuasions are conscious that the foundational interpretive materials of Islam have no universally acknowledged essence. Some of the problems derive from the materials' nature, some from the manner of their perceived role in Islamic civilization, and some from the way Muslims have applied them. For example, it is well known that the principle normative materials, that is, those essential to the subsequent building of the Islamic system, are not systematically structured nor organizationally consistent. The Qur'an, Islam's holy scripture, is regarded as the unalloyed Word of God, but there are very few passages in it that logically develop a theme or a behavioral model. The hadith, those pronouncements and customary practices of the Prophet that also became paradigmatic for the community and that are the basis for much of Muslim family codes, are not organically connected, and they cannot be used without great interpretive sophistication. Within the hadith, there are important variations as to emphasis and reliability.[2]

Despite these problems, the Muslim scholarly tradition has utilized these materials for its characterization of Islam; they have provided the building blocks for what we know of literate Islam. Western scholars, especially humanists who have been trained in the literary-oriented mold, have usually accepted the Muslim scholarly Islam as the "real" Islam, and have differed only in what they see as the patterns and significance of the constitutive elements. They have chiefly studied the so-called orthodox, official and essentially elitist tradition. Those trained in social sciences like anthropology, however, have criticized this method, arguing that nowhere in the Muslim world does one find Islam practiced according to this model. Popular, non-structured and eclectic, the Islam of the field-worker sometimes bears only marginal reference to the theological cohesion of the literate tradition. The two models still comprise the major thrusts of Western scholarly research on Islam.

They do not sit contentedly together, and they compound the difficulties of the entire enterprise of scholarly research. Western notions of religion, based upon doctrinal assumptions and nurtured by theology, do not fit the Muslim experience. Scholars like Wilfred Cantwell Smith

have moved to redefine religion along "faith" lines in order to accommodate Muslim priorities (Smith, 1963) attempting to reach an understanding of religious meaning beyond western limitations, while followers of Clifford Geertz opt for a definition of religion drawn from
symbol theory (Geertz, 1973). The model preferred in this chapter is
to understand religion as an underlying system of sacred values and
cultural directives that orient the believer in a fundamental manner. A
fruitful method of examining religious material is to follow one of its
basic patterns; the tensions and centrifugal forces of society are offset
by the opposite pull of cohesion. One way to read religious history,
then, is to note the continuous story of this interaction in the life of a
people. This view accords place to the official tradition as having normative force in society, but it also acknowledges that the operative
principle is the dynamic relationship between the religious ideals and
the cultural components that make up the community.

This method has direct relevance for the study of the Muslim family.
Neither Muslims nor Western researchers are able to explicate the essence of Islam, for it is the collectivity composed of the elements in the
dynamic. Nor, on the same grounds, do Muslims come to the United
States and Canada with fixed cultures. We must also acknowledge that
the role and quality of religion has been changing somewhat in North
America in recent years, especially with the impact of the Moral Majority. It is highly ironic that Islam is developing in that environment at
precisely the same time. Should secularism be seriously challenged as
the official viewpoint of North America, clashes of varying types of religious conservativism are possible. In addition, these factors are central to the scientific study of religion and culture, for our methodological tools are scarcely sophisticated enough to deal with current
changes, let alone to provide adequate analyses of a religious tradition
that sees fundamental conflicts with its worldview in that science. Such
issues must be kept in mind as we attempt to survey how religion and
ethnicity are the focal points for Muslim adaptation in North America.

## ADAPTATION OF THE FAMILY TO
## NEW ENVIRONMENTS

The major interpretive medium for Muslim family life has been the
law. Sunnis recognize four legal schools, and the Shiᶜa have additional

favorite codes.[3] But rather than make the task easier, such multiplicity raises questions concerning authority. For if the Qur'an or the hadith explicitly state a principle, does that make it authoritative? What if there are conflicts between the two? If there is no explicit statement, can an analogy be the grounds for legal rights and judgments? What of the assumptions that seem to lie behind the principles? Are they of divine sanction while the offending principle is held to be relative to contemporary understanding?

After so many centuries, such problems would seem to belong in the dusty haunts of lawyers and archivists. But they have very real significance for Muslims in North America. Consider the notion of women's equality. Objectively regarded, some statements the Qur'an and hadith about women make it impossible to deny in several respects that a woman's position was conceived of as lower than a man's. If these authoritative sources must be restated in the contemporary situation in view of revised opinions about female roles, how should this be done? Should it be grounded on the norms of international equality or of traditional views? If the latter, why should endogamy be enjoined upon women and not upon men? This particular issue has direct and sometimes heartbreaking significance in the North American milieu, as other discussions in this volume make clear. In short, the application of Muslim normative patterns within North American society not only calls for creative response from Muslims living here, but it also raises basic methodological problems for the researchers dedicated to studying them.

Muslims come into an environment that has an impact on them at several key religious levels. They respond with loyalty to their own tradition by trying to adapt it to the new environment, because they know there will be no future for their children in North America if they do not. Their attitudes vary greatly toward both the environment, and their own tradition. Some Muslims are consciously North American in identity and behavior. Some have been here so long that the third or fourth generation has a very meager connection, or none at all, with any overseas Islamic community. And some of them have scant connection with mosque or Islamic organizations. As well, in the United States, an indigenous Islam has grown up among people who regard themselves as black Americans, with no connection to any other place or time. A more restrictive attitude is found among others. They respond to North American culture by attempting to build organizations that will preserve and enhance their tradition on this continent, and their relationship to those organizations is much tighter than is the case with most believers in the major centers of Muslim population abroad. Some Muslims build closed communities, that is, they concentrate on establishing bridgeheads on the continent and look for their spiritual sustenance and community sense in a faraway land. Whatever the stance assumed, it is evident that the evaluative process must deal with a welter of variables, beginning with attitudes toward the tradition, the length of time separated from the Islamic homeland (if, indeed, there was a separate homeland), the cohesion of the group and the dominance of individualism among them, the impact of religiously validated reactions to North American culture and the negative responses they have received from it. Above all of these, however, stands the single cardinal fact: Muslims are adapting.

This investigation will focus upon three interrelated dimensions of the adaptation process. First, there are a number of religio-cultural factors in North America that aid Muslims in adapting. Second, there are certain critical differences between Canada and the United States that are relevant to the Muslim process of adaptation. Finally, ethnicity has a considerable impact on the adaptation process.

## COMMON RELIGIO-CULTURAL FACTORS AIDING MUSLIM ADAPTATION
### The Religio-Cultural Setting in Contemporary North America

North America is ostensibly secular, yet its heritage belies that assertion. Indeed, some studies would suggest that North America fares well in religiosity when compared internationally (Sigelman, 1977:293). Thus, the Muslim immigrant does not face the prospect of an environment hostile to matters of faith. While neither Canada nor the United States accepts discrimination on the basis of religion and the individual's religious commitment theoretically plays no role in any official relationship with the state, in securing employment, or in being considered for immigration, etc., the secular world accepts the normativeness of the majority religion and has an acknowledged relationship with it: Christian values, history, and influence result in state sanction of Christian holidays and heritage.

Having been derived from a common Abrahamic root, Judaism, Christianity and Islam have had such a long and complex relationship that they share values and beliefs at both the conscious and unconscious levels. Islam was avowedly self-conscious in its reaction to its older sister traditions, and set about carving out a distinctive identity while acknowledging the validity of the others. Even that self-assertiveness presupposed a degree of religious interplay with Judaism and Christianity, and the interaction between the three has had a marked effect on them all. With much the same conception of religious ultimates, with long histories of similar social organizations, with a fund of common literary/religious stories, and, even, common assumptions about religious language, their bonds are complicated. In short, a whole compendium of relationships, from theology to internal conflict to the mutual rebuttal of materialist ideology, has woven them together. When Muslim immigrants come to North America, they are not venturing into an environment whose religious and cultural legacy is unknown. Indeed, their anticipations may be based upon a long tradition of tolerance and mutual acceptance within home cultures, relationships that have been sanctioned within the Holy Writ itself and that have been adjudicated over time (Goitein, 1955; Bell, 1926).

Moreover, since North American culture places its primary emphasis on personal achievement and aggrandizement, no essential religious ideology need be upheld in order to function effectively. The complicated relationships, laced with religious values, that so determine standing in the homeland, need play no role in the immigrant's drive for success. Most assuredly, there is a conformity requirement, most notably an "Anglo-conformity," but it is not overt enough to involve confrontation with religion per se.[4] North American culture may indeed free the immigrant from the bondage of a tradition that is not changing fast enough for individual tastes.

### Traditions of Tolerance

A religious viewpoint that stresses a personal relationship with God, common to all Abrahamic religions and essential to Islam, will not encounter structural problems within North American culture. Indeed, such diversity of opinion exists about religion, and so many organizations exist for religion's expression, that one more can hardly be of great significance. Religious pluralism guarantees a certain autonomy for believers and allows them to pursue religious ends to the extent they themselves determine. Having choice with regard to commitment may be an attractive trait to those who wish to promote their own beliefs, so Muslims may regard the religious diversity of North America as an opportunity to promote their own perception of Islam, an activity sometimes unacceptable in the home environment where religious boundaries are often strict.

Both Canada and the United States have constitutional guarantees allowing religious worship, and both states and provinces have additional legal mechanisms to ensure religious autonomy for their citizenry. Educational institutions, such as universities and colleges, have departments that stress the significance of the Muslim tradition, such as political science, anthropology and religious studies, and educational media provides the opportunity for ethnic and religious programming. No curbs are placed on religious publications unless they libel other religions, so Muslims may create their own religious press and foster their own religious programs. While the state has certain legal requirements that interface with religious practice, especially in the area of marriage and divorce, the law is such that religious organizations can work under the general oversight of the law. Thus, for example, the imam acts as a mediator between state and individual when he completes official legal documents of marriage, and the government leaves details of the contract to the religious authorities. The leader of the mosque is generally accorded the same position as a priest, minister, or rabbi in public functions, and his role is perceived in much the same sense. At the official level, then, a Muslim family would appear to have few concrete roadblocks in carrying out its religious obligations.

Religious tolerance has been part of the environment in North America since the early days of European immigration, and movements within Christendom have encouraged such diverse activities as common days of prayer, ecumenical movements, and dialogue. While most of these interfaith relationships have been superficial, they have been based upon intellectual currents of some significance and antiquity within Western religious traditions.[5] Since Vatican II, the Roman Catholic Church has set up a special mechanism to effect dialogue with Islam[6] and organizations once avowedly committed to the conversion of Muslims now concern themselves with understanding.[7]

North America has seen its share of radical religious movements in the last two decades, movements that have lead to tragedies like Jonestown and the conflicts of the mind-control cults. Some of these groups have been social rejectionists and hence unsympathetic to the principal trends of North American religion. In contrast, Muslims have sought to contribute to the social order, by espousing North American culture yet maintaining a certain distance from it. This positive view of church-state relations makes Islam far more pro-North American culture than many other groups. Muslim adaptation is thus founded upon positive predispositions between religion and state.

## DIFFICULTIES FACING THE MUSLIM IN NORTH AMERICA
### Stereotyping Islam

If the above points to a structural coalition with North American culture, there are marked disjunctions. The differences between the ideals of the North American religious system and the realities are as great as anywhere in the world. Western religious culture has had a strong anti-Muslim tone, and the legacy of the Crusades still haunts Muslim-Christian relations.[8] Political events involving Israel, terrorism, and oil embargoes have exacerbated these latent hostilities to such an extent that Islam and Muslims have become stereotyped in the public mind. Several recent studies have documented these stereotypes in popular and educational literature (S. Abu-Laban, 1975; L. Kenny, 1975; S. Al-Qazzaz, 1975).

### The Unconscious Skewing of Media

Perhaps of even greater significance has been the latent skewing of Islam by both media and academia. Muslims have insisted that their culture has been ignored or denigrated by those who should be more objective, and, in the recent past, analyses have detailed how a wide range of writing is flawed in its assumptions about Muslim culture.[9] The result has been that the intellectual community has abandoned the word "orientalism" and taken great pains to examine the basic propositions of social and cultural study. But the lingering animosity of the popular press is more difficult to address. The Muslim who comes to these shores may not be convinced that the media is doing anything more than representing what most North Americans think.[10]

*The Latent Racism of North American Society*

It is a more sinister antagonism that prompted the growth of the Black Muslim movement. The inherent racism that blacks have felt and condemned in the United States provided the catalyst for Elijah Muhammad and his distinctive Muslim group, a movement that has had far greater impact on North American religion than any other Muslim organization (Lincoln, 1968). It is in the name of Muslim principles of equality that this same movement, a large section of which is under the leadership of Warith Din Muhammad, has moderated some of the original leader's radical policies and has developed a more orthodox position vis-à-vis the nature of Islam. But such a dramatic redirection should not hide the fact that it was the violent rejection of white racism that provided the background for the growth of the movement to begin with, a racism that takes its most offensive pose in Ku Klux Klan organizations. Nor is Canada free from its own types of racial prejudice.[11] In short, the immigrant Muslim will not be immune to the dark underside of social antipathies present in North American culture.

*The Destruction of Assimilation*

If these difficulties are posed at a more or less conscious level, there are other, more subtle hazards for the community. Demerath and Theissen have indicated that foreign-oriented minority churches are generally to be defined as "precarious":

> The term "precarious" is appropriate for any organization that confronts the prospect of its own demise. The confrontation need be neither intentional nor acknowledged. The only important criterion is a threatened disruption of the organization such that the achievement of its goals and the maintenance of its values are so obstructed as to bring on a loss of identity through deathly quiescence, merger, or actual disbandment. (1970: 241)

Islamic groups, with the exception of the Black Muslim organizations, have depended to a large degree on foreign-born imams and mosque officials. While boards and mosque organizations may have indigenous participants, the burden of the leadership is from abroad. Mullins did a study of the Japanese Buddhists in Canada, and concluded that, in contrast to the claims of Isajiw and Hansen (1975, 23; 1952, 495), ethnicity and a return to the social solidarity of a religious organization is not the experience among third-generation Japanese Buddhists:

> Progressive assimilation of each generation within minority churches, the strongest ethnic institutions in the post-war Japanese community, indicates that the proverbial "melting pot" more accurately represents what is happening to the Japanese in Canada. Evidence for a pattern of ethnic rediscovery is not to be found among third generation Japanese. The loss of ethnic language ability and the unusually high rates of intermarriage demonstrate that the preservation of ethnic ties and heritage is a low priority for the vast majority of Sansei . . . it is almost certain that without significant replenishment by new immigrants Japanese Buddhist churches face a loss of their identity either through de-ethnicization or eventual disbandment. (Mullins, 1987:35)

While no similar study has been done on immigrant Muslim groups, and there are significant differences between them, the pattern may be applicable. Requiring spouses to convert may retard the assimilation, but unless there is indigenous growth of leadership, and continuous migration from abroad, the future of a North American foreign-oriented Muslim community remains clouded. This situation is particularly true in Canada, which has no indigenous Muslim sect, although there have been converts across the spectrum of Muslim groups. In all, the pressures to assimilate constitute a grave issue for the Muslim immigrant, an issue of which he may not initially be aware. As a result of the hidden forces at work in North America the Muslim family may find itself in situations for which it has no preparations, and it may only vaguely comprehend the ramifications. Religious bias or racism may thus be easier to handle; a process that leaves the family weakened without an obvious source may be considered more diabolical from the perspective of the *umma*'s continuation.

### Structural Antipathies

In addition, there are structural problems. The late Ismail al-Faruqi noted one in conversation in 1982: insofar as American identity is tied to a particular religious orientation, just that far does a Muslim have a problem in regarding North America as home. In effect, commitment to being Muslim requires a social milieu with Muslim presuppositions in order for the believer to feel comfortable. Since America does not have that milieu, the Muslim is constantly challenged about why he is working out his Islam in an environment foreign to the dictates of the tradition. Al-Faruqi plainly felt that the immigrant was in danger of losing his soul for his own aggrandizement. He believed that Muslims have to develop a personal vision of the meaning of life in America, particularly solutions that do not betray the essence of the faith. Others may not agree with his analysis.

For example, it is a recognized reformist position that there are elements in Islam hostile to North American orientation. Currently, Iraq is only the most vocal of a number of countries where the philosophy of Islam is interpreted as being hostile to Western secularism. Even if this hostility is discounted as resulting from the imperialist policies of Western nations, there is also an underlying antagonism derived from superiority beliefs that play a role.

Not all reformist thinkers in Islam acknowledge a structural conflict with the West on the basis of state characteristics. Many have argued that Islam cannot be identified with a state. Mawdudi is one who doubted that modern nation-states could be claimed to be "Islamic."[12] Taken to its logical conclusion, this argument would mean that Islam cannot be embodied in any state—it remains above and beyond the political realm as it presently exists. This view implies that there is no structural conflict between Islamic belief and any modern state, even one informed by a different religion, or none at all. Until such time as the true Islamic society appears, the nation-state is acceptable. But, in actuality, few contemporary Muslims argue vigorously for this separation of religion and state. They point to the state of Muhammad's time as a model. It follows that a strong tradition in Islam affirms the need for an Islamic state, with the obvious corollary that only an Islamic state is acceptable. Thus some deeply held convictions about the nature of Islam actually lead to an antagonism toward North American statecraft.

Despite the weight of this religiously-encoded resistance, a continuing Muslim presence in North America depends upon some form of assimilation. Elkholy argues that Muslims in the United States have been more successful in enduring as a community when they have made significant accommodation to American customs (Elkholy, 1966). Thus, whatever the religious ideology might claim, adaptation requires some modification of deeply held convictions.

There is another structural issue of particular significance in the Canadian case. Government policy has fostered multiculturalism as an essential marker of Canadian identity. Funding and policy assistance is directed toward its maintenance and development. While multiculturalism might be seen as a recognition of the ethnic "facts of life" in Canada, it may also be a cloak for conformism to a secular ideology, either Anglo or Franco. Barclay explicitly disavows the official Canadian view that Islam and Canadian-style multiculturalism are compatible:

> I would argue that such a multi-cultural society is a myth and the Muslim example demonstrates this argument. In Canada Muslims are in no sense free to practice their traditional Muslim law. Polygamy and divorce Muslim style are prohibited. The forces of the establishment speak loudly and clearly against the doctrine of male priority, of seniority by virtue of age, of the patriarchal family, of arranged marriages, and the belief that marriages are contracts between groups and not individuals. (Barclay, 1978:110)

According to this view, the Canadian emphasis on multi-ethnic community as an expression of a common identity rests ultimately on political ideology and cannot provide the basis for a nation's soul. Hence, Islam, at least as traditionally known, cannot be practiced in Canada.

### The Conflict of Values and Beliefs

A number of traditional values are also challenged in North America. Family traditions, such as the clear-cut role separation of the sexes, status differentials, and achievement markers are all subject to modification. Muslim holidays are ignored by the society as a whole; there is no place for Ramadan or for prayer during the work day. Girls are under peer pressure to conform to dating and friendship codes frowned upon or rejected by traditional Muslim societies. Conservative banking practices requiring that interest not be charged on loans are virtually impossible to follow. Family structure, where decision-making is in the hands of the eldest male, is directly challenged by the North American code of success: he who flourishes financially has the power. Public food manufacturers pay no attention to the use of pork or pork-related products, and often something as innocent as a cookie may technically be forbidden to a Muslim because of its contents. Strong pressures to accept modifications of these values confront the Muslim every day.

Thus, a range of elements, some forthright and others hidden, challenge the Muslim immigrant. North American culture is not passive; it is present in every medium and through a whole range of goods and services. The social situation affects the male immigrant who has come just to further his own economic success as well as the closely cloistered woman in a traditional home. In the workplace the Muslim is always under the jurisdiction of a foreign culture. The greater the success, the more the immigrant may feel marginalized. Whether to return home to a situation in which personal opportunity is limited or to stay in North America and be subject to a" foreign" set of values confronts the sincere follower of Islam from the moment he/she arrives. For some it remains a permanent disjunction in their lives.

## SIMILARITIES AND DIFFERENCES BETWEEN CANADA AND THE UNITED STATES RELEVANT TO MUSLIM ADAPTATION

While Muslim immigrants may make little distinction between Canada and the United States and the two countries share a number of common values, they also differ in significant ways. Some of these similarities and differences affect the religious practice of the Muslim family.

Neither Canada nor the United States has an establishment church, and both have a rich denominational history. Religion is evidently important to the people since about 40% attend church weekly (U.S. forty-two percent; Canada thirty-nine percent) (C.I.F.O., 1974). Moreover, the two countries have a similar religious culture in that over 90% of the believers belong to some form of either the Christian or the Judaic tradition. They have also experienced common developmental patterns, such as the growth of the frontier.[13] The legal foundations and legislative traditions, the European roots, and common ideas in intellectual, political, religious and ethical history, all provide markedly similar configurations. In addition, although some analytic distinctions traditionally were held to signal differences between the two [such as the mosaic (Canada) and the melting pot (U.S.)], these are no longer accepted as universally applicable,[14] the fact is that Muslim commitment to a unique lifestyle and doctrine would predispose the receiving culture to the mosaic model. Insofar as each country accepts and promotes this model, Islam as a religion may flourish. On the other hand, insofar as Canada and the United States are different culturally, so the range and types of adaptations will differ.

There are also significant contrasts between Canada and the United States. For example, one real difference is the relative lack of diversity in Canadian institutional religion. The Anglican, United, and Presbyterian churches constitute 70.7% of the Protestants in Canada. To achieve similar percentage in the United States would require as many as twenty-one church populations. Merger and centralized polity is widely accepted in the Canadian milieu. Discussions about merger have even taken place between the largest Protestant denominations, the Anglican and United, but such a possibility would be very remote in the United States. For the Muslim family, the impact of this difference may be negligible. But there are ramifications for developing organizational structures; the dominance of a few churches in Canada makes formal religious relations far easier and far more direct. Winning the approbation of national religious organizations allows for program development on a nationwide scale. At the same time, the strong denominational boundaries mean that Muslim groups can define themselves vis-à-viz this national church character in a direct manner. They may even be required to do so in order to take their place in the official pantheon of religions. On the other hand, the very diversity of the American religious scene allows for initiative at the local level, with the attendant possibilities of different local relationships with Christians. This situation could be either positive or negative depending upon the character of the Christian church and the attitude taken to the Muslim tradition by local authorities. It also means that ad hoc programs have much greater potential because of regional interest and involvement.

In contrast to the United States, the churches in Canada have always played a key role in immigration. Some sent clergy to the frontier before the new immigrants arrived; some provided entire groups for homesteading a region. Both the Catholic and Protestant churches developed vigorous missionary programs aimed at Christianizing the nation, because both believed that the moral fiber of the citizenry was essential for a civilized nation. This radiation from center to periphery has continued to exercise a restraint on schismatics, and even small cult groups follow the centralizing model of the larger institutions. None of these ingredients has played nearly such a commanding role in the United States. So far, it is not clear that Islam is following a similar pattern. Islam may fail according to the Canadian model, or it may be building a new and different form.

Even though there is no establishment church in Canada, there continues to be an establishment mentality among the churches. The Roman Catholic church has always had a strong grip on the French-speaking population; right from the time of the Company of New France, which permitted the establishment of French colonies, the Catholic church was given exclusive privilege to bringing its adherents to the new world. The clergy saw the advantage in the joining of English-speaking, Protestant Upper Canada with French Lower Canada as a means of offsetting the influence of the United States and of maintaining the hegemony of the Catholic vision. The resulting "balance" between Catholic Quebec and Protestant Ontario continues to play a role in the national consciousness. This balance did not extend to the Prairies, where each religious group tried to outdo the others in providing settlers and clergy. The competition meant that settlement on the Prairies was intimately tied to the "national" church, in direct contrast with the United States, where individuals and sects looked to settlement for religious and personal freedom. Hence, organized religion has asserted a far greater role in the shaping of Canadian identity. While the importance of the church in matters relating to immigration has declined, there remain strong connections between the ideals of Christian aid and national immigration policy. These factors are directly relevant for the development of Islam. First, if Canadian identity is marked by the impact of a quasi-national church, where will Muslims fit in that system? Second, if immigration still requires progressive attitudes on the part of the church, how dependent is Muslim identity on immigration should the attitudes change? Third, can Islam flourish within the Canadian context without a national religious presence?

### The Conflict of "Manifest Destiny" and Islam

Where America developed a sense of "manifest destiny" that had religious overtones and to which the churches made their collective contribution, the Canadian churches set as their goal making Canadians into good Christians and by so doing, creating a "good" nation. Catholic and Protestant urged and promoted legislation to reflect their moral concerns. Since Canadian governments often responded favorably, Canada has been formed implicitly by this idealistic vision. Eventually social activism embodied in legislation secularized the mission legacy of the churches, giving Canadian legislative bodies an appearance of liberalism and community sensitivity. Long after the impact of the mission had withered, the moral responsibility lived on in loyalty and commitment to the betterment of the community.

The Muslim would find this sense of responsibility and, indeed, the emphasis on community goals close to his own. Islamic tradition has stressed the role the committed believer must play in making his community more Muslim, and it is well established in law and behavior that the responsibility for moral rectitude falls on the head of the family. In effect, then, there is much compatability between the underpinnings of religion in the Canadian experience and Islamic conviction. This compatibility can translate into a sense of commonality with the host culture.

On the other hand, national goals in the United States have also provided a transcendent meaning to the American believer. By participating in America, the churches shared its manifest destiny. America, in effect, had religious reasons for being what it was, and these reasons were intimately linked with the Christian faith. The primacy of this national vision provides an identity lacking in the Canadian experience and raises interesting problems for the immigrant Muslim, for Islam has had its own international destiny carved out in a distinctive history. Its previous glory is not connected to the American dream. Is it possible, then, for an American Islam to fit the traditional pattern?

### Canadian Identity in Relation to Islam

The community-oriented Canadian experience has not stressed entrepreneurial individualism, and it is, therefore, far less particularistic than the American. The wild west is a fitting example. Canada's west was very dull indeed compared to its counterpart south of the border. Law and order, represented by the specially formed Northwest Mounted Police, preceded the immigrants, extending a sense of tradition and mediating between groups when they came in conflict. The law was held to be the expression of the moral dimensions of society, so it came to represent an encompassing super-value system, including religions. Respect for law remains one the the chief traits on which Canadians pride themselves, whether this pride can be justified by the facts or not.

Here, too, there are similar emphases in the Muslim experience, for Muslim society from the beginning has stressed the corporate identity of the believer, affirming his participation in the umma regardless of his station in life or the group to which he belonged. The Muslim sense of law, also conceived the truths of the tradition in a system of rights and responsibilities rather than in creeds and statements of faith. If Muslim society had a singular foundation, it was the law, which provided the formulae within which people were to live their lives. It would be fallacious to claim that the Canadian sense of law is equivalent to that experienced by the traditional Muslim, but it may not be too far from the truth to point out that the notion of propriety in Canadian society has similar resonances in Islam. The Muslim immigrant will not feel alienated by this Canadian sense of public propriety experience.

While some would argue that the respect for law and tradition has stifled Canada's development, the fact remains that Canada is conservative in responding to new religions. No indigenous Canadian religious group has attracted widespread interest; nothing compares with Mormonism, or Scientology, or the Black Muslims. Moreover, conversion to a new religion is not widely accepted in Canada; only fifty odd groups comprise the identifiable Christian diversity in the census figures. Americans, on the other hand, join and convert to hundreds of different Christian persuasions. On this ground, it might seem that America would be a far more sympathetic environment for the growth of Islam than Canada.

Then again, Canada has never developed an equivalent to the "manifest destiny" of the United States. Since no new group has arisen in Canada, it follows that no religious group has linked its identity with Canada as a nation. Religionists have not been concerned with the fact of Canada's existence, but they have been exercised about the character which the country embodies. Since the accepted values were held to be the finest from the past, Canada could not be conceived of as a "lively experiment." The spiritual patriotism that marks the American church is absent in Canada, and the messianic mythology behind the civil religion of the United States is also absent in Canada. Unlike most Americans, the average Canadian does not gain an entree into the national identity by participating in a local religious organization. The acknowledgement of ethnic and racial pluralism has placed severe limits on the church as a viable identity element. For the Muslim family in Canada these limits can have a positive value in the process of adaptation. They can retain close connections with the homeland and may look to it for renewal and replenishment without having to face issues of identity conflict or appearing disloyal to the new home. Moreover, their religious convictions need not collide with the will of a "national" religion such as Faruqi encountered in the United States.

### The Role of Civil Religion

Studies in the American academy have continually refined the notion of civil religion in the United States (Jones, 1987). These studies affirm that nationhood has drawn to itself many of the loyalties normally associated with a national church or common religious destiny. While we have little concrete evidence, some very real conflicts must exist between the loyalties of the recent Muslim immigrant, with his identity based upon a strong national or quasi-national religious consciousness and the civic character of American awareness. It raises the question of whether an immigrant mosque organization could thrive in the United States without a sufficient number of converts with roots in America, who could then become dominant in the organization.

While there are elements of civil religion in Canada, they are closely linked with ethnic identity; Quebec society, for example, has embodied a messianic vision of French culture in North America, and it has given this vision form and substance through state festivals, legendary heroes, and popular epics. The result has been a kind of "grand" destiny. Such a collective concern has continued to play an effective role, even after the province became far more ethnically divided and certainly more secular than it was during the formative days of New France. The civil religion of the other provinces is far more ambiguous. A Protestant civil piety survived, even when immigration brought non-Christian traditions, but it has provided a kind of Canadian value system that transcends sectarian consciousness. Whether it functions in the same manner or even with the same kind of moral constraints as the

Muslim immigrant would find in the homeland is doubtful. Scholarship has thus far not dealt with the issue.

According to Canadian artists, what does unite the nation is a collective response to the natural environment. There is, then, a kind of "geopiety"[15] that integrates groups into the whole. Various writers have tried to articulate the nature of this relationship with the environment. The first missionary priests, the Jesuits, wrote of Canada as a country of almost paradisiacal dimensions.

But more recent writers have explored the alien, even sinister character of the land, as does F.R. Scott (1966:38):

Hidden in wonder and snow, or sudden with summer,
This land stares at the sun in a huge silence.
Endlessly articulating something we cannot hear.

These visions of the environment are not new, since they played an important role in the philosophical and religious viewpoints of the native peoples. But they do indicate a shift towards a consciousness rooted in a common psychological response, a response that is being defined artistically in terms of ambiguity and loss.[16] The Muslim family encounters the same environment, and he expresses many similar reactions. The difficulty is that it is not clear whether this reaction is generated by the environment of Canada, or whether it derives from a sense of loss of homeland and the inherent alienation of a foreign culture in which the believer must live. It is not difficult to imagine that the Muslims of the Near East, so long associated with a particular piece of geography and highly sensitive to the symbolic and sacred meanings of land, in their daily prayers toward Mecca could relate to the Canadian psyche in this regard. But there are few studies on this aspect of Muslim and Canadian interaction with a "sacred" environment, and the material must await future research.

Nevertheless, it is evident that the civil religion of Canada differs significantly from that of the United States, and indeed, the reaction to the United States itself is an ingredient in it.[17] The importance of this factor for our study should not be lost; immigrant groups and religious consciousness are bound to play somewhat different roles in Canada than those of kindred groups in the United States. This is one reason why Abu-Laban was able to suggest that a Muslim future was not guaranteed in the Canadian situation (1983:76). It is also the cardinal reason why the Muslim family situation may differ considerably in the two jurisdictions.

## ETHNICITY AND ISLAMIC TRADITION IN NORTH AMERICA

Most researchers believe ethnicity to be constituted of several elements, the most common being group identity and common history. Some, like Aronson, find such analyses faulty, basically because each can be resolved into a more generic term or because such elements do not really elucidate the phenomenon (1976:9-12). A number of alternatives have been proposed, from asserting that ethnicity is ideology to abandoning the term altogether (Wellerstein, 1972:15). In Isajiw's consideration of twenty-seven ethnic studies, ten accepted a subjective definition, that is, they saw the term only in relation to groups who either regarded themselves or were regarded by others as being distinctive. Of that ten, eight included religion among ethnicity's attributes (1974:12).

Isajiw holds that religion cannot be subsumed under ethnicity, preferring to give it its own definition (1974:1). Moreover, it might even be argued that the "new ethnicity," the ethnicity that affirms a history and culture even if the group makes few demands because of it and belonging requires little distinctive behavior (Weinfeld, 1981:78-79), is hardly the same as that which made great religious or cultural demands on a group in the past. On the other hand, perhaps this kind of ethnicity is but a species of North American religiosity. For example, Canadian commitment to this new ethnicity, officially called "multiculturalism" has striking similarities to revivalism in the United States during the 1950s, which had an explicit civil dimension focusing on American idealism (Gold, 1976:410; Anderson & Frideres, 1981:39). If the similarities appear to be more than coincidental, it might derive from Canadian commitment to a religiosity with an ethnic coat.

If the relationship between religion and ethnicity remains problematic, religion also has difficulties standing on its own. For example, religion has declined among some groups as the medium of identity, French-Canadians being the most evident group fitting this description (Gold, 1976:409). Such affirmations may relate more to the paucity of comprehensive studies of Canadian identity than to the real position of religion in society. Perhaps it takes a national crisis for a genuine religious consciousness to become evident. In Lebanon, religion returned to dominate identity when ethnic groups faced violence and destruction (Picard, 1986:172).

It is quite possible that the model of the relationship between group and religion used here is essentially weak. Perhaps it is better to stress the dynamics between groups rather than to assert either a Canadian or an American identity into which the various groups assimilate. Anderson and Frideres point out that even though Canada is unicultural (i.e. Anglo or French, depending on whether you are in Quebec or the rest of Canada), bicultural (large minorities of French or English in the other's area), and multicultural, ethnic identity really changes more often than such categories imply. They hold that ethnicity changes from generation to generation (1981:115). Or, as Hannerz argues the American case, boundaries can shift as different groups interact and interpret each other (Hannerz, 1976:435; Higham, 1983:17-25). In the articles in this book, many factors affect Muslims as they interact with and react to the larger cultures. Consequently, Muslims themselves shift or find society shifting according to a number of influences. Some of these are summarized here.

### Internal Differentiation Factors by Muslim Groups

Muslims distinguish themselves from each other by a number of factors, not all of them strictly religious in character. Some of the distinctions are quite ancient. Probably the oldest is that between the Sunni and the Shi'a, the basic division that goes back to the first century. Organization, doctrine, piety, and cultural dimensions are affected by this division. But some others may play a more direct role in the life of the average believer. Thus, in the United States, there are decided distinctions between indigenous Islam (that is, those of the American Muslim Mission or so-called Black Muslims) and that of the immigrant. There are distinctions between the more proselytizing organizations and the benign service groups (e.g. the Ahmadiyya are quite aggressive in advocating Islam for North Americans, while some mosques serve only the immigrant population.) There are distinctions formed around the word "Islam" itself. Most Isma'ilis prefer to be regarded as followers of

the Aga Khan and designate themselves as Isma'ilis primarily. Like-
wise, many Sufi groups play down traditional Islamic connections.
There are also a series of differences between militantly conservative
Muslims and more acculturated believers.

"We worship together but then the Pakistanis go back to their cur-
ries and the Arabs to their kebabs," one Pakistani leader told Haddad
(1978:80). The comment highlights the ambiguous relationship between religion and ethnicity experienced by most Muslims in North
America. Faced with an indifferent attitude by the host culture and isolated from home by distance and psychological factors, the immigrant
reacts in divergent ways. Depending on the date of immigration and
the socio-economic level, a spectrum of responses obtains ranging
from clinging to a "package" of ethnic and religious markers to the uti-
lization of Islam as one feature (Abu-Laban, 1980:230-32; Haddad,
1978:93). A key ingredient in the process is the conception of identity
in the homeland; a Muslim from village India has a decidedly different
conception from that of a counterpart from Lebanon (Khalidi,
1986:395-403; Hudson, 1978:39-40). Generational differences also
give rise to contrasting views (Haddad, 1978:92). In summary, questions of self-perception cannot be solved by reference to a distinctive
Islamic identity to which an admixture of ethnicity has been added.
Consequently, we must deal with a reality whose participants are not
able to separate elements that are peculiarly ethnic from those of religion.

Socio-economic differences also have an impact on intergroup relations. Immigration patterns in this area demonstrate dramatic contrasts. Most of the early Arab immigrants came from the Levant, and
most had little education. They opted for labor-related jobs. Recent
immigrants have been from among the better educated, many of
whom are professionals (B. Abu-Laban, 1980: 98-127). Departments
of immigration, of course, favor these people. Moreover, since the professionals interact at a business level with others and tend to be profi-
cient in English or French, the process of assimilation takes place more
quickly and with greater depth.

On the other hand, there is division over the kind of Islam, in terms
of values espoused among the various groups. Some argue that it will
take almost herculean will to carve out a place in North American society for Islam, and the result of this view is to promote different doc-

trinal foci, with a more radical means to establish the community. A sense of this can be gleaned from the conflicts between Louis Farrakhan and Warith Din Muhammad's American Muslim Mission (Mamiya, 1983:242), although the presence of conservative radicals have been felt among even the most innocuous groups. The disparate socio-cultural backgrounds of Muslims cause some to wonder whether a truly religious Islam can ever be made of these "Islams" (Haddad, 1978:80).

Funding from abroad also causes division. Since many mosques and mosque organizations receive funding from Muslim countries, various alliances and even personnel from those countries tend to accentuate an ethnic identity. Splits also arise over attitudes towards home values; for example, it is a critical problem whether mosque attendance should follow the home pattern or adopt the North American pattern. Some youth have raised issues (for example, having dances in the gymnasium of Islamic centers) that have caused dissension. Then there are subtle distinctions, those imposed by social and political movements within the homeland or within international Islam. Some of these are based on religious sensitivities. For example, an Egyptian social organization, designed to foster cohesion among Coptic and Muslim Egyptians in Edmonton foundered over the presence of alcohol at club meetings. Some Copts argued that they should respect Muslim sensitivities, while some of the Muslims felt alcohol should not in itself be an issue, especially since some of the Muslims drank socially anyway. The dilemma brought the club down, because Muslims felt they could not have their children see the activities of such a club and maintain traditional attitudes toward alcohol. Political issues in Muslim countries have also left an impact. Many Muslims who had no connection to Iran lauded the Imam's revolution in its early days, but a strong antipathy set in as it became evident that the regime was wilful and violent.[18] A different sort of political problem is highlighted by the Ahmadiyya sect. Denied true Islamic participation by law in Pakistan, the group has tried to promote Islam in the disapora, but they remain very sensitive to Sunni criticism. When the Department of Religious Studies at the University of Alberta refused to continue to sponsor a Religious Founders speaker's forum, which brought together many different faiths in debate under the general guidance of the Ahmadiyya group, who represented Islam, the group was nettled. Certainly there had been lobbying by the local Sunnis, but the reasons for ceasing sponsorship had nothing to do with that fact. Nevertheless, the group accused the department of bowing to Sunni pressure.

All of these ingredients are present in the process of adaptation within North America. They indicate that the strategies for relating to the host culture are moderated and mediated by a number of religious, social and political conceptions, and traditions. They add to the tensions and strain linkages already present in North American society with regard to Islam.

### Differentiation Between the Muslim and Larger Society

Diffentiation also develops out of interaction with the larger community. Since most immigrant Muslims move from majority Muslim areas, they are faced immediately with religious status reversal. They also come into an environment that is largely indifferent to their religious boundaries. Indeed, Muslims tend to speak of the traditional boundaries, at least with outsiders, as if they are deemed of little significance. One example is the Sunni/Shiʿa division, which tends to play a less significant role in public identity, especially the more remote the generations are from the homeland (Aramco, 1986:16-33). Distortions of the Muslim image in the media, education, and politics have, on the other hand, heightened the awareness that Muslims have of their heritage. They have had to switch to voluntary organizations in order to preserve their sense of identity, since that is both the norm for religious development in North America and the means of providing support. Continuity without the effort of organization cannot be guaranteed. Various strategies to indicate that their group is equal to Judaism and Christianity are adopted, such as pressure on news media to carry information about Muslim holy days, etc., and participation in festive activities in common with those traditions (such as having a Christmas tree and presents) stress common religious notions. On the other hand, adaptation to different laws must be made, such as those that apply to marriage, divorce and the position of women. Whether Islam will develop as a genuine "religious" community within North America, apart from its ethnic connotations, is still not clear.

Differentiation also takes place in other, often less evident ways. If Muslims represent a relatively "new" religion in North America, the quality of the immigrant's Islamic commitment is also measured by those "back home." Thus, in returning home the immigrant Muslims have to be more religious than the home people in order to compensate for living in a non-Muslim environment. They must "prove" that they have lost none of their dedication to the tradition.[19] The need to "represent" makes the North American Muslim susceptible to the political activities of Muslim governments. Such representational demands may result in withdrawal from open engagement in the Muslim community or a shift toward militancy. Like Jews and the policies of Israel, this has the potential for great personal ambiguity and trauma. Another dimension is added by the relative ease of travel back and forth between homeland and North America. Movements, ideas and religious influences are easier to transmit to North America with the resulting enrichment or fragmentation of the community here. Thus movements like the Tabliqis can translate their reformist and Islamization campaigns to the North American environment. The voluntarist nature of religious organization once again puts the onus on the religious group.

Attitudes towards trends in culture here, such as feminism also impact on Muslim society. Distrust of Muslim girls brought up in North America sends many families back home for suitable mates for their sons, leaving North American Muslim girls trapped between the code forbidding marriage to those out of their tradition and the unavailability of Muslim mates. Even if the stated reason for returning home for spouses is couched in religious terms, ethnic qualities may be the real reason. But it is nearly impossible to argue that this is so in any given case.

Events in the Middle East associated with Islam can trigger anti-Islamic feelings. The antipathy towards Arab/Muslim causes on the part of the host cultures has the potential to impact negatively on self-identity. This, in turn, places curbs on Muslim enthusiasm for identification. The involvement of the United States in the support of Israel makes Muslims particularly susceptible to this process.[20] The result is that Muslims who have little or no relationship with the Arab cause are categorized and thus sensitized to being someone associated with a group totally beyond their personal awareness. Stereotyping creates an identity that makes them "other," even when they might have little idea of how they became that other, or what constitutes its character. In effect they become treated like an ethnic group without being in any way related to a particular ethnic group.

A variety of these differentials impact on every Muslim in some way, making it clear that ethnic identity can only partially account for the sense of being Muslim. Hence ethnic analysis can not totally accommodate Islamic traditions. Thus, whatever definition is given ethnicity, religious elements will continue to push it past ethnic boundary markers.

Ethnicity and religion continue to pose a problem for investigators. In this section we have seen that ethnicity can play a number of roles in the adaptation process including giving a character to Islam that is lacking at the conceptual level. On the other hand, the Muslim family realizes that ethnicity can only partially account for the sense of their distinctiveness, and any attempt to understand the growth and development of the strategies for accommodation which the family uses under the guise of ethnicity would misrepresent their religious convictions. Ethnic boundary markers are not fixed either, and change with time and circumstance. Hence ethnicity is only an imperfect tool in uncovering the meaning of Muslim family life in North America.

## The Muslim Family and the Process of Adaptation

Our examination of the process of adaptation indicates that there are a collage of positive and negative elements, within the host culture as it relates to Muslim families and Islam, among Muslim families as they relate to their host cultures and among Muslims themselves as they struggle with several kinds of identity. Moreover, we have encountered a number of variables that affect both the rate and range of the adaptation process, some of them directly related to Islam. It is evident from our survey that there are many positive factors that could attract the Muslim family as it attempts to find a firm footing in the new world. On the other hand, there are long-standing issues and attitudes that militate against the success of the process, some of them internal to the Muslim community itself, and some deriving from the ethos of the two nations to which Muslims come. Muslim families who are the subject of our discussion may have as much separating them from each other as divides them from the host societies of Canada and the United States. Particularly in the Canadian case, the controversial nature of ethnicity in national identity binds the Muslim to his ethnicity, while sidestepping the critical role of religion to his character. The result is that the Muslim family experiences religion through a nationally accepted ethnicity, but not in terms that would allow the religion itself to be identified as part of the *raison d'être* of the host cultures. The ethnic content of Islam marginalizes the tradition to the foreign. Thus the adaptation process may incorporate the Muslim family into North America, but the import of Islam in that integration remains elusive.

Our current level of understanding allows us to see the rough outline of the adaptation process, but the nuances and subtleties are not clear. Our survey may have uncovered more lacunae than given directions. Nevertheless we have been able to situate the Muslim family as it maintains itself with its essential norms and values over against the forces both within and without that would fragment it. Specific understanding of that process will require further probing of elements we have identified here and, indeed, others before anything like an effective profile can be offered.

## Notes

1. For an interesting discussion of the issue, see Richard C. Martin, 1983: 41-57.
2. The best general survey on the issues is in the article *Hadith, Encyclopedia of Islam*, edited by M. Th. Houtsma *et.al.*, 4 vols. and supp. Leiden: E.J. Brill, 1913-38.
3. The best short introduction to the development of the shari'ah or Islamic law is Joseph Schacht, 1964.
4. The source of this Anglo-conformist may go back to the early leadership of the colonies; the elite leadership of Upper Canada had been from England, and hence were members of the Church of England. This church had hopes of being a state Church in Canada, but this never materialized. (Armstrong: 1981:22-37).
5. A survey of this tradition is found in Jacques E. Desseaux, trans. M.J. O'Connell, New York, 1984.
6. Pontificio Istituto di Studi Arabi e d'Islamistica, Rome. The publication from this institute is *Encounter, Documents for Muslim-Christian Understanding*.
7. The best example has to be Samuel Zwemer's Hartford Theological Seminary, and particularly his Journal, now known as *The Muslim World*, which has become more and more a journal of academic study of Islam around the world.

8. The best study of the crusades from the western standpoint is Steven Runciman: 1951-54. On the legacy of animosity between Muslims and Christians see Jacques Lanfry, Penn: 1985, pp.15-27.
9. The trend is usually associated with the name of Edward Said and his book *Orientalism*.
10. As many conservative reformers have argued. For an overview see W.C. Smith, Princeton, 1957 or H.A.R. Gibb, *Modern Trends in Islam*, Chicago, 1947.
11. The most recent example has been Jim Keegstra, in Alberta, who taught for several years in the public school where he was employed that the holocaust never occurred and that there was an international Jewish conspiracy. But native groups have claimed for years, with evident good reason, of the prejudice in Canadian society. Studies on this and other dimensions of prejudice, see section IV, "Ethnic Origins, Prejudice and Bureaucracy," in *Ethnicity, Power and Politics in Canada*, Dalhie and Fernanda pp. 233-91.
12. See W.C. Smith, 1946 for analysis. For a dissenting view on the formation of nation-state and Islam, see James P. Piscatori, 1986.
13. The classic study is associated with Frederick J. Turner, who proposed his famous "frontier thesis" in 1893. See evaluations in Robin W. Winks, 1971.
14. A historical summary of the movement within social scientific discussions is provided by Robert P. Swierenga, 1977:31-45.
15. Attributed to David Carpenter at a conference in Banff, Alberta, subsequently published as *Crossing Frontiers*, edited by Dick Harrison, Edmonton, Alberta: University of Alberta Press, 1979.
16. For example, Margaret Atwood, Toronto, 1972; For an overview of this motif, see also Margaret E. Yeo, 1969.
17. Anti-Americanism is a continuing theme in Canadian attitudes. The roots of this tendency go back to the Loyalists; see Murray Barkley, 1975: 3-45, but the whole notion of the border between Canada and the United States has immense significance for Canadians. Eli Mandel, 1979:105-121.
18. As indicated in Yvonne Y. Haddad, "The Impact of the Islamic Revolution in Iran on the Syrian Muslims of Montreal," in *The Muslim Community*, Waugh et. al., 174ff.; on the negative impact, the Canadian-born religious leader at the Edmonton Sunni mosque paid a visit to Iran immediately after the revolution, and despite his Sunni convictions, was overjoyed at the revolution. When questioned a year later, he would not speak of the revolution, saying only it was not Islam that was motivating the regime.
19. See, for example, the father who returned from a trip home to acknowledge that he limited his daughter in a much more strict manner than he found "back home," Haddad, 1978:93.
20. See Anthony B. Toth, 1986:15 where the death of the al-Faruqis is given

*Part Two*

# From Generation to Generation: Transmitting the Tradition

◆   ◆   ◆   ◆

◆ ◆ ◆ ◆

This section deals with the important task of conveying the tradition to another generation. A number of critical issues are touched upon which indicate that the belief system continues to function as an identity marker beyond the first generation immigrant. There are significant elements that unify the articles but distinctive problems and characteristics are also identified.

The first overriding element to be noted is the success that Muslim families have had in North America as nuclear families. In contrast to the religious importance placed on the larger community, the North American setting is more likely to stress the autonomy of the smaller kin groups. Some settings act to harmonize these units. Ross-Sheriff/Nanji indicate that centering the community life on the jamatkhana, which brings the entire family together through ritual and educational activities, serves to strengthen the Islamic context of the family's meaning.

The second element indicates the interaction of the family in the process of education. Barazangi suggests that the family passes on both general information about the tradition, and more subtle aspects, such as attitudes and convictions. Schubel underlines the importance of the ritual activities of the young in coming to terms with the tradition and discovering their religious identity. A factor that unites several of the papers is the role of the mother in assuring that the family's values are transferred to the younger generation.

The third element is the role of ritual and/or social interaction in the process of passing on the tradition. This characteristic is best seen in the juxtaposition of Schubel and Ross-Sheriff/Nanji, where the creation of a community is dependent upon the enriching and developing of the community at worship. This would seem to indicate that the role of institutions in preserving and enhancing tradition is very significant, and that Muslim families have recognized the essential role of an institution in providing the tradition to the youth. These papers indicate that ritual forms can be utilized to reduce distance from the homeland and provide a sense of continuity for all age levels.

The fourth element concerns the role of different age groups in the whole process. It is evident that children and youths, through their contacts at school, face the potential for conflict with the larger society. It is also clear that Muslim families have assumed the critical role of the religious community for providing direction to children although specific youth programs have not always been available. Rather, the age-old structures of community and family ritual are relied upon to provide support for the young. In this context, the role assigned to elders in the educational process, particularly evident in the Ross-Sheriff/Nanji contribution, is noteworthy.

Finally, although patterns and traditional roles may be shifting in response to the North American setting, this section illustrates the continuous role of the family unit in the development of identity and the transmission of tradition.

# Islamic Identity, Family and Community: The Case of the Nizari Ismaili Muslims

Fariyal Ross-Sheriff

Azim Nanji

◆   ◆   ◆   ◆

The Nizari Ismaili Muslims are recent arrivals to North America. The majority of them, like many others from Asia and Africa, came in the 1970s following reforms in American and Canadian immigration laws that allowed a larger number of people from the so-called Third World to enter these countries. In one dramatic episode in 1972, several thousand Ismaili Muslims from Uganda were forced to find refuge in North America after the Asian population of that East African country was expelled by then president and dictator, Idi Amin. In time, the community has grown to more than 50,000. While they have come mainly from African countries including Kenya, Uganda, Tanzania, the Malagasy Republic, South Africa and Zaire, as well as from Asian countries such as India, Pakistan and Bangladesh, they share a common religious heritage.

Ismailis are part of the Shiᶜa branch of Islam, and they are found today in some twenty-five countries all over the world. The majority of those in North America, however, trace their ethnic roots to the Indo-Pakistan sub-continent, where Ismailism has had a long and checkered history, dating back to the ninth century. In the nineteenth and twentieth centuries, some migrated and established permanent homes in what were then the British colonies and territories of Eastern Africa. When these countries became independent in the early 1960s few Ismailis living there imagined that they would soon be leaving. Independence, however, brought in its wake the turbulence that has often accompanied the search for national identity and development goals.

Political and economic instability eventually caused (and in the case of Uganda, forced) Ismailis to find new homes in Canada and the United States.[1] Thus, in just over a century, two out of four generations had suffered the traumatic experience of dislocation and disruption in their lives. It may be argued that such an experience could have made them more capable of adapting to sudden change; however, community organization and stability take time to evolve and, in the case of transition to the Western cultural context, the move was unlike any shift that the Ismailis had undergone before. The metaphor of *hijra* (based on the Prophet Muhammad's migration from Mecca to Medina) is an important element in Ismaili historical self-understanding, and, as in the past, it provides an important frame of reference for recreating patterns of community and personal life.

The interchange between this common understanding of the past with its relationship to core religious values and a new cultural context within which to effect such a vision represents the overall perspective within which family life among the Ismailis must be considered. In using such a perspective, it is not necessary to emphasize unduly the model of assimilation that has generally been followed in studying ethnic groups, for it polarizes the incoming and host cultures into an either/or dichotomy. Rather, the emphasis here is on how a group like the Ismailis draws upon their religious tradition as well as modernity to shape new forms of organization and provide an equilibrium upon which to build their lives.

## THE HERITAGE OF FAMILY VALUES

Whether in North America or elsewhere, Muslims are by no means a homogeneous religious group. Historical, cultural, and geographical factors have played a large part in determining their past experience. Ismailis, like their co-religionists, however, do have a shared sense of what "ideal" family life in Islam ought to be, primarily as it is reflected in precepts of the Qur'an, and in the evolution of their interpretation of the shari‘a. Religious groups, characteristically, tend to project such an ideal back into the past; in the case of Muslims, either to the historical beginnings of Islam, or to the immediate past context which is viewed as approximating such a pattern. Thus, they are still in the process of developing strategies for a new context within which their own historical experience can be fully understood and related.

In the case of the Ismailis, the ideal of family values relates very closely to the organization of community life under the guidance and leadership of a living Imam.[2] In modern times, guiding principles came to be outlined, in a framework of rules and regulations of conduct referred to as a "Constitution." Such constitutions provided a degree of continuity and a means of balancing past values with the requirements of the legal systems of colonial administrations and subsequently, those of the new independent nations, whose personal laws they also complemented.

Ismailis, like other Shi‘i and Sunni schools, have evolved an identifiable framework for implementing the values of Islam. The role of the living Imam as guide has been perceived as embracing both material and spiritual spheres of life. As guardian and interpreter of these two foci, the Imam seeks to guide his followers in ways that will enable them to implement the total Islamic vision. The constitution emphasizes the centrality of family life referring to the Personal Law that has evolved within the Shi‘a Ismailis school of thought. Such guidelines were also provided for Ismailis living in India, Pakistan, and elsewhere, where rules also had to be adapted to national legal systems.

One aspect of the overall policy that had major implications for family life, particularly in Africa, related to women's roles. Steps were taken to prepare women for a greater public role. The enabling factors were encouraging modern education, and de-emphasizing specific cultural and social traits that had discouraged work outside the home. The reorganization of Ismailis institutions allowed women greater participation in the public sphere of community life. The emphasis on female education was also an important part of the development of the Ismailis community in the sub-continent. The changing role of women did not cause the Ismaili family to undergo any transformation; however, psychologically there was a change of perception— the family was no longer seen as being limited by male and female spheres of action.

The newly developing ideal allowed roles to become more complementary; women were still regarded as the anchors of family life, but they began to be viewed as more than just child-bearers and mothers. In time their roles acquired greater social and economic significance.

Family life among Ismailis in East Africa was reinforced by other institutions that provided mutually supportive bonds. One illustration is the way in which the community took the initiative to set up programs to provide adequate family housing in major urban centers. In Nairobi and Mombasa, Kenya, for example, there were several such programs. In both cases, efforts were made to provide financing at a reasonable cost and to create environments that offered comfortable housing and also made it possible to develop community solidarity further. At one level, the leadership of the community stressed the importance and significance of contributing to national development and of full participation in national life. At another, it sought to recognize the pluralistic and diverse nature of African society and the role of private initiative in ensuring the continuity of the community's Muslim identity and progress. The effort to balance these two levels constitutes the heart of Ismaili institutional strategy in East Africa. Within the larger boundary that was being created to blend community development into national development, there was also an inner boundary, where Islamic identity and tradition was being preserved and extended. One of the centers of community interaction and activity is the *jamatkhana*.[3] An urban morphology that is often evident in Muslim environments seeks to juxtapose places for religious practices, housing, and the market-place so that each zone is linked to the other but still has an autonomy of function and space in the conduct of faith, work, and family life. Such a model, of course, varies with geographical conditions and historical factors, but in the environments created for daily Ismaili life in East Africa and eventually in India and Pakistan, it was oriented towards sustaining a balance between Islamic family, social and spiritual obligations.

Against this background, this paper focuses primarily on three topics: the Ismaili family today in an institutional, community context; the particular concerns of the youth and the elderly as they seek to adapt to changing contexts and roles; and community programs and strategies for creating an enabling family environment. The data for this study is based on field work done among various Ismaili communities in North

America over the past four years (1982-86) and we are grateful to the members of the various communities and officers in the United States and Canada of the National and Regional Councils and other community organizations for their cooperation and assistance.

### ISMAILI FAMILIES TODAY
*Settlements Patterns*

Most North American Ismailis arrived during the last quarter of a century in one of three waves. First there were college students and immigrants from India, Pakistan, Bangladesh, and various African countries; some of them subsequently became permanent residents. The second wave consisted of refugees from Uganda and entrepreneurs from newly independent African countries, who came with their families in the early 1970s. The most recent Ismaili immigrants are relatives and dependants of previous migrants as well as people in business, managerial, professional, and service categories. Thus from a mere handful twenty-five years ago, the Ismaili population has grown rapidly, and its institutional development has provided it with a stable and recognizable identity.

The background of educational attainment, business experience, and professional skills, combined with fluency in English and other European languages and past exposure to diverse cultures, predisposed many Ismailis to make a successful transition. In keeping with the general trend among recent immigrants, Ismaili families have mostly settled in large cities: Calgary, Montreal, Toronto, and Vancouver in Canada, and Atlanta, Chicago, Dallas, Houston, Los Angeles, Miami, and New York in the United States. However, there are communities in smaller cities or towns.

*Structural and Cultural Adjustments*

Ismaili families have tried to synthesize traditional and contemporary family values within their structure and processes. The notion of tradition requires some elaboration, particularly since certain Eurocentric models in the social sciences have tended to view it as a hindrance in the path of progress and individual freedom. More recent analyses of tradition have focused on its role in shaping experience and values and in providing an anchor and a framework for dealing with and adapting to change. Edward Shils, for example, refers to tradition's capacity to provide stability while at the same time it is in continuous flux.[4] In the Ismaili case, tradition is best embodied in the concept of exteriorising through community institutions, the ethics of Islam, thus, offering a frame of reference within which to chart individual and collective life.

Islamic tradition includes an emphasis on certain primary family values: the importance of marriage and children, participation in social activities as a family unit, respect for authority of the elderly and parents, mutual dependence and group harmony. Contemporary Western family life, on the other hand, reflects a move toward egalitarian family roles in which there is greater individualism, emphasis on self-reliance, self-direction and independence in selected aspects of life, such as educational and occupational pursuits. The balancing of these two dimensions is a crucial ingredient in the adaptation of Ismailis to the North American situation.

At the structural level, adaptation has been fairly rapid because of the skills for global survival that Ismailis have developed in the past. The relatively high level of employment, industry, and family cohesion evident among them, together with acceptance of the commitment to their adopted homeland, and formal support from international Ismaili institutions has enabled most Ismailis to make rapid structural adjustments to American society and in becoming a productive group in North American society.

The cultural adjustment of Ismaili immigrants presents far more complex problems and is particularly acute for adolescents and the elderly. For adolescent stress results from having to adapt their historical and cultural background to a new set of contexts: the worlds of school and peers, of the home, and the world of the community. For the elderly, especially those living in isolated areas, stresses arise from such factors as lack of mobility, limited opportunity for socializing, perceptions that they receive too little attention from adult children (especially daughters and daughters-in-law, who might, in their countries of origin, have remained in an extended family), loss of their traditional position of authority in the family, and lack of access to a regular and formal religious environment.

While most parents take pride in the educational accomplishments of their children, many also express fear about the negative influences of popular culture and the consequent erosion of the family traditions. The most serious cultural conflicts experienced by Ismaili youth arise from the negative attitudes towards Muslims in the larger North American society that have become especially prevalent in recent times.

One Ismaili educator used the following example to illustrate the pervasive influence of mass media on Muslim teenagers. When asked what words or images come to their minds when they heard the terms "Muslim," "Shiᶜa" or "Shiᶜite Muslim," a number of Ismaili youth responded with terms like "terrorists, Muslim extremists, hijackers, etc." Though at one level, most teenagers were conscious that their own background was being subjected to distortion and stereotyping, at another level they were imbibing, perhaps subconsciously, negative images about Muslims from their peers, who, they believed, held such opinions. As a result, some of these adolescents sometimes felt hesitant to be identified as Muslim. However, when they were questioned about issues that related to their self-perception of the relationship between their faith and prospects for success in their lives as North Americans, a large proportion (75 percent) expressed feelings of confidence (Ross-Sheriff, 1985). Similar results on identity were reported by Tomeh (1983), who noted that most of the Ismaili youth she interviewed identified themselves as American Ismaili Muslims. Only longitudinal research will indicate whether those who expressed some unease with cultural and religious practices do so as a result of being adolescents and will change with age, or whether it is a more long-lasting characteristic of these young immigrant Muslims. Parents and community leaders are addressing these tensions and making efforts to instill religious self-awareness and develop a positive Muslim self-identity.

Before the activities of the majority of Ismaili families are described, two minority tendencies evident among all North American Muslim groups need to be noted. One of these groups imitates the perceived pattern of cultural values in the host society as much as possible. Such families or individuals seek to disassociate themselves from other Ismailis and establish friendships and support networks mainly with non-Ismailis. This is the least common adaptation pattern, and it is found among a very small group of professional, affluent families and, in some cases, among unsupervised teenagers or young adults from families overburdened by the stresses of adjustment. Another minority pattern involves resistance to the North American lifestyle and a withdrawal to what are regarded as the "old ways." Such families make explicit efforts to socialize exclusively with families with Asian backgrounds or to participate only in cultural activities that promote this cultural heritage and to limit contacts with other groups or individuals except those required by work and school. Such patterns have been observed among other groups of immigrants to the United States as well. (Alvarez, Dean and Williams, 1983), but they are not endorsed by the Ismaili community's leadership, which emphasizes a policy of building cultural bridges with other groups and stresses the common Judeo-Christian-Islamic values that are shared with many other North Americans. This vision of the community's future has been addressed by a variety of programs developed specifically for the youth.

## CREATING A NORTH AMERICAN MUSLIM IDENTITY
### The Family

Most of the parents want their children to adopt Islamically-oriented moral, social and cultural values. As a result, they encourage them to participate in religious activities and programs that sustain an awareness of Muslim identity.

Within the home, parental efforts are apparent from the attitudes of the youth who for the most part take pride in stating that they are Ismaili Muslims. Parents also take their children for religious education to jamatkhana and obtain materials that they read to them. In addition to such efforts to cultivate religious knowledge and identity, almost all parents are eager that their children receive a good secular education, which they see as a route to success in North America. However, there are differences among Ismaili families in use of resources such as nursery schools, libraries, zoological gardens, summer camps, theaters, sports and recreational programs that reflect differences in educational background and level of integration in American society. Some mothers, still attempting multiple roles, said they felt overwhelmed by their responsibilities—jobs, homemaking, and child-rearing—with little or no support from extended family or household help, both of which were typically available to their parents in the country of origin. However, we are not aware of any child abuse or neglect or of interventions among Ismaili families by legal, medical, or social welfare agencies.

The second method Ismaili families use to socialize children is family activities, a significant method for other cultural groups in North

America as well (Mindel and Haberstein, 1983). Participation in religious and recreational activities is predominantly done as a family group. Thus, many Ismaili teenagers observe that their non-Muslim friends go to parties with classmates, while they are often accompanied by their parents. In addition, Ismaili children and adolescents are expected to be actively involved in entertaining their parents, friends, and families at dinner parties in their own homes though some express dissatisfaction that their classmates meanwhile spend weekend evenings partying with each other.

Parents often have considerable influence on which group of young people their child will associate with and whom they will visit. By this means the children are directed into preferred social groups and encouraged towards preferred marriages. Those families that are isolated geographically and socially from other Ismailis expressed fear that their children might be absorbed into the surrounding culture. Thus, when possible, they arrange to visit relatives or friends as a family unit.

Ismailis are also dealing with problems adjusting to the North American environment through adaptations at the family level. Among these adaptions are changes in the roles of individual family members and informal networks among friends and extended family members that reach across cities and continents. For example, it is not uncommon for husbands to help their wives with household chores or for them to share the responsibility of child rearing. It is also not uncommon for many families to send their youngsters to spend summer vacations with extended family or friends in cities with large jamats in other parts of the country or even in other parts of the world. Young families with children feel the need to maintain family networks because it helps with child rearing and the socialization of young children. However, many do not want to live in the traditional extended family under one roof because of the social obligations and responsibilities entailed in such living arrangements. The pattern among young families is to adopt the nuclear family mode, while retaining contact through community and social networks.

*Programs and Institutions at the Community Level*

Two types of programs have been established by Ismailis in North American cities. One imparts Muslim education to young children and youth, primarily by voluntary teachers. Almost all jamats with young children and adolescents have religious education centers that are open at least once a week. The curriculum used for these classes is standardized at a national level through efforts of religious education specialists in both the United States and Canada. The teachers receive periodic training in curriculum content and in modern teaching methods that are compatible with those that the youngsters experience in their secular schools.

The second type of program is socio-cultural and recreational. These are organized at local levels and periodically at regional levels to help link communities. Some of the events that bring together Ismaili adolescents and young adults are sports tournaments, debate competitions, and cultural events. Arrangements are made for visitors to be hosted in homes of individual families or in a motel or hotel owned by Ismailis. Most of these events are well attended by families from host jamats, and almost always they end with a communal get-together and feast.

To combat possible erosion of identity and to prepare Ismaili youth to address problems of cultural conflict, a cultural-religious educational summer program entitled "Al-Ummah, an Experience in Islamic Living" was initiated in the summer of 1983 at the national level in the United States. Similar programs have been developed for youth in Canada.

### Ismaili Elderly

Ismaili elderly have had to make two major adjustments: relocation from their country of origin to North America and a change in lifestyle from one immersed in a community environment to one that is predominantly secular. Conceptual frameworks for explaining the behavior of the aged in North America—disengagement (Cumming and Henry, 1961; Cumming, 1976) and activity theory (Havighurst, 1963: Lemon, Bengtston, and Peterson, 1976) may be partially appropriate in explaining the behavior of Ismaili elderly. Disengagement is a process in which the elderly and society make "a gradual and mutual" withdrawal, a process that is inevitable. As a result, the elderly are freed from the constraints of earlier life norms and are content to live with symbols of the past. Activity theory maintains that the norms of middle years remain consistent throughout the later years of life and that the level of satisfaction with aging depends on the extent to which roles and relationships of earlier life can be sustained. Thus morale and life satisfaction are determined by continued active participation in important spheres of life. While these theories are helpful, it is important that a historical perspective (Rey, 1982) also be incorporated in developing a further understanding of behavior and adjustment, since such a perspective includes the environmental, social, and institutional contexts affecting the elderly.

Historically, the elderly worked within the family structure, and when they became physically unable to work, were taken care of by the extended family network. In this "welfare system," financial and social support of older Ismailis was the responsibility of the family with the primary responsibility often falling on the eldest son. For those who did not have living children or an extended family the responsibility fell on the larger Ismaili community. This support arrangement has always constituted a major ingredient of family life among all Muslim groups. Most Ismailis over sixty years of age migrated to North America as dependants of their young and middle-aged children. Despite the dispersion of extended families, most of the elderly live with one of their adult children, their spouse, or other family members. Though some live alone, hardly any, to the knowledge of the authors, live in institutions. Thus, among the first-generation Ismailis in North America, the family has assumed collective responsibility of the elderly.

However, a number of factors associated with the socio-economic milieu have caused Ismailis, like other immigrants, to respond on a more individualistic basis. This pattern of family autonomy in urban and suburban environments has resulted in both stress and modifications of Ismaili family life. For example, when the elderly are dependent on their adult children, they can occasionally be a source of friction, especially during the initial period of adjustment to North America. At the same time many have been a great asset to young families in two primary roles: as religious advocates/teachers who impart family values and traditions, and as child-rearers for young families with two working parents.

Ismaili elders rely heavily on their family members to perform instrumental, personal, and social functions. Instrumental support involves help in carrying out day to day tasks such as shopping for personal effects, transportation to visit friends, going to jamatkhana and meeting health needs through interaction (communication, transportation, interpretation, etc.) with physicians and health care institutions. Personal support refers to emotional networks that reinforce family ties. In the country of origin, most Ismailis lived in neighborhoods or planned communities, and such support was part of the milieu. In contrast, their living environments here are totally lacking in such networks, and the burden thus falls on immediate family members. The elderly also have more personal time at their disposal, and consequently, a greater need for attention from their adult children. For the elderly Ismaili, the loss of a sense of belonging that is experienced by other immigrants (Rack, 1982) is compounded by two additional losses—the loss of status and the loss of opportunity to practice their faith in an environment analogous to the traditional one. The loss of role status is perceived as the general lack of deference towards the elderly evident in North America as well as to change in economic status that some have undergone because they lack skills necessary to succeed in the North American economy.

For personal and cultural reasons, most elderly Ismailis have neither established significant ties with other Americans nor participated in established programs for the elderly. They say that their American neighbors and acquaintances are generally helpful in providing instrumental support, but very few have developed strong social ties or personal friendships with them. Apparently this is the result of reciprocal perceptions about cultural differences. Ismaili elderly believe that other Americans have insufficient time or interest in developing personal relationships with them. Efforts on their part to befriend their non-Muslim neighbors often fail because of cross-cultural communications problems, and they feel that their neighbors do not understand or accept them. In turn, they also are unwilling to discuss personal or family problems with outsiders since these are spheres of private life that are not easily shared outside the family boundary.

The most critical problem confronted by a majority of elderly Ismailis is the lack of opportunity to participate in what they regard as a total Ismaili Muslim environment, a problem they share with the elderly from other Muslim migrant groups. They describe the loss of the traditional milieu in terms of having lost the crutches they need to lean on.

Child-rearing is perceived by elderly Ismailis as one of the principal functions of grandparents. Almost all of those who had grandchildren under the age of five indicate that their presence enabled their daughters or daughters-in-law to seek employment outside the home without having to worry about the quality of care provided to their children. Both grandmothers and grandfathers with school-age grandchildren report that their most important responsibilities are to teach the grandchildren their ethnic language and traditional customs, morals, and religious practices and to impart religious knowledge. In addition, they provide after-school care and supervise homework. A majority of the elderly stress the importance of encouraging formal education even though many say that they do not fully understand American ways of education. Some disapprove of the liberty their adult children give to the grandchildren and feel remorse about the loss of cultural and religious values and behavior among their children and grandchildren that are the results of acculturation.

The elderly who are grandparents of adolescents and young adults mention traditional roles of grandparents, such as the role as family historian or the responsibility to pass on traditional information concerning the use of herbal medicine and techniques of massage that relieve stress and related illnesses. Youngsters attending colleges and universities are divided equally among those who turn to their grandparents for traditional knowledge and those who feel that their grandparents may become a burden to them since their parents expect them to help provide support. An example of such traditional expectations is reflected in a statement by one parent:

> My parents help not only with child-rearing and teaching language, cultural and religious practices to my children, but they enable our children to develop maturity and responsible social behavior . . . our children are required to respect their grandparents and help them with daily chores.

In most cases families who migrated to the United States and Canada in the 1960s and early 1970s have now established roots through jobs, purchase of residential property, long-term settlement in a specific location, establishment of jamatkhanas, and secondary migration to larger cities. They feel that their success in achieving economic and social adjustment in North America including familiarity with available resources, has put them in a position to begin making a significant social contribution while sustaining an integrated family life. Their efforts are directed towards the re-establishment of family rituals and of family and community networks to meet the needs of changing family situations including the critical groups of adolescents and elderly parents.

A new pattern of interaction with the extended family emerges through contacts developed during regular visits. Access to auto, rail, and plane travel and to instantaneous communication through the telephone has made it possible for family members to remain in regular contact and sustain a network of assistance. Many elderly who were initially perceived as being a burden to the family now regularly visit their children and siblings during such significant life events as births, marriages, and deaths and during Muslim festivals. Such visits not only serve as reminders of kin obligations but also maintain family ties. During such visits all the family members share a residence. Not only elderly and adolescents, but also adult children state that they talk more, maintain higher levels of interaction, mutual self-disclosure and interpersonal closeness during these occasions. They also engage in more recreational activities. The disruption of normal routine during such visits is not generally considered a source of tension; rather, it is considered an opportunity. Whether in their own city of primary residence or in other places while they are visiting adult children or siblings, the elderly mostly participate in religious festivals with other family members. Social interactions during these times—preparation, gatherings for meals, exchange of gifts, also reinforce relationships. Thus, these functions bring elderly, adult children, and adolescents together in a positive and enriching manner.

Despite the drastic changes experienced during the move from a supportive, well-established Muslim community in Africa or South Asia to a predominantly secularized and unfamiliar environment, most Ismaili families have managed to retain supportive family structures. Although the processes of acculturation are making the practice of a traditional lifestyle impractical, especially for a majority of the elderly, the cultural values have not disappeared. Rather, they are being modified to fit the changed economic, social, and environmental conditions.

In cities with large Ismaili populations, young volunteers provide transportation to community activities. Events such as luncheons, picnics, and special gatherings to promote folk and cultural practices are planned periodically for special weekends to provide social opportunities for the elderly, who are also regularly involved in observances of Muslim festivals and holy days. Recreational activities are also planned to enable them to visit other centers with large Ismaili populations and to travel across the country to visit places of interest. Social programs are coordinated to facilitate interactions between the hosts and the visitors. These services and activities are particularly helpful in alleviating the sense of isolation created by geographic separation and the dispersion of families to various parts of North America and by the altered lifestyle of their adult children's nuclear families. Thus, the restructured family and larger Ismaili community has assumed collective responsibility for the elderly.

## CONCLUSION

On the whole it appears that the Ismailis have addressed the process of integration into North American life successfully. The foresight of young parents, adult children, and community leaders have facilitated the initiation of programs to meet the religious and intercultural needs of children, youth, and elderly. The adjustment has benefitted from community support networks and proven traditional coping strategies. Some difficulties have arisen because of intergenerational differences, pressures on both parents to work, and other stresses involved in adapting to a highly industrialized and differentiated society. For most Ismailis, their traditional Muslim heritage remains the critical resource that they turn to when they encounter problems. Longitudinal and comparative research may provide a better understanding of the long-term impact and the need to develop new mechanisms to sustain family and community cohesion and foster a moral vision that reflects the distinctiveness of a North American Islamic identity.

The establishment of a major Ismaili Center in British Columbia suggests the direction that the community is choosing. Its architecture and function symbolize a synthesis between the Islamic heritage and North American resources. In that sense, it serves as a bridge between the Muslim roots of the community and the cultural values of the West that it has deemed appropriate to its vision of living in the New World.

The emergence and articulation of a more well-defined Islamic identity, adapted to this new Western context and enriched by shared humanistic goals, lies in the future. The quest for this identity among Ismailis, as among other Muslims in North America, will involve addressing a complex set of problems that will affect the future structures and ethos of family life.

The so-called "secularization" thesis has held that in modern industrialized society religious belief came to be given less credence and that as a result the influence of religion in social and cultural life diminished. Several recent studies (Stark and Bainbridge, 1985; Bellah, 1985; Cox, 1982; Mol, 1986; Nanji, 1986) have shown this thesis to be inadequate not only in Western contexts, but also globally, and they have argued, on the contrary, that instead of declining, religion has rather tended to be reaffirmed and revived in different forms and ways. The response to change in modern times has caused religious groups to accommodate to as well as contend with secularizing forces, and to redress imbalances that have affected their sense of identification with the past. In a pluralistic society like North America these responses are varied and reveal a whole spectrum of attitudes ranging from withdrawal and separation to accommodation or affirmation of selected aspects of modernity.

This study has focused on ways in which religious identity, family values, and community development are interconnected, and we have consciously avoided the tendency to follow an assimilationist model of analysis. Such models have tended to assume that proper explanations of ethnic and religious groups derive mainly from studying the impact of the majority and the consequent erosion of the minority's value system and traditional organization. Because of this focus, most sociological analysis tends to ignore the role of tradition as a source and method for shaping responses to new conditions. Such analyses also minimize the critical role that religious values and institutions play in maintaining equilibrium and continuity and overemphasize the more measureable social control aspects of religion. The recent study, by Bellah and his colleagues *Habits of the Heart* (1985), argues that transformation in American culture and society involves a change of consciousness through individual action, which in turn is nurtured by groups that carry a moral tradition. This study of the Ismailis provides an instance of a group seeking to transform social ecology through its own moral vision linking past, present, and future. It is in the pursuit of that common endeavor that their experience and success may contribute to the larger Canadian and American societies of which they have now become a permanent part.

### Notes

1. For the general background and history of Ismailis in North America, see Azim Nanji, "The Nizari Ismaili Muslim Community in North America: Background and Development," in *The Muslim Community in North America*, eds. Earle H. Waugh, Baha Abu-Laban, and Regula Qureshi (Edmonton: University of Alberta Press, 1983).
2. At present, the Ismailis acknowledge His Highness Prince Karim Aga Khan as their hereditary forty-ninth Imam, or spiritual leader, in direct lineal descent from the Prophet Muhammad, through the first Imam Ali and Fatima, the Prophet's daughter. He became Imam in 1957, succeeding the internationally well-known figure, Imam Sultan Muhammad Shah, who had led the Ismailis for over seventy years.
3. Literally "a house of assembly," which has traditionally served among the Ismailis as a center for community activities, social gatherings and superogatory religious observances. Each congregation may be referred to as a jamat. Congregational activity in the initial stages of development in North America has often centered on available sites, such as school halls and other locations, which have served in place of jamatkhanas during the period of transition. More permanent locations are being obtained gradually and with due regard to changing demographic patterns in the community.
4. E. Shils, *Tradition* (Chicago: University of Chicago Press, 1981), pp. 4-25. See also J. Pelikan, *The Vindication of Tradition* (New Haven: Yale University Press, 1984).

# The Muharram Majlis: The Role of a Ritual in the Preservation of Shi'a Identity

## Vernon Schubel

◆　　◆　　◆　　◆

The most important ritual of public devotion for Twelver Shiʿi Muslims of South Asian origin in North America is undoubtedly the *majlis* or lamentation assembly. This ritual is most commonly associated with the annual commemoration of the martyrdom of Imam Husayn in the lunar month of Muharram. While the majlis is essentially a devotional ritual, it is also a fundamental vehicle for the maintenance of Shiʿi culture.

In cities and towns throughout South Asia, the first day of Muharram ushers in a ten-day period of intense religious activity for the Shiʿi community. Shiʿi precincts take on a somber hue as black banners are hung in the streets and people don the black dress of mourning. Mournful poetry in memory of the martyred grandson of the Prophet can be heard continuously through loudspeakers. Large and ornate replicas of the coffin and tomb of Imam Husayn are carried through the streets in processions to shouts of "Ya Husayn" and "Ya Abbas." At night, families attend majlis in the *imambargahs*—the communal religious centers of the Shiʿa. During the majlis, both parents and children listen to the religious discourse of the *zakir*—the majlis reader—as he sits upon the *minbar* flanked by the ʿ*alams*-standards of Husayn—each topped with the five-fingered hand symbolic of the *Panjatan Pak* (the five pure ones): Muhammad, Fatimah, ʿAli, Hasan, and Husayn. These five are the quintessential *ahl al-bayt*—the household of the Prophet— and the paradigmatic Muslim family.

The longest portion of the majlis is usually an oral exegesis of Qur'anic verse. Much of what the zakir says may be profound and complex, drawing on points of history, theology, and literature well beyond the grasp of the smaller children in attendance. But at the culmination of this discourse the zakir begins the *gham*—the lamentation for the martyrs of Karbala—in which he emotionally recounts the story of the murder of Husayn, the last survivor of the immediate household of Muhammad. At this point in the majlis, children may see their parents begin to weep. They are witness to the tearful sobbing that fills the imambaragah and to the *matam*—the rhythmic beating of the chest with the hand—which follows it. Thus, even before Shiʿi children can fully comprehend the meaning of the events of Karbala, the intensely emotional ritual responses of the adult community to those events provide incontrovertible evidence of their power.

As children grow older, attendance at majlis becomes a means of religious education. The Muharram majlis provides each successive generation with the religious instruction necessary for the continuance of Shiʿi identity. Throughout the year the verity of the emotional experience of Karbala that begins in childhood is repeatedly reaffirmed. Although these activities occur on a much smaller scale in North America, their function remains essentially the same as in South Asia.

## SHIʿI RITUAL IN NORTH AMERICA

North America is home to a sizeable and heterogeneous community of Muslims of South Asian origin. Although the majority are Sunnis, there is also a sizeable number of Shiʿi Muslims, who have continued many of their traditional devotional practices. In so doing they have found an effective means for maintaining the cultural allegiance of the next generation as the Shiʿi community adapts to the realities of North American life.

In 1982 at the Zainabiyyah Hall in Toronto, I had my first opportunity to attend Muharram majlis. Since that time I have had the opportunity to examine the performance of majlis much more closely, including a year of field research in 1983 that centered on the role and function of such mourning rituals among the Shiʿa of Karachi, Pakistan. The structure of these rituals provides for the kind of creative reflection that allows a religious minority to adapt to changing circumstances.

Shiʿi devotional observances are of two types—private and public. Private or household rituals include the recitation of formulaic miracle stories (*kahanis*), which serve as the basis for spiritual vows (*mannat*).[1] The public rituals consist primarily of majlis and *julus* (processions), both of which are generally associated with the martyrdom of Imam Husayn. While the household rituals are more obviously "family" occasions, the public rituals are perhaps even more important as foci of family activity. They are centered in the imambargahs; as in South Asia, North American imambaragahs are communal centers that serve a wide variety of religious needs. They may contain a mosque for prayers, a *ziyarat khaneh* to house the religious artifacts symbolic of the ahl al-bayt, meeting halls for the performance of the majlis, schoolrooms for the religious education of the young, and facilities for the preparation of the dead for burial. Thus, the imambargah is a place where families can surround themselves with the ethos of Shiʿi piety.

## SHIʿI PIETY: THE PIETY OF PERSONAL ALLEGIANCE

Shiʿism is the Islam of personal allegiance to the Prophet Muhammad and his family. For the Shiʿa, this devotion is of such crucial importance that rejection of it is seen as a rejection of the faith itself.[2] The Prophet, his daughter Fatimah, his cousin and son-in-law ʿAli, and their two sons, Hasan and Husayn, constitute a special familial constellation. Together with the Imams—or spiritual leaders—who follow Husayn, they make up the *maʿsumin* (those protected from sin).[3] The last of these is Muhammad Mahdi, the Twelfth Imam, who remains in hiding as the receptacle of the millenial hopes of the community and who is expected to return eventually to establish a just society. It is allegiance to these persons that defines the parameters of Twelver Shiʿism.

Most Western scholars have focused on the political roots of the distinction between Sunni and Shiʿi Muslims. In doing so they mirror the Sunni point of view. For the Shiʿa, however, the source of the discord is not the Sunni rejection of ʿAli's right to the caliphate, a political office, but rather their rejection of him as Imam, a position of intrinsic spiritual authority. Shiʿism places great emphasis on the supernatural authority of the ahl al-bayt. The Shi'a hold that both Muhammad and 'Ali were taken from a pre-existent Light before creation.[4] The Panjatan Pak are the most complete manifestation of that Prophetic Light in the world.[5] Furthermore, on the basis of the Qur'an, the Shi'a conclude that because they were martyred, the Imams continue to exist in a spiritual state that allows them even now to intercede on the behalf of their devotees.

The Prophet, Fatimah, and the Imams are thus understood both as historical and "meta-historical" personalities. Rather than being relegated to an existence in some distant historical past, they are instead thought of as living presences. Their paradigmatic virtues have been revealed in history, but their spiritual existence is not bounded by mere historicity. The Prophet and Imams therefore inhabit a spiritual realm parallel to that of normal waking consciousness that humanity may, at times, contact. One important means of achieving contact is through the performance of ritual.

The centrality of personal allegiance in Shi'i piety has made narratives of the exploits of the ma'sumin foci for reflection in these rituals. The retelling and remembrance of sacred or miraculous events in the lives of the ahl al-bayt allow for the possibility of emotional encounter with them. The most important of these narratives recalls the martyrdom of the Prophet's grandson, Imam Husayn, at Karbala. There the Imam and his family were cut off from water and then cruelly killed by the larger forces of Yazid, an event seen by the Shi'a as a watershed in history. The yearly rituals of grief and mourning during Muharram are not simply remembrances of Karbala but opportunities to evoke it.

For the Shi'a, this ritual encounter is crucial for establishing the parameters of their communal identity. According to the Shi'i view of history, the majority of the nominally Islamic community, from the earliest period of Muslim history, rejected Islam as intended by God and his Prophet. Not only did they reject those persons to whom the granting of allegiance was requisite for membership in the Islamic community, but also they murdered those who were beloved of the Prophet. For the Shi'a, the expression of grief and sorrow over the sufferings of the members of the Prophet's household is an act of solidarity with Islam as truly intended. Thus, the Shi'a define themselves as the true Muslims.

The first step in the process of transmitting Shi'ism from one generation to the next, therefore, is to convince the children of the necessity of allegiance to the ahl al-bayt. Secondly, they must be educated in the consequences of that allegiance, that is to say, the manner in which they should live their lives. Devotional rituals such as majlis accomplish both of these purposes.

## ANALYSIS OF THE RITUAL PROCESS OF THE MAJLIS

Although majlis occurs throughout the year—particularly on Thursdays and on the birth and death anniversaries of the ahl al-bayt—it is most closely associated with Muharram. Clifford Geertz has defined religion as

> a system of symbols which acts to establish powerful, pervasive and long-lasting moods and motivations in men by formulating conceptions of a general order of existence and clothing these conceptions with such an aura of factuality that the moods and motivations seem uniquely realistic. (1973:90-91)

This definition is particularly useful when looking at Shiʿi Islam. Shiʿi rituals evoke the system of symbols related to the authority of the ahl al-bayt in such an emotionally charged fashion that the verity of those symbols seems unquestionable.

Such rituals allow one to step momentarily out of normal time into the realm of "what if" and "what could have been" (Turner, 1982:62-64). Through the ritual of majlis, mourners enter into a sacred history, but one which contains the possibility of certain alterations. For example, in the processions, the unburied Husayn is represented by a coffin, even though he was denied burial by Bani Umayyad (Yazid's tribe). The majlis allows the mourner to experience Karbala and ask the question: Had I been at Karbala would I have had the courage to stand with Husayn? This is part of the reason behind such acts as flagellation and firewalking—a desire to demonstrate physically the willingness to suffer the kinds of wounds that would have been incurred at Karbala. The majlis allows for this entrance into a subjunctive realm removed from ordinary reality by creating a separate ritual space—a liminal arena where one's attention can be focused on the symbolic paradigms that transcend the particular historical moment. The ritual allows for individual and communal reflection upon the actors in the Karbala drama. It leads not to a simple reaffirmation of stated truths but rather to an experience of what Turner has called "root paradigms" in ways which allow for cultural adaptation and change.[6]

The majlis is not a static event but rather a dynamic process. It generally takes place immediately after the evening prayer. Women and men are seated separately. At the Zainabiyyah Hall in Toronto the forward section is reserved for men, with the women seated in the rear section. In some imambargahs, women are seated in an upstairs room. Girls and very small boys sit with the women; older boys sit with their fathers. In certain imambargahs loudspeakers or television monitors are placed in the women's section so they can follow the majlis.

Having performed ablutions to separate themselves from the realm of the ordinary and profane, mourners further separate themselves by saying prayers, thereby drawing nearer to the sacred and recreating the actions of Husayn on the eve of his martyrdom. Following the prayers, the crowd begins to move gradually—a few at a time—into the majlis hall proper. Upon leaving the masjid, they may enter the *ziyarat khaneh*, where they are confronted with objects connected with the ahl al-bayt that evoke Karbala, and they may touch or kiss them. The visual focus of the majlis hall is the minbar, a moveable staircase-pulpit draped in black. The minbar is located at the *qiblah* so that the audience faces towards Mecca. As they settle in, poetry recitations may take place. Generally, the reciters sit or stand to the side of the minbar. These poems of mourning create an auditory environment that evokes Karbala. Participants in the majlis thus walk through a series of "doorways," all the time surrounding themselves more and more completely with sights and sounds that reinforce the sense and presence of Karbala. It is as if the events of Karbala are always occurring just underneath the surface of everyday existence and as if the act of going to hear majlis pulls back a veil, revealing a reality that is in many ways more real than the world in which we normally live.

It is into this already charged atmosphere that the *zakir* enters to recite the majlis. He usually comes in to the shouts of *"Salavat"* for the family of the Prophet. He delivers his address from the minbar, seated on the next to the top step, as the highest step is traditionally reserved for the Imam. The minbar is thus itself symbolic of the authority of the Prophet and the Imams. It may be flanked by standards bearing the Fatimid hand—yet more symbols that evoke both the battle of Karbala and the authority of the ahl al-bayt. Everything in the room serves to focus the attention of the audience away from the mundane and towards the events of the sacred narrative.

Once the zakir has taken his seat, he initiates a quiet communal recitation of *Sura Fatihah*. This evocation of the Qur'an serves to make the environment even more sacred. The zakir then begins with a verse of the Qur'an, and the rest of his discourse acts as an exegesis of it. During the ten-day mourning period, the zakir will deliver a series of discourses linked in theme and subject matter. Although the majlis is oriented around a Qur'anic verse, the subject matter varies a great deal, and it may cover a wide range of topics. Throughout, the zakir continues to evoke the name of the Prophet, calling on his audience to offer salutations to the Prophet and the ahl al-bayt. People may spontaneously call for shouts of "Ya ʿAli." During this portion of the majlis, some may already weep. The zakir uses his arms and the timbre of his voice to emphasize important points, and by the time the discourse has ended, the room is thoroughly charged with emotion.

The dramatic culmination of the majlis is the gham or lamentation, which consists of an emotional narrative of the sufferings of the family of the Prophet. The transition to the gham may be abrupt, but the most talented zakirs find ways to blend it skillfully into the context of the theme of the discourse. On each of the ten days the majlis is traditionally linked to a specific martyr or event. For many the gham is the central portion of the ritual. As soon as it starts, people begin to sob and wail. As the incidents of Karbala are told, the crying becomes more and more intense. People will strike their foreheads and chests. Generally, when the gham ends, the zakir is overcome with emotion.

The gham is in many ways the crucial part of the zakir's performance. Here he must recreate the atmosphere of the events of the battle itself. Usually in tears, sometimes speaking in the present tense as if the events were happening before his eyes, the zakir attempts to evoke strong emotion from his audience. Many become grief stricken at the first mention of the events of Karbala. The Shiʿa believe it is evidence to non-Shiʿa of the remarkable character of these events that they can still bring people to tears after fourteen hundred years, and they take this as a proof of the truth of their religion.

On certain occasions, the gham is followed by matam—the physical act of mourning. From the seventh through the tenth of Muharram the matam is extended. Young men who stand near the minbar sing rhythmic and musical variations of poetry. The crowd joins in a calling pattern of repetition. The rhythm of the matam is carried by striking the hands against the chest. Between the recitations of the different lamentation poems, simple chants of "Ya Abbas" or "Ya Husayn" are called out and the sound of hands on chests becomes louder. Matam varies in length depending on the evening. On the last three nights, matam may take the form of *zanjir ka matam*, in which young men flagellate themselves with chains and knives. This activity is relatively rare in North America. In a few communities, in South Asia as well as North America, it has become more fashionable to donate blood to blood banks.

On the last four days of these rituals, small processions take place within the imambargah. Implements related to the stories of the martyrs are carried throughout the crowd. These may take the form of coffins wrapped in white and stained in red, a *calam* staff bearing a Fatimid hand or perhaps a silver waterflask symbolizing the standard of Hazrat Abbas, the slain standard bearer of Husayn.

The entire process of the majlis is brought to a close by the recitation of ziyarat, in which the entire congregation turns in the directions of the tombs of the ma'sumin while reaffirming their allegiance to the family of the Prophet by reciting salutations to the Imams ending with Imam Mahdi, the living Imam while facing the qibla (direction of prayer). Following the ziyarat, the crowd breaks up slowly. Food or tea is served, and people have a chance to ask the zakir questions informally or simply to visit with each other. Sometimes books about Islam are distributed. There is time for everyone to reflect upon their own experience before returning to their usual routine—each taking away a personally distinct and yet communally shared experience of the event.

### THE MAJLIS AS FAMILY RITUAL

The importance of the majlis as a family ritual among Shi'i Muslims in North America is difficult to overestimate. As in the rest of the Shi'i world, the events of the first ten days of Muharram are the most intense religious activities of the year. Engaging in these activities brings to the forefront the crucial distinctions between the Shi'a and other communities. These periods of celebration are therefore important opportunities for families to provide clear demonstrations to their children of what their community stands for.

The majlis serves two interrelated purposes. The first is devotional or soteriological; because of the cosmic dimension of the tragedy of Karbala, weeping for the sufferings of the ahl al-bayt is taken as a true sign of Islam. Unless one's heart is hardened, one cannot help but cry. The inability to cry over such a heinous crime may be taken as evidence that one is spiritually lost. It is commonly believed that Fatimah and Zainab (the sister of Husayn) appear at the majlis and gather the tears of the mourners in their skirts; on the Day of Judgment they will present these tears to God as proof of the sincerity of those persons. According to hadiths of the Imams compiled in the popular Urdu work *Tahufat-al ʿAwam*, mourning for Husayn can lead to the forgiveness of sins and the blessings of God.[7]

The devotional aspect of the majlis is in many ways its heart. On questions of Shariʿa there really is little of consequence that separates Shiʿi and Sunni Muslims. Styles of dress, propriety, and marriage are very similar. The devotional attitude toward the ahl al-bayt is the clear mark of distinction between the two groups. To attend the majlis is evidence of membership in the Shiʿi community. In South Asia, it proved to the Shiʿa that their particular vision of Islam is true. In North America, it stands as a yearly lesson to the younger generation that the sacred history of Shiʿism demands allegiance even in a non-Muslim environment that continuously competes for attention.

Devotion to the ahl al-bayt has its consequences. If one loves the ahl al-bayt, then one should strive to live in a manner which is in harmony with them. One should be aware both of the Shariʿa as it has evolved from their practice and the general moral principles by which they lived. The second function of the majlis, therefore, is to educate-didactically, inspirationally, and environmentally. Didactic education is most clearly seen in the discourses. At least once a year Shiʿi Muslims are exposed to highly developed religious discourses. Often these deal with the issues of the proper manner of Islamic practice in the contemporary world. In South Asia, they serve to provide the listener with the types of arguments that the Shiʿa might need in order to answer the religious objections of the Sunni majority. In North America, they speak to larger Islamic questions as well, since the majlis also forms a link back to general South Asian Islamic culture.

Given this connection, it is not surprising that Sunni Muslims in North America will occasionally attend Shiʿi majlis. Although there exist several "mother tongues" within the community, Urdu has been the *lingua franca* for public religious rituals. It allows Muslims from many parts of the sub-continent as well as East African/Asian communities to congregate together for religious observances. Thus, for the Sunnis as well as the Shi'a, majlis is a chance to hear Urdu used in a religious context. General questions of Islamic piety, as they are addressed in the didactic portion of the majlis, are not necessarily specifically Shi'a.

In North America, both Shi'a and Sunni Muslims are faced with similar crucial questions about adaptation. Which South Asian customs should be continued? What constitutes essential Islamic practice? How can Islamic verities be translated into the North American idiom? One man told me that he was disturbed that children tended to greet their parents with "Hello" rather than the traditional Islamic "*Salaam Alaikum.*" These questions are not specifically Shi'i in nature; they are universal to North American Islam.

The majlis also commonly contains arguments from both Sunni and Shi'i classical sources and seeks to prove that the Shi'i interpretation of history is the valid one. This type of education is particularly important to a religious minority that must regularly defend its position. Thus the majlis educates its listeners about both Shi'ism and the general South Asian Muslim tradition.

These primarily didactic eductional functions are clearly related to the devotional and inspirational ones. For example, arguments about the necessity of conforming to the Shari'a are amplified by the fact that one should obey religious law out of love for the ahl al-bayt, who were themselves willing to die for the maintenance of Islam. Observing their sacrifices provides a powerful incentive for practical piety.

This observation is not done in isolation. Majlis is a communal and family event. Although the women and men sit separately, they arrive and depart together. Extended family relationships are reaffirmed both at the majlis and afterwards in family get-togethers. The battle of Karbala itself was a familial experience, and women play an important role in the narrative. They survive as witnesses and are thus the historical links to the event; most dramatically, it is Zainab who takes temporary leadership of the community after the martyrdom and who publicly accuses Yazid of his crimes. Thus, the battle of Karbala allows individuals in the community to reflect upon the "root paradigms" of behavior for men *and* women in a variety of relationships. Models of familial behavior are provided. There are examples of the correct behavior for a son, a bridegroom, a wife, a sister, and so on. Within the drama there are any number of possible hierarchical relationships-father-son, mother-daughter, wife-husband, uncle-cousin. The men were on the battlefield and the women were in the tents, but they all played important roles in the drama. In the majlis the behavior of the paradigmatic Muslim family is articulated, experienced, and reflected upon.

Another way in which the majlis educates is through the creation of a Shiʿi environment. In the midst of the secular world of contemporary North America, the majlis creates not only the meta-historical Karbala but also a miniature South Asian environment. Here children observe the practice of Islamic etiquette and propriety firsthand. They also witness the power of the Karbala narrative and the truth of the authority of the ahl al-bayt. The ability of the majlis to teach in this way is linked to familial participation in it. Children witness the effect of this ritual not on distant strangers but rather on people whom they love and respect. As one Canadian Shiʿa told me, when he was very young, he would attend the majlis and watch his father cry. When he became a bit older, he would pretend to cry so as to emulate his father. Now he cries automatically upon hearing the gham. It has become a response that is beyond his control, compelling evidence of the power of the Shiʿi religion.

There is no single clear-cut message to the majlis. The number of characters in the Karbala drama and the richness of its symbolism imbue it with multivocality. While the zakir may intend a specific didactic message to his majlis, the more subtle inspirational and environmental educational processes may yield more individual responses. In particular, the emphasis on the gham and its narrative allows for a great deal of interpretation. While all Shiʿa may agree that allegiance to the ahl al-bayt is crucial, there is a great deal of disagreement over precisely how to manifest that allegiance. While the virtues of the Karbala martyrs-courage, self-sacrifice, piety, devotion-are agreed upon, the proper means of articulating them are more controversial. Thus, the majlis becomes an arena for intense communal discussion as well.

When I witnessed the series of Muharram majlis in Toronto, it was a time of agitation within the Shiʿi community. Debates about the proper attitudes and behavior for North American Muslims were at the center of much of the discussion. In the imambargah, before and after the majlis, several of the concerns of the community were debated. For example, there was the question of the community's response to the

events of the Iranian Revolution, which were having important rever-
berations throughout the Shiʿi world. Some of the young men were
particularly interested to see the majlis used for political statements
supportive of the revolution. Other persons were more interested in issues closer to home.

One issue that generated much concern at the time shows clearly the
importance of majlis in the maintenance of Shiʿi values. The majority of
the community in this particular imambargah had always known Urdu
as the language of the majlis, and some felt that the power of the majlis
was linked to its use. Others argued vigorously that the power of the
majlis was to be found in the narrative of Karbala itself and that its
power could not be diminished. They argued that because so many
children could not speak Urdu fluently, the didactic portions and even
much of the gham were lost on them. This crucial issue was addressed
in English on the last evening.

On that final evening, the zakir broke tradition and before reciting
the gham, he addressed the congregation in English. He related a discussion with a child who told him that the part she enjoyed best was
the gham because she knew that the majlis was almost over. Having
learned the story of Karbala in the religious "Sunday School," she
knew what was happening in the gham, but the rest of the majlis was
basically unintelligible to her. The zakir urged the congregation to allow majlis in English. While conceding that English was not yet an Islamic language, he argued that Urdu did not begin as one either. He
argued that North American Muslims must make English an Islamic
language if Islam is to take firm root in North America.

It is significant that this argument took place within the context of
the majlis. The social drama of religious change within the community
was taking place within its ritual drama. In the last few years, the community has changed its position, and half of the majlis is now read in
English and half in Urdu. This adaptation shows a clear commitment
by the community to link the the devotional and educational purposes
of the majlis by increasing its effectiveness as an educational tool.

## CONCLUSION

For North American Shiʿi Muslims, the majlis is a link both to South
Asia and to the larger Shiʿi world. Its structure offers the possibility of
combining religious devotion with soteriological consequences and

education about Islamic practice. As one important Indian zakir and ʿalim has argued, it would be impossible to fill imambargahs for simple lectures on Islamic law and history. But the elements of the majlis provide wide audiences for instruction in these topics.[8] In order for the majlis to be effective as an educational tool, it needs to maintain its power as a ritual devotional performance. The yearly experience of the majlis provides Shiʿi children with a sense of the power of their religious heritage that perhaps gives the Shiʿa an advantage over their Sunni brothers and sisters in educating the next generation of Muslims about Islamic values. Furthermore, because of its multivocal character, the majlis educates in ways which allow for creative reflection and adaptation.

One of the remarkable features of Islam is that it has produced not one uniform civilization but a series of vital cultures that share certain universal values. Similarly, within Islam, Shiʿism has maintained a great deal of diversity within an overarching unity. In South Asia the majlis has provided a way for a minority community to continuously adapt its religious sensibilities in the midst of a Sunni majority. Likewise, in North America, the majlis facilitates the community's readaptation to the changing cultural climate. As the majlis speaks to the specific needs of its North American audience, it continues to pass on universal Shiʿi values. The continuation of the majlis in North America is not the simple recreation of South Asian custom. In fact, its very dynamism may well facilitate the development of a truly North American Shiʿism just as it previously helped to produce a uniquely South Asian Shiʿi Islam.

### Notes

1. The *muʿjizat kahanis* or miracle stories are an important part of piety for Shiʿi women. The recitation of these short Urdu tales, particularly the stories of *Bibi Fatimah* and *ʿAli Mushkil Kusha*, in order to evoke the intercession of the ahl al-bayt is clear evidence of the popular belief in the supernatural existence and accessibility of the ahl al-bayt.

2. This is not to say that the Sunni do not also venerate the Prophet or see him as a paradigm of behavior. But the Shiʿa attach certain metaphysical associations to him that are not necessarily shared by the Sunnis.

3. Although the term *ma'sum* is usually translated as "infallible," I prefer the translation used by A.A. Sachedina of "protected from sin and error."
4. Interestingly, they often argue this belief upon an hadith from Bukhari, a standard Sunni source. It is common for the Shi'a to attempt to prove their position from standard Sunni sources.
5. This is clearest in the famous *Hadith Kissa'*, in which the Prophet gathers the five together under his cloak and the concentration of light attracts the Angel Gabriel from the heavens.
6. Turner defines root paradigms as cultural models that

> have reference not only to current state of social relationships but also to the cultural goals, means, ideas, outlooks, currents of thought, patterns of belief . . . which reach down to the irreducible lifestances of the individuals, passing beneath conscious prehension to a fiduciary hold on what they sense to be axiomatic values, values literally of life or death. They are multivocal and clothed with allusiveness, implicitness, and metaphor.

While Turner originally developed the concept in order to explain social dramas, it is clear that "root paradigms" lie at the liminal center of religious rituals as well where individuals encounter, in an immediate sense, the powerful multivocal symbols that underlie their religious systems (see Turner, *Dramas, Fields and Metaphors: Symbolic Action in Human Society* [Ithaca: Cornell University Press, 1974], p. 64.)

7. *Tahufat al-'Awam Maqbul* (Lahore), pp. 242-43.
8. The South Asian 'alim 'Ali Naqi al-Naqvi makes this argument in "Sawal-o Jawab Besilsileh Yas-o Yadgar az 'Ali Naqi Al-Naqwi," *The Safarez Weekly, Lucknow* (1976):5-13.

# Parents and Youth: Perceiving and Practicing Islam in North America

## Nimat Hafez Barazangi

◆ ◆ ✦ ◆

This chapter examines how some Arab Muslim youth and families in North America perceive themselves both as Arabs and as Muslims in the context of Canadian and United States societies. Parents are concerned with how best to transmit the Islamic ideological and Arab cultural heritage to their children. One of their problems derives from differences among Arab Muslims, who come from varied national origins and hold several interpretations of the Islamic view, not all of which are based on the Qur'an; as a result, they also have different nationalistic attachments to an understanding of Arab heritage. A second problem arises between immigrant parents and their American-reared children. The children may participate in American culture to a greater extent than their parents, and they are constantly faced with the conceptual need to accommodate potentially conflicting points of view. Effective identity transmission requires the determination of the nature and extent of the different interpretations held by parents and their children and of the ways these interpretations are reflected in their practice of Islam and association with the Arabic heritage.

This paper focuses on a small sample of Arab Muslim youth aged fourteen to twenty-two and their parents. They were a sub-sample of a larger group who participated in my study of North American Muslims' perception and practice of the Islamic belief system.[1] These youth are first-generation children of immigrants who came to North America during the 1960s and 1970s.

The aim of this effort is threefold:

1. To gain a greater understanding of the differences in the ways immigrants adjusted by examining the effects of preconception of identity on both the adjustment process of the immigrant parent and the transmission of identity to his or her children.

2. To explain the differences between the social (modification of behavior) and the conceptual (modification of worldview) accommodation or assimilation process.

3. To explicate the role of the search for conceptual integration[2] as a more lasting factor than social integration, whether it is the parents' adjustment to the Western environment or the youths' attempt to acquire an Arab Muslim identity in the context of Western societies.

The argument of this paper is built, therefore, on two propositions:

1. Not all immigrants—even those coming from the same region and adhering to the same religion—can be assumed to experience the same accommodation/assimilation process.

2. Conceptual accommodation and assimilation are the reverse of social accommodation and assimilation. People who assimilate socially may very well accommodate conceptually by modifying or changing their worldview in the same way as they modified their behavior to fit the environment in which they assimilate. Those who accommodate socially and assimilate conceptually modify the environmental behavioral norms and/or worldview.

I have concentrated on Arab Muslim youth who are children of the last wave of immigrants in order to examine the complexity of this identity problem at its roots, at the learning process. The basic questions are: What makes the present first generation of Arab Muslim youth associate with two conflicting, yet integrative, identities, Arabism and Islamic/Muslim, and how do these youth perceive this dual-identity association in the reality of North American societies?

## STYLES OF IDENTITY DETERMINATION

Contemporary Arab Muslim immigrants may perceive themselves as having at least four different identity associations at the same time.

They may identify themselves as Islamic, Muslim,[3] Syrian (or Iraqi, Ye-meni, and so on), Arab, or American/Canadian[4] at different times and in different contexts. These four aspects of identity can result in a mini-mum of twelve different combinations when the person attempts to describe his or her association, such as Arab Muslim American of Syr-ian descent or Muslim Arab Syrian who resides in America, and so on. The Iranian revolution indirectly added to the list of descriptive terms. With its emphasis on Shi'ism, a fifth identity association was added to the other four.

This complexity has had different social and political meanings since the early twentieth century, and particularly since the post-World War II growth of Arab nationalism and the Arab world's resistance to the creation of Israel. But even more interesting is the development of Is-lamicity[5] over the past decade. This term, which North American Mus-lims hitherto primarily used to refer to a religious affiliation, has now taken on a new religio-nationalistic and ideological meaning. (See Ak-bar Muhammad's account of the heightening and attraction of Ameri-can Muslims to the political and religious sentiments of the Arabic-speaking world.)[6]

The establishment of sub-Muslim or sub-Arab organizations did not help resolve identity confusion, and, in fact, it may have added a new dimension to the problem. For example, the Muslim Arab Youth Asso-ciation, the Malaysian Students Association, and others came into exis-tence in the late 1970s, and since they differ in political tone, they also have different identity associations.

There is a wealth of studies treating attitudinal religio-social and be-havioral adjustment.[7] Whether or not they relate specifically to immi-grants, these studies are concerned mainly with the social accommoda-tion/assimilation process of the individual or the group. Social accom-modation is understood generally to indicate that the person modifies the new behavior/environment/ attitude instead of his or her own when attempting to integrate them. Social assimilation is understood to indicate that the person complies or conforms with the new behav-ior/environment/attitude instead of modifying it.

Very few studies, however, have dealt with the conceptual aspects of attitudinal and behavioral adjustment. Baha Abu-Laban[8] touches on this level when he suggests reviving *Ijthad*, or independent reasoning, to help reconcile Islam, as a body of theological doctrine and beliefs, with the new environment. This paper approaches the task by adapting from three sources (the reconstruction of religious thought,[9] the philosophy of science,[10] and conceptual change theory[11]) a model of Islamic/Arabic integration within the context of North American societies.

## CONCEPTUAL CHANGE THEORY

Evidence from recent work on the learning of concepts in science and mathematics[12] suggests that beliefs about the nature of reality (metaphysical commitments) and about the nature of knowledge (epistemological commmitments) may play a role in what is learned and how. Although the mechanism of this interaction is unknown, the learning theory underlying these studies may be useful in understanding Arab Muslim youths' determination of their identity.

Conceptual change theory assumes that an individual's learning process is at least in part a rational process[13] of altering or changing ideas or concepts. To understand learning as a rational process, one must take into account a person's existing conceptual structure (what he or she already knows), his or her belief about the nature of reality (metaphysics), and his or her beliefs about the nature of knowledge (epistemology). Together, these may shape the reasons for what and how a person learns.

In contrast to Elkholy, Lovell, and other students of immigrant groups,[14] who approach the adjustment from historical, anthropological, sociological, or psychological points of view, here these factors are taken into account, but within the framework of the learning/adjustment process. That is, the parents who are attempting to maintain themselves in a new (Western) environment go through a learning process. Whether it is called adult learning or adjustment, it is a process of assimilating new concepts and/or accommodating previous concepts.

The same learning process applies to Muslim youth, with three differences. First, their epistemology (that is, belief or formative thinking) has not been fully established and is less complex or advanced than that of their parents. Second, they are being reared in two different environments at the same time, the familial/communal Muslim or nationalistic Arab and the school or host-societal secular. Finally, their social and conceptual accommodation/assimilation processes are interwoven in a complex balance that varies depending on their parents' adjustment process and transmission of the Islamic/Arab heritage.

It is essential to realize that both parents and youth, but particularly parents, may have formed their epistemological view of Islam in another environment. It is possible, therefore, that they may go through an unlearning and learning process when they have contacts with other Muslims and Arabs and are exposed to new conceptions of Islam and of Arabism.

## APPLICATION TO THE STUDY

The theoretical question, hence, may be restated as concerning how an Arab Muslim's view of Islam and its different practices and of Arabism might affect how he or she learns the basic principles and their practice in a particular context. For example, Islam might be thought of as a faith in which the teachings are considered as an absolute list of "dos" and "do nots." A person with that view might accept and practice the codes and might think that they cannot be modified or changed to accommodate to the new environment or way of life. On the other hand, Islam may be seen as an intellectual view of life that encompasses certain guidelines, and Arabic custom may be regarded as a tool or a manifestation of these guidelines. A person with that view might recognize not only the Islamic principal elements but also the variation in the ways they may be applied. He or she might take an approach to everyday activities that is different and perhaps less strict or dichotomous than that of the Muslim with an absolutist view. If, however, a person chiefly thinks of Islam as codes representing the Qur'anic teachings, he or she may learn them but keep them separate from or opposite to his or her practice in the real world. If this view is combined with a perception of Arab and Arabic as the only appropriate social manifestation of Islam, such a person may view Islam as being only the rituals and customs practiced by "Arab" Muslims.

## THE METHOD

Members of fifteen Arab Muslim families of varied nationalities were interviewed in five major cities in Canada and the United States as part of a larger study. The total number of subjects who were interviewed and who completed two sets of questionnaires was seventeen parents (eight fathers and nine mothers) and seventeen youth (eight males and nine females) who could be matched for data analysis. The criteria for selecting families in the sample were that they were willing to participate in the study and that they had youth of the age fourteen to twenty-two years who were raised mainly in North America.

### Participant Observation

In many large North American cities Muslim groups have established centers/mosques where their major religious activities take place. Most Islamic/Arabic education programs also take place in these centers. The investigator spent at least a two-day weekend in Toronto, Montreal, Buffalo, New York, and Washington, D.C., to get a picture of community activities and to get acquainted with the people who associate with various centers. The weekend was chosen because most activities in Muslim centers take place then, beginning with Friday Prayer, and most Muslim families can be reached easily only through these centers.

### Questionnaires

Two sets of questionnaires were used. In the first, closed and open-ended questions were developed to gather information about the individual's age, sentimental attachment to the culture, identification preference, nature of education, family status, patterns of practice, length of residence, and exposure to mass media.

In the second, forced-choice and open-ended questions tested the hypothesis that perceptual differences among Muslims, parents and youth alike, are associated with their understanding of the principles in Islamic teachings. The belief items tested were: monotheism and human role; prophethood and sense of mission; the Hereafter and accountability; the pillars of Islam and significance of application; the Scriptures; moral teachings, social systems, and social institutions; and beliefs about knowledge, inquiry, and education.

### Focus-Group Interview

Four basic principle of Islam—Allah (God), Islam (as a worldview), Taqwa (Consciousness of Allah), Islah (construction)—and eight other issues, such as why teach/learn the Arabic language, what do you mean by "practicing Islam?" and so on, were probed in taped focus-group interview sessions. Fathers, mothers, and youth who responded to the questionnaires individually were interviewed in small groups of like members. Also, each interviewee was asked, at the beginning of the interview, to write on an index card what he or she thinks, feels, or does when each of the above principles is mentioned.

## THE FINDINGS

A model of Islamic/Arabic integration guided the analysis and the interpretation of data.[15]

The results are summarized under two major headings, the parents' responses and the youths' responses.

### The Parents' Conception and Practice of Islam

1. Although the parents in this study tend to regard themselves as "Arab Muslim" or "Muslim Arab," the majority of them identify primarily with their countries of origin. Yet, most do not want to be identified with their country of origin within the general context of American society.

In response to the question "What is your cultural heritage?" 82 percent identified themselves with their country of origin. Only 12 percent identified themselves with pan-Arabism, and 6 percent identified themselves with Islam.

In response to the question "How do you see yourself when you are among non-Muslims?" only 11 percent identified themselves as "Arab first," and no one identified him or herself as "Muslim first." The majority of parents identified themselves as "American."

2. Most of these parents practiced Islam as a "religious" duty (in the narrow sense) before their arrival in North America. When they expressed some identity association with "Islam," it was mostly a reflection of their idealized view of the past or of ethnic customary experience.

In response to the question related to family practice, emphasis, and reaction to their children's obedience in practicing "religious" obligation (conditional concepts), the majority argeed with their family's em-

TABLE I.

Parents and Youth Frequency on Conception and Practice

| | Domain—Conception | | | |
| | Parents | | Youth | |
| | High (%)* | Low (%)** | High (%) | Low (%) |
| --- | --- | --- | --- | --- |
| Central Concept | 82 | 18 | 88 | 12 |
| Conditional Concepts | 70 | 30 | 53 | 47 |
| Human Interrelation Concepts | 82 | 18 | 88 | 12 |

| | Domain—Practice | | | |
| | Parents | | Youth | |
| | High (%)* | Low (%)** | High (%) | Low (%) |
| --- | --- | --- | --- | --- |
| Central Concept | 18 | 82 | - | 100 |
| Conditional Concepts | 82 | 18 | 82 | 18 |
| Human Interrelation Concepts | 18 | 82 | 24 | 76 |

\* High: at or above mean score 4.5 on a 6-point scale.
\*\* Low: below mean score 4.5 on the same scale.

phasis on religious obligations and supported a strong reaction when these religious practices become lax.

In response to questions related to family emphasis on scholastic and professional achievement, the majority of these parents agreed that their family valued such achievements. Yet, when they were asked about valuing Islamic knowledge of moral and social principles, very few indicated that their families emphasized this practice, but they had no quarrel with it.

In response to the question "What does practicing Islam mean to you?" the predominant themes among parents were related to overt behaviors that accompany belief, such as behaviors "the Prophet used to conduct himself and deal with others," or outward appearances, such as dressing Islamically (60 percent), and the basics or the Pillars of Islam, such as "following al Sunnah (footsteps) of the Prophet," or Salah (prayer), Zakah (tax on wealth), read and learn Qur'an" (30 percent).

3. When parents join organizations with Islamic, Muslim, or Arabic names, they tend to politicize "Islamic" ideals or "Arabic heritage" in order to advocate personal views that are mostly the result of abstract nationalistic, ethnic, or sectarian sentiments.

For example, in response to the question "Why do you value teaching Arabic to your children?" only 25 percent of the parents emphasized the value of Arabic for understanding the Qur'an. Fifty percent emphasized Arabic as a means for keeping the heritage and for reading Arabic history books, and 25 percent emphasized the spoken dialect for easy communication with grandparents and relatives.

As Table 1 shows, parents in the study tended to score higher on questions that asked them to state Islamic central concepts and human interrelation concepts (82 percent in each case had mean scores at or above 4.5 on a 6 point scale) than on the practice of those same concepts, on which the great majority of scores fell below 4.5. This trend was reversed, however, in the case of the conditional concepts, on which the majority of the parents scored below 4.5 on conception and at or above that level on practice.

4. When these parents attempt to transmit their Islamic/Arabic heritage to their offspring, they transmit either definitions of principles and ideals or a mixture of socio-cultural customs of religious practices.

In response to the question "If you were to present the concept of 'Allah' to your youth, what are the first four meanings that you think of?" for example, 90 percent responded with themes related either to the description of Allah's characteristics (for example, Creator, Master of the Universe, has no partner) or to the relationship of the concept "Allah" to the Hereafter (for example, "because we have to return to

Allah one day, and we have to give an account of what we do, then we have to follow his instructions"). Only 10 percent responded with themes related to human role in relation to the conception of Allah (for example, "God gives you guidance that you can follow"; "because you need something to love and something that you can depend on").

In response to the question "If you were training your youth to become "muttaqi" (to be conscientious about Allah and to practice the role of viceregency), what are the first two meanings that you would stress?" 50 percent replied: "Think that this is not the real world, what's after is," and the other 50 percent responded: "Feels good by doing what you're supposed to be doing, such as a prayer, fasting, etc."

In response to the question "If you were teaching your youth to be a "muslih" (a person who undertakes constructive acts), what are the first three actions that you produce as a role model?" 60 percent of the responses were related to the Hereafter (for example, "realizing accountability for constructive acts in Hereafter helps present society"), and 20 percent were related to worship (for example, "prayer is for your own soul, between me and God").

### The Youths' Conception and Practice of Islam

1. Parents' idealization and/or abstraction of "Islamic/Muslim" and Arabic is reflected in the youths' confusion concerning identity association. In response to the question "What is your parents' cultural heritage?" 35 percent of the youth identified themselves as being of Arabic origin, 29 percent identified themselves as being of Muslim or Islamic origin, and 18 percent identified themselves with the country of their parents. The remaining 18 percent responded by checking "None of the Above."

The variation among siblings is interesting and indicates some uncertainty and confusion. For example, in one family, the oldest, who was in his mid-twenties, identified himself as Arab. The second child, who was in her early twenties, did not respond to the same question: "How do you see yourself when among non-Muslims?" The third child, who was in his late teens, identified himself as Muslim.

2. In response to the question about practicing Islam, the predominant theme among youth was to identify themselves as Muslims among non-Muslims (55 percent). There were two aspects to this

identification, a positive one, such as "You have to identify yourself a Muslim among non-Muslims by telling everyone you have a separate identity," and a negative aspect, "You can't pray five times a day in front of others."

The same theme, "being different," dominated the responses to the question "What does it mean to you to dress Islamically?" Yet, Muslim youth of Arab descent are more uncertain about being different than non-Arab Muslims who participated in my larger study. All the Arab girls who responded to this question agreed with the observation: "It is hard for us girls to dress Islamically because people will make fun of you."

3. The youth responses also reflect different perceptions from those of the parents even when they have scores similar to those of their parents. As can be seen in Table 1, youth tended, like their parents, to score higher on questions that called for them to state an Islamic central concept and/or human interrelation concepts (88 percent in each case had mean scores at or above 4.5 on a 6-point scale) than on the practice of those same concepts, where the great majority of scores fell below 4.5. Youth scored higher than their parents on questions related to the conception of human interrelation and on questions that called for them to state an Islamic central concept, but lower on questions that called for them to state conditional concepts. The youths' trend was, like the parents, reversed in the case of conditional concepts, where 47 percent scored below 4.5 on conception and 82 percent scored at or above that level on practice.

4. As these youth attempt to conceptualize and practice Islam and the Arabic heritage as presented to them by their parents within the framework of Western secular society, they tend to become confused by their parents' application of the Islamic principles or of the "Arabic heritage."

In response to the question concerning the meaning of Allah, for example, 65 percent of the youth responded with themes related to the human role (for example, "It is the concept of wrong and right. Right is what God wants you to do. It is the only way you can identify with Him" [God]).

In response to questions related to the meanings and actions toward the concept "Taqwa" (consciousness of Allah), 80 percent of youth responded with themes related to inner consciousness (for example, "It is the inner conscience and not the external factors that make one act rightly or wrongly") and to human interrelationship (for example, "It is always in the back of my mind that I'll be judged by my actions).

In response to the question on "Islah" (constructive acts), 60 percent responded with themes related to worship as a reminder for human interaction (for example, "Prayer is a reminder that we are watched by Allah, so we should keep in mind [His orders] before acting").

## IMPLICATIONS FOR INTERGENERATIONAL TRANSMISSION OF ISLAMIC/ARABIC IDENTITY

Social assimilation of Arab Muslim youth in North America is only a symptom of a more basic problem, namely, conceptual accommodation. Their inability to perceive Islam as a system and Arabic heritage as one manifestation of this system is a probable reason for their difficulties in practicing that system in the new context.

The assumption that the group's cultural heritage can be preserved by maintaining the socio-cultural customs of the old country, though not unique to Arab Muslim immigrants, is seen here as one of the reasons for the inability of American Muslim immigrants to span the gap between the old and the new generations. That is, no matter how tolerant the old are to the young or how compromising the young generation is to their parents' socio-cultural customs, they will never be able to meet on the ideational level. The parents' ideas, sentiments, traditions, and interests are not the same as those of their American-reared.

The parents' perception of Islam as abstract and/or as religious duties (in the narow sense) is a central factor in their children's confusion in identifying with and practicing the "Arab Muslim" cultural heritage. The meanings, weight, and articulation the youth attach to the concepts "Arab" and "Arabic heritage" and to the Islamic system is another leading factor in the process of identity transmission.

This confusion suggests that the youth will either reject the parent's beliefs about Islamic/Arabic practice and the principles or the worldview that come with them; continue to have unresolved conflicts between cultures and belief systems; try to compartmentalize by having two or three sets of behavior, namely Islamic/Arabic and Western; or reject the advocated practices and attempt to find, by themselves, a new means by which they can apply Islamic principles and/or the Arabic cultural heritage.

It follows that any attempt to reverse the situation requires first a change in decision makers' and/or in parents' perceptions of "Islamic" and "Arabic." This change in perception may be achieved by one or all of the following strategies:

1. Bring to the attention of decision-makers and/or parents the fact that as long as their conception and practice of Islam are limited to some rituals or to the Five Pillars only, they will not be able to relate these practices to their day-to-day interactions with the Western environment. Moreover, youth may not be able to relate to this limited perception because they are mainly raised in the Western way of life.
2. Help decision-makers/parents as well as youth gain a realistic view of Western values, their consequences in practice, and the ways they actually differ from or resemble identical Islamic values.

The second prerequisite is to recognize the socio-political changes that are occurring rapidly in the countries of origin as well as in North America and how these changes are reflected in the immigrants' adjustment process. Parents need to address the practice of Islam and the achievement or retention of Arab Muslim identity in the North American context. The strategies may include:

1. Helping parents acquire the skills and understanding needed to deal with the Western environment so they will not have to compartmentalize conceptually the three aspects of cultural interaction, the Islamic, the Arabic, and the Western.
2. Making parents and youth aware that Islamic/Arabic identification and worldview can be integrated into the Western environment without compromising Islamic principles or divorcing oneself from Arabic heritage.

Because of the small sample, this study can only be suggestive. Further research is needed on North American Arab Muslim youth who are in the second, third, or fourth generations of immigrants from the Arab regions and who adhere to Islam as a religion or worldview. It is clear, however, that the conceptual change approach used here provides both explanations and guides to practice.

It is equally clear that unless Arabs and Muslims in general, and Arab Muslims in particular, identify and reconcile the ambiguities that exist in the conception and practice of Islam and in its relationship to the Arab heritage, attempts to transmit the Arab Muslim identity to the next generation will falter. Some parents succeed despite the difficulties described above. Understanding why they do may contribute to modifying the conceptual framework proposed and open the door for more sophisticated research on this key socialization issue.

### Notes

Special thanks are due to two persons who have contributed significantly to the shaping of ideas, statement of concepts, and reporting of results: Robert L. Bruce of Cornell University, my academic adviser, and the late Isma'il R. al-Faruqi of Temple University, an ad hoc member of my graduate committee.

Others have also contributed directly or indirectly to the outcome of my research. In particular, I wish to acknowledge Omar Afzal, Muslim adviser to Cornell University and surrounding communities; George J. Posner and David S. Powers, members of my graduate committee at Cornell; and Sid Doan, who helped me prepare the manuscript.

1. The reader is referred to the author's Ph.D. dissertation, "Perceptions of the Islamic Belief System: The Muslims in North America" (Cornell University, 1988).
2. Integration is used here to indicate the ability to maintain the Islamic belief system at its central concept level, Tawhid, and to objectify this belief system in the Western secular environment without compromising the Islamic principles or the Arabic heritage, living triple, but separate, lives (Islamic, Arabic and Western), or withdrawing from the outside society.
3. The distinction between Islamic and Muslim is essential to understanding the variation in the individual's or the group's conceptualization and interpretation of Islamic principles. These principles can be interpreted and practiced within the particular Qur'anic context (Islamic) or within the particular socio-psychological context (Muslim).
4. To avoid further complexity, the word American will be used to indicate the association with Canadian and United States societies.
5. Islamicity may have different meanings to different individuals or groups. It is used here in the widest sense, in which an individual or a group may associate with as his or her worldview or ideological belief with reference to Islam as a way of life.
6. Akbar Muhammad, "Muslims in the United States: An Overview of Organizations, Doctrines and Problems," in *The Islamic Impact* ed. Yvonne Haddad et al. (Syracuse, N.Y.: Syracuse University Press, 1984), pp. 195-217.

7. See, for example, S. Bochner, ed., *Cultures in Contact: Studies in Cross-Cultural Interaction*, International Series in Experimental Social Psychology, vol. 1 (Oxford: Pergamon Press, 1983); R. Laurence Moore, *Religious Outsiders and the Making of Americans* (New York: Oxford University Press, 1986); and E.K. Lovell, "Islam in the U.S.: Past and Present," in *The Muslim Community in North America* eds. Earle H. Waugh, Baha Abu-Laban, and Regula B. Qureshi (Edmonton: University of Alberta Press, 1983), pp. 93-109; and Abdo A. Elkholy, *The Arab Moslems in the United States; Religion and Assimilation* (New Haven: College and University Press, 1966).

8. Baha Abu-Laban, "The Canadian Muslim Community: The Need for a New Survival Strategy" in *The Muslim Community*, eds. Waugh, Abu-Laban, and Qureshi.

9. Sir Muhammad Iqbal, *The Reconstruction of Religious Thought in Islam* (Lahore, India: Muhammad Ashraf, Publisher, reprinted 1962.)

10. T. Kuhn, *The Structure of Scientific Revolutions* (Chicago, Illinois: University of Chicago Press, 1970.)

11. This theory is represented in George J. Posner, "A Model of Conceptual Change: Present Statues and Prospect," in *Proceedings of the International Seminar on Misconceptions in Science and Mathematics*, eds. H. Helm and J. Novak (Ithaca, N.Y.: Department of Education, Cornell University, 1983); and in K.A. Strike and G.J. Posner, "Understanding from a Conceptual Point of View" (paper presented at the annual meeting of the American Educational Research Association, Montreal, Canada, 11 April, 1983).

12. See examples of these studies in G.J. Posner, "A Model of Conceptual Change;" in J. Confrey, "Conceptual Change, Number Concepts and the Introduction to Calculus." (Unpublished doctoral dissertation, Cornell University, Ithaca, NY, 1980); and P.W. Hewson, "A Conceptual Change Approach to Learning Science" *European Journal of Science Education* 3:4, pp. 383-96.

12. See examples of these studies in Posner, "A Model of Conceptual Change."

13. See K.A. Strike and G.J. Posner, "Understanding from a Conceptual Point of View," for an explanation of what they mean by learning as a "rational activity," where they distinguish their view from the behaviorist's view of learning rather than exclude other factors in learning.

14. See, for example, Nathan Glazer, *American Jews* (Chicago: University of Chicage Press, 1972); and Yih-Chyi Nina Lin, "Educational Needs in Intergenerational Conflict: A Study of Immigrant Families in New York Chinatown" (Ph.D. diss., Cornell University, 1978).

15. The model, developed by the author, consists of four parts. First, the central concepts (Tawhid), accepting the Islamic worldview that human being is God's viceregent and that Allah is the only God (Qur'an 1:16). Second, the conditional concepts ('Ibadat), the fulfillment of religious obli-

gations, such as believing in the unseen, prayer, fasting, and so on (Qur'an 2:1-4). Third, the human interrelation concepts (Mu'amalat), in which transactions are based on the belief that all humans are equal except in their conscientious constructive character (Qur'an 29:39). Finally, the outcomes (A'mal), a society that is free from harmful acts (Qur'an 2:5).

# Part Three

## The Dynamics of Family Formation and Process

◆　◆　◆　◆

◆   ◆   ◆   ◆

Enshrined in Qur'anic legislation and reinforced by Islamic tradition, the institution of marriage is clearly recognized as central to Muslim social existence, with its essential impact extending from the individual to the community as a whole. Too crucial to be left solely to individuals, marriage has been a societal responsibility, and a strong religiously sanctioned ethic of individual interaction governs two dimensions that make it possible to carry out this responsibility successfully. At the center is the ethos of restricted interaction between marriageable young people, based on two notions: one is the complementarity of the male and female domains, the other is the special vulnerability of women. The second ethical dimension is the fundamental consensus of respect for parents and elders as the guardians of societal norms.

This section shows that the view of a global socio-religious dynamic of marriage and family continues to inform Muslim families in North America, regardless of their ethno-cultural background. All four writers show a high degree of awareness of the need for Muslim families to protect and cultivate this special dynamic. For those groups emanating from a traditional Muslim society, marriage is also crucial as a determinant of family continuity across the generations, an idea most clearly manifested in Regula Qureshi. As such, marriage is a pivotal concern, not just for the partners involved, but also for parents and community leaders, and its pursuit activates complex social processes involving a number of actors. Set against Islamic marriage norms, the eloquent statements from community leaders and parents that Hogben presents reveal a suggestive palette of such social processes in the context of their relevance to preserving Muslim family identity in North America.

On the other hand, Muslims emanating from North American society must pioneer new social processes to bring a Muslim character and dynamic into their families, as is shown by Akbar. It is appropriate here to single out this contribution on African-American (that is, "Black") Muslims. Written from within the tradition, it represents a rare view of a Muslim community with a uniquely North American identity. Akbar conveys both a flavor and a problematic of family formation quite distinct from the other three authors, who deal with a dynamic of traditional Muslim immigrant communities.

How communities and individuals actually deal with marriage-related social processes in the North American environment is illustrated in all four contributions. Clearly, the North American norm of direct mate selection through dating confronts Muslims with a potential threat to their traditional norms and to the established practices aimed at socio-religious guidance or control. Qureshi details how highly cohesive families of South Asian origin adapt Muslim norms to this situation by orienting mate selection quite exclusively to their own ethno-religious group, either in North America or in the home country. How individual young Muslims confront the opportunities of free interpersonal contact emerges from the broad-ranging survey of Ba-Yunus; how parents attempt to deal with these potential influences is an important theme in both Ba-Yunus' and Hogben's chapters. A different perspective arises from the special situation of Muslim converts from North American society itself. Akbar provides insight into the dynamics of families who strive to strengthen their new religious identity by adopting Muslim family values.

All four articles address the potential conflict of values between Muslim marriage norms and North American standard practice and to its effect on the Muslim identity of the family, but they differ in approach and in the nature of the information presented. Complementary in their methodology, they include two surveys, one a sociological, statistically-based survey covering Muslim students across the United States (Ba-Yunus), the other a personally-based survey of Canadian Muslims (Hogben). They also include two community studies, one an anthropological study of a South Asian-Canadian Muslim community based on participant observation (Qureshi), the other a case study of African-American Muslims by a clinical psychologist (Akbar).

Equally significant is the difference in topical focus that reflects the duality of religion versus ethnicity—already discussed in the Introduction—and reveals each author's own vantage point. Thus, both Ba-Yunus and Hogben address their inquiry to all Muslims regardless of origin, while Ba-Yunus disregards local or ethnic background altogether. Hogben brings in such information where he considers it relevant; Qureshi and Akbar, on the other hand, focus on Muslims with reference to a particular ethno-cultural identity.

Because the Muslim community in North America is so young, many essential questions remain about the long-range outcome of the local adaptation of marriage norms and processes discussed in this section. One is the extent to which ethno-cultural identity can continue to contribute to Muslim social cohesiveness, and to appropriate partner selection, as in the case of Muslims of South Asian origin. Conversely, in the absence of such a social buttress for individual Muslim families, can their sense of a shared Islamic identity draw them together into a pan-North American Muslim social universe, embracing ethnically diverse Muslims and including marriage partners from the majority culture?

# Marriage and Divorce among Muslims in Canada

## W. Murray Hogben

◆    ◆    ◆    ◆

Two of the greatest causes of suspicion and even of censure of Muslims by non-Muslims concern the Islamic laws and traditions of marriage and divorce. Non-Muslims often believe that Muslim men are probably licentious and (just possibly) fortunate because they can have up to four wives at a time and because divorce for them is apparently only a matter of thrice repeating "I divorce you." Muslim women, according to the same misconception, must be either the delightful damsels of Hollywood harem scenes or the shapeless figures seen on the television news—in either case people without rights or independence of mind.

The historical and religious context of these marriage and divorce customs are not commonly known to non-Muslims, but they have their roots in Islam's early seventh-century Arabian beginnings, distant in time and place from the happy scenes of monogamous wedding ceremonies or the less happy proceedings of the divorce courts of late twentieth-century Canada which frame the topics of this paper.

Specifically, who is marrying whom among Canada's roughly one hundred thousand Muslims, 75 percent of whom are foreign-born? How important is the traditional arrangement of Muslim marriages in the New World? How insuperable are the barriers to marriage outside

Islam for men and women: to marrying someone of a different sect, of different ethnicity, or of different socio-economic background? And what about divorce? Who is divorcing whom among Muslims, and why? What is happening to the religious status of the children of Canadian and foreign-born Muslims, and how do Muslim parents feel about their young people socializing with and even dating other Muslims and non-Muslims who are potential spouses? Finally, what concerns Muslim leaders about present Muslim marriages and divorces, and what do they feel is needed to produce satisfactory results in the future?[1]

It is not the purpose of this paper to explain Islamic marriage and divorce in much detail, let alone to argue the case for laws found in the Qur'an, in the traditions of the Prophet Muhammad, or in the later jurists' decisions. However, as background, it should be noted that among the traditions or sayings of the Prophet was one in which he said that "he [and presumably she] who marries completes half of his [or her] religion,"[2] and that for God "the most detestable of all things permitted is divorce" (Abu Dawud, 13:3, cited in Ali 1951: 284).[3] Also, the following verses from the Qur'an should help to set the stage for the subsequent discussion of marriage and divorce in Canada:

> Wed not idolatresses till they believe, for lo, a believing bond-woman is better than an idolatress though she please you; and give not your daughters in marriage to idolaters till they believe, for lo, a believing slave is better than an idolater though he please you. (2:221)

> And the chaste from among the believing women and the chaste from among those who have been given the Book before you [that is, the Jews and Christians] are lawful for you when you have given them their dowries, taking them in marriage, not fornicating, nor taking them for paramours in secret. (5:5)[4]

These verses state quite clearly that aside from not marrying the idolaters, with whom Islam was locked in a life-or-death struggle in its early years, Muslim men were encouraged to marry other Muslims or Jews or Christians. Presumably this sanction was given because women were then taken into their husbands' families or tribes, and hence their children would be raised in the faith of their fathers—in this case

Islam—even though the women were allowed to retain their beliefs. Muslim women were expected to be put in the same situation if they married non-Muslims, and they are forbidden in the Qur'an to do so, in order that they and their children would not be lost to the Muslim *umma* or community.

More controversial than these strictures is the permission for Muslim men to marry more than one wife under certain circumstances:

> And if you fear that you will not deal fairly by the orphans [apparently widows and orphans left after the early battle of Uhud], marry of the women who seem good to you, two or three or four; and if you fear that you cannot justice (to so many) then one (only) or (the captives) that your right hands possess. Thus it is more likely that you will not do injustice. (4:3)

This latter verse is one which obviously would lead to censure from the non-Muslim even if he or she were well informed about the theoretical qualifications and limitations placed upon its implementation. In theory, additional wives were supposed to be clothed, fed, housed and provided for equally well, as well as equally loved.

However, the prime reasons for encouraging marriage were to provide a moral basis for relations between sexes and a secure family setting for raising children and to avoid more socially destructive promiscuous sexual liaisons and fatherless children in a society that was less willing or less able to absorb single mothers and their offspring than our slightly more tolerant contemporary society. Two hadith to support this view are:

> He who is able to marry should marry, for it keeps the eye cast down and keeps a man chaste; and he who cannot, should take to fasting, for it will have a castrating effect upon him. (Bokhari 30:10, in Ali, 1951:268)

> The conditions which are most worthy that you should fulfill are those with which you legalize sexual relations. (Bokhari 54:6, in Ali, 1951:273)

As for divorce in Islam, the Qur'an states in one controversial passage:

> Men are in charge of women, because God has made the one of them to excel over the other, and because they spend of their

property (for the support of the other). So good women are the obedient, guarding in secret that which God has guarded. As for those from whom you fear rebellion, admonish then and banish them to beds apart, and scourge them, Then if they obey, seek not a way against them. . . .

And if you fear a breach between the two (man and wife), appoint an arbiter from his folk and an arbiter from her folk. If they desire agreement God will make them of one mind. (4:34-35)

More complex are the legalities in Islam for pronouncing divorce upon a wife, although a wife can also sue for divorce. Basically, if reconciliation is impossible, then a divorce is allowed and it should be effected with kindness and without later stigmatization (2:232; 4:20; 65:2).

Before proceeding further, I should state that my interest in marriage and divorce among Muslims is more than academic because I am a Canadian convert to Islam of more than a quarter-century's standing and am married to a Muslim woman. Also, since we hope our three children will marry Muslim spouses in due time, I am especially interested in how the younger generation is likely to fare in the marriage sweepstakes. I have also been involved with local and national Islamic organizations, and so my approach is that of the "participant observer," as sociologists term it.

First, it is important to state that polygamy is not endemic among Muslims in Canada, and it is even dying out almost completely in the more modern portions of the Muslim world overseas. My own impressions and those of several community leaders suggest that there have been only a few isolated examples of Muslim men with more than one wife in Canada, where it is against the law. All in all, the incidence of polygamy is probably no higher than that of bigamy among the rest of the Canadian population.

It is also important to estimate how powerful the tradition of "arranged" marriages is. Certainly, the rate of family intervention in the choice of marriage partners among Muslims is higher than it is among the general population, except for a few equally traditional immigrant groups. The proportion of arranged marriages naturally varies with the community in question and with the length of time its members have been in this country. Some leaders suggest that arranged marriages that are purely an affair between families are extremely rare, but they say that there are a good many "semi-arranged" marriages, where the parents prepare the groundwork for the meeting of young couples, and estimates of the general level of arrangement range from five percent to fifty percent. A prominent leader and spokesman, resident in Canada since the early 1960s even estimated that real arranged marriages accounted for twenty-five percent of Muslim marriages, partly arranged for another fifty percent, and personal choice for the remaining twenty-five percent. Personal choice would account for less than ten percent of marriages in his homeland, Pakistan, he added. In the thirty-seven responses to my own small survey of Muslims across Canada, about one-third said their marriages were "western love marriages," one-third, "traditional Islamic marriages," and one-third, "a combination of the two."

Just as the number of arranged marriages is hard to pin down in statistical terms without further study, so it is hard to be sure how much family intermarriage is prevalent. In Muslim societies there is traditionally a good deal of marriage between cousins for the sake of family ties and certainty of blood and character. A Montreal leader puts it this way:

Muslims like to marry their relatives because they know very well what kind of atmosphere they are coming from and what is the background they have. For example, I married my son to my deceased sister's daughter.

A Canadian-born Western Ontario leader recalls:

In marriages within the community when I got married [about 1960] there was a predominant number in which there was at least some distant relationship. It may not have been very close, maybe second or third cousin, but that doesn't happen as much now as it used to.

A Montrealer says:

Yes, it's a very common thing, because as you know, in our religion first cousins can marry. It is getting popular because of the divorces, because people are afraid now to marry outside [the family]. If you see the percentage of Pakistani divorces or separations now compared to even 15 years ago there is a tremendous increase in it.

Obviously it depends upon whom one knows. A Turkish-born community leader says family endogamy is rare in his Western Ontario area "because people don't have their extended families here," adding that even in his homeland this tradition is disappearing.

Marriage with kin may also depend on other factors suggests an Eastern Ontario leader: " . . . the unfortunate ones who aren't so pretty have a harder time finding husbands so they go back to the old country or ask their parents to find them husbands [among their relatives]."

If as many as half the Muslim marriages in Canada are "arranged" to some extent, and some are with cousins, depending upon the ethnic community, there are still a proportion in which arrangement cannot have been very evident or, at best, only after the fact in terms of welcoming a son-in-law or a daughter-in-law into the family—whatever their religion.

Arrangement is obviously unlikely in exogamous or "outmarriages" where young Muslim men marry whomever they wish, theoretically at least, from among Christian and Jewish women. According to the 1981 Census of Canada figures, 18.7 percent of Muslim husbands and 7.7 percent of Muslim wives were married outside Islam at that time,[5] the latter despite the Qur'anic injunction against doing so. However, as Abdul Rashid points out, these rates are "heavily weighted by the immigrant families, most of whom arrived as family units with very few inter-faith unions".[6] Over 97 percent of the Muslim husbands, or 23,380 men, were born outside Canada and a majority of the 17.5 percent of them who married a non-Muslim wife probably came to Canada as students or very young immigrants.

Although the numbers involved are quite small, still the real surprise is the 60.8 percent rate of exogamy among the 625 Canadian-born Muslim husbands. If we further assume that the 405 Muslim wives married to Canadian-born non-Muslims were also Canadian-born (a sweeping but plausible assumption), then the rates of exogamy among both husbands and wives were over 60 percent, abnormally high by any standards.

Of the 2,230 lone-parent families, the father is a Muslim in 440 cases, and the mother, in 1,790 cases—four times the rate of men. However, their birthplaces are not mentioned, nor do we know the religious status of their spouses when they were married.

Much of the evidence concerning exogamy obviously relates to more "nominal" Muslims, those who have little or even no contact with the organized communities—at least when they are still single or without children. For example, a Montreal leader of a more traditional community says there is little exogamy that he knows about, "not even 1%." Further he knew of no Muslim women who married non-Muslims, but his strict views were well known, and they would not likely have approached him.

A leader of another Montreal organization noted that the percentage of outmarriages had apparently dropped from an estimated 10 percent to 5 percent lately because Muslims were getting "more and more conscious" of Islam, which was supported by rising attendances at his center. He added that the number of women who married non-Muslims was "negligible . . . maybe in a year one or two marriages."

But another Montreal Muslim leader says that organized groups such as his are probably in touch with only 10 to 15 percent of the total Muslim population, the rest being "nominal Muslims":

> . . . these people never go to the mosque and they never observe Islam. But when it comes to a cultural identity, they identify themselves as Muslims and they would definitely go after marrying among their own as far as possible . . . the marriageable population is just starting to come into the marriage market and the crunch will come then. These are the children who have been brought up in this culture from day one and are now 19 and 20 years of age. I think the [outmarrying] proportion will increase but I think probably we could have the same thing as the Jews have—that in spite of their irreligiosity or areligiosity they will continue their cultural identity as such, and so even though it will increase, I don't think it will increase by much.

Ethnicity and length of stay in Canada obviously affect the rate of outmarriage in different groups. For example, the very high rate of exogamy among Canadian-born Muslim men and women is recorded among a very small proportion of the total Muslim population. There were only 1,035 Canadian-born husband-and-wife families in 1981 in which one or both parents were Muslim: in 245 cases both parents were Muslims; 380 had only a Muslim father; and 405 only a Muslim mother (Rashid, 1985:59). These Canadian-born husbands and wives were largely the children of the small, mostly Lebanese communities that existed before the great multi-ethnic immigration waves of the 1960s and 1970s. Only 530 Muslims came to Canada in the decade from 1946 to 1955—probably because of exclusion policies—and only 890 from 1956 to 1960 (Rashid, 1985:17).

Among one such pre-1960s Muslim community, a leader confirms that there is a "fairly significant" rate of outmarriage, especially among the children who were born in Canada. As an example, he says that in his own Canadian-born family, half have married outside Islam and half have stayed within its bounds. But he added that:

> An interesting phenomenon is happening in the last two years—that more seem to be marrying within the community but at a much older age. That is what's happening among the Arabs, but I can't speak for the Pakistanis.

Again, in an Indian West Indian community one leader estimated that outmarriage was at the rate of about 10 percent in his group:

> . . . more males in the population are tending to marry non-Muslims because of exposure to North American society, the relative laxity in terms of social interaction between girls and boys compared to the Islamic background, and society allows a boy to date more freely. Parents also tend to keep a little tighter rein on girls than they do on boys.

In discussing the Ottawa region, a marriage officer also estimates that about 10 percent of Muslims marry outside Islam in his experience and that the number of girls who did so was "very, very small," adding that there were only a dozen such cases in that city.

A Western Ontario marriage officer said that

> Unfortunately for the last few months there is an alarming phenomenon where we find even Muslim girls attracted to non-Muslim boys. Amongst the youth this is becoming a very serious problem to deal with.

However, deal with it he does, recounting how he had managed to convert a Catholic man to Islam:

> They had no intention of getting married, but Alhamdolillah, God opened his [the man's] heart and he accepted Islam and then

I convinced him it was his duty to marry because in Islam he has to marry to complete his faith.

These references to conversion and marriage bring in one of the more complex issues related to Islam, one which arises in connection with other fairly demanding faiths. For example, a Montreal leader in a more traditional group said that four non-Muslim women had accepted Islam in the previous week and that in his five years there, more than three hundred women had converted before marrying. The question arises whether these numbers were simply *pro forma* or serious conversions.

A Toronto leader notes that a number of non-Muslim potential spouses are:

> converted mostly under pressure from the [Muslim] family, but unfortunately not many of them continue. I don't think it's because they want to be something else. In many cases, it's because they're really nothing. They're not good at Islam or at whatever they were before either. Again it's just because they never really make an attempt because the other party, the Muslim boy or girl, didn't really know much about their own religion. That's the problem. If they felt very strongly about their religion they would try to teach the other partner.

However, this view gives less credit than it might to the people for whom conversion was not simply a ritual. Some have even become community leaders themselves.

Not as severe a hurdle is the question of marrying outside their own Islamic sect, or "school of thought," as some Muslims put it more delicately. The principal sectarian division between the Sunni majority and Shiᶜa minority and the various subdivisions has been a serious matter since the religio-political events of the first century of Islamic history. In most parts of the Muslim world, there is an uneasy truce between the two groups, and yet the barrier of sect is also continuously crossed in marriage overseas and here in Canada, where its significance is much less strong, especially among the younger generations.

On the importance of sect, a Canadian-born leader says:

> I can just speak to my own case: my wife is from a Shiᶜa family and I'm from a Sunni family, and I know that in our community

[the Lebanese] it's hardly ever talked about, and I don't know if people are even aware of it except in recent days in the news. The community doesn't make a distinction. We have Sunnis and Shiᶜas coming to the mosque and no one really knows it.

A Montreal leader says that crossing the sect barrier is "very, very common":

In my own family, my background is from a Shiᶜa family and my wife is Sunni. I've got eight brothers and five sisters and I would say that half of them are Shiᶜa and half of them are Sunni. And I've heard the same thing is found in other families too [even among these arranged marriages]. . . . It is vanishing.

In Montreal, another says that back in Pakistan:

these kinds of differences between sects are very deeply entrenched and people are very fearful of crossing the boundaries, but here, with the close affinity among Muslim groups, these differences are not so much emphasized.

A Montreal leader of a more traditional community does not agree with these impressions about the frequency of sectarian boundary-crossing in marriage. He said it was "very, very seldom" that there was inter-sect marriages, despite the presence of many Iranian Shiᶜa in the congregation, and he could think of only two such marriages over the years.

A Western Ontario leader also supports this stand:

There's no problem in marrying a Sunni and a Shiᶜa . . . but when it comes to the new sects and new types of divisions within the Shiᶜa faith, such as the Ahmadis, it is a big problem, first of all because we don't know much about the Ismailis and as for the Ahmadis the Muslims declare them non-Muslims. I am aware of one problem and InshaAllah we will try to solve it. I myself do not perform mixed marriages between Muslims and non-Muslims, but Sunni and Shiᶜa is no problem . . . but I refuse between Sunni and Ismaili and I absolutely refuse between Sunni and Ahmadi.

Just as inter-sect marriages are seen at varying rates in differing Muslim communities, so are marriages that cross ethnic lines. For example, while sect seems to matter little among the long-established and Canadian-born, ethnicity is a stronger barrier to marriage, as one leader says:

> You would find that Arabs would marry Arabs and it would be very rare that you would find a Lebanese marrying a Pakistani. It's more likely that they would marry an Anglo-Saxon, if they were going to marry outside [their ethnic group] and probably not a Muslim. I would say that the odds against them marrying outside their ethnic community are less than marrying someone who is not a Muslim.

A Montrealer supports this view:

> It definitely does happen [cross-ethnic marriage], more frequently than before, but not very frequently. I would say of all the marriages that you see there are much more of the local marriages—say French-Canadian or English-Canadian girls and outsiders from various ethnic groups—than marriages between the different Muslim groups, between other Arabs and Palestinians, for example. There is still more hesitation in an Arab marrying a Pakistani. Somehow they find it more of a cultural clash than an Arab or a Pakistani marrying a French-Canadian.

While almost all those interviewed suggest that inter-ethnic marriages form a small minority, they are happening, especially among the Canadian-born or those who have grown up here. Among my respondents, twelve had married across ethnic lines, seven with converts, and a number of leaders mention that it is a highly desirable trend, as does one Arab-Canadian:

> I am preaching that, because the only way to strengthen the Muslim umma is to create these mixed marriages and I am trying to arrange the maximum number of them because we are divided into Pakistanis and Egyptians and Palestinians and Indians.

Just as inter-ethnic marriages are relatively rare, even if increasing in number, so are marriages that significantly cross socio-economic barriers. Most people of any group tend to marry others of their own ethnic, religious, and socio-economic group. The same holds true even more strictly of immigrants, but virtually all those interviewed said that socio-economic levels matter here, but less so than they do in their homelands. One said that while his community was still too young to be a useful basis:

> I do not think social status or financial position is that important really. I think educational achievement seems to be more dominant than financial. If the boys and girls want to marry, they want to marry someone of equal intellectual or educational background rather than marry a less intellectual person with a lot more money.

And a Montreal leader says socio-economic barriers matter more among the Indo-Pakistanis than among the Arabs because there is still a lot of stratification among the former. He says barriers, particularly social ones, are "definitely" less important in Canada than in the homelands:

> I think mostly it is out of necessity and partly it may be also that frankly they are living in a society where this kind of barrier is not encouraged and where they are not reinforced. Mostly it is necessity—you have to get married and so on—other things like education and other factors seem more predominant in their thinking than social class.

This reality is being helped along by marriage officers such as this one, who says that socio-economic barriers do not exist—at least for him:

> In all the marriages I perform, the *mehr* [dowry] is one dollar and I pay it! For my part, I try to stick with the hadith, marry them even if they are poor because Allah Subhanuhu-Ta'ala will give you the necessary support.

In Toronto, one leader finds among his more Westernized community that socio-economic barriers are not very important:

> because there is a shortage of marriageable Muslim boys. I think if there is a person of a higher socio-economic status with a daughter they would prefer the daughter marry a Muslim even if he was of a lower socio-economic stratum than they would have liked. They would have to condone it.

Another Toronto leader suggests that perhaps a quarter of Muslim marriages here cross these lines, and a Montreal one says it is often the case where Muslim boys marry outside Islam, the girls having lower socio-economic and educational backgrounds in this case. "Somehow people [Muslim boys] do not find spouses in their own social class. That has been the case lately. This applies to boys marrying non-Muslim girls." But he says:

> people are more open-minded here. Society is not very rigid with respect to marrying outside one's own class or one's sect. Back home these things are very rigid and it's very difficult for people to overcome—an important reason being that most marriages are arranged.

With the possibility here of marrying outside Islam and outside all the constraining barriers of more traditional Islamic societies, cases of contemporary Muslims not marrying because they could not find a Muslim spouse should be uncommon.

In contrast, many of the early Muslim arrivals in this country were single men from Lebanon-Syria, for example, and they married local girls who did not convert to Islam, nor, probably, were they encouraged to because the Qur'an allowed exogamy, because the women had no personal knowledge of Islamic theology, and because there was no Muslim community to support such conversion. However, some did; one Western leader had an American mother with a strong Christian background, but she converted to Islam early in this century when she married an Arab trader. The son recalls how his mother never allowed pork in their frontier home and how she broke a bottle that another peddler brought into it on one occasion. But to illustrate the point further, the Canadian-born son said that while his father said his prayers and read the Qur'an, he never passed on much or any of Islam's message, and so the son had to wait until the Depression forced him to spend hours in the public library, where he suddenly stumbled upon translated verses of the Qur'an in a book on the literature of the world, after which he never looked back.

But even now, when there is a Muslim population of about one hundred thousand, there are still many who apparently cannot find a Muslim spouse.

One of those interviewed recalls that in Cambridge:

I came across many, many friends—who were getting very concerned that boys and girls were getting older, older than the
range of mid-20s to late-20s, and that they had not been able to
find proper spouses. Their problem is more predominant in large
communities. . . . I think it's the most serious potential problem
in Canada.

Another Ontario leader finds that the problem of a lack of suitable
spouses is more prevalent among women:

I know a lot of girls around who are in their mid to late-20s who
haven't married. I think it's more prevalent among the women
than among the men.

And a Montrealer backs this statement up from his experience:

There is a fairly significant number of those people in their 20s of
marriageable age. . . . One of the problems that is bothering
many people who are settled here is that many of the Muslim
boys—when it comes to marrying—go back home rather than
finding a bride right in Canada.

But another Montrealer says that he has not heard of people in his
community who cannot find spouses:

For the girls, if the parents feel that they aren't getting a match
here, the parents go back home and soon they find a suitable boy
and they perform the marriage or they invite him to come to Canada and he comes and they perform the marriage here. . . . [But]
There are a lot of instances of girls looking for boys and boys
looking for girls, but the community is limited and their activities
are limited and so there is not much they can do.

Given the barriers to marriage in terms of religion, sect, ethnicity,
and socio-economic status, what do the community leaders think
about these kinds of barriers in general?

A Western Ontario leader of Indian background says:

There are two types of people—one is those who are inward-
looking, for them it [barrier] does matter, it is important for
them to stay within Islam and the Punjabi so they only marry
Punjabis. . . . But people who are a bit liberal or outward-

looking, because of their liberal approach they wouldn't mind getting their daughter or son married as long as it's to a Muslim.

Another Arab-Canadian in the same area supports this estimate:

From my experience I found the Muslims who are practicing Islam, those who pray regularly, they pay no attention to these barriers. . . . Another thing, those who hold to their faith strongly, they believe it is very important to bring these gaps to the minimum so we can establish the Muslim *umma* strongly in North America. Thirdly, we are trying, especially those who have decided that Canada is their own country, to live in for the rest of their lives, to think in terms of Canadian Muslims rather than Pakistani, Egyptian or Arab Muslims, and Alhamdolillah, there is progress in this line.

These attitudes perhaps reflect the view of the future held by the more acclimatized and the more progressively "Islamic" individuals, who think they see to the heart of the matter—putting adherence to Islam above other considerations as a limitation on who can marry whom. However, there will probably continue to be many others for whom these barriers of religion, sect, ethnicity, and socio-economic class will continue to matter to a considerable degree, at least, as long as they remain an immigrant community.

But if Muslim immigrants are changing their attitudes towards marriage to varying degrees under the influence of the North American society's liberalism and theoretical disdain for distinctions, so they are having to face a rising divorce rate. According to the 1981 Census of Canada statistics, a slightly higher percentage of Muslim men are married and a slightly lower percentage are separated and divorced than among the total population. Muslim women are also married at a slightly higher percentage rate and separated and divorced a little less (see table below). However, Rashid said that a simple comparison may be misleading for general reasons. Since separation and divorce are a function of marriage, their incidence should be compared only after excluding the "never-married" population. Furthermore, these statistics do not tell how many of the married, separated, divorced or widowed have been in any of each other's shoes earlier on.

TABLE I
Percentage Distribution of Population, 15 Years and Over
by Marital Status, Canada, 1981

| Marital Status | Total Population | | Canadian-Born | | Foreign-Born | |
| --- | --- | --- | --- | --- | --- | --- |
| | Total | Muslim | Muslim | Other | Muslim | Other |
| Male | | | | | | |
| Married | 62.6 | 67.0 | 36.3 | 59.8 | 68.5 | 74.5 |
| Separated | 2.2 | 1.9 | 2.2 | 2.2 | 1.9 | 2.3 |
| Divorced | 2.2 | 1.9 | 2.5 | 2.2 | 1.9 | 2.2 |
| Widowed | 1.9 | 0.8 | 0.8 | 1.7 | 0.8 | 3.0 |
| Never Married | 31.1 | 28.4 | 58.4 | 34.2 | 26.9 | 18.0 |
| Female | | | | | | |
| Married | 60.4 | 70.3 | 53.9 | 58.9 | 71.2 | 66.6 |
| Separated | 2.8 | 1.8 | 4.0 | 2.8 | 1.6 | 2.6 |
| Divorced | 3.1 | 1.7 | 3.7 | 3.2 | 1.6 | 3.0 |
| Widowed | 9.2 | 7.1 | 2.5 | 8.0 | 7.3 | 14.2 |
| Never Married | 24.5 | 19.2 | 35.2 | 27.1 | 18.3 | 13.6 |

Source: 1981 Census of Canada, table 7, in Abdul Rashid, *The Muslim Cana-dians, A Profile* (Ottawa: Statistics Canada, 1985), p. 27.

Also, he adds, the relative youth of the Muslim population makes comparisons very unrealistic, as does the fact that more than 60 percent of the total Muslim population immigrated here in the 1971-81 decade (1985:17). Mostly they were married when they came, and hence they are likely to stay that way because they cling to each other and their children in a new world.

Despite these serious statistical quagmires, it is at least interesting that these figures show that although the Canadian-born Muslims of marriageable age are a very small proportion of the total Muslim population, the percentage of separated and divorced is higher among them than among other Canadian-born men and women. When the foreign-born Muslim men and women are compared to other foreign-born men and women, they show a lower percentage of separation and divorce.

But who is getting divorced and why? Rather than trying to calcu-
late the incalculable, it may be more useful to register some of the impressions of Muslim leaders on separation and divorce rates in their
communities. An Indian from the West Indies says:

> I would say that the number of Muslims in our community that
> would be divorced in one year would be less than two or three
> out of 5,000. That is not to say that they are not having prob-
> lems, but they tend to stick together. . . . I would say in many
> cases the problems would have been economic pressures because
> one breadwinner is not sufficient to maintain the household, con-
> sequently both parties have to share the workload . . . Now the
> female is out working and bringing in an income. She feels more
> independent and so she can take off and support herself, and so
> there is no real pressure to stay within the marriage if it is uncom-
> fortable.

Another said, "There seems to be an increase in separations, but I've
not really heard of that many cases of divorce. . . . Among the Muslims
it would be less than half of one percent." And another thought less
than 2 percent. A third says from his experience in Montreal that while
the divorce rate might only be 1 or 2 percent in Pakistan, it would be
closer to 5 percent here, which was "a considerable increase":

> I think it is just easier now, because the woman knows she can go
> to court and she can get alimony and so on, and I think she is
> more able and more likely to take the step. Also, I think I have
> seen more divorces among people where the man went home and
> got married, and already had a girlfriend to begin with and has
> not adapted to his marriage.

He does not think there are necessarily more marriage breakdowns
among marriages with Canadian spouses than otherwise, but he suggests that the chances of success depend, to a considerable degree, on
how the couple stand in regard to cultural adaptation to the North
American way of life. If one or the other partner is not so North Amer-
icanized, then there is more chance of difficulties arising.

One Canadian-born community leader says divorce is now occurring in his area too:

If you had asked me that two years ago I would have said there isn't any, but there seems to be a lot more now. It's less than among the general population, but it's no longer unheard-of. . . . I used to think that because of our faith and the way we were brought up that we were less susceptible to the kind of social pressures that exist and the things that cause divorce among the general community. I think as time goes by it seems to be that's not really the case and that the religious ties are slackening off a little bit and people are more likely to be affected by what goes on around them and as the family breaks down in the general community we're likely to be affected by it too.

The religious leader and marriage officer of one more traditional Muslim community says cases of divorce spring up "very seldom" in marriages between Muslims from Pakistan or Egypt, for example:

Mostly [they occur] with the boys who are marrying the girls here, the girls who have been brought up in a certain atmosphere and certain surroundings and they have a particular way of living and the Muslims have different styles of living, different ways and even different eating habits. For example, if before she married she is used to going dancing, she is used to alcohol, she is used to smoking and watching TV for hours everyday, but the boy doesn't want this . . . He explains and she tries to correct herself but it is not possible for her, then ultimately you know how it ends up.

He adds that when marriages seem to be breaking down in this community, certain men try to help in reconciling the couples involved, which usually works. If reconciliation is impossible, then they suggest how to follow the Islamic divorce procedure before finalizing it in the civil courts. "You can't simply say you divorce a women three times. You can do it, but it is prohibited," he points out.

The Muslim divorce procedure, he says, requires the divorcing party to say before witnesses that he or she is divorcing the other. This is the first "divorce," which is followed by a month of continued co-residence and hoped-for reconciliation and the completion of a menstrual cycle—usually a month—followed by a second "divorce" and another month of waiting and possible reconciliation. Then comes a third "divorce" and a final month before the parties can marry anyone else. That leader had stated earlier that it is either Canadian-made or exogamous marriages that are the most likely to end in divorce, and other leaders said much the same thing.

One leader in the same city but in a different community says, "the frequency [of divorces] would be much higher in Muslim and non-Muslim [exogamous] marriages, but even between Muslim spouses divorce is no longer a rare case." Another in Western Ontario adds that he knows of "quite a few" divorces and separations in his area, and he adds that "most of the ones I know of are mixed [exogamous] marriages but I know of at least two Muslim families that have been divorced too."

In discussing divorce, another leader in Eastern Ontario says:

I would say the main reason [for divorce] is the husband. He starts to fool around, looking for some easy-going Canadian girls and so the marriage starts to disintegrate.

But for him, the biggest cause of divorce is exogamy:

They [Muslim men] may not care initially about religion and they say "Oh yes, that's all right, Islam allows me to marry a non-Muslim girl and Islam doesn't mean much to me." But when they start having children and they want to raise them as Muslims the subconscious differences in cultures and sometimes languages and traditions and habits appear. These differences don't show up initially, but after a while when they get used to one another, then they have a chance to come through.

If many Muslim marriages are in trouble in Canada—whether Islamically exogamous or endogamous, whether Canadian-made or formed overseas, whether with converts, members of different sects or ethnicity or socio-economic background—what about the religious status of the children of these marriages? Abdul Rashid's statistics give the Muslim community cause for alarm; unless present and future conditions are different for the children of the foreign-born majority than they were for the Canadian-born minority, the declared or enumerated Muslim proportions may decline radically within a few generations.

As can be seen from table 2, of all 44,920 children of all 27,870 husband-wife and lone-parent families, some 39,350 are listed as "Muslim" and 5,570 as "other"; therefore, 87.6 percent are Muslim as a percentage of all children. Then, among the total of 25,640 husband-wife families where, respectively, both parents, only the father, and only the mother are Muslims, the percentages of Muslim children are, respectively, 99.3 percent, 36.2 percent and 22.7 percent. In 24,605 of all husband-wife families, the father was foreign-born. Among them, 99.5 percent of children of both-parents-Muslim families are listed as "Muslim," 38.9 percent of children in the father-only-Muslim families were Muslims, and 24.2 percent in the mother-only-Muslim families. Therefore, while two Muslim parents could seemingly ensure that their children retained their religion, women who married outside Islam appear to have had an even harder time than their male counterparts in keeping the faith of their children Muslim. Among the Canadian-born minority the chances of maintaining Islam were even slimmer. For example, among the families with Canadian-born fathers, 83.1 percent of the children in both-parents-Muslim families were registered as "Muslim," dropping sharply to 9.1 percent in father-only-Muslim families and rising only a little to 17.1 percent in mother-only-Muslim families.

These last figures are the ones that might cause alarm among the largely immigrant Muslim community in Canada, suggesting to its members that when their children grow up, they will be destined to a high rate of exogamy—even among women—and a devastating loss of faith among their children. However, as Rashid points out, this concern need not drive Muslims back to their homelands to safeguard the faith of their children and grandchildren:

> The high rate of interfaith marriages is surprising and, if continued, it will result in a more or less complete assimilation of the Muslim Canadians in two or three generations. However, the earlier Muslim immigrants to Canada were very small in number and lacked a sense of community and communal support. During the last decade, as their numbers grew, the Muslim Canadians have quickly established centres in most urban areas across the country. These centres not only provide the new generation of Canadian-born Muslims with religious education but also act as

TABLE 2

Distribution of Families and Children
by Religious Status of Parents, Canada, 1981

| Religious Status of Parents | Number of Families | Number of Children | | | Muslim children as a percentage of all children |
|---|---|---|---|---|---|
| | | Total | Muslim | Other | |
| TOTAL | 27,870 | 44,920 | 39,350 | 5,570 | 87.6 |
| *Husband-Wife Families* | | | | | |
| Total | 25,640 | 40,915 | 35,715 | 5,200 | 87.3 |
| Both Parents Muslim | 19,530 | 33,555 | 33,320 | 235 | 99.3 |
| Only Father Muslim | 4,480 | 5,380 | 1,945 | 3,435 | 36.2 |
| Only Mother Muslim | 1,630 | 1,980 | 450 | 1,530 | 22.7 |
| Canadian-Born | 1,035* | 1,230 | 385 | 845 | 31.3 |
| Both Parents Muslim | 245 | 325 | 270 | 55** | 83.1 |
| Only Father Muslim | 380 | 495 | 45 | 450 | 9.1 |
| Only Mother Muslim | 405 | 410 | 70 | 340 | 17.1 |
| Foreign-born | 24,605 | 39,685 | 35,330 | 4,355 | 89.0 |
| Both Parents Muslim | 19,280 | 33,230 | 33,050 | 180 | 99.5 |
| Only Father Muslim | 4,100 | 4,885 | 1,900 | 2,985 | 38.9 |
| Only Mother Muslim | 1,225 | 1,570 | 380 | 1,190 | 24.2 |

*Lone-Parent Families*

| | | | | |
|---|---|---|---|---|
| Total | 2,230 | 4,005 | 3,635 | 370 | 90.8 |
| Muslim Male Parent | 440 | 890 | 750 | 140 | 84.9 |
| Muslim Female Parent | 1,790 | 3,115 | 2,885 | 230 | 92.6 |

Source: 1981 Census of Canada, in Abdul Rashid, *The Muslim Canadians, A Profile* (Ottawa: Statistics Canada, 1985), p. 59.

Notes:

\* 1,035 is the result of rounding to protect confidentiality.

\*\* The original table had a typographical error (255).

social and communal institutions for the Muslim Canadians. It is therefore expected that the incidence of inter-faith marriages is likely to be smaller in the future than in the past. (1985:60)

Interestingly, in the last table's 2,230 lone-parent-Muslim families, the rate of retention of Islam is apparently quite high, 84.9 percent for fathers and 92.6 percent for mothers, suggesting that Muslims who are single parents for whatever reasons have a much better chance of ensuring that their children retain or are claimed to retain their faith to a much higher level than if one parent in a husband-wife family is a Muslim. Possibly, after the loss of a marriage-partner, the surviving Muslim is eager to make sure the the children are not allowed to drift off too.

Considering these statistics and the perceptions of the difficulties of marriage in North America, it would not be too surprising if Muslims decided to stress the need for endogamy among the faithful. But given their varying degrees of acculturation, how do they propose to encourage their children to marry other Muslims? How do they feel about their children socializing with and even dating Muslim young people and non-Muslims? Do the largely urbanized Muslim communities provide scope for religious endogamy, let alone ethnic and sectarian endogamy?

Let us start with the most strictly orthodox Islamic point of view, which has traditionally discouraged the mixing of the sexes unless they were related. A Montreal community leader states quite categorically:

The first thing is that this [mixing and dating] is strictly forbidden. Even the Canadian girls accepting Islam we tell that this kind of friendship between boys and girls is not allowed. So certainly in our centre—and I'm sure in any other *masjid* [mosque]— we do not allow our young generation to meet with the other sex . . .

A little less stringent is the view of another Montreal leader:

It is possible in a way. If some chaperoning is going on then I don't think anyone would mind. But Muslim parents who really are religious or know their religion—I'm not talking about people who are Muslims but don't care about their religion—I don't think they would like it that there would be dating. But they won't mind if there is a gathering and some meetings going on [like youth groups].

A third Montrealer is more realistic about what may be going on despite the strictures of the elders and the traditions of Islam:

> ... it is happening covertly, but if you ask most of the people they will say it is not happening at all, because they don't see it. Mostly it happens when you are going to school and college and you meet in the cafeteria and so on, or you have these Muslim camps and you meet there or you talk on the telephone. There is not much of the regular dating—going out in the evenings and at night and having dinner and so on—happening here, at least in my experience. Between Muslims and non-Muslims yes; among Muslims and Muslims it doesn't.

Searching for alternatives, a Western Ontario leader and marriage officer says dating

> is not acceptable; however, last year we started a new experimental thing. For example, a gymnasium where young people go and play once a week. We have teams for girls. . . . We try to separate them as much as we can, but they will have a chance to see one another and to talk to one another. . . . They play volleyball and basketball but no mixing. They don't play against one another— perhaps volleyball but not basketball. . . . We do not accept dating but we organize parties within the families so that some young people can meet with one another under the supervision of their parents.

Attitudes are changing. Some community leaders speak of the more or less organized meetings of Muslim youth, of the Council of Muslim Communities of Canada (CMCC) camps where relations are on a brother-and-sister basis, but swimming classes and some other activities are quite segregated, and of allowing a certain latitude in group activities if not in one-on-one dating.

When it comes to dating or socializing with non-Muslims, Muslim opinion is much more united that it is over mixing with other Muslims. As a Canadian-born community leader says:

> Dating outside the community is discouraged. Again it varies from family to family. Within our own family situation we haven't forbidden our kids to do it, but we let them know we weren't happy about it, and I guess in our circumstances it hap-

pens occasionally. It's not a very frequent thing and our sons are 16 to 23. . . . There are other families who absolutely forbid their kids to do it and so they sneak out and do it.

Another says that "the general community seems to be against it, but it's yet to be seen how much they are able to control or monitor that." One suggests that force must be used if necessary, but basically all but the most liberal are opposed to dating.

Of course one of the biggest fears among Muslim parents—and probably in many other communities as well—is that the socializing or dating will lead to a daughter's loss of virginity—or worse. In Toronto years ago an Albanian Muslim father killed his daughter because she became pregnant—the worst scenario in a community that stresses outward morality to such a degree. In the wake of the sexual revolution and tolerance of cohabitation, how strict is the maintenance of virginity as a *sine qua non* for marriage? How far have Muslims gone beyond the public display of a bloodied bedsheet as a sign that all was well and "honor" was upheld?

One community leader says that he has not heard of the issue being raised but that it was expected that neither sex would get involved in a sexual relationship before marriage. "But there is a double standard for boys," he adds. "It's not really okay, but maybe it's overlooked or maybe accepted in some cases." Another says it is not an insuperable barrier to marriage:

> I don't think it is, particularly if dating or whatever you want to call it prepares for that and then that loss of virginity is not that much of a problem for people who are growing up here. It is happening, I presume, even back home in certain areas and in certain strata of society and . . . nobody else knows about it and it's nobody else's business and that's it.

But one leader links real or imagined loss of virginity with the need for women to look outside Islam for husbands. He states that there is a particular code of dress and behavior for Muslim women and that those who have gone beyond it in effect get a reputation that makes it difficult for even the less observant or nominal Muslim men to marry them. Hence the men seek virgin brides from their homelands, while the women left here have to find acceptance from non-Muslim husbands. This situation may well explain why some community leaders note a rise in exogamy among women as well as a larger number of women seeking husbands in vain, while their male counterparts marry inside or outside the faith and inside or outside the country.

As a result of the growth of marriage problems and divorces among the Muslim communities of Ontario and Quebec, where most of them live, leaders are calling for marriage counseling before, during and after marriage. As one put it:

> . . . in many, many cases Muslims who come and get married are first-generation [immigrant] Muslims or came here as children and grew up in this society. After they get married they are finding that the traditional type of male domination in the society which they may have grown up with doesn't conform with the female's point of view and they are going to have problems. They aren't going to solve them unless they have communication and I think the communities ought to have more enrichment programs to help these young couples to solve their problems. Again in the old society with the extended family there were always the parents around who can advise and help pave the way for a smoother marriage, but over here that situation doesn't exist so they haven't got the support to make their marriages work.

One leader confirms that there is a lack of support for people in troubled marriages:

> I think back home, say in Pakistan or Egypt, couples have so many avenues to vent their frustrations, their difficulties. Here I think the husband and wife are stuck with each other, and as a group I think we have to open up those avenues.

A Western Ontario leader extends the need for counseling to the whole family on occasion:

> . . . there are conflicts within the families going on and what is really needed is more family counseling, whereby some professional could bring the couples together and counsel them on family problems and bringing up children also. . . . It's not only wife-beating but there is some frustration among wives about staying home, not getting enough opportunities to go out and get the

same opportunities for mental development as the men are getting.

The other solution to the problems of marriage and divorce for Canadian Muslims is to ensure that young Muslims are allowed to meet each other at least as often as they meet their non-Muslim friends at school, university, or work. Since most young people will not be parties to overtly arranged marriages or be married to someone from their parents' homelands, then this more "Canadian" solution is probably the most likely.

In talking about the prevalence of outmarriage in one Lebanese community, the Canadian-born leader says:

> I think it's fairly significant, particularly among children born in this country of immigrant parents. I think there is a general alienation of the young and the old. I guess they used to call it the "generation gap," and in this case it's more accentuated because there is no fundamental understanding of the position the kids are in, and the kids don't understand the needs of their parents in terms of wanting to retain their culture and extend it through their children and their grandchildren. There isn't enough dialogue on that so consequently when the issue is raised it's usually in a confrontational setting rather than one of dialogue and understanding.

Another West Indian-born leader observes:

> I would say that we would have a problem on our hands in terms of the values of the present generation growing up here and the values that their parents bring with them. Somehow or other the Muslim community must generate activities to assist in maintaining Islamic values and that really means evolving activities around the youth—both social and educational activities.

And a Montreal community leader warns of the urgency of establishing Islamic structures in Canada if Muslim youth are not to be lost to the group through more and more "mixing":

> I do not think that the Muslim can survive the way they are going at this point, as a Muslim group, for more than two generations, unless Muslims establish more institutions and Islam becomes more acceptable.

He cited, as an example of this non-acceptance, a recent book on the religions of North America that ignored Islam while covering a variety of small Christian and Jewish groups.

Another man suggested sending Muslim children back to visit their parents' homelands to teach them about their religion. The cost of these trips should not be seen as expenses but as investments in the future, he said, having just welcomed back his own daughter, on whom such a visit had had a "tremendous" effect. But, obviously, it depends on the family and the homeland, because many situations in the Islamic world overseas could have a counterproductive effect on young Canadian Muslims.

Finally, another leader stresses the need for increased social contacts among young Muslims, more camp activities, and marriage-counseling services. Evidence of the need for a marriage bureau of some sort—or, indeed, an effort to fulfill the need—is found in the back pages of the Islamic Society of North America (ISNA) journal *Islamic Horizons*, which carries advertisements of *Muslimahs*, or women, seeking, for example, "matrimonial correspondence from educated professional Muslims, age 35-40, for Pakistani Muslimah (Sunni), Urdu speaking, age 30, M.A. accountant." These ads usually mention the ethnicity and sect of the seeker and their educational and economic standing; they sometimes offer piety and often request "photo first letter" (*Islamic Horizons* [August 1985], p. 19).

In conclusion, what can one say about the present and future state of the Muslim marriage and divorce in Canada? What are the chances of more exogamy—or less—given the recency of the arrival of most Muslims and the average youthfulness of the Canadian-born community? How important will religion, sect, ethnicity, and socio-economic status be for the next generation?

Until more sociologically directed and well-funded research projects can be launched, we will not know very much about this small but growing community. However, it will take a generation or two for the new Canadian-born and child-immigrant Muslims to discover whether their children will be listed as Muslims in the census of 2001 or 2011 and whether their own faith and works will be well known and respected across the land. Probably, despite the faith of the individuals, the relationships that lead to marriage and divorce will become more "Canadianized"—for better or worse—and lead to statistics comparable to those of the general population. Careful research will also have to be done on the actual degree of religious adherence or observation among the range of "Muslims," from the wholly nominal to the completely engrossed, because until then it will be very difficult to suggest where the future generations are headed.

It is reasonable to suppose that just as some of the younger generation's members who are marrying endogamously are already crossing lines of ethnicity, sect, and social class, so the Muslim community may come to form its own mini-melting-pot as the earlier Islamic community did in their expanding homelands as conquest, settlement, and trade mixed all sorts of races and groups. Many Muslims are discounting the importance of ethnicity and sect environment and are stressing instead the need for the faithful to live up to their egalitarian and non-racist instincts. Nevertheless, since a majority of Muslims are still immigrants, ethnicity and sect will continue to loom very large. The marriage of Muslim men with Christian and Jewish women has had negative effects on community solidarity, while the prohibited exogamy by Muslim women has only occasionally brought husbands and children back to the Muslim umma. Hence, endogamy for both sexes has been frequently stressed by community leaders.

The answers to these questions will lie in the impact of the growing Islamic institutions here. Societies and organizations, centers and mosques, part-time and full-time schools, summer camps and youth groups, programs and publications, and so on were non-existent or only scattered and minimal before the late 1960s, so it is not surprising that exogamy and divorce were very high among the Canadian-born minority of the past. It now seems unlikely that the difficult pre-1960s experience will be repeated.

### Notes

I must gratefully acknowledge the support received from Le Collège militaire royal de Saint-Jean, Quebec, since my sessional appointment there in the summer of 1985. My telephone interviews and typing could not have been managed readily without it.

1. Originally I distributed a long and detailed but anonymous questionnaire to gain information and views on Canadian Muslims' pre-marital, marital, and post-marital experiences to more than two hundred married people.

After months of waiting and cajoling I received thirty-seven responses, for which I am very thankful.

Since this result was not sufficient for my purpose I pursued the community-leader-interview technique, which provided answers on a more generalized basis. The range and suitability of my interviewees can be seen from the following list. I have placed the names in alphabetical order: Zafar Abaas, president, Islamic Centre of Quebec, Montreal; Dr. Mohammed Amin, M.D., president, Muslim Community of Quebec, Montreal; Dr. Mahmoud Ayoub, executive director, Canadian Institute for Advanced Islamic Research, Toronto; Khalil Bakhsh, secretary, Council of Muslim Communities of Canada, Kingston; Mohammed El-Farram, president, Islamic School Teachers Association of Canada, Brantford; Hanny Hassan, vice-chairman, Ontario Multicultural Advisory Council, London; Mohammed Manzoor Khan, Imam, Islamic Centre of Quebec, Montreal; Sadaqat Lodhi, president, Muslim Association of Saint-John, N.B.; Qasem Mahmud, chairman, Islamic School of Ottawa, Ottawa; Izhar Mirza, general secretary, Pakistani Association of Quebec, Montreal; Dr. Muin Muinuddin, past chairman and past secretary, Council of Muslim Communities of Canada, Toronto; Dr. Fuad Sahin, M.D., chairman, Council of Muslim Communities of Canada, Niagara on the Lake; Haroon Salamat, president, Toronto and Region Islamic Congregation, Toronto; Abdul Hamid Shaikh, president, Majlis-e-Shura, Muslim Association of Hamilton, Hamilton. I am grateful for their time and effort.

Concentration of interviewees in Ontario and Quebec is reasonably justified by the fact that 53 percent and 12 percent of Canadian Muslims respectively live in these two provinces, about two-thirds of the total.

2. This is the form I have long been familiar with, and another one is "He who marries completes half his religion; it now rests with him to complete the other half by leading a virtuous life in constant fear of God".
3. Maulana Muhammad Ali, *A Manual of Hadith* (Lahore: Ahmadiyya Anjuman Ishaat Islam, 1951).
4. Adapted from the English of Mohammed Marmaduke Pickthall, *The Meaning of the Glorious Koran, An Explanatory Translation* (New York: New American Library, n.d.).
5. Abdul Rashid, *The Muslim Canadians, A Profile* (Ottawa: Statistics Canada, Ministry of Supply and Services, 1985), table 22, p. 59.
6. Ibid., p. 57. He notes:
    When families are analyzed by the characteristics of an individual in the family, by convention the individual chosen is the husband in the husband-wife families and the parent in the lone-parent families. It is on this basis that the 26,235 Muslim families were analyzed. For the purposes of analysis of inter-faith marriages, the religious status of both husbands and wives was taken into account. Table 22 presents the relevant data.
    I should also acknowledge my great debt to the author of this important

analysis of the 1981 Census statistics for his patience with my questions. He is not responsible for any errors I have made in their reproduction or further mathematical analysis based upon them.

# Marriage Strategies among Muslims from South Asia

## Regula Burckhardt Qureshi*

◆　　◆　　◆　　◆

Most crucial to the survival of any social institution is its reproduction from one generation to the next. This chapter focuses on marriage as the primary strategy toward achieving family consistency and continuity among Muslim North Americans of Pakistani and Indian origin. How marriage can serve these goals is contingent on the socio-religious configuration which characterizes South Asian Muslim society and which results in a unique pattern of adaptation to North American conditions. In particular, this inquiry will show how a traditional set of norms and practices is put to use in order to serve the achievement of desired social goals through comprehensive long-range strategies that quite deserve the epithet "social engineering." The shared fundamentals of Muslim social structure across the Indian subcontinent and, equally, the basic homogeneity in the social environment of North America, make possible generalization across the two realms. The main data for this chapter, however, comes from the Prairie Region of Canada, particularly from the province of Alberta, where a thriving South Asian Muslim community is settled, principally in Ed-

*I gratefully acknowledge the research assistance of Azra Ahmad, as well as the contribution by Yasmeen Nizam.

monton and Calgary, Alberta; Saskatoon and Regina, Saskatchewan; and Winnipeg in Manitoba. The majority of this community originates from Pakistan, with a minority coming from India, and it includes South Asians from Eastern and Southern Africa.[1] The shared language and lingua franca, Urdu, articulates a strong common cultural and religious identity.

Based on both participant observation and extensive eliciting, this inquiry has both a formal synchronic and an informal diachronic dimension. In formal terms, systematic data was gathered on fifty-four marriages from thirty-two families situated within a larger group of fifty-five families with a total of ninety-seven adult children.[2] In less formal terms, this is part of a long-range study of South Asian Muslims in Canada extending over the last 15 years and very much based on personal involvement (Qureshi, 1972, 1983). Because of the personal and private nature of the data, care is taken here not to reveal identities; summaries are used, and where necessary, constellations of facts are changed, without, however, distorting their substance. This distancing mode of presentation, though out of tune with present trends in ethnography (Clifford and Marcus 1986), is one with which my friends and collaborators are comfortable, for it enables us all to share their way of living without exposing personal lives.

## MARRIAGE IN THE CONTEXT OF THE COMMUNITY[4]

At this juncture (1987) a good number of families have adult children, though families with younger children are more numerous. The second generation, then, is in the beginning of its adult phase, and the marriages investigated here represent the start of a process that will become more widespread within the next five to ten years. What characterizes the children of the older group is the considerable number of them who were born before immigration took place and who therefore often had early socialization by grandparents in the home country. In addition, the parents were both fully socialized, and married, in the home country. The importance of this fact needs to be seen in reference to certain special characteristics of South Asian social structure and the priorities these characteristics have generated. In addition, it also needs to be seen in reference to the religious norms established by Islam.

Most of the families marriageable children find themselves in are, for the most part, relatively stable and prosperous, especially those of the professional elite. The parental generation is fully adapted to take advantage of economic and social opportunities, and their children are on the way to doing the same by acquiring education and training and by striving to enter professions that have high socio-economic and status value.

In social terms, these families form part of well-established social groups that mostly share a regional background and are compatible in class and culture. Within these groups there is much visiting, which generally takes the form of an intense, reciprocal system of large informal dinner parties, in which children are normally included. These groups are subsumed within what their members themselves call "the community." In all larger cities, the community is formally organized in one or more "societies," usually under the name of Pakistan or occasionally Islam. There societies organize larger social and religious events, a number of which are usually connected with, or held at, the local mosque. These events, too, families normally attend with their children.

The vast majority of families from South Asia have made Canada their permanent home and look forward to a future here, as much as they maintain family ties with their homeland. There are, however, some exceptions who see themselves returning for retirement and who therefore retain a strong sense of belonging to a larger familial unit back home. Naturally, their view of the marital future of their children is also part of this more general focus regarding the family's future.

South Asian society, though comprising several widely differing religious groups — principally Hindus and Muslims — shares a common principle of group endogamy in a socio-economic system where division of labor, occupational specialization, and hierarchical control of resources are all based on the coexistence and continuity of separate social groups. Less rigidly practiced among Muslims, the endogamy principle nevertheless predominates, especially among occupational groups, whereas among the upper strata of Muslim society, given their small numbers and the incentive for political alliances, endogamy is less localized.

A concomitant to endogamy is societal control over the choice of marriage partners in the form of parental arrangements. The rules that govern these arrangements differ among Indian social groups primarily on the basis of religious tradition. For Muslims, the Islamic norms are put into operation, as follows:

1. Men carry the ultimate responsibility for societal arrangements, including marriage. This responsibility is reflected at two levels. First, marriage is contracted and witnessed by men, including a male representative of the bride — an established principle of Islamic law. Second, a marriage is initiated by the male side, that is, by the parents or agents of the groom. The female side must wait to receive "proposals"; the parents or agents of the bride can at best work informally to elicit them.

2. Women are in charge of carrying out the actual marital arrangements; underlying this practice is the general principle of allocating the public social sphere to men and the private domestic or familial sphere to women, which implies the social separation of women from non-related males — an established principle of Islamic social tradition.

3. Compensation for the restrictiveness of the above separation comes from the acceptability of marriage within the family, including marriage with first cousins of all categories. This practice is in keeping with the Islamic tradition, sanctioned in the Qur'an itself, although the Arab preference for patrilateral cousins (especially father's brother's or sister's daughters) is not shared by South Asian Muslims.[5]

4. Marriage within the kin group is further broadened in partner choice by the important principle of bilaterality that traditionally governs the reckoning of Muslim kinship, notwithstanding its strong patrilineality. This broadening has important implications where local contacts are unavailable — as is the case in the community under consideration here. Interestingly, the bilaterality principle too is rooted in Islamic social tradition.[6]

5. This bilaterality, however, does not extend to post marital residence. There the patrilocal principle predominates and extends to the general notion that offspring belongs to the patrilineage, another principle of Islamic legal tradition.

6. Women retain their identity after marriage. This norm is expressed in the fact that they retain the right to personal ownership, including both property and inheritance. Also included is the right to initiate divorce. While South Asian tradition is weak in implementing

these rights outside of a married woman's ownership of personal belongings (gold jewelry figures prominently), they are theoretically recognized as being laid down in Islamic law.

7. Procedurally, the marriage contract makes it possible to separate legal marriage (*nikah*) from physical marriage (*rukhsati*, or the bride leaving her natal home).

Commensurate with the background socialization and the socioreligious norms of South Asian Muslims,[7] it is clear that marriage in that group forms part of a societal or communal or familial strategy planned and carried out by its responsible adult members—that is, the parents of marriageble children. These children have traditionally no initiative to take and little to say beyond agreeing or, in the few families where this option exists, disagreeing with their parent's choice. Exceptions, of course, occur, especially where cousins know and choose each other, but they rarely run counter to the established rules of parental authority.

In accordance with these facts, I have, perforce, had to make the parents the focus of my study, although I have supplemented my findings with personal inquiry into the responses and viewpoints of the children, both married and unmarried. My own participant observation and sharing predisposed me to adopt this focus, for experience made clear to me a premise that formal eliciting might not have revealed in its full depth. It is this premise that I have developed into the following hypothesis:

> Among South Asian Muslims in North America, marriage is the culmination of a "social engineering" process that begins at the birth of a child and is designed to reproduce the family and the socio-cultural matrix it requires for survival. This process is rooted in the home society; men and women socialized in that environment become the social engineers who adapt this process to their new situation as first-generation immigrants in North-America.

The North American situation is characterized by two factors that make it differ from that of their home community: the children to be married have spent all, or at least some, of their lives living and being educated in North America; the parents' own life experience includes up to thirty years as settlers in North America. These factors and their implications present a serious challenge to the entire social engineering process: the challenge is marriage. Parents, especially mothers, are fully aware of this challenge and are ready to meet it; a good number have already done so. This paper focuses on the strategies of these marriages by examining their results and by inquiring into the process leading up to these results.

## PARENTAL GOALS

To begin with, parental goals for their children, as they are modified by the immigrant situation, need to be understood, for marriage forms part of the future vision parents have for their children, and that vision informs the actions taken in connection with marriage. At a general, "abstract" level, three such goals may be identified in the following order of priority:

1. The prime goal a parent pursues is to get the child "settled." Ideally, this process takes the form of an improvement in material and social status or at least its maintenance at a level equal to that of the parents. Implied here is success in the world of the majority society, but that success is validated in the immigrant community.

2. A second and equally essential goal for many parents is to retain the bond between themselves and their children, so that their own lifestyle is reproduced and they are able to live out their own lives according to the traditional pattern as parents of married children and later as grandparents. Implied in this goal too is community recognition and improved status as successful "elders."

3. From the second goal flows a third, which is, however, seen as subsidiary to the first goal and therefore may become subject to modification, or may even be abandoned outright. That parental goal, or desire, is to retain a controlling role in the lives of their children in the sense of the traditional life-cycle pattern in which the young are guided by the old: members of the group move from childhood and young adulthood, in which they are controlled by their parents, through marriage into parenthood and grandparenthood, in which they are able to be in control of their own and their children's lives.

In the North American environment, achieving the first goal means successful performance and interaction in a culturally and socially different world; indeed, it may mean adopting norms and practices different in form, if not contrary to those at home. Such adaptations are only seen as a problem where they interfere with family goals. Otherwise, the outside world can be given its dues, as it always has been, even in the home country. As an example, it is quite acceptable for women, especially married women, to work, even if that requires contact with men, since such interaction will be kept at a non-personal, public level.

The primary means of achieving material and status improvement is education and professional training, with particular preference given to professions deemed to be superior in status. These are, in order of general preference: medical doctor, lawyer, engineer, and accountant (now computer specialist). The main point to be made in this connection is that parents make sure to indoctrinate their children, especially boys, so that they will pursue these professional goals by building the identity of the child from an early age and by reinforcing their expectations rigorously, the specific form of this reinforcement varies from simple exhortation to detailed attention to the educational process.

Given the traditional separation of the male and female spheres whereby men are in control of the "outside" world, and women are in control of the "inside" world of the family, it follows that the approach taken toward realizing both principal parental goals calls for quite different methods of implementation vis-à-vis sons and daughters. Sons, who will become breadwinners and status bearers, need, above all, to be successfully educated. Parents generally spare no effort in achieving this goal, recognizing that, in addition to formal education, boys need to have initiative and competence to manage life in the public domain. Much is expected from sons once they are adults; to this end parents do everything to build up their goodwill. Boys generally grow up feeling secure and privileged; their dominant behavior is reinforced from early childhood, while duties, expectations, and responsibility are added gradually.

Restrictions on outside contacts are strong during early childhood; later, pragmatism generally prevails. Jobs are encouraged once high-school age is reached. In general, controlled or formalized activity is always given preference outside the home, as is activity with a profitable result (money or advancement in education). Higher education or professional training is a first priority for a boy; parents will do all they can to facilitate it, including buying the son a car when he starts university or medical school or investing heavily in sending him to a medical college back home if that is the only way to enable him to become a doctor.

A girl, on the other hand is traditionally raised for the "inside" or family sphere, although she, too, is seen as a potential achiever in terms of education and professional status, especially in professional families and in families where there are only daughters. Restrictions, however, are far more severe for girls than for boys throughout childhood. In the words of one mother: for a boy the answer is mostly "yes," for a girl it is always "no."

Considering now the second goal: In order to achieve the goal of maintaining family ties, family values, and practices and in order for parents to be able to live out their lives according to their expectations, they must bring up their children in a way that conditions them to accept fully the parental priorities and guidance. Essentially, work has to be done on two fronts. Most important, the values and practices of the family need to be inculcated and reinforced in order to create and strengthen the children's sense of identity. Secondly, outside influences potentially detrimental to the parent's goals need to be curtailed, neutralized, or kept at bay altogether.

Both sons and daughters are raised to expect an arranged marriage. From an early age, a negative evaluation of any free mixing of the sexes beyond the immediate family is clearly laid out to children, as are traditional values generally; seniority and experience qualify parents to guide their children's destiny, and social experience reinforces these teachings. Thus, the sexual spheres are clearly delineated, from separate seating at parties to everyday social activities in which boys naturally get drawn close to their fathers and girls to their mothers, resulting in very clear same-sex role modeling. In fact, sons and daughters are socialized very differently; hence, the process needs to be discussed separately.

## SOCIALIZATION
### Daughters

Starting from early childhood, girls are socialized into the traditional feminine role. Specific codes of dress and demeanor are encouraged, as is participation in the female sphere — care of family and home. Social occasions with community friends play an important role as a place where the girl's identity is validated. She sees herself and her role model—her mother—reaffirmed there, sharing in a celebration of the social universe in which her home life belongs and getting adult approval and admiration. In that setting, she can also share her personal experience with others raised like her, where she is safe to express positive and negative feelings about her home environment and its restrictive effect on life outside. Mothers are keen to shape their social life to include their children, especially their daughters.

On the other hand, outside social contact is discouraged. Generally, their only independent activity outside the house is going to school, though some families allow controlled outings like lessons and other organized education-related activities. The remaining time is spent at home studying or participating in home-related activity or in outings with the family, such as shopping and visiting. Parents encourage friendships between their children and will make the necessary effort to drive them to each other's homes. These relationships, however, are more common among the more numerous families with younger children; they have a larger group in which to find compatible friends than do the young people whose marriages are being considered here and who grew up in relatively greater social isolation.

Since schools are co-educational, girls are strictly instructed to stay away from dating of any sort or from any mixed-sex socializing that centers on boy—girl interaction. Parents find themselves in a truly difficult situation in this matter, since they know that their daughter's comportment must generate a reputation that comes up to the rigorous standard of their traditional society. Even here, the initiative for marriage proposals is entirely in the hands of the parents of sons. As a result, a family is intimately concerned with the reputation of its female members. The acute worry this situation generates leads some parents of growing daughters to take—or at least to consider seriously taking —such extreme measures as sending the daughter to school in the homeland, moving the entire family back home, or, most commonly, marrying their daughter at the earliest age possible.

Girls raised in these families, then, are fully prepared to accept a marriage arranged by their parents. The possibility of marrying an outsider is as unreal to most of them as is participation in the mate selection system of "white" society. They look forward to marriage as the start of a life of their own. As for a girl's own say in the choice of a partner, she knows that it is limited to the proposals actually received, which, in turn, are predicated upon factors which she knows to be beyond her purview. Indeed, behind her acceptance of her parents' role as her agents is the larger acceptance by a girl's family that success in the marriage process is ultimately a matter of fate (*qismat*).

### Sons

The traditional social role of boys is far more loosely defined. Beyond the structural acceptance of seniority, their domestic role is limited and distinctly less demanding than that of girls. As well, their participation in community social occasions is a relatively lower priority, especially as they grow towards adulthood, although for them too, this arena functions as a setting for the reinforcement of their social identity. For boys, affirmation and support from adults is less important than solidarity with peers, other boys like them, which lead to friendships that can be pursued independently. In addition, what those occasions of family socializing articulate for boys is the general pattern of the friendly separation between the sexes that they experience between themselves and girls their own age.

Outside home and community, boys have the freedom to make social contacts. Parents rely on the socialization process to ensure that, ultimately, their son will accept a traditional marriage arranged by them. Since their first priority for a son is to see him well educated, his interaction with outside girls is generally tolerated as long as it does not lead to deeper attachments. Once he is near adulthood, this may be part of a necessary amount of freedom he must be granted in order for him to achieve that first priority. At the same time, parents do their utmost to provide their son with home support that will help keep him attached to his parents and to the familiar home life that only his mother or, once he is married, a wife from within the community can provide.

A few families grant a similar amount of freedom and devotion to daughters who are in very demanding professional training programs, mainly medicine. In fact, parental expectations of these daughters appear to have the same priority as those of sons, with marriage temporarily taking a secondary place. At the time of writing, it is still too early to assess how the marriage issue will be dealt with by their parents.

Complementing the appropriate socialization of sons and daughters is the process of creating the social conditions that will activate potential marriage links. Doing so requires both general and specific action. At a general level, family socializing is carried out with a view to making the most of status and linkage. This strategy may operate only within the context of the local — that is, the North American — community, or it may also extend to relatives in the original home community, although there it is less crucial since family identity makes general status considerations irrelevant and the fact of living in Canada is itself an indication of high status. In particular, parents of girls must build up a desirable identity and establish appropriate links long before marriage partners need to be found. In the words of one mother: "You have to have those links to get those proposals."

The second strategy concerns the child directly: giving him or her social exposure. It is primarily important for girls and takes the form of mothers having their daughters accompany them to gatherings where other parents or possible intermediaries can see them and interact with them. The same strategy is an even greater priority if marriage partners are desired from the home country. In this case, the family will take a trip home or arrange a stay for the girl with a trusted close relative. Such a stay also reinforces traditional socialization. What is important is "to let people see that their daughters are growing up."

Finally, there is the all important economic dimension: parents must arrange for the necessary resources, especially where a son-in-law is sought from the home country. These include travel funds for all concerned, dowry, and resources for getting the immigrant established in Canada. It is striking to which extent South Asian Muslim parents are willing to invest everything they can in their children's progress, including both their education and their marriage.

## CRITERIA FOR CHOOSING A PARTNER

Parents have a constellation of criteria for selecting a partner for their child which, of course, are assigned different priorities by different individuals; they are described here in order of the general preferences. Like the socialization process and the process of establishing and managing social links, this enterprise is primarily in the hands of mothers and women generally.

For a son-in-law, two major criteria are agreed upon. One is competence, education or training that will enable him to provide a daughter with economic and social assets equal to or better than her parents. The second criterion is that there should be close ties between son-in-law and daughter's family. This criterion is ideally fulfilled by the son-in-law living in close proximity to his in-laws. Alternatively, a son-in-law who already has close family ties may be chosen even though he lives in the home country—provided he is well situated there. Underlying this set of criteria is the parental ideal of keeping close ties with their daughter even though the traditional social structure does not support this aim.

For a daughter-in-law, the major criterion relates to her integration into the son's existing family given the norm of patrilocality; it includes her adaptability to the son (and his parents), and, if possible, patrilocal residence. Since it is the son who will be provider, her education is more a social enhancement than an essential socio-economic asset.

The special situation of the immigrant family contains certain assets and liabilities that individual parents have learned to use to the best advantage. Two fundamental characteristics emanate from this situation, one negative and one positive. The separation from the larger family and home community is negative; the normal relationships are replaced by a very limited group of non-related nuclear families whose children, in the majority of cases, are as yet too young for marriage. Of course, there is the trend toward extending the family by means of sponsorship. However, in Canada, unlike the United States, only "dependants," that is, aged parents and children under twenty-one years of age can to date be sponsored. As a result, older young adults can only be brought in as non-earning students, an expensive and temporary proposition. And even sponsoring a sibling under twenty-one years of age requires prior or concurrent sponsorship of the parents—an undertaking of major social and economic proportions.[8]

The local community thus has a severely limited choice of possible marriage partners. There is, of course, the wider North American community of South Asian Muslims to which local communities have ties through other national and religious societies as well as through individual links. But these ties are seldom close enough to be activated for such a personal purpose as marriage.

In addition, there is also the larger Muslim community in North America—people of the same religion but a different culture area. Then there is the larger South Asian community—people from the same culture area but of different religions — and, finally, there is the larger Euro-Canadian majority, people different on both counts. Normally, all three fall outside the accepted boundaries of endogamy, even though the first is theoretically acceptable, for all Muslims, as is the marriage of a Muslim boy and Christian or Jewish girl, which would theoretically make a Euro-Canadian girl an acceptable choice for a son. But none of these choices are considered serious options by most South Asian Muslim parents, even though such partners were chosen by several of the girls who married on their own.

The positive characteristic emanating from the immigrant's situation is the very fact that he has a permanent right to live in the West, which by itself, in most cases, raises him above the rest of his family. And even if the family at home is equivalent in prosperity, the North American immigrant has access to international opportunities that even considerable prosperity in the home country could hardly match.

The key, of course, is permanent resident status. Obtaining such status is at present nearly impossible on the basis of professional qualification or even political exigency. Since family sponsorship is also highly restricted, marriage is the one great opportunity. Parents can use this powerful attraction in finding the best possible match for their child. This boon has several important dimensions. To begin with, the marital partner will get sponsorship himself. Obviously, this opportunity is most attractive for educational or professional advancement, both of which are more relevant for men than for women, given the traditional role expectations. In addition, once they are permanent residents, immigrant partners can sponsor their dependent relatives. For both men and women this can mean the beginning of moving other family members out of the homeland, a priority for South Asian Muslim families living in minority situations where political change has caused loss of status and insecurity.[9]

Clearly, the North American parent looking for a match in the homeland holds a position of great potential strength over his counterpart at home. This strength is particularly important for the parents of a girl, whose traditional position is relatively weak. While it does not change the traditional procedure in which the boy's parents play the decisive role, there is a special feature built into the assets of a North American girl's parents that differs from those of even a rich family in the homeland. That feature is the necessary bonding of the groom with his wife's family—given his initial dependence on them—along with the physical separation from his own.

Parents of the potential groom may, in fact, see this as a detriment, and so may the groom himself. The bride's parents can offset this feeling by offering their assets with extra liberality; they can afford to do so in the certainty of having the young couple within reach of their exclusive guidance. On the other hand, North American parents looking for a bride in the homeland will generally find that the traditionally expected separation of a married daughter from her natal family works to make her move to North America acceptable, as long as ties between the parents exist that would ensure visits. In addition, the opportunity for a daughter to sponsor her family's immigration can become an important motivator for agreeing to such a marriage.

With this background, it is now possible to examine actual marriage strategies using composite case descriptions. Together, these cases present what has so far emerged as the range of North American adaptations to the South Asian Muslim marriage pattern. Collectively, this range of strategies should allow some conclusions to be drawn about their impact on the South Asian Muslim Family in North America.

## MARRIAGE GOALS REALIZED: THE DATA

Tables 1 to 6 in the Appendix summarize the data assembled for this study. The marriage sex ratio clearly shows that the marriage of girls is a priority. This conclusion is supported by the fact that daughters invariably get married before sons, as is indicated by the number of married daughters who have unmarried adult brothers. There is also a disproportionate number of girls in the control group of unmarried young adults. There actually are more girls; but more important are the respective ages at which girls and boys are considered marriageable. Girls are traditionally considered ready for marriage by age sixteen or seventeen, boys not until at least their early twenties. Since the upper age range of both sexes is equally limited by the average age of the parents, the result is a considerably larger number of marriageable girls. Including only boys and girls of the same age range in the sample would have been mechanically accurate but socially irrelevant, for my purpose is to present a picture of the present composition of the marriageable young people in the community.

Given this situation, the marriage issue has clearly centered mainly on daughters, since far fewer sons have reached the age of marriage. A survey of both married and unmarried girls within the community reveals a two-pronged debate that has been surfacing among mothers of daughters: should marriage take precedence over education or vice versa? A good number of parents have opted for education, among them parents of only or several daughters. Of course, marriage plans have not been abandoned, only deferred. Some parents who decided on marriage for their daughters, also wish for them to continue higher education. But this goal is not proving easy to achieve, partly because of the role expectations of a wife, and partly because there is often a more pressing need for the young wife to earn money if she is to be active outside the home.

The vast majority of the marriages are arranged, as is to be expected. At the same time, the fact that about one-quarter of the marriages are not arranged needs to be put into perspective. Five of the ten families whose children married on their own, raised a total of eight daughters to be independent beyond the bounds of traditional society. A variety of factors account for this, among them a difference in the mother's religion (Christianity) or ethnic origin (Anglo-Canadian). Also, almost all the young women who married on their own are a number of years older than even the oldest among the arranged group. This is not to explain away unarranged marriages, but to place them in the perspective of the total group studied. It appears that these unarranged marriages lacked some factors that are essential prerequisites to successful marriage arrangements of a traditional kind.

Thirty-two of the fifty-five families examined have married children, twenty-seven of them by arrangement. On the other hand, twenty-three families have not chosen marriage for their adult children. The total number of girls married is forty, twenty-seven of them by arrangement, and thirteen on their own. The total number of boys married is fourteen, all by arrangement.

The arranged marriage, central, dominant, and socially valued, is what parents strive for, but this does not mean that they are unmindful of their children's wishes. On the contrary, most recognize their Western-raised children's increased autonomy, and they seek ways to allow them to express themselves in this matter. All the methods used, however, are solidly founded in the socialization process which makes the child confident that the parents will choose the best possible partner and reinforces that an independent search is inappropriate. Thus, parents will generally not involve the child in the selection process, but they may let him or her get acquainted with the chosen partner by correspondence, telephone, or even personal meeting. In effect, what is offered is the choice of refusal, but with the understanding that the preselected partner is the best the child can hope for. All this presupposes a great deal of solidarity on the part of the child, which is generally forthcoming. Equally, it presupposes a commitment of resources and devotion on the part of the parents which is forthcoming as well.

To show the actual marriage process and its result, I have constructed a set of representative composite cases from the data, so as to put flesh on the bare bones of the figures provided.

## CHOOSING FROM THE HOME COUNTRY
*Son-in-Law*

While there are some families in the home country, as well as in North America, who object on principle to marriage between close relatives, many accept and even favor it where suitable partners are available. Clearly, from a long-distance perspective, the prospect is particularly attractive because a closely related son-in-law belongs to the same "inside" sphere. The privileges and support he will be given thus constitute a direct contribution to the family. Such support may even include sponsorship for his parents, especially where one of them is the arranging parent's own sibling, a most desirable prospect for him or her. In addition, such a choice strengthens the truncated family's ties to the larger family in the homeland.

There are, of course, two families in the homeland: the father's and the mother's. But in the couple's absence, there is no active link between the two, and on the few visits home, time is usually strictly divided between the two "sides." While the father's family normally receives precedence on joint visits, the mother never develops the close ties with her in-laws which co-residence would have led to. For the father the reverse is even less the case, but since marriage-arranging is essentially in the hands of the wife, her priorities are more relevant. The data clearly show that mothers naturally select among their own close relatives: the largest single group of partners chosen are children of the mother's sister or brother. The mother's sisters or brothers are also the primary allies in finding a partner from a wider circle.

The actual process leading up to marriage will likely consist of an initial visit by the mother, possibly with the daughter, who can then be seen by the family. The daughter, too, will see her probable partner and possibly choose among several related boys, considering mainly their educational assets. On the other hand, an agreement for a marriage between their children may have been made by two siblings years ago. That would leave only the external arrangements to be made.

If no suitable choice is available—or desired—within the immediate family, the search is extended, usually with the help of a trusted close relative, since the North American parents will not have been able to maintain extended links in the homeland. In this situation bringing the girl home for a visit is an important strategy, especially if there is a family wedding where she will be seen by a wide circle of women who might be on the lookout for a bride. A North American mother is most likely to enlist her sister for help in eliciting and evaluating proposals, whether they come from distant relatives or from a family linked through friendship, profession, or common local origin. On the whole, the connection in all cases is far more likely to be one with the mother's rather than the father's family.

Since the understanding is that the boy will live with the bride in North America, the girl's parents will be more concerned with him than with his immediate family, as would be the case if all parties lived in Pakistan and close ties between the daughter and her in-laws were expected. The new position of strength North American parents of daughters find themselves in have resulted in new strategies that innovative parents pursue in their daughters' and their own best interests. The fact that traditional society frowns somewhat on a son-in-law dependent on his wife's parents does not seem to deter either side in planning marriages where sons from the home country move into their in-laws' exclusive sphere of control. The cultural assumption remains that the young man will assert his independence eventually, which should also enable him to extend the benefits of his North American residence to his natal family.

It is, of course, possible that the boy or his family may be opposed to emigrating and that the girl will have to move to the home country. In the case of a close relative, this alternative can be acceptable, especially where the parents are thinking of returning to the homeland on retirement. More immediately crucial is the financial ability of the Canadian parents to provide the resources for an immigrant son-in-law to get trained and established. If they cannot do so immediately and if for this or other reasons the couple is to live in the home country, sponsorship still remains an asset to be offered the boy's family, as is the girl's access to the material bounty of North America in the form of earnings acquired up to the marriage, the prospect of visits there, and access to medical care, including child delivery, which will also ensure that the children become Canadian citizens.

Thus, all possible future considerations are part of the planning of a marriage. Once an agreement is reached, the engagement ceremony is carried out and also the marriage, if the girl is present and old enough. Then the family returns to Canada, and the daughter sponsors her husband for immigration.

*Daughter-in-Law*

The few daughters-in-law chosen so far are almost all close relatives. Given the difference in priorities used in choosing a daughter-in-law the selection pattern is not surprising. Only three of the eleven arranged marriages involve family members, but those three are all first cousins. In other words, the priority of having a close family link and good family adaptation are asserted here, especially where a mother is able to choose for her son a daughter of one of her own siblings. This clearly is part of a mothers' strategy to ensure future closeness with her son's family, including the prospect of permanent co-residence or of sponsorship of the mother's sibling, that is, the girl's parents or possibly her younger sibling. Even in the case of a girl from a more distant family, sponsorship may form part of the marriage agreement, especially if that family is living in a minority situation. Otherwise, well-settled families are often reluctant to let their daughter be married abroad, since it generally means near-permanent separation.

Choosing a partner outside the immediate family requires an intermediary. Since compatibility and adaptability are high on the list of prioritities, the choice, particularly of a girl, needs to be made with the help of a woman. Here, too, weddings are prime occasions where mothers and their contemporaries can see and evaluate the girls. More recently, with the increase in the number of educated girls and the demand for them as brides, mothers have begun to rely on their daughters to find suitable brides for their brothers among fellow students and their families—another pragmatic adaptation of a traditional process.

## CHOOSING FROM EXPATRIATES

The very few cases that exist indicate two possibilities. One is to choose a relative (or family friend) already living in the West. This is clearly a desirable option, because the partner is already adapted to North American life, yet there are traditional ties that satisfy the need to reinforce the family's identity and lifestyle. For residents of Europe, where residence is hardly ever permanent, the additional advantage is that marriage in North America leads to citizenship and socio-economic opportunities.

Conversely, where the young person's family is well-settled elsewhere in the Western world, there may be less of an incentive for him or her to join a distant spouse. The limited data seems to suggest that the crucial factor is family support, that is, that there are relatives who can be relied upon to negotiate and back up the agreement. This potential problem is, of course, avoided if the young man can visit and then be dealt with directly.

## CHOOSING FROM THE LOCAL COMMUNITY

Arranging a marriage locally is, so far, a very secondary option, taken principally in response to one or more special situations. One is the absence of parents; instead, an older married sibling arranges a marriage for a younger brother or sister living with him. A local choice is made since the arranger has neither strong past ties with the home community nor a strong desire to keep his sibling very closely attached to him. A local arrangement is also a way of dealing sensitively with special conditions such as divorce or children from a previous marriage.

The other major motivation for a local arrangement is immigration for a non-permanent resident. Once again, as with home-country marriages, this case is advantageous for the family choosing a son-in-law, although as a local resident, he already has his own associations with friends or family and is thus not exclusively dependent on his wife's family.

So far, the age composition of the community does not allow enough selection to make a local marriage arrangement a viable alternative; but the situation is bound to change within the next few years.

## PARTNERS CHOOSING THEMSELVES

Although parentally arranged marriages are the norm, the sons and daughters of Muslim South Asians also partake of opportunities to choose their own friends through their contacts with the larger society around them. It is among children who grew up better integrated in the larger society that the skills and incentives to make their own choices appears to be present.

The fact that all unarranged marriages have been made by girls constitutes, I believe, an important statement about the primacy of marriage in a girl's socialization, even where traditional forms of marriage were not chosen or not available. The socialization of boys, on the other hand, gives marriage a secondary place after education and status achievement. Also, the far less restrictive upbringing of boys makes it possible for them to assert themselves creatively in the outside world and thereby to express their individuality vis-à-vis family tradition without breaking out of it. Since the restrictive socialization of girls allows minimal scope for such a move it follows that girls might well see "marrying into" the outside world as the only, though drastic, alternative. Furthermore, in Canada, as elsewhere in the Western world, girls are generally subject to male initiatives, whereas boys have to take such initiatives themselves —not an easy matter for many South Asian Muslim boys.

### THE MARRIAGE
*Partner from the Home Country*

The Muslim legal tradition of recognizing a legal marriage contract (*nikah*) as separate from its implementation (*rukhsat*) provides a flexible framework for marriage arrangements made over a longer time period, and it therefore facilitates long-distance marriages that require immigration sponsorship. Especially the provision that the Muslim marriage contract can be sealed by proxy makes it an adaptable tool for the situation of the immigrant family. Thus, after the choice of a partner is made, an engagement (*mangni*) is entered into; it, however, is only socially binding and has no legal validity.

Marriages are family occasions of prime importance, and in the home tradition great amounts of a girl's parents' resources are expended on its celebration. In the case of North American immigrants, however, the parents' community is now in North America, and they will properly wish to celebrate the marriage there. Before that can happen, however, the boy has to be sponsored, and that can only follow, not precede, his marriage. Here the separation between contract and consummation is put into play: the *nikah*, surrounded by a minor amount of ceremony, is carried out by proxy, using the telephoned consent of the groom in the homeland—a so-called "telephone nikah." On the basis of this contract, the girl can then sponsor her new husband. Once he arrives, a proper wedding celebration will be held, marking the start of the couple's married life. Essentially the same procedure is followed where the boy is an expatriate living in the West.

For the parents of a son, the situation differs, for it is the bride in the home country who is responsible for the wedding. Normally, an engagement takes place after the selection is made, and at a suitable time parents and son visit the home country for the wedding. Legal and physical marriage are generally part of the same celebration. But sometimes the arrangement is legally sealed first, possibly to initiate sponsorship early, or to create security for either side if no previous tie exists between the families. Then the *nikah* ceremony can be held by telephone. Choosing this option also allows for arranging the wedding in accordance with the financial ability and holiday opportunities of the groom.

As with a son-in-law, the arrival of a daughter-in-law will be followed by a lavish dinner party, traditionally given by the groom's family after the marriage has been consummated: the *valima*. Either way, the local family invites the community to witness and to celebrate the arrival of a new family member and to rejoice in the parents' successful completion of this most important step toward replicating their family.

## ESTABLISHING MARRIED LIFE
### Daughter and Son-in-Law

Parents with a son-in-law from the home country initially support the couple entirely. Even if the girl works, establishing a separate residence must wait until the groom can well support himself. If the parents can afford it at all, the groom will start by obtaining appropriate training, for most South Asian professional qualifications are not valid in North America. Even if he has the prized medical training, he will study for the necessary exams and then try for an internship. Engineering and other technical qualifications also require some local training for him to qualify for professional practice. Otherwise, the groom needs either to start a training course from the beginning or to establish himself in a particular line of work through employment.

In all situations, initial dependence on the in-laws is inevitable. Parents realise it can create stress, given the negative value the culture attaches to such dependence. One method of alleviating the situation is for the parents to help finance a separate living arrangement for the young couple. Then the wife can work while the husband gets the necessary qualifications. If there are children, the girl's mother will look after them so that the young wife can continue to earn.

### Son and Daughter-in-Law

For the newly arrived daughter-in-law to move into her in-law's house is a traditional norm that is followed here, given the fact that the son, too, has continued to live at home. In this way, the girl can be introduced to North American housekeeping and also to the opportunities available to her educationally and professionally. In comparison with the parental generation when young wives joined single husbands in North America, these young women escape the loneliness and insecurity that often beset their mothers-in-law, for there now exists a community welcoming them with open arms.

In unarranged marriages, the couples live separately, though some keep equally close links with their parents and enjoy both financial support and babysitting services.

## FAMILY AND COMMUNITY INTEGRATION

An integral part of getting the young couple established is for the parents to introduce the new partner to the community and to help both partners to assume their new social role as a couple. Tied in with this is the new role this implies for the parents themselves. They have achieved the crowning conclusion of successfully bringing up their child: getting him or her appropriately married. This fact alone visibly raises a couple's status in the community, and it adds to their self-confidence and their social authority, enhancing the seniority that comes with the adulthood of their children. What this enhancement will amount to depends on the qualities displayed by daughter- or son-in-law. For a son-in-law, professional qualification and success is primary. For a daughter-in-law, good looks and social demeanor come first; education is also a prime asset. For both, in addition, deportment and social skills become a crucial index of social standing. These assets come into play as the integration process takes place by means of the social currency already referred to earlier: the dinner party.

After the wedding, where parents introduce the new member of their family to the community, their friends, in turn, undertake to welcome the new couple into their homes, thus including them in their social group. "The proper" occasion is a grand dinner party given for them and their parents. The round of parties is carried out enthusiastically because other couples, most of whose children are younger, rejoice in the successful achievement of a goal that is shared by all. In the young couple, they see the embodiment of an ideal and proof that it can become reality despite the pitfalls of life in the "diaspora." Thus, the young couple is warmly included in the social group of the parents.

In turn, the new couple is, in time, also expected to assume its own social responsibilities by attending community functions and condolence gatherings. Unless they have their own home, however, they are not expected to extend independent invitations, although when they do so, it represents a measure of their stature as full members of the community.

The birth of a child represents a further step in enhancing the seniority of both grandparents and parents. It also solidifies traditional ways and values, since these can now be recreated in the process of the baby's and child's socialization that will begin under the grandparent's influence.

In sum, what we witness in the Muslim community from South Asia is a process of community-building, extending into the second generation by means of marriage. The process is a testimony to the social skill and commitment of community members, most of all of mothers, who undertake the full responsiblilty for its management. As for their children, there is so far no indication that they are in disagreement with their role in this process, even in the case of those who have married on their own—at least where their partners have the necessary cultural affinity, religious or social. Significantly, partners of Western origin seem to be the exceptions here.

## CONCLUSION

In the entire discussion of marriage strategies, two essential dimensions have been rather neglected if not ignored outright, for the simple reason that it has been possible to outline the marriage process by making scant reference to one and by ignoring the other. The first and obvious dimension is the vantage point of the young people who are the subject of the marriage strategies discussed. It appears to assert itself mainly when expressed in action against the traditional intent of parents. For a few girls this has taken the form of independent marriages outside the community. For boys, even this indication is missing. Yet, in discussing marriage with young people, married and unmarried, it becomes clear that they do have opinions on the qualities of partners. And they consider it desirable to marry after higher education; indeed, many girls see marriage and the schooling or training process as mutually incompatible. But these opinions are subsumed within a larger view of marriage as being a matter properly to be handled by parents or elders generally—as coming from above, so to speak. The marriage partner they see as someone to be accepted as one accepts one's sister or brother.

However, this does not mean that marriage has the immutability of sibling ties. After all, Muslims have the provision for separation and divorce, and it is recognized by children as well as parents that a marriage choice may turn out to be wrong. Muslims have a great deal of healthy realism regarding bad marriages! Nevertheless, the process of acquiring a spouse is one these children will leave to their parents, and they accept that it may take place with a minimum of input on their part.

The other dimension is contact with the larger North American community, especially in the case of children who have had their schooling in North America. South Asian Muslims certainly do not live in complete isolation from the majority community, yet in matters of marriage the larger society is not involved; their own community is very much the focus of reference.

This fact points up a crucial reality about the nature of the South Asian Muslim family as a bilaterally extended kinship sphere surrounding the nuclear family. The concern with marriage as a community-oriented process is really the expression of a *family*-related need: the need to situate the nuclear family within what amounts to an extended network of family-like relationships, for it is within such a network that marriages are traditionally arranged. Here in North America, such a network has had to be created between non-related nuclear families. However, this network cannot, at least at this time, supply an adequate choice of marriage partners. It needs reinforcement from the "real" extended family in the home country. The fact that these choices can include marriage partners related only by the remotest of ties highlights the fact that association, not actual blood ties, constitutes the active principle of the bilateral extended family that enables members to activate the most tenuous link by mutual consent. At the same time, that principle can operate only upon a solidly established base structure of descent and marriage. In North America such a structure is presently absent, and, ultimately, only intermarriage within the North American community can begin to create it. That process is perhaps beginning to take place, although marriages within the community so far seem mostly to have taken place in response to special needs rather than as a result of preference.

What we have seen is how senior members are acting to create a new generation for the immigrant community through marriage arrangements, and then to integrate the new members into this "family" constituted by the circle of their friends. However, whether the "community" will continue to play the role of an extended family into the adult life of the second generation remains to be seen, or, indeed, whether the new nuclear families arising from the marriages discussed will continue to need the "community" in that role. Certainly, the first generation of immigrants is doing its utmost to generate such continuity and, though marriage strategies, to pass on the social climate of well-being and mutual support that sustains them as individuals in their life within the larger North American society.

## Notes

1. The Bengali-speaking majority of Muslims from Bangladesh form a somewhat separate community not dealt with in this paper.
2. For a summary of the data, see Appendix, Tables 1 to 6.
3. For a repetition of this process in North America, pp. 207-8.
4. For a discussion of the dynamics underlying the development of this community, see Regula B. Qureshi and Saleem M.M. Qureshi, "Pakistani Canadians: The Making of a Muslim Community," in *The Muslim Community in North America*, eds. Earle H. Waugh, Baha Abu-Laban, and Regula B. Qureshi (Edmonton: University of Alberta Press, 1983), pp. 127-48.
5. The only stated preference my own research in South Asia has revealed—but no more than sporadically—is for mother's brother's daughter.
6. Robert Murphy and L. Kasdan, "The Structure of Parallel Cousin Marriage," *American Anthropologist* 61 (1959), 17-29.
7. Abul Hasan Ali Nadvi, *The Musalman: Social Life, Beliefs and Customs of the Indian Muslims* (Lucknow: Academy of Islamic Research and Publications, 1972).
8. It is worth noting that the difference in sponsorship laws in the U.S. seems to have something of a beneficial effect on the marriage perspective, at least on the basis of informal observation.
9. Whether or not they will actually do so in the end is not relevant here.
10. See Qureshi and Qureshi, "Pakistani Canadians," for a discussion of this process.

## APPENDIX: DATA TABULATION

*Table 1. Cases Studied*

|  | Daughters | Sons | Total |
| --- | --- | --- | --- |
| *Families* |  |  | *55* |
| with married children |  |  | 32 |
| *Children* (of |  |  |  |
| marriage age) | *66* | *31* | *97* |
| Unmarried | 26 | 17 | 43 |
| Married | 40 | 14 | 54 |
| arranged marriage | 27 | 14 | 41 |
| unarranged | 13 |  | 13 |

Table 2. *Marriage Partners: Origin*

a) *Arranged Marriages*

| | Husband (for daughter) | Wife (for son) | Total |
|---|---|---|---|
| South Asian Muslim | 27 | 14 | 41 |
| Home Country | 22 | 9 | 31 |
| Euro-America | 4 | 1 | 5 |
| Local Community | 3 | 2 | 5 |

b) *Unarranged Marriages*

| | | | |
|---|---|---|---|
| Home Country | 1 | | 1 |
| *Local Community* | 12 | | 12 |
| South Asian, Muslim | 4 | | 4 |
| South Asian, non-Muslim | 1 | | 1 |
| Non-South Asian, Muslim | 1 | | 1 |
| Majority Community | 6 | | 6 |

Table 3. *Arranged Marriages: Initiators*

| | |
|---|---|
| *Parents* | 34 |
| No specific initiator | 7 |
| Mother initiated herself | 15 |
| Mother initiated through relative | 12 |
| Sibling | 6 |
| Daughter | 3 |
| Other kin | 3 |
| *Married Brother* | 4 |
| Wife initiated | 3 |

Table 4. *Arranged Marriages: Relatives Chosen*

|  | Husband (for daughter) | Wife (for son) | Total |
|---|---|---|---|
| *Mother's Relative* | 9 | 3 | 12 |
| Sister's child | 2 | 2 | 4 |
| Brother's child | 2 | 1 | 3 |
| Brother's wife's brother | 1 |  | 1 |
| Maternal cousin's child | 1 |  | 1 |
| Distant kin | 3 |  | 3 |
| *Father's Relatives* | 4 | 2 | 6 |
| Sister's child | 1 | 1 | 2 |
| Brother's child |  | 1 | 1 |
| Sister's husband's brother | 1 |  | 1 |
| Distant kin | 2 |  | 2 |

Table 5. *Arranged Marriages: Residence*

|  | Daughter (with husband) | Son (with wife) | Total |
|---|---|---|---|
| With parents | 9 | 4 | 13 |
| Near parents | 3 | 4 | 7 |
| Separate | 15 | 2 | 17 |
| Home Country | 4 |  | 4 |

Table 6. *Arranged Marriages: Wife's Occupation*

|  | Daughter | Daughter-in-Law | Total |
|---|---|---|---|
| Housewife | 7 | 7 | 14 |
| Studying | 8 | 1 | 9 |
| Working | 12 | 2 | 14 |

# Family Stability among African-American Muslims

## Na'im Akbar

◆    ◆    ◆    ◆

### BACKGROUND FACTORS

The social and historical factors that have shaped the African-American family are so potent that any subset of those families must be viewed in the broader context of these factors. Much of the contemporary structure and the stability, or problems these families face have their origin in factors that have affected all African-American families. At best, the African-American Muslim family has a unique arena of solutions and ideals that may not be available to the more traditional African-American Christian family.

African-American families have occupied the center of much social science research and controversy over the last one hundred years. DuBois (1909) and Frazier (1934, 1939) produced the first meaningful scholarship, focusing on their economic conditions and the "problems of family by disorganization." Daniel P. Moynihan (1965) found himself in the heat of controversy when he attributed most of the problems in the black community to the nature of black families.

In recent years, a more progressive trend among African-American scholars has produced a literature focusing on the adaptive strengths and positive aspects of the black family. Scholars such as Billingsley (1968), Hill (1971), Ladner (1971), McAdoo (1981), Nobles (1974, 1976), and Staples (1973) have demonstrated in their work that many of the negative images that exist are the result of imposing Euro-American ethnocentric values on black family life.

Most prominent has been the work of those scholars who have argued for an understanding of black family life as "African root and American fruit" (Nobles, 1974:10). This argument adopts the position that African-American families (and their life in general) must be understood as being African in nature and American in nurture. Their important features represent a continuity of African patterns of family life within an American context. The African-American family is not a variation of the European-American family structure.

There is growing historical evidence that the vast majority of West Africans who were made slaves in America came from either Islamic African or traditional African religious backgrounds (Austin, 1982). Few were Christian before contact with their European-American slavemasters. In fact, Austin has documented that there were highly influential African Muslims in antebellum America.

Combining these two areas of research on the historical influences on African-Americans reveals some important points of connection. If African-Americans are fundamentally African in their worldview (Nobles, 1972), then there should be an even more evident affinity for the Islamic values among this displaced group. This study will not be directed towards the elaboration of the "African genesis" hypothesis; rather, the concept provides a workable context for understanding some important aspects of the African-American Muslim family.

Four fundamental aspects characterize these families:

1. The African-American Muslim family shares with other African-American families the characteristics of a family structure whose roots are African.

2. The American slave experience and subsequent oppression have altered this historically functional family style in fundamental ways, making it unlike its parent African structure and unlike the European-American model to which it is often compared.

3. The problems encountered in the African-American Muslim family are very similar to those found in the African-American Christian family.

4. Islam as established in the forty-year history of the Nation of Islam and the more contemporary structure offered through the concepts

of its inheritor, Imam W.D. Muhammad and his followers, has offered a socially and historically significant remedy for many of the problems found in African-American family life in particular and for human family life in general.

## THE DEVELOPMENT OF THE "BLACK MUSLIM" FAMILY

Between 1933 and his death in 1975, Elijah Muhammad built one of the most impressive social reform movements in the African-American community since the work of the Honorable Marcus Garvey. This movement, known as the "Nation of Islam," was based on a rather idiosyncratic interpretation of the religion of Islam as it was taught to Elijah Muhammad by an Arab silk peddler named Wallace Fard Muhammad in Detroit in the early 1930s. The movement grew to a membership of several hundred thousand (some estimate that as many as half a million people were members at the height of the movement) over the course of the forty years that Elijah Muhammad led it. There were congregations of Nation of Islam converts throughout the United States, Canada, and the Caribbean Islands. The movement controlled millions of dollars in assets and huge parcels of land, and it also had an international educational system.

The membership of the Nation of Islam was restricted to African-Americans, and this restriction was the source of most of its negative publicity. Through the best-known treatise on the Nation of Islam, written by noted religious sociologist, C. Eric Lincoln (1961), the group came to be known in popular parlance as "Black Muslims." Despite the fact that the group was never identified with the initiation of violence, there were militant reactions against it because of its provocative and strongly anti-white rhetoric. Imam W.D. Muhammad in subsequent years characterized the Nation of Islam as follows:

> The Nation of Islam was a religion and a social movement organization. In fact the religion as it was introduced to the membership was more a social reform philosophy than Orthodox Islam. (Marsh, 1984:51)

Elijah Muhammad's social reformation was certainly directed towards the African-American family. Much of his instruction and many aspects of the organization were directly geared towards improving its conditions. Family life was primarily associated with the effective role of the African-American woman. Elijah Muhammad wrote that

> Until we learn to love and protect our woman, we will never be a fit and recognized people on Earth. . . . My beloved brothers, in America, you have lost the respect for yourself. You won't protect her; therefore you can't protect yourself. Your first lesson comes from your mother. If you don't protect your mother, how do you think you look in the eyes of other human beings. (1965:58-59).

Elijah Muhammad equated womanhood with the source of good family life and said that the role of the man was to ensure the respect and protection of the woman. His analysis concluded that slavery and oppression in America had damaged the family by undermining respect for the African-American woman as well as by causing her to lose respect for herself. He operated with the assumption that the restitution of family life in the African-American community could be accomplished by the restoration of respect for the woman (Akbar, 1984). He encouraged the black woman to avoid self-negating identification with white women. Mr. Muhammad instructed his followers to:

> Stop women from trying to look like them. By bleaching, powdering, ironing and coloring their hair; painting their lips, cheeks and eyebrows; wearing shorts; going half-nude in public places; going swimming with them and lying on beaches with men. . . . Stop them from going into bars and taverns and sitting and drinking with men and strangers. Stop them from using unclean language in public (and at home), from smoking and drug addiction habits. Nothing but Islam will make you a respectable people. (1965:60)

These prohibitions were similarly reinforced for men in the relevant areas of conduct. Striking in most of his teachings was the constant reminder that Islam was the instrument that would make a difference in the lives of African-American people.

To enforce these standards of conduct, Elijah Muhammad established classes for women called "The M.G.T.G.C.C." (Muslim Girl's Training and General Civilization Classes). These classes taught basic domestic skills such as housekeeping, child-rearing, and hygiene. Women in the organization were required to adhere to the following rules, referred to as the laws of Islam:

1. Do not use lipstick or makeup.
2. Do not wear hair up unless wearing long dress.
3. Do not smoke or drink alcohol.
4. Do not commit adultery.
5. Do not use pork in any form.
6. Do not cook in Aluminum utensils.
7. Do not wear heels over 1 1/2 inches.
8. Do not dance with anyone except one's husband.
    (Marsh, 1984:59-60)

These laws were enforced by public exposure and suspension or expulsion from the movement.

Muslim men were instructed in proper conduct in the men's classes called the F.O.I. (Fruit of Islam). There were similar rules for them to follow and similar means of enforcement. In these classes men were taught respect for women, the importance of supporting and protecting women, and the value of family responsibilities.

Family life was identified as the only proper Islamic life. Premarital and extramarital relations were strictly forbidden. Marriage and family life were considered as fundamental religious responsibilities of the Nation of Islam, and the community served as the primary source of enforcement for the strict marital code of the Nation of Islam.

The irony is that all evidence suggests that despite these stringent moral codes, the Nation of Islam held considerable appeal for young people, primarily young men. Dr. Lincoln observes in his important document:

> A suprising number of young people are attracted by the Muslims' redefinition of the roles men and women should play in the home and in the religious life of the sect. There is a strong emphasis on the equality of individuals irrespective of sex, but each sex is assigned a role considered proper to itself. The trend in our larger society today seems to be toward blurring the distinct line between the traditional social roles of men and women. The Muslims, on the other hand, claim to have restored the woman to a place of dignity and respect, while restoring to the man his traditional responsibilities as head of the family. Muslim women seem to welcome this security and protection implicit in this arrangement and the men seem to exhibit a deeper sense of responsibility than is common to others of the working class. Children seem to

profit the most, for among Muslim children, delinquency is un-
heard of. (1961:33)

There is little empirical evidence on how successful the Nation of Islam was in accomplishing its goals. The protected and carefully
guarded inner world of Muslim life during the time of the Nation of
Islam did not permit very many social scientists to examine the personal behavior of the Muslim community. One of the very few such
studies was conducted by sociologist Harry Edwards (1968). He used
focused interviews to compare a group of Nation of Islam families with
a matched group of lower class "Negro Christians," and he looked at
four areas of family relations: husband-wife, extended kinships, parent-
child, and family-community. The most striking evidence of the success of the Nation of Islam in restructuring critical family relations for
the African-American community is found in Edward's study.

The Muslim families in Edward's sample reported that all major decisions, such as where to live and what purchases to make as well as
when to make them, were made by the male. This finding contrasts
with the situation in Christian families, where the females made the decisions. Edwards concluded that:

> The Muslim families, by contrast, through family role definition
> prescribed by Black Muslim dogma, have established for them-
> selves a more patriarchial family system. This role clarity appeared
> to reduce intrafamily conflict considerably. Muslim respondents
> regarded intrafamily conflict of any type as totally unnecessary
> and by contrast, the Christian respondents thought such conflict
> to be unavoidable and some physical violence inevitable if two
> people lived together long enough. (1968:606)

Though Edwards's study only included fourteen Muslim families
and an equal number of Christian families, the trends he reported were
consistent with impressions from other observers (Lincoln, 1968;
Essien-Udom,1962). Edwards draws a rather interesting conclusion
that "in the area of family-community relationships, the Muslims typified the wage earning, non-criminal, middle-class ideal to a greater extent than did other Christians." He continues:

> Although the Muslims are shown to be lower class in terms of in-
> come, education and general environment, they are very middle

class in many other respects—especially with regard to such issues as sex practices, the value put upon education (with some qualifications), personal hygiene and grooming, the high value placed upon work and industriousness, and their intense interest in developing and maintaining a high degree of mental and physical alertness. These are clearly not the characteristics typically found to exist throughout the lower class Negro-subculture. (1968: 606)

Another aspect of the teachings of Elijah Muhammad was the emphasis on racial purity in marriage and family relationships. One objective of the Nation of Islam was not only the restitution of family life but the restitution of racial pride. Implicit in Mr. Muhammad's philosophy was the idea that the deterioration of African-American family relationships resulted from the absence of racial pride and an identification with European-American values and standards of beauty. He believed strongly that the racial pride of African-Americans had been systematically destroyed during slavery and the subsequent years of oppression. He emphasized that self-love was fundamental:

One of the greatest handicaps among the so-called negros is that there is no love for self, nor love for his or her own kind. This not having love for self is the root cause of hate (dislike), disunity, disagreement, quarreling, betraying, stool pigeons and fighting and killing one another. How can you be loved, if you have not love for self? Love yourself and your kind. (1965:32-33).

He spoke firmly against interracial marriage:

The most foolish thing an educator can do is to preach interracial marriage. It shows the white man you want to be white. . . . What are we going to integrate for? What do you want to marry a white woman for, when we are black men? That is going to ruin our family. We will spot up our family. What does she want a black man for? Or what does the black man want the white one for? (1965:60)

Marriage difficulties and divorces did occur in the Nation of Islam. A family and marital counseling system was readily available through the leaders of the women's and men's groups (the M.G.T.G.C.C. and the

F.O.I.). When family conflicts occurred, the captains of these respective groups were ready resources for assistance in resolving them. Many of these marital problems were produced by the economic and social positions of poorly educated and economically indigent members of the Nation of Islam. Community leaders could not resolve these problems, but when families sometimes found themselves in severe financial straits, the "Temple" was a source of refuge. Financial aid was available only in very dire circumstances because everyone was encouraged to provide for himself and his family.

## THE CHANGES OF W.D. MUHAMMAD AND
## THE GROWTH OF AFRICAN-AMERICAN ISLAM

With the death of Elijah Muhammad came radical changes in the forty year-old Nation of Islam. Most of the customized interpretations that were structured to address the unique problems of the African-American community were eliminated with the entrance of Elijah Muhammad's son, Warith Din Muhammad, into the leadership of his father's organization. Imam Muhammad described his new organization (which for a brief period of time was renamed the World Community of Islam in the West) in the following terms:

> The W.C.I.W. is an organized social movement and a religion but in line with Quranic teachings. The old Nation of Islam was not in line with the Quranic teachings. (Marsh, 1984:89)

Imam Muhammad's concept of how to restore strong family life in the African-American community was quite different from that of the Nation of Islam. He radically altered the dress, the codes, the rituals, and the concepts of the group. For example, as Marsh observes:

> There is also a change in the nature of the Muslim Girls' Training and General Civilization class. Traditionally, the classes taught " . . . the basic principles of keeping the house, taking care of the children and taking care of her husband." The class has been changed in name and substance. . . . "The Muslim Woman's Development Class" established by Wallace Muhammad, looks at life in a broader sense. She is encouraged as a woman to fulfill her

mental capabilities. . . . Wallace Muhammad justifies the new status by saying, "We cannot make any distinctions between men
and women in terms of intelligence, spirituality or moral nature.
Women are equal with men and they are not to be treated any differently." (1984:96)

By 1979, the women's and men's classes were eliminated altogether.
We shall say more about the current role of women in our discussion
below.

Despite the radical change in concepts and practices, Imam Muhammad did not alter his commitment to the establishment of strong family life among his followers. Imam Muhammad emphatically teaches
the Islamic foundation and necessity of family life. In a lecture addressed to the responsibilities of the Muslim male, he observes:

> Some of you are afraid of marriage because you are afraid of
> obligation. If you want to improve your situation the best way is
> to marry. Prophet Muhammad (PBUH) said "marriage is half
> your religion." Now you brothers who are not married, how do
> you feel living just half of your religion, if you are living that half?
> What is the other half? He said the other half is service to Allah.
> He said half of the religion is marriage and the other half is ser-
> vice to Allah. So you have to take care of your family and then
> serve Allah. (1986:5)

Imam Muhammad follows the lead of his father in seeing the family
as a social and tribal function as well as a religious obligation. He observes:

> The key to strengthening the community is strengthening the
> home. The key to strengthening the race is to strengthen the
> household and it begins with the man's responsibility. The mem-
> ber of the family that's the most responsible person is supposed to
> be the male member, the adult male member in that household;
> the husband, the father. (Ibid.)

Despite the disappearance of the F.O.I. and the M.G.T.G.C.C. under
the leadership of Imam Muhammad, he continues to offer instruction
on appropriate family conduct and male and female roles. It is these

concepts which stand as the best characterization of the image of family life present among the largest indigenous Muslim group in North America.

## CONCEPT OF FAMILY ROLES

The ideal of the Islamic family epitomizes the doctrinal changes that Imam Muhammad has tried to instill into his altered structure of the former Nation of Islam. His emphasis has consistently been an orthodox Islamic one, suggesting that the only proper practice of the religion follows the instruction of the Qur'an and the example of Prophet Muhammad (PUBH). These changes have not occurred without some criticism, but the open challenge to his doctrines has been limited.

One major oppositional challenge comes from the former spokesman of the Honorable Elijah Muhammad, Minister Louis Farrakhan, who has garnered considerable publicity over the last several years. His major effort has basically been to maintain the strong social and ethnic emphasis of Elijah Muhammad's doctrines, while acknowledging the importance of orthodox Islamic ideas. He views these ideals as normative for an Islamic society, but he finds the more traditional doctrines of Elijah Muhammad to be more relevant to the particular needs of the African-American Muslim community. Though there is evidence that his movement is still growing, it is very small in comparison to the following of Imam W.D. Muhammad. Minister Farrakhan has maintained the men's F.O.I. classes and the women's M.G.T.G.C.C. classes as a means of teaching proper male and female conduct. Though the dress and conduct of Minister Farrakhan's followers are closer to those of Elijah Muhammad's original movement, there have been some notable changes, probably as a consequence of the radical shifts made by Imam Muhammad in his movement.

Dr. Dorothy Fardan, in a book based upon Imam Muhammad's teaching, describes Imam Muhammad as teaching that the "basic institution of any society is the family" (1981). An obvious responsibility of these families is the parenting role. According to Imam Muhammad:

> The parents are supposed to provide shelter, or home, food, clothing and an education. In our religion, parents are obligated to provide an education for their children. (1986:5)

The family roles are more explicitly identified as they relate to male and female responsibilities within the family. Imam Muhammad says of the man's role:

The male parent should look for opportunities to get into some kind of employment that will enable him to take care of the needs of his children. He should never accept the kind of situation in his life where his children are needy and he is doing nothing but tolerating a situation like that. That's not Islamic. In this religion . . . there is no way for you to escape your responsibility. Don't say "I can't find a job." You have to keep looking for a job. You have to look for a job every day and spend all day looking for it. . . . Keep looking because you are responsible for your wife's food, clothing and shelter. You are responsible for your children's food, clothing, shelter and their education. You shouldn't rest until you find a way to earn enough money to pay for your child's Islamic education. (Ibid.)

In addition to the economic responsibility that Imam Muhammad describes for the Muslim man, he is also clear in contrasting this responsibility to that of the Muslim woman:

If the woman will help you, good. If she will share some of her money with you, good. If she'll work sometime and help, good. If she'll take a full time job, that's good if you really need that. But you can never take the position as a Muslim that she owes you that. She does not owe you that. In this religion, you owe her to keep you from having to do that . . . the more you leave your woman dependent upon outsiders, the more you are going to leave your race dependent upon outsiders. If you want to get your race out of dependency on outsiders, start right in your home and get your woman from being dependent on outsiders. (Ibid.:5-6)

This quote also shows that Imam Muhammad has not completely deserted his father's emphasis on the need to deal with the ethnic community problems within the religious context.

It is also evident that despite the assertion of equality between men and women which is a prominent aspect of orthodox Islamic doctrine as taught by Imam Muhammad, the differentiation of roles between men and women is in no way diminished. Dr. Fardan characterizes Imam Muhammad's position as follows:

> A woman can experience mentally whatever a man can, in her own way; but in day to day life, she is more often concerned with the affairs of children, home, feeding, caring for, looking after. Her mind moves in unison with this natural pattern. But man is by nature inclined towards the open marketplace, the arena of social affairs; he has no babies to carry from here to there; is not required to stop for nursing a baby. He must lead everyone and himself, or at least make a good try. . . . Man, not woman, is in his essential nature the producer of worlds (social or mental worlds). He is by nature the leader of society. Woman is by nature not the leader of society. Woman is by nature the womb or reflector of the leadership. (1981:110-11)

As in the teachings of the Honorable Elijah Muhammad in the early Nation of Islam, the emphasis is placed on the role of the woman as the mainstay of the family. In much the same sense, there is a focus on the importance of dignity and respect for the woman as a foundation for strong family life:

> Al-Islam gives true liberation to the woman by highly honoring her role of wife and mother in the society as a most sacred and essential one. Western society does not present dignity and respect for the role of wife and mother as Allah guides us. Al-Islam not only establishes honor for the woman in the home but also assures her right to grow from her primary role to roles in the outer society. Husbands can bring leadership to the family and the society by helping the wife see and value the great role Allah has given the woman.
>
> It is through the degree of superiority that Allah has given the man, the greater the physical strength and more freedom to amass wealth, that he is able to maintain and protect the family and grow to leadership in the community. This provides the woman the security and the means to establish the homelife and rear the children.
>
> Mothers must bear in mind that Allah has entrusted the young life to the mother to shape and mold for the society. (El-Amin, 1985:9)

Not only is there an appeal to the dignity of womanhood, which is a strong Islamic tradition both in Orthodoxy and in the Nation of Islam, but also there is a strong sense of liberation presented to the woman as well.

Though there is no M.G.T.G.C.C. under Imam W.D. Muhammad's leadership, there are still some rather explicit expectations about the Muslim's woman's conduct. One of Imam Muhammad's appointees and assistant editor of the *Muslim Journal* newspaper is Imam Nuri Muhammad. In a recent article entitled "The Muslim Woman's Dress," Imam Nuri Muhammad specifies some of the details:

> The Muslim woman should conduct herself to maintain the strength of character required to carry out the responsibility of being the first teacher, and to maintain the influence she should have in general.
> 1) The Muslim woman (as well as the man), is discouraged from gazing into the eye of the opposite sex.
> 2) Not mixing freely with men in such a way that their bodies come in contact with them.
> 3) Her clothing in public must conform to the standard prescribed in Islam, that is: her garment should cover her entire body; they should not be light, thin or transparent revealing what is underneath; her dress should not be so tight as to define parts of her body; she should not wear styles of clothes which are specifically designed for men; in the choice of clothing, Muslim women should not imitate non-Muslims. (1986:6)

Some of these requirements are very similar to those under the Nation of Islam and, of course, to those among orthodox Muslims in general. However, without the strong organizational support system that existed in the Nation of Islam, there is much less adherence to this code than existed when the dress code was strictly enforced by the M.G.T.G.C.C.

In the same article, Imam Nuri Muhammad observes:

> The morals and manners of the Muslim woman is quite different than the non-Muslim woman. Though among all people can be found aspects of goodness and congeniality, the guidance which the Muslim woman accepts from Islam is holistic and therefore is

reflected in all aspects of her life. The Muslim woman is chaste, dignified, self-respecting and modest while the trend today is for women to be vain, showy and anxious to display their attractions. Many women who fall into this trap of vanity are many times unaware of the effect of the media on creating the images by which they live.

In these days of heightened feminism, such traditional characterizations of the role of woman do not escape criticism from both Muslim and non-Muslim women. It is interesting to note, nevertheless, that very few, if any, women followers of Imam W.D. Muhammad have voiced critical opposition to these descriptions of women, which have brought intense reactions from Christian women, both European and African-American. Imam Alauddin Shabazz, another follower of Imam W.D. Muhammad, observes in a *Muslim Journal* article:

An issue on which al-Islam is somewhat regularly attacked is with regards to the status of women. It is purported by both overt and covert enemies of Al-Islam that according to the teaching of our *din* (i.e. religion) women are considered inferior to men, have no rights and were created solely to be instruments of sexual pleasure and child breeding. This report is false. As Muslims, we must combat such lies. (1985:7)

Karima Omar takes a Moroccan Muslim feminist to task for her attack on the sexist practices of the religion. She observes:

her condemnation of al-Islam, the religion of Asiya, Aisha, Khadijah, and Naseba; of Humama and Safiyya and Zunaira and a host of heroic women is inexcusable, absurd, and utterly self-defeating. She has fallen head-long into the trap which so many non-Muslims slip into—that of confusing al-Islam with the (mis)actions of Muslims. (1986:13)

Another issue that has resulted in some controversy among African-American Muslims is the Qur'anic authorization for more than one wife. During the time of the Nation of Islam, this was a privilege limited to the leader of the movement, the Honorable Elijah Muhammad, who maintained several wives and their children. It was an established fact among the adherents that this was a permissible practice in the religion, but that it was one which only the leader was able to practice in a just and correct way. Except in some isolated cases, it did not arise as an issue in the Nation of Islam. Polygamy had long been an appealing aspect for large numbers of indigenous American Muslims, who were attracted to other Sunni sects, particularly after the early 1960s. It became a real issue for the World Community of Islam in the West (and the subsequent American Muslim Mission) only after Imam W.D. Muhammad instituted orthodox Islamic authority over his followers. Large numbers of his followers sought and established polygamous marriages, which they viewed as consistent with the orthodox Islamic doctrine that Imam Muhammad had firmly authorized for his followers. Consequently, Imam Muhammad had to speak out against the practice, while still maintaining its legitimacy as a Qur'anically authorized activity.

His supporters occasionally found it necessary to defend Imam W.D. Muhammad's contradictory behavior in this regard. Imam Nuri Muhammad, for example observes:

> Imam Warithhuddin of Masjid Elijah Muhammad in Chicago has strongly discouraged his community from entering polygamous relationships. For this he has been criticized by some Muslims in the United States. The criticism, however, is unfounded and is based on the allegations that the Imam, by discouraging polygamy, is making haram (prohibited), what Allah has made halal (permissible). However, to discourage a thing is not equal to making it prohibited. The Imam has not said that polygamy is haram; he has said that the kind of Islamic environment for the proper practice of it is not available and that the laws of the United States do not recognize such marriage and therefore offers no protection against its abuse. (1986:6-7)

## FAMILY STABILITY AMONG AFRICAN-AMERICAN MUSLIMS

As yet there has been no systematic effort to assess how successful the followers of Imam Warithhuddin Muhammad have been in implementing the high Islamic values discussed above. Certainly, at the observational level, African-American Muslims are no longer easily distinguishable on the basis of the clean, modest appearance and industrious conduct that characterized the followers of the Honorable Elijah Muhammad and that even, to some extent, characterizes the followers of Minister Farrakhan in his new version of the "Nation of Islam."

Some insight into family stability may be gained by examining the *Muslim Journal*, which still speaks primarily to the followers of Imam Muhammad, who in April 1985 dissolved the organization of the (then named) American Muslim Mission which was the progenitor of Elijah Muhammad's Nation of Islam. The *Muslim Journal* carries a weekly article written by Mildred El-Amin, who acts as a "Dear Abby" for what remains of this organization. Mrs. El-Amin's weekly "Family Life" series responds directly to questions from readers regarding their personal problems. Apparently she consults frequently with Imam Muhammad regarding her responses, and it can reasonably be assumed that her answers represent his thinking on the issues she addresses. Her columns also provide a sampling of problems that exist within this community or, at least, among persons who are willing to seek help through this anonymous form of correspondence. If the Muslim Community is like other groups in this regard, those who are likely to write express in milder ways some of the difficulties that exist to a greater extent among the wider community. There is no way to determine how prevalent these problems are, but we are certain that at least some of Imam Muhammad's followers give voice to concerns that are typical throughout the society, particularly among poor African-American families. In fact, the kinds of concerns are very similar to those raised in other open formats. What differs is the kind of advice that is given, the source of authority for that advice, and the values that are summoned in addressing the concerns. Some examples from Mildred El-Amin's weekly "Family Life" column will give an idea of some concrete issues confronting African-American Muslim families.

A not unusual question is this one from a Muslim Sister:

Question: What should a sister do when she is trying to follow al-Qur'an but after almost five years of marital difficulties she has run out of tolerance, patience, understanding and trust in her husband. We have lived in houses without water and lights, and in unsanitary conditions. We've been put out-of-doors, gone without food and it wasn't the month of Ramadan and had no T.V., radio or telephone. He is suspicious of me and other people. He does not believe a woman should work outside the home.

(Partial) Answer: If the marriage contract is not being fulfilled, as Allah has designed, you should ask yourself is this really a marriage? Do we have a true marriage in the sight of God? Qur'anic permission to terminate the relationship is only given if it becomes absolutely impossible for a couple to continue together. (1985,10,50:9)

Not all questions come to the "Family Life" column from sisters in distress. A significant number of letters come from brothers with problems such as the following:

Question: We have been married for 15 years, been in the Muslim community 13 years and have three children. What am I to do? My family life is falling apart. My wife and her sister, if not together physically, are talking on the phone day and night. Her sister's husband and I disapprove of this because we cannot live our own lives. When my house is upset or we are having a disagreement, her sister's home life is also in disagreement. My wife's sister leaves her husband out of anger, my wife leaves too, and they both go home to their parents. They are non-Muslims but good people.

(Partial) answer: The Holy Qur'an cautions one against interfering with or hindering the marital success of others. Persons outside the marital union, whether invited or uninvited, can come in and bring confusion which may cause problems and division between a couple. (1985, 11,1:9)

Mrs. El-Amin seldom quotes secular authorities as a source of information for resolving family problems. She is strict in her adherence to the idea that the Qur'an, the traditions of Prophet Muhammad (PBUH), and the teachings of Imam Warithhuddin Muhammad provide the strongest guidance for family problems. A typical example is the following:

Question: How can a husband and wife Islamically carry on the negotiations that continuously are required in a marriage?
Answer: The discussions, compromises and agreements that are necessary in marriage on an on-going basis require mutual respect and balanced input on the part of the husband and wife. Most of the problems human beings have in relationships

whether it be a business relationship or a sacred one such as marriage, come from not speaking in straight and open words, explains Imam W.D. Muhammad. By fearing to speak an open straight word, Imam Muhammad cautions, God is telling us that this makes for a lot of trouble.
There is no relationship closer than that of husband and wife. Therefore, there is no room for secrecy in a marriage. The first secret begins to untie the marriage knot. (1985, 10,47:9)

Many of the questions that come to "Family Life" also suggest that the Muslim community is not as successful in enforcing its code of conduct as the Nation of Islam was. Questions like the one below speak very directly to the occurrence of unchecked adultery within some relationships:

Question: My husband and I (married for 15 years) have for a lot of years experienced difficulties. Some problems resulted from his being unable to provide sufficiently and his adultery. My feelings and love for him have badly deteriorated. I'm still married because of the children and because he is against divorce where there are children. I am afraid it may be affecting the children in a negative way. I feel caught up with no right answer or solution.
(Partial) answer: Islamically, every effort should be made to save a marriage, especially when children are involved. But, Islamically, the liberty of man and woman to have a divorce should not be restricted. Al-Islam recognizes the woman's right to seek an end to an unsuccessful marriage. "If their intention is firm for divorce, Allah heareth and knoweth all things," says the Holy Qur'an (2:227). The Qur'an clearly sets forth the laws governing divorce. (1985: 11,5:9)

As is the case in the broader society, one seldom hears of the successful cases, but only the problematic ones. The fact that a considerable number of people continue to look to Imam Muhammad for leadership suggests that there is a successful contingent of African-American Muslims who are applying the teachings of the holy Qur'an and of Imam Muhammad to the problems of marital and family life. On the other hand, it is clear that this group is no longer the exemplary group described by Harry Edwards, C. Eric Lincoln and Essien-Udom in their writings on Elijah Muhammad's "Nation of Islam". They seem to be much more like the ordinary American family and to share the unique adjustment difficulties of other members within their sub-group, that is, working-class African-American Christian families.

Several characteristics appear to stand out in this survey. First, there is a strong connection between the values espoused by the Muslims and family stability. Thus, commitment to the notions of an ideal family propounded by both Elijah Muhammad and W.D. Muhammad has provided a viable environment within which to develop positive family values. Secondly, in some ways the reformist doctrines have served to integrate African-American Muslims into a class structure consonant with other working-class people in America, so that there are no essentially different status markers between them. Moreover, the African-American Muslim family has become more at one with all those whose roots are African, including the larger black Christian community. Thirdly, leadership has played a crucial role in setting the standards and interpreting them for rank and file believers. Indeed, without such quality and vision the family of which we speak might not have existed. Finally, much additional research must be done to determine the specifics of the impact that religious ideology has had on the African-American family and to suggest where that will lead in the future.

# Muslims in North America: Mate Selection as an Indicator of Change

## Ilyas Ba-Yunus

◆ ◆ ◆ ◆

This study examines the mate selection experiences of North American reared Muslim youth in comparison with traditional Islamic practices. Korson (1969:155) has suggested that "if one were to predict the source of change from the norms of a society one would look to the younger generation to initiate such change in an area which so vitally affects them, viz., mate selection." Accordingly the issue of change is examined by focusing on the young, marriage eligible men and women born to more recent Muslim immigrants.

### BACKGROUND

Muslims are no strangers to North America. Historically there have been at least three major episodes of Muslim migration to the United States and Canada. First, although there are few records available, there is a strong conjecture, especially among blacks, that a number of slaves trapped in West Africa and subsequently sold in the east coast colonies were Muslims. Alex Haley's *Roots* (1976) fictionalizes this very theme. Secondly, there were sizeable migratory chains in the nineteenth century from such predominantly Muslim areas as Syria, Turkey, and the Punjab (Nyang, 1983). Thirdly, and most important here, there has been a great influx of students from Third World countries, including a number of Muslim countries especially during the post World War II period. Only a few of these students were allowed to settle in North America before immigration laws were relaxed during the period 1965-71. Many of those who were finishing their higher education in Canada and the United States at the time decided to take advantage of this opportunity and eventually become citizens. Benefitting from the same relaxation of these laws, many professionals working in their home countries were also able to immigrate. There has never been a total count of the North American Muslim population. According to Ghayur (1981), during the twenty-year period following 1960, at least two million Muslims were admitted, and the process is still continuing, presumably with a pyramidical progression.[1]

What is significant about these relatively new immigrants is that most of their children have been born on this continent, and those who were not have mainly been raised in North America. Many of these children are already in college.[2]

Like many other immigrant groups who do not readily assimilate, Muslims in general seem to cherish community life, but unlike other ethnic groups, they do not generally live in physical proximity. The evidence of the existence of a sizeable and active Muslim community is the existence of a mosque. Except for those that are located at or near large campuses with active chapters of the Muslim Students Association, most mosque activities are held on weekends. Mosques come to life on Fridays at congregation time and they offer a number of programs oriented toward children's education in the Qur'an and such other Islamic sciences as law, history and morals. They are also used for festivities, including marriages, and community dinners. With their well-furnished halls and other meeting rooms, they serve primarily as symbols of Muslim existence, much as churches signify the Christian life around them. Hence, mosques are a matter of great pride among Muslim communities. But they also reflect a sense of ambiguity, of fear as well as hope, particularly among the new immigrants with respect to their children. At some level, all Muslim parents—even those who are successful and benefitting from living in North America—are afraid of what they consider to be North America's inferior moral standards, especially the sexual laxity, criminality, and drug abuse among juveniles. They hope that by offering community-based education at weekends, their children will develop a degree of Islamic identity that could shield them from this perceived moral decay (Ba-Yunus, 1975).

In short, Muslim community life in North America is aimed at maintaining a certain amount of Islamic behavior, especially regulating sex and family life. As an ideology, Islam deals mainly with the regulation of three institutions: the polity, the economy, and the family. An Islamic polity is impossible in a non-Islamic society, and practicing an Islamic economy is also difficult, if not impossible. As a result, the family sphere, according to al-Faruqi (1972), is by far the most significant for Islam in minority situations. It is little wonder, then, that morals and rules regarding sex life and marriage constitute a fundamental aspect of Islamic community education in North America.[3]

## MARRIAGE AMONG MUSLIMS

Although marriage is not imposed as a duty upon its followers by Islam, *hadith* (Sayings and Traditions of the Prophet Muhammad) emphasize marriage in no uncertain terms.[4] Hence, there is a great abhorrence of celibacy among Muslims, and it is believed that all normal persons marry. Eligible males and females must marry as soon as their circumstances allow; the individual who does not marry without apparent reason, must have something wrong with him or her (Bean and Afzal, 1969; Kirk, 1966).

There are four major elements in Islamic marriage that have a bearing on this study. Firstly, marriage is strictly a social contract between the principals; it is not a sacrament. Thus, like any other contractual situation, marriage often involves a protracted period of negotiations among relatives, neighbors, and other go-betweens who may benefit if and when the marriage is finalized. Also, like any other civil contract, the marriage contract must be witnessed by at least two adult, sane Muslims. It must be officiated over by a *qadi* (literally, a judge), who acts on behalf of the state. More significantly, the explicit consent of the principals is required; they are given a veto power that can negate the whole marriage proceedings if one of the partners does not voluntarily agree to the conditions of the contract.

Secondly, the marriage contract cannot be finalized without mentioning *mehr*, a sum of money or a piece of property which the groom gives to the bride at the time of the wedding or promises to give to her later, on demand. "Under Muslim law, a marriage without mehr is not legal, so some amount is always specified in the contract" (Prothro and Diab, 1974:37). Mehr has been translated as dower, but it must not be confused with the bride price. In Islam, mehr is the right of the woman alone. No one else, not her father, her guardian, or her husband, can legally claim it, nor has anyone else the right to mehr. According to Levy (1962:5), mehr reflects a stage in the emancipation of woman from concubinage and slavery through bride price to the Islamic stage, where a gift is paid to the bride alone. Thus, Korson points out:

> The dower is paid to the bride at the time of the marriage, or payment can be deferred to a later time, either on demand or at the time of separation or divorce. Should the wife predecease her husband, he is freed of his obligation to pay the balance of the dower. Should the husband predecease the wife, then, the unpaid portion of the dower serves as a lien against the husband's estate and is due her in addition to her share of the estate. In any case, dower is irrevocable. It provides a form of security for the woman should the marriage fail and a separation or divorce occur. (1969:154)

What this means is that a woman enters her marriage as a propertied person in her own right. Marriage, according to this Islamic injunction, signifies a change not only in her social status but also in her economic status.

Thirdly, marriage in Islam is basically a family rather than an individual affair. The right of consent or the veto power on the part of the marrying partners notwithstanding, men and women in Muslim society are not allowed to make their own selection in the marital market place. The reason for this apparently paradoxical situation lies in the Islamic injunction against the mixing of unrelated males and females, which effectively segregates the population into two separate worlds.[5] In a more strict sense, this segregation makes it next to impossible for eligible men and women to have premarital social and sexual proximity. Only when the young eligibles are near relatives is this restriction relaxed to some extent, allowing them some limited room for premarital romantic rendezvous. Or, as Lipskey (1959:53) pointed out, it is quite possible for a young man in the desert to see a young woman "among the camels" and become infatuated with her looks. In urban environments, where today men and women meet in places of education and work, they may "like" each other to the extent that they directly or indirectly inform their parents of their wishes. However, such situations are not a norm in an Islamic society. Even in modern Muslim cities, the norm is to let the parents and kin initiate and decide the matter while the young person maneuvers to give the final consent. It should not surprise us, then, that even college-educated youth in countries like Pakistan do not think it necessary for them to see their future spouses before they are married (Korson,1969).

On the surface, it might seem that mehr would strengthen the role of the principals in the marriage. In fact, quite the contrary is true; the mehr is typically decided by the father or the mother, who then conveys the decision to the child (Prothro and Diab, 1974:34).

Thus, although no marriage would be consummated without the expressed consent of the principals, parents play a crucial role in the marriage of their children. To say that marriage among Muslims is a family affair, then, is to say that the family members on both sides play roles as brokers, negotiators, and decision-makers to such an extent that even in cases of self-selection, due respect to the parental authority has to be maintained.

Fourthly, the restriction on social and sexual proximity between the sexes indicates that love is not highly valued as a primary reason for marriage. In fact, as Lipskey pointed out:

> the general attitude is that love should grow out of marriage, not precede it. Not romantic love but proper social arrangements and satisfactory material circumstances are regarded as essential foundations for a successful marriage. (1959:53)

This negation of love as a prelude to marriage in a "purdah society" (Papneck, 1971) does mean that there are a greater number of restrictions imposed on women. However, these restrictions automatically constrain the male maneuvers also. Thus, in describing the society, Goode observes that

> Ideally, the Arab groom could not choose his own bride, since he never had an opportunity to see her until the marriage contract had been concluded; he usually waited until the wedding day itself. (1963:88)

Marriage in Islam, then, has generally followed parental preferences. Once parents and other relatives on either side finish their job and the marriage takes place, it is hoped that love will emerge at first sight between the groom and bride, who most probably have never had a heterosexual encounter in their lives before.

## METHODOLOGY

The 245 responses that form the basis of this analysis were derived from a sample consisting of 136 males and 109 females whose parents were recent immigrants to the United States and Canada (1960 and after). About 50 percent of them (N = 132) were born on this continent, while the remainder were minors when they arrived with their parents. With the help of the Muslim Students Association, which maintains active chapters at nearly all larger campuses, the main sample was drawn from four American campuses and one large Canadian one. These students were given a ten-page questionnaire which focused on a number of political, economic, and social issues, including their present and future marriage prospects. The data were then subjected to a $x^2$ analysis mainly in order to see if there were any sex differentials regarding these issues.

## FINDINGS

The findings that are presented below pertain to three main issues in Islamic marriage, namely, premarital heterosexual contact, parental role in marriage, and attitude toward mehr.

## PREMARITAL CONTACT

Since close encounters between unrelated and especially unmarried males and females are not permissible in Islam, we wanted to know whether or not, and to what degree the North American college environment, which promotes premarital dating, has a pulling effect on our subjects.

Table 1 shows that a majority of our subjects (56.3 percent) do not date; and if we collapse the "Hardly Ever" category and combine it with the "Never" category, this percentage goes to more than 66 per-

## TABLE I
## Frequency of Dating

| | | Quite Frequently | Not Very Frequently | Once in a While | Hardly Ever | Never | Total |
|---|---|---|---|---|---|---|---|
| Males | N | 28 | 22 | 22 | 13 | 51 | 136 |
| | % | 20.6 | 16.2 | 16.2 | 9.5 | 37.5 | 100 |
| Females | N | 11 | 0 | 0 | 11 | 87 | 109 |
| | % | 10.0 | 0 | 0 | 10.0 | 80.0 | 109 |
| Total | N | 39 | 22 | 22 | 24 | 138 | 245 |
| | % | 15.9 | 8.9 | 8.9 | 10.0 | 56.3 | 100 |

$x^2 = 58.95$     df = 4     p < .01

Percentages are rounded to the nearest whole.

cent or about two-thirds of the sample. However, what is striking here is the difference between the males and the females ($x^2 = 58.95$). While 37.5 or close to 40 percent of the males said they have never dated, 80 percent of the females fell into this category. In fact, if we collapse the "Hardly Ever" category and combine it with the "Never" category, the proportion of the non-dating males still remains below 50 percent while that of the females reaches 90 percent. There are also some other notable differences between the two sexes in the sample. While 20 per-cent of the males said they date quite frequently, only 10 percent of the females fall into this category. Also, while there are infrequent and ca-sual daters among men (31 percent), there are no such females.

The second interest we had was to find out from those who date their reasons for doing so.

TABLE 2
Reason for Dating

|  | | Males | Females | Total |
|---|---|---|---|---|
| 1. Soon you are going to | N | 20 | 8 | 28 |
| marry the person you date. | % | 23.5 | 36.4 | 26.2 |
| 2. You are engaged to marry | N | 31 | 3 | 34 |
| the person you date. | % | 36.5 | 13.6 | 31.8 |
| 3. You like the person that you | N | 10 | 0 | 10 |
| go out on a date with. | % | 11.8 | 0.0 | 9.3 |
| 4. You like to go out with nice | N | 7 | 0 | 7 |
| people. | % | 8.2 | 0.0 | 6.5 |
| 5. You go out on a date only | N | 17 | 11 | 28 |
| when you are invited to a | % | 20.0 | 50.0 | 26.2 |
| party. | | | | |
| Total | N | 85 | 22 | 107 |
| | % | 100 | 100 | 100 |

$x^2 = 14.22$     df = 4 p<.01
Percentages are rounded to the nearest whole.

Table 2 shows the $x^2$ analysis. Close to 60 percent of those who date do so because they are engaged to or are going to marry the person they go out with. Likewise, if we combine the response to the first three items in Table 2, close to 70 percent of our subjects who date do so probably with the same person because they are going to marry him or her or because they have a great liking for that person. However, the $x^2$ analysis shows a significant difference between the two sexes. Females date because they are going to marry or because they have been invited to a party (presumably by the person they go out with). Other reasons for dating, such as "I like the person" or "To be with nice people," are non-existent. Males, on the other hand, have a much wider spread of reasons. Although a majority of them (more than 70 percent) seem to be "steady" daters because of future marriage plans or because they like a specific person, the rest of them do it for the sake of companionship or partying.

We also asked our subjects if they had gone out on dates with non-Muslims.

A majority of them (64.5 percent) reported that they had never done so (Table 3.), but if we combine "Hardly Ever" and "Never" categories, the percentage of those who avoid dating non-Muslims is slightly over 70 percent. Among the rest, frequent dating with non-Muslims was rare (1.9 percent), although casual or infrequent dating was not uncommon (10.3 percent and 16.8 percent respectively). Although the $x^2$ analysis shows that there is no significant difference between males and the females in this respect, more males (65.9 percent) than females (59.1 percent) seem to avoid such situations. However, those females who went out with non-Muslims did so extremely infrequently, whereas males did so with a visibly higher frequency.

## PARENTAL AUTHORITY

Table 4 is based on the responses of the seventy-four subjects who reported that they are going to marry soon or are engaged to be married. Here, we wanted to know how important a role their parents played in the selection of the future mates for their children. In the light of the finding that about 66 percent of the subjects either do not date or avoid dating, the findings in Table 4 are not a surprise. This table shows that fully 77 percent of the subjects indicate strong parental authority in mate selection. What is surprising is that despite this strong parental role, sixty out of these seventy-four, or close to 84 percent are dating—some of them, including females, quite frequently.

TABLE 3
Dating Non-Muslims

| | | Quite Frequently | Not Very Frequently | Once in a While | Hardly Ever | Never | Total |
|---|---|---|---|---|---|---|---|
| Males | N | 2 | 11 | 13 | 3 | 56 | 85 |
| | % | 2.4 | 12.9 | 15.3 | 3.5 | 65.9 | 100 |
| Females | N | 0 | 0 | 5 | 4 | 13 | 22 |
| | % | 0 | 0 | 22.7 | 18.2 | 59.1 | 100 |
| Total | N | 2 | 11 | 18 | 7 | 69 | 107 |
| | % | 1.9 | 10.3 | 16.8 | 6.5 | 64.5 | 100 |

$x^2 = 8.346$    df $= 4$  p $> .05$

Percentages are rounded to the nearest whole.

TABLE 4
Mate Selection

|  | | Males | Females | Total |
|---|---|---|---|---|
| 1. Your parents chose your future spouse and then informed you. | N | 2 | 0 | 2 |
| | % | 3.5 | 0 | 2.7 |
| 2. Your parents chose your future spouse after they consulted with you. | N | 14 | 5 | 19 |
| | % | 24.6 | 29.4 | 25.7 |
| 3. You left it up to your parents to choose a future spouse for you. | N | 28 | 8 | 36 |
| | % | 49.1 | 47.1 | 48.6 |
| 4. You chose your future spouse after you consulted with your parents. | N | 3 | 1 | 13 |
| | % | 17.5 | 17.6 | 17.6 |
| 5. You chose your future spouse and then informed your parents | N | 3 | 1 | 4 |
| | % | 5.3 | 5.9 | 5.4 |
| Total | N | 57 | 17 | 74 |
| | % | 100 | 100 | 100 |

$x^2 = 0.735$    $df = 4$    $p > .05$
Percentages are rounded to the nearest whole.

The $x^2$ analysis in Table 4 shows that male and female would-be-marrieds do not differ significantly ($p > .05$) with respect to parental authority. Only 23 percent show autonomy in this respect. Finally, although it may be only a chance occurrence, the two subjects who reported the strongest parental role in their future marriages were both male.

Because of the general absence of mate self-selection in Muslim society, the fixation of mehr is a parental responsibility that further enhances their authority in the marriage of their children. Not surprisingly, then, the findings in Table 5 reinforce those in Table 4.

TABLE 5
The Fixation of the Mehr (Perceived)

|  |  | Males | Females | Total |
|---|---|---|---|---|
| 1. Your parents would fix the mehr in your marriage and then would inform you. | N | 0 | 0 | 0 |
|  | % | 0 | 0 |  |
| 2. Your parents would fix the mehr in your marriage after having consulted with you. | N | 41 | 51 | 92 |
|  | % | 30.1 | 46.8 | 37.6 |
| 3. You would, most probably, leave it to your parents to fix the mehr for you in your marriage. | N | 61 | 41 | 102 |
|  | % | 44.9 | 37.6 | 41.6 |
| 4. You would fix the mehr in your marriage after having consulted with your parents. | N | 25 | 12 | 37 |
|  | % | 18.4 | 11.0 | 15.1 |
| 5. You would fix the mehr in your marriage and then would inform your parents. | N | 9 | 5 | 14 |
|  | % | 6.6 | 1.8 | 5.7 |
| Total | N | 136 | 109 | 245 |
|  | % | 100 | 100 | 100 |

$x^2 = 7.96$    df = 4    p > .05
Percentages are rounded to the nearest whole.

Table 5 shows that close to 80 percent of our subjects perceive a strong parental role if not authority in relation to their marriage. Only about 20 percent of our subjects show some autonomy in this respect. Although the $x^2$ analysis does not show much difference between the sexes regarding this issue, at the extreme end of the scale, the males tend to show a relatively greater amount of independence than the females (6.6 percent vs. 1.8 percent).

## ATTITUDE TOWARD MEHR

After we saw how our subjects perceived the actual role their parents would play in the decisions regarding mehr in their marriage, we wanted to know what our subjects thought was the ideal role their parents should play.

TABLE 6
Fixing the Mehr (Ideal)

|  |  | Males | Females | Total |
|---|---|---|---|---|
| 1. Your parents should fix the mehr in your marriage and should then inform you. | N % | 0 0 | 0 0 | 0 0 |
| 2. Your parents should fix the mehr in your marriage after having consulted with you. | N N | 34 25.0 | 17 15.6 | 51 20.8 |
| 3. You should leave it up to your parents to fix the mehr for you in your marriage. | N % | 52 38.3 | 40 36.7 | 92 37.6 |
| 4. You should decide about the mehr in your marriage after having consulted with your parents. | N % | 38 27.9 | 42 38.5 | 80 32.7 |
| 5. You should decide about the mehr in your marriage yourself and then inform your parents. | N % | 12 8.8 | 10 9.2 | 22 8.9 |
| Total | N % | 136 100 | 109 100 | 245 100 |

$x^2 = 4.689$    df = 4    p > .05
Percentages are rounded to the nearest whole.

The findings presented in Table 6 show that a relative majority (92 or 37 percent) of the subjects think that ideally they should leave it up to their parents to decide this issue; and although none of them would like to leave this matter exclusively in the hands of their parents, 32 percent thought it would be ideal if they made the decision in consultation with them. There is also a minority (8.9 percent) which would like ideally to see a great deal of independence from their parents in this respect. Finally, although there is little difference between the sexes, relatively more females (about 48 percent) than males (about 37 percent) would like to see a greater role for themselves with respect to this issue in their marriage in the future.

For the sake of comparison, we also ran a $x^2$ analysis between the marginal totals in Table 5 and 6. This analysis shows a rather large $x^2$

TABLE 7
Attitude toward Mehr

|  |  | Males | Females | Total |
|---|---|---|---|---|
| 1. There is no room for mehr in this day and age. I think that it must be abolished completely. | N | 11 | 0 | 11 |
|  | % | 8.09 | 0 | 4.49 |
| 2. Mehr is like buying or selling a woman. I do not like it. It must not remain mandatory. | N | 17 | 0 | 17 |
|  | % | 12.50 | 0 | 6.94 |
| 3. I do not have any opinion about this matter one way or the other. | N | 39 | 30 | 69 |
|  | % | 28.68 | 27.52 | 28.16 |
| 4. With such a high divorce rate these days, mehr must be continued as mandatory. | N | 33 | 42 | 75 |
|  | % | 24.26 | 38.53 | 30.61 |
| 5. Whether you like it or not, mehr is provided by God. Just for this reason alone, it has to be continued. | N | 36 | 37 | 73 |
|  | % | 26.47 | 33.94 | 29.80 |
| Total | N | 136 | 109 | 245 |
|  | % | 100 | 100 | 100 |

$x^2 = 27.59$     df $= 4$     p $<.01$
Percentages are rounded to the nearest whole.

value (29.76), a considerable difference (p<.01) between the two totals. A glance at these two tables shows that this shift from the perceived to the ideal role that parents could play in deciding this issue is mainly the result of a hope for more liberalization among our subjects. (Table 6 shows that more than 40 percent of our subjects opt for the last two categories compared to only 20.8 percent in these categories in Table 5.)

Finally, we wanted to know whether or not our subjects would like to see the practice of mehr continue as a necessary element in Islamic marriage.

Table 7 shows that while slightly over 11 percent of our subjects are against the continuation of this practice, fully 60 percent of them are in favor of it and about 28 percent do not have any opinion. On the other hand, the $x^2$ analysis shows a significant differences between the sexes (p.<01). This difference may be attributed mainly but not entirely to a greater conservatism among the females in our sample. While none of them is against the practice of mehr, more than 70 percent of them are in favor of continuing it for pragmatic as well as for purely religious reasons.

## SUMMARY AND CONCLUSIONS

This is one of the first empirical studies on the Muslim family in North America, and consequently it is exploratory in nature. There was no hypothesis to test and no theory to present as a by-product. Likewise, the Likert type of scaling and the $x^2$ tests applied in data collection and its analysis are some of the least rigorous and sensitive techniques in social science methodology. Thus, the findings must be read with some caution. There have to be many more studies before any definitive statements can be made about the problems of adjustment among recent Muslim immigrants to North America.

These shortcomings notwithstanding, this research has yielded some easily discernible patterns that deserve consideration. For instance, our subjects show an overwhelming reluctance to depart from prevailing Islamic practices with respect to all the dimensions that we considered, that is, dating, parental authority in marriage, and attitude toward mehr. First, more than 66 percent of them either do not date or hardly ever go out on a date (Table 1). Also, 77 percent of our subjects who are going to marry soon or who are engaged to be married report a strong parental role in the selection of their future spouses (Table 4). Likewise, close to 80 percent of them foresee a strong role played by their parents in the decisions of mehr at the time of their marriage (Table 5). Moreover, relatively fewer but still a majority (58.4 percent, Table 6) think that parents should play a strong role in this matter, with only a tiny minority that wishes for a subsidiary parent role in this regard. Lastly, an absolute majority of them (60 percent) are in favor of keeping the practice of mehr as a necessary element in their marriage.

Although males and the females in our sample do not differ in many respects, females in general seem to be more conservative. For instance, while less then 50 percent of the males in our sample never or hardly ever date, the proportion of the females reaches the neighborhood of 90 percent (Table 1). Also, while only 40.7 percent of the males are in favor of keeping the practice of mehr, more than 72 percent of the females support it for pragmatic as well as religious reasons (Table 7).

On the other hand, we found some strong undercurrents of departure from the Islamic ideals among our subjects. For instance, although males are definitely more active among those who date, females who date do so quite frequently and not occasionally as many males do (Table 1). Likewise, it may be small comfort for the Muslim community elders that 60 percent of our subjects who date do so as a prelude to their future marriages (Table 2). Although it has been reported that in some places in the Muslim world going out alone with a person you marry later is not uncommon (Prothro and Diab, 1974:34), going out with an unrelated person is still anathema to Islam. It may be even more intriguing, on the surface at least, to see that 50 percent of the females who date do so with a high frequency (Table 1). However, a comparison of Tables 1 and 2 shows that these frequent daters among our females are actually the ones who are going to marry or are engaged. This leaves us with 50 percent of the females who are "partying" (Table 2), but perhaps these are also the ones who "hardly ever" go out on a date (Table 1). This means that those of our females who date quite frequently mostly do so with their future spouses; and those who do so very infrequently do not go out alone but in public. Perhaps this also explains our female subjects going out with non-Muslim dates. They do it quite infrequently, and even if they are with their non-Muslim friends, they do not go out alone. Otherwise, dating non-Muslims is generally practiced by the male subjects (Table 3).

Such a high frequency of dating among those who are engaged or are going to marry soon is somewhat strange, especially in view of the fact that 77 percent of them show a strong parental role in the selection of their future spouses. It seems rather strange that parents who play such strong roles in the selection of their children's future mates allow a great majority of them (compare Tables 2 and 4) to date each other quite freely.

It is mainly in the case of mehr that we find distinct adherence to the Islamic practices among our subjects. Very few of them think that they would and should play roles in the fixation of mehr itself, and only a little more than 11 percent do not favor it (Table 7); the proportion of those who are undecided about this matter is close to one-third (28.16 percent). Do the subjects with no opinion in fact represent a move from favoring to ultimately disfavoring this practice?

To summarize, our subjects seem to distinctly observe and support Islamic values regarding mate selection and marriage. Their socialization within their families and, perhaps, Muslim community education seem to have been quite effective. In this respect, our subjects differ from other similar groups in North America. Research among Japanese Americans, for example, shows that the Issei (new immigrants) cling to tradition, but that the Nisei (their children) shy away from it and that the Sansei (third generation) rediscover it (Osako and Liu, 1986; Kefer, 1974). Our subjects clearly do not conform to this pattern. However, there has been one big difference between our subjects and other similar groups in North America. Children of most other immigrants have been upwardly mobile from the bottom that most of their parents occupied on the socio-economic hierarchy in this continent. Such social ascendancy among the children of the immigrants, as Goode (1970) pointed out, is apt to create intergenerational strain or value conflicts. On the other hand, most of the parents of our subjects were educated professionals when they migrated to North America. Hence, our subjects were not expected to experience any radical departure from the status of their parents; furthermore, they must experience a greater status dependency on their parents. Children of other immigrants were experiencing just the opposite i.e., they were quickly assuming status independence vis à vis their parents' generation. Thus, while status independence among other immigrant explains intergenerational value conflicts, status dependence among our subjects explains intergenerational value convergence. This hypothesis is further augmented by the fact that it is mostly the females in our sample who are supposed to be relatively more dependent on their parents, and they are the ones who tend toward conservatism.

To conclude, it seems likely that a changeover to North American practices is beginning to take hold among those of our subjects (mostly males) who are relatively more status independent of their parents. Even among them, this change is not a leap from one value system to another. Rather it is piecemeal and perhaps even cautious. These North American practices which are more tempting (dating for example) are adopted with some rationalizations (marriage, for example). As to other practices (mehr, for instance), many of our subjects are quite visibly sitting on the fence.

### Notes

1. That these new immigrants were admitted mostly for their skills, education, and professional expertise has been considered and discussed by a number of demographers and others. For a detailed account, see John R. Weeks (1987).

2. According to estimates made for the project of which this paper is only a partial report, in ten large universities in North America (Columbia, Rutgers, MIT, Chicago, University of Michigan, Michigan State, UCLA, Berkeley, University of Toronto, and University of Ottawa) there were 9,760 Muslim students. Of these 2,160 or close to 20 percent were citizens of or had immigrant status in the United States and Canada.

3. There are more than three hundred student and non-student chapters affiliated with the Islamic Society of North America (ISNA), the largest organization of Muslims on this continent. However, there is no uniform or standardized curriculum followed by these affiliates of ISNA in their weekend schools. Moreover, there are at least seven hundred other communities with established mosques that are not affiliated with ISNA. Each one of these communities follows its own curriculum according to their needs and customs in their countries of origin.

4. "There is no celibacy in Islam," so declares Maududi (1970:83). Quoting from the hadith, he reaches the conclusion that marriage is not a duty upon Muslims but that celibacy is not to be regarded as a virtue either.

5. Social science literature on women written by women is rather scarce. Literature on Muslim women is even more so. See Papaneck (1973).

# Part Four

## Muslim Women: Gender in Socio-Religious Context

◆   ◆   ◆   ◆

◆   ◆   ◆   ◆

It is primarily in the private sphere, through the roles of *women*, that the family is nurtured and sustained. It has been argued in fact that "*family* is a code word for *mother*" (Spiegel, 1982:95). Moreover, religion generally has been seen as the "single most important shaper and enforcer of the image and role of women" (Reuther, 1974:7). Not infrequently, women's adherence to religious principles and practice is seen as concomitant with the stability and strength of the family unit itself. In Islam, as in Christianity, where there are concerns about the "state" of the family, these are often focused on normative evaluations of the behaviors of wives, mothers, and daughters. For these reasons, women's roles are particularly important to understanding Muslim families.

The three papers in this section examine different elements of the dynamics between women's roles, the family, and Islam. In her contribution on the women of Dearborn, Michigan, Aswad contrasts the lives of two groups of Arab Muslim women in closely knit ethnic communities. Aswad's work suggests the value of comparisons *between* Muslims in an attempt to isolate the factors associated with maintenance of faith. Her work sets up interesting contrasts between Yemeni and Lebanese women. The two groups differ from each other in terms of education, nativity, and phase in the family cycle. In many ways, the lives of the first-generation Yemeni women are closest to what their lives would have been if they had never emigrated. In contrast, it is the first- and second-generation Lebanese women who claim *greater* adherance to Islam, and they are more likely to read the Qur'an and to be active in organizations linked to the mosque. A surprisingly high percentage of the Yemini women report that religion is not very important to them. Aswad's study suggests the need for closer attention to the impact of such factors as the North American replication of the ancestral culture, national origin, and immigrant cohort on the intensity of ties with Islam.

In her paper, Cainker focuses on second-generation Americans born and raised in Chicago. Cainker takes a modified life course perspective in examining her subjects' exposure to religion. As children, living outside an ethnic community, they had few opportunities for formal exposure to Islam. In this early phase their religious development was similar to that of their brothers. But by adolescence, gender asymmetric socialization was clearly apparent. Teenage daughters experienced severe parental restrictions on their personal freedoms; conflicts resulted as parents attempted to create "good Muslim women," keepers and transmitters of traditional culture and religion. These young women moved from childhood ignorance about Islam and a generalized assumption that they were not very different from non-Muslims through adolescent conflicts over the family clampdown on their social life and its emphasis on their distinctiveness as young Muslim women to an eventual coming to terms with their altered identity. In this transition, their socialization was quite different from that of their brothers. Cauliku argues that the North American setting exacerbates ethnocultural and religious gender asymmetry. Further, contrary to popular assumptions, the Western setting may, in fact, *decrease* the status and personal freedom of Muslim women. While young Palestinian Muslim males are "allowed to be American," their female counterparts are compelled to restrict their lives in the service of family image and honor. The religious standing of the entire family is seen to be reflected in the behavior and conduct of daughters. The irony is that their brothers, not held to the same restrictions and free to date like other American youth, often reject endogamy and select a non-Muslim mate or marry a "real" Palestinian Muslim, that is, someone born in the Middle East. As a consequence, this cohort of American-born Palestinian Muslim women, constrained by the requirement of female endogamy, has been left with a limited pool of potential marriage partners. Many women have remained single.

Waldman brings a historian's perspective to the examination of Muslim families and the roles of Muslim women in North America. Historically, Waldman observes, Islam, like Christianity, has generally occupied a hegemonic position. In Muslim majority countries, family religious values are reinforced by dominant social and cultural forms. In contrast, in the United States and Canada, both pluralistic societies, Muslims find themselves in a minority position for which there are few precedents. They face pressures to adjust their family life to the dominant patterns of the culture. Not the least of these pressures is that North American Muslims must depend on secular law to protect their minority religious rights. In some ways, this fact puts the Muslim family at risk; where rights can be protected by law, there is the threat that some practices may also be prescribed by it. The forms of marriage, marriage arrangements, grounds for divorce, child-custody, child-parent relations, husband-wife relations, inheritance rights, and burial customs are some of the areas where there is the potential for heightening conflict, particularly should the strict interpretations of Islam continue to gain support.

The three contributions belie the stereotype of a static, unchanging Islam. The Lebanese-American, Yemeni-American, and American-born Palestinian women discussed in this section suggest some important considerations: there are significant pressures on women to *reflect* the religiosity and moral status of the family; there are commonalities among Muslim women in North America, but there are also differences between them; religious identification is not the only factor in the lives of Muslim women. As it is reflected in the family lives of women and girls (and, by extension, of men and boys), Islam in North America is dynamic and can be both initiative and responsive.

# Yemeni and Lebanese Muslim Immigrant Women in Southeast Dearborn, Michigan

## Barbara C. Aswad

✦　✦　✦　✦

The Arab women in the southeast region of Dearborn represent different generations of immigrants and are from different countries of origin. They share a Middle Eastern, Arabic, and Muslim background. With the exception of some recent Lebanese immigrants, the vast majority are from peasant backgrounds or from families who had recently been peasants. They have all migrated to a lower- to middle-income urban industrial region where male employment in the auto industry dominates the mode of production. Thus, they share certain similarities, but they also differ in their adaptation experiences.

The change in the role of women through migration is the focus of the study. It is based on intensive interviews in 1984 with forty married immigrant women, half from South Lebanon, and half from the Yemen Arab Republic (North Yemen).[1] The interviews took place in their homes and usually required several visits. Selection was done by snowball sampling, adjusted for different periods of migration among the Lebanese. In a number of cases an interpretor assisted the interviewer. The study is also based on participant observation since the writer has been involved in numerous activities in the community over the last fifteen years.

The "Southend" community, numbering approximately five thousand persons, borders the Ford Rouge industrial complex and has been a depot for immigrant groups since the Ford factory was first built in the 1920s. It has served as home to Italians, Eastern Europeans, and southern whites as well as to many other ethnic groups. An Arab population was present in the 1920s, but it started to become significant in size in the 1950s; today, it constitutes approximately 75 percent of the whole. The area borders Detroit and is geographically isolated from the more affluent regions of Dearborn. The largest group in the community is the Lebanese Shi²a, followed by the Yemeni, both Zaidis and Sunnis, and the Sunni Palestinians. Reliance on the auto companies for jobs is so great that in the 1980 depression, estimates of unemployment were 30 percent to 40 percent. Emigration, movement to other states, welfare, and entry into other professions such as gas station ownership have emerged as alternative economic strategies.[2]

Socially, the community is a primary ethnic community with much face-to-face interaction. It is characterized by strong kin and neighborhood networks, which have acted to reduce the random crime, rape, and murder that terrify some adjoining Detroit neighborhoods. (See Aswad, 1974a; Abraham, Abraham, and Aswad, 1983; and Aswad and Gray, 1990, for further discussion of the community.)

PREVIOUS STUDIES

Although the study of migration has a long history, the specifics of the effects on family organization and women has been given more attention in the West since the political rise of feminism and the pursuit of academic studies relating to women. Safia Haddad (1969) was one of the first to concentrate on the Arab women's role. Cainkar (1985) has described the roles of Palestinian women in Chicago whose families owned small stores and who were not brought up in Arab communities, while Naff (1985) has examined the life of early women immigrants, particularly those involved in peddling. Y. Haddad and A. Lummis's extensive survey (1987) on Islam in the U.S. explores many female attitudes in relation to religion and family.

In the Middle East, the pattern of labor migration has added to the increased interest in the field. In the 1960s Abu-Lughod noted the decrease in the role of women who migrated from villages to the cities in Egypt (1961), citing the reduction in their workload and social life and their confinement to the neighborhood, at the same time, men's work often increases and is less solitary, and it typically takes them out of the neighborhood. Joseph's (1978) work on the importance of the neighborhood for urban women's activities in Lebanon also notes the importance of the neighborhood in relieving boredom. In her sensitive study of women in a Yemeni town, Dorsky (1986) shows that economic, social, and age differences are less significant for women's networks than they are for men's. She discusses the many ways in which women help each other: in raising children, in providing comfort in an illness, and sometimes in taking collective action against a man. I found in a study of the Southeast Dearborn neighborhood in 1974 that when men were asked why they wanted to stay in the neighborhood, most answered because their wives wanted to stay near female friends and relatives. A major contribution to the understanding of changed family relations during migration comes from the work of Browner and Lewin (1982), who compared Colombian women and immigrant U.S. Hispanic populations in relation to control over resources. They found that as women became less dependent upon their husbands, their major bonds of affection and alliances were with their children rather than their husband.

There have been numerous studies of Middle Eastern Turkish women who have migrated to Europe. Most of them were guest workers and worked in factories. Kosack (1976), Kiray (1976), and Kudat (1975) found some increase in the participation of women in family and community affairs. Kosack noted that while wage-earning allows women increased decision-making, they were still supressed as lower-class workers, as females, and as foreigners. Their participation in the workforce also gave them increased information, made them more questioning, and often led to family conflicts. Abadan-Unat (1977) noted that there were two trends. The first promoted the emancipation of women through the increased importance of the nuclear family and the establishment of bank accounts. However, the second, increased consumption, was a change of pseudo-emancipation and also migration sometimes reinforces tradition and religion (1977). In discussing the splitting of the family, Kiray notes that the main base is where the woman is living; this crucial position involves the woman in trying to hold the nuclear family together as a unit. As a result, she acts as a major decision-maker in the nuclear family (1976:221).

Discussing Turkish women who accompany men to Denmark where some are employed and others are not, Mirdal (1984:998) agrees with Abadan-Unat that women are not emancipated, but more dependent on their husbands. Taken from their more structured roles and either isolated or given double jobs, they face stress raising children in a different country.

In this study, the women have basically accompanied the men; they are not primarily employed, nor are they brought to the United States to be employed. Thus, they more closely fit Mirdal's pattern. As well, there are some emancipating conditions and some constricting conditions. As Morokvasic (1984) notes, the effects of migration are a result of the interaction of the old and the new environments. They are often complex, with both negative and positive results. Also, it is important to remember Kiray's point that immigrant families are constantly changing their composition.

There are also several recent studies of the effects of male migration on women's roles in villages of the Middle East, including those by Taylor (1984), Khafagy (1984), and Myntti (1984). Their analyses of factors affecting women reveal a complex set of variables, among them the nature of the local economy, the type of migration—whether recurrent, seasonal, short- or long-distance—the number of visits, the possibility of local reinvestment, the class of the migrants, and the stage of the family cycle. These works are reminiscent of Nancy Gonzales's classic study (1961), which correlated various types of migration with family organization. Writing on the effect of male migration on women left in Egyptian villages, Taylor and Khafagy both emphasize women's acquisition of new power. Khafagy (1984) mentions the increase in managing finances, disciplining children, and dealing with outside institutions. In the area of social relations she found that the husbands began to depend on their wives more and that the wives developed a stronger relationship with their brothers-in-law, who, while not receiving the remittances, acted as advisors. Taylor (1984) found a similar change in decision-making but added that it only occurs if the wife establishes a home outside the extended family of her husband and that that only happens when she has a child. Taylor also notes that the independence seems temporary, disappearing when the husband returns. In most cases where a woman heads a nuclear home, she escapes some of the dominance of her mother-in-law. Mirdal (1984) asked the Turkish wives in Denmark how they had felt in the villages without their husbands and found that some had felt liberated but that others feared they would lose their husbands to European women. They also feared irregular remittances and poverty and reported disciplinary problems with children. In the area of work habits, Taylor found that the intensification of agriculture with new investments meant that a woman's role in agriculture was unrelieved; she remained as a full participant. In Yemen, on the other hand, Myntti (1984) found that the increased remittances allowed middle peasants to acquire the habits of the rich peasant and hire male and female labor to replace their wives in the fields and in other arduous tasks. Thus, stratification increased; those who did not receive remittances worked for those who did, and the wives of the immigrants became more restricted to the home.

This investigation of the changes in function in Dearborn will examine the history of migration networks, the role of women in the home and their relations with their husbands, employment and attitudes toward outside work, women in public, women and Islam, and health problems, social assistance, and other major problems that face women. The Yemeni and Lebanese women will be discussed separately in order to form a profile of each group.

## HISTORY OF MIGRATION AND SOCIAL NETWORKS

Most of the women in the southend community come from a tradition of middle peasantry, that is, from families who owned medium-sized farms and did much of the labor themselves. A minority come from small merchant families in small towns. The ethic of the middle peasant involves cooperation and reliance on the extended family, but it also contains a spirit of individual hard work and of personal management of one's own share of the land. In contrast, rich peasants do not do manual labor and scorn it; they are principally managers who hire poor peasants and laborers (see Aswad 1981). In the middle peasantry, women have a central role in food production. For example, Myntti reports that in Yemen women had a dominant role in grain production. Whereas men ploughed, threshed, and applied chemicals, women planted, thinned, weeded, harvested, winnowed, pulled roots, and applied manure. Women were also involved as food processors and hauled water and firewood (1984:12). They held a large amount of responsibility for managing the household. However, many of the North American families interviewed say that families at home have adopted the organization of the rich peasant because of increased remittances from migrants abroad. Thus most informants reported that life used to be harder for women in their families in Yemen than it was now, and as a result of the remittances, the roles of women vary. A second important factor of work for village women in an extended and sometimes polygamous family was that they shared jobs. If there were no other women, the wife would have to spread the work out.

The customs of Arab peasant culture emphasize patrilineal ownership of property, patrilineal involvement in politics, planned marriages, preferred first cousin or other cousin marriage on the father's side, family honor, and female chastity before marriage. Women are allotted half the share allotted to their brothers and often do not take even that share in case marital problems require them to return home (Aswad, 1981). In addition, the culture involves a loyalty to village, region, and religion. Lebanese and Yemeni migrants both come from mountainous regions that have a history of regional political autonomy and in which family and kin ties are more extensive and organized than they are in societies characterized by centralized governments and class divisions, such as Egypt. Kinship ties also provide a major means of migration to and social establishment in the host country, and planned marriages are one of the primary migration mechanisms. The Middle Eastern traditions of sexual segregation in most work roles and public functions and the modesty required in public affairs limit women in certain endeavors. But these aspects tend to be overemphasized by Westerners in their appraisal of women's roles and power, particularly since the role of the family is diminished in the West. That is, since the traditional family is a strong unit of organization in the Middle East and women are important to it, they have a considerable degree of power and respect.

The family is structurally biased toward male control, but female networks, the power of gossip, the socialization of children, and the enforcement of honor and shame, or *'ayb*, which controls the majority of social behavior in the family and the community, are also important. Women have extensive female networks, some of which are formalized (see Aswad 1974b), others not. A woman's role and status are defined not only in terms of the domains of herself and her family, but also in terms of her relationship to the public arena. As Nassal shows in her research on the institution of shame in Arab society, the Arab woman "should not become an object of scorn or ill-repute, or the subject of adverse public opinion, for that in itself serves to relegate her to an inferior status" (1986:8).

The important questions in this study relate to what happens to women's networks and their roles and statuses as they migrate to a different environment. For first-generation women the extended family networks are disrupted. Because males migrated before females in both the Yemeni and Lebanese cases, men have more relatives in the United States than women do. Thus, many women report that they have to do most of their work alone and that they miss their mothers, sisters, and aunts. They have to rely on people around them, neighbors and friends. There is a difference, however, between the Lebanese and Yemeni. When the Lebanese first came to Dearborn in the 1920s and 1930s, there was no large community of Muslims; they were on their own, and the climate in America favored assimilation. There was less pressure to adhere to the social mores of the Middle East, and they pushed their children to assimilate. They gave them both Anglo and Muslim names, pressured them to learn English, and generally lived in a bicultural tradition. It was not unusual for their sons and a few daughters to marry non-Arabs and raise a much more assimilated second and third generation.

Soon the Lebanese families brought their relatives, and very large clans and village organizations were established in the community. The majority of those interviewed reported having from forty to two hundred relatives living in the Southend. With this change, women became more involved in family and kin networks. Today, most Lebanese fleeing the warfare and destruction of their country arrive into established networks, and first-, second-, and third-generation women are involved in organizations that reflect the religious and political problems in Lebanon as well as local ones. These networks have also served in many cases to reinforce concepts of 'ayb.

The Yemeni women, on the other hand, have come within the last ten years, and most have no extended family networks. They typically report that they have from four to ten relatives living here, although 80 percent of them have fathers or brothers among the primarily male Yemeni community. Their ages range from twenty-three to forty, and they are involved in raising young children in nuclear families. They do not have a second or third generation to assist them in assimilation. Generally their educational level is lower than that of the Lebanese, and many Yemeni feel that the Lebanese look down on them. There are some clear exceptions in which the two groups have assisted each other, but most Yemeni women have formed close neighborhood networks with others within the Yemeni community.

### YEMENI WOMEN
*Migration*

About 1910 a few Yemeni seamen found their way through the St. Lawrence Seaway to Detroit, but the primary migration has occurred since the 1950s when the men increasingly came to work in the auto industry as unskilled laborers. They engaged in a pattern of "recurrent migration"; that is they worked in the United States or elsewhere for several years, returned home for a stay, and then migrated abroad again. Many variations of this process are visible, but most men were married before they migrated and did not bring their wives. Recently they have begun to bring their families. Thus, men had established networks with other Yemeni and Lebanese to assist them in obtaining jobs, and women who came moved into a subcommunity which usually contained their father or brother, but few other relatives. Furthermore, the community, made up primarily of single men, was somewhat isolated from a number of American and other Arab-American institutions.

The migration to America disrupted the extended family more than migration in Yemen, owing to the great distance involved and the small size of the Yemeni subcommunity. Women voiced their opinion that both their major problems and opportunities involved the disrupted family situation. They miss their mothers, sisters, and male kinsmen, but they felt free from their husband's family, particularly from their mothers-in-law. Thus, the freedom to manage their families on their own, to walk in public without the veil, and to consider education and increased health care for themselves and their children is exciting.

Divorce and remarriage are much more common among the Yemeni than among the Lebanese. Divorce is not stigmatized as much, and thus there are more options for a divorced Yemeni woman than there are for Lebanese. But the choice of a new husband seems to remain with the male members of the patrilineage, either the woman's father or her brother. Sometimes the remarriage involves bringing another relative to the U.S.

In addition to problems associated with the husband's unemployment and health care, a Yemeni woman's frustrations involve the lack of female relatives to help with household duties and raising children and her lack of English and industrial skills and education. There are also special problems in raising children who learn English before their mother does, in a culture where dating is so extensive that the mother fears for their reputations and, as a result, for her own. Should they have marital problems, the few women without male relatives in Dearborn, can be at a disadvantage.

The women try to solve their problems by building extensive friendship and neighborhood networks with other Yemeni women; they visit extensively, depend on each other for assistance in raising their children, go to English classes together, and keep in touch with their families back home by phoning frequently. They seldom leave their neighborhood, and they do not have outside employment, depending upon their husbands or patrilineal kinsmen for maintenance and mobility. Some also seek assistance from religious leaders, and recently some have sought assistance from social workers in the local community center ACCESS (Arab Community Center for Economic and Social Services), which has established a family counseling unit. Because the center is located in the heart of the community, the husbands allow their wives to attend. Otherwise, the women complain, their movements are frequently restricted by their husbands.

### Role of Women and Relationships in the Home

These women are definitely in charge of caring for the home, however, 40 percent said that their husbands helped around the house, though only a minority indicated that the assistance was significant, such as helping with the cooking. For most it meant that the men helped out occasionally, most commonly when the children were young.

Sixty percent of the women said they shared in decision making, but all indicated that their husbands made the major decisions. Several said they made the major decisions regarding children's affairs. The vast majority indicated that their husbands controlled the money and that they were given spending money. None ever went to the bank. Their inability to read and write either Arabic or English certainly contributes to this lack of control. Women generally leave their inheritance in the trust of their brother or another member of their patrilineage in the village, which is why it is important that they be near a member of their patrilineage for security. As with all immigrants, they lose some control over property left at home.

The world of Arab women is intensely social. Most reported that they visit frequently, at least three times a week and often every day. Visiting is almost always segregated by sex among the Yemeni. Hospitality is important, as are manner of greetings, respect for age, and etiquette. Living rooms are kept very clean for visitors, and much money is spent on them, while kitchens may not be as neat among women who have come from villages and who are used to more open cooking areas. Children are welcome in groups of sitting women, but they primarily listen and observe. One never sees women playing with children in public. Women also reported watching an average of three hours of television daily. Some videos they watch are in Arabic, but most of the television is in English, and they learn some colloquial English through this medium. As the author was interviewing one woman, others came into the room, and the interviewee seemed not to mind answering rather personal questions with up to nine other women and many children listening and amending her answers. Sisterhood is an organizational strategy brought from the Middle East, and it is used extensively to adapt to a new environment.

Some women are bored. With their jobs confined to the household and their restriction to the Southend area, there seems to be a need for other activities. Perhaps one reason for the enthusiasm for the ACCESS classes is that they help the women get out of the house as well as offering self-improvement. All the women vehemently expressed their dislike of polygyny and felt it was unfair, while 41 percent said that sometimes their husbands threaten them with it. There are several cases of illegal polygyny in the community. The women also expressed their abhorrence for wife-beating and added that it happens in the community too often. In a recent study of client visits to the newly established Family Counseling Program at ACCESS, the writer found spouse abuse was not often mentioned and that there was more mention of women being abused by brothers or children than by husbands (Aswad 1987). They said that in Yemen they could be beaten, although there is a new law which puts men in jail for six months and allows a woman to get a divorce if her husband beats her. They all knew about the law, but the vast majority did not seem to think that it was effective. A third of the women said that their husbands yelled loudly at them, and 20 percent indicated that they yelled back. They were more tolerant of the idea of yelling at children (35 percent), and 20 percent said it was all right to hit them. They were very interested in the American law that allows women to obtain permanent custody of children in the case of divorce, a situation impossible in Yemen. Twenty percent indicated that they thought a woman should get custody until the children were eighteen.

There also seems to be a rise in the number of divorces, both real ones and those faked for reasons of citizenship and migration, for welfare, and in some cases to escape abuse. The rise is more notable in the Lebanese community, as will be explained later. In most cases the women keep the children; however, men often attempt to keep the daughters to protect their honor and let the sons stay with their mothers if they must give up some children.

Seventy-five percent of the marriages were arranged, and half of them were either with their father's brother's son or with a second cousin on their father's side. The majority felt that a girl should refuse if she did not like the boy her parents proposed, but they added that there was little one could really do to influence the outcome if the parents wanted it. They would be obliged to respect their parents' wishes. Most of those who had arranged marriages named their father as the primary arranger. The 25 percent who did not have arranged marriages mentioned marriage for love as a reason and marriage as a result of love that had grown through letter-writing.

When they were asked about a woman's rights in a marriage, the women felt most strongly about: financial support, visiting relatives, fidelity, and equal treatment in the case of polygamy. There was less support for the liberty to control their own possessions or to sell them. Under the category of a husband's rights, they rated (in order) fidelity and management of the home, with little value placed on the wife's obedience to her husband or on deference to the husband's mother and father.

When the women were asked about their major concerns, they most frequently mentioned their children's problems, such as whether they were having difficulty in school with language or the level of classroom achievement. They were concerned if their children did not obey them and were rebelling. They frequently discussed whether they should send them back to Yemen, who they would stay with there, and how they would miss them. A number of families are in fact split. One woman has not seen two of her four children for five years and grieves over this fact. Another is taking care of her husband's children from a previous marriage and wants children of her own but says he does not.

Those who have teenagers are concerned about the influence in the schools of dating and drugs. They want their daughters to get an education, but feel they should send them to Yemen or marry them early in order to avoid problems. They treat their sons more leniently, but they also talk about sending them home.

Thus, families that migrate with young children are perhaps strengthened, but those with older children are vulnerable to role reversal. In addition, the proper socialization of children remains the mother's responsibility. She is blamed if her daughter is not brought up well. In the case of the Yemeni women, their distance from female members of their families who could help them, places increased responsibility on their shoulders.

The women are also clearly concerned about their own futures and about their lack of English, education, and knowledge of illnesses. Their primary desires are for classes in child-rearing, health care, sewing, English, typing, and nutrition.

When asked about political events in the Middle East, half indicated that they were very concerned, and half said they were not that concerned, but all said that Middle Eastern politics bothered their husbands a great deal, and that they in turn worry about their husbands' conditions.

Although the women are fairly young, a few were concerned about the health of their parents abroad and their inability to assist them. Such feelings were more typical of Lebanese, whose relatives were in obvious danger, and among those who were middle-aged and had elderly parents.

Thus, because they are younger and because their homeland is more

stable, the Yemeni demonstrate a sense of freedom that is partially a result of lesser responsibilities although these will increase as their children become teenagers and their parents age. They also have greater
protection from husband abuse because they are not isolated from
their brothers and other male kin.

### Women in Islam and Women in Public

Half the women described themselves as not religious at all, 40 percent
as very religious, and 10 percent as somewhat. The majority indicated
that their husbands used religion and the religious authorities to control them. All observed Ramadan and 40 percent said they prayed regularly; however, only 10 percent went to the mosque regularly, and because of their high rate of illiteracy, most said they were not able to
read the Qu'ran. The mosque which most Yemeni men attend is primarily a male institution in the Southend currently, although in the
1960s under second-generation Sunni Lebanese control, it operated in
the fashion of many American churches. Another mosque outside the
community, which many of the Shiᶜa Lebanese attend, is more integrated, and the women have some power through their organizations.
In the local mosque, which is predominantly Yemeni, the women sit
separately from the men. There is a small women's study group, but it
is not as powerful as the Lebanese women's groups.

The women do veil if they attend the mosque, but it is the only place
that they do so. They see the Southend community as their village, and
one would seldom see a veil there. In Yemen, women veiled when they
went to town but not in the villages; only women of lower status
would not veil in the town. All the women wear either long dresses or
knee length dresses over pants. They cover hair with scarves. This typical Middle Eastern peasant dress should not to be confused with the
newly popular "modest dress" of many urban women in the Middle
East, which is associated with the rise of religious fundamentalism.
The daughters of Yemeni women wear scarves and long-sleeved
dresses to school.

The women seldom leave the Southend to shop. They cannot drive,
and their husbands seem to restrict them more than the Lebanese husbands restrict their wives. Perhaps the women are also concerned
about wearing their peasant dresses in shopping centers. Their lack of

mobility confirms the importance of the social service center, where 128 Arab women take English classes.

The Yemeni women universally want their children to marry Muslims, and 90 percent strongly prefer that they marry other Yemeni. Only a few said it is not as important for their sons to marry Muslims as for their daughters. The patrilineal orientation of descendents makes the double standard apparent. Regardless of who the mother is, the children of the sons are Muslims. If a daughter marries out, it is supposed that her children will follow the faith of the father.

Parents who discuss sending their children back to Yemen until they marry, especially their daughters, feel that away from the Dearborn High School, they would not be exposed to strangers or to dating practices. However, the parents are torn since they want a good education for their children, and the children strongly want to stay in the United States, especially those who want to continue in school. Several of the women felt that it is necessary to marry their daughters at an early age to keep them out of trouble.

Yemeni women have no visible impact on local politics, and the Yemeni men have also been peripheral in the community because their stays have been transient and there is no significant second generation. But the women and men are not uninterested in local conditions. The men have been sporadically active in labor union issues, but they still feel dominated by the Lebanese in local organizations, and they also feel discriminated by other Americans because of their color, small size, and language problems.

### Outside Employment

Only one woman was employed. One of the few with an education, she assisted the English teacher at ACCESS. All of the women had a strong desire to work outside the home and to learn English in order to do so. Half of them felt their husband would not mind at all if they worked and would welcome the money. The majority of this group indicated that their husbands were on welfare. The other half felt that their husbands would be strongly opposed to their working. Sixty percent would permit their own daughters to work, but they preferred that they work with women. Several with small children said they had to stay home until their children were older since they did not have kinsmen to help them, and a couple had previously worked in stores with their male kinsmen. The majority (80 percent) felt that their husbands would not like them working in factories alongside men.

The women felt that ideally their husbands would like them to work in a store with their male relatives, but since this kind of work does not really exist, the men prefer them home. Thus, the ideology of modesty and that of the rich peasant are evident and limit women as does their lack of skills; however unemployment has moderated the ideology among both women and men.

### Health and Assistance

Since the Yemeni women are young (sixteen to thirty-five) and in their child-bearing years, they are concerned with pregnancies and having children, which in a patrilineal society is crucial for a woman. The lack of children, especially male children, is often the cause of divorce or the taking of a second wife. Twenty percent of the women were not able to have children, and both partners had gone for medical assistance. Since coming to this country, the tendency to fault the women primarily in such cases has lessened as a result of new knowledge and there has been some reduction in social pressure. About 30 percent had had miscarriages, and 60 percent had not received prenatal care, only going to a doctor or hospital if they had problems or toward the end of their pregnancy. One had carried her baby dead for two months before she knew about it.

All of those interviewed had health coverage either through the auto companies where their husbands work or through the government. However, there are members of the community who are not covered. Recent immigrants have numerous problems. All go to the closest hospital, Oakwood, although a few had traveled many miles to see specialists. Half had regular doctors, and the others said they went to the emergency room. This corresponds to Bowker's findings that there is a heavy reliance on emergency care in this community (1979). Generally the women seemed pleased with their ability to get to hospitals easily and with the medical service they receive. They actively seek out doctors and they have a great interest in medical information. They agreed wholeheartedly that they would like to have classes in Arabic on health problems.

Generally, the women rely on their husbands or other male relatives to drive them to doctors and hospitals, which sometimes creates problems, particularly since women tend to be the primary caretakers for children. They will also ask neighborhood assistance for transportation if no relative is near. For reasons of modesty, there is reluctance to allow a wife to be alone with a male doctor. This custom may sometimes inhibit a trip to a hospital, however more likely it will inconvenience the doctor, who may have to examine a woman with her clothes on or with her husband also in the room. Another area of concern for the medical staff is that frequently the husband or other family male answers for the women when she is asked questions about her health, even when it is not a matter of translation.

Much of their experience and views relating to health care must be seen in the light of their experience at home in Yemen, where the services were very limited, and they did not use preventative medical practices extensively, except through customary medicine. There are several women in the community who are sought out for healing and the casting of spells.

Yemeni women were not accustomed to social services and did not know how to use them initially, but once they are aware of the opportunities they are eager to make use of them. Ninety percent of the women I interviewed had gone to the community center for English classes, federal food subsidies, translation of documents, or assistance from social workers. The latter are used primarily for problems with their middle and teenage children and for their marriages. Two-thirds found it difficult to accept welfare or the idea of it, although a quarter of the sample were on welfare. Most of the others said it would pose no problem, but a few disapproved of it since they said others were lying and cheating and should not be on it anyway. A pattern that Browner and Lewin found among Hispanics—divorce in order to receive welfare—has begun to be evident in the community. Some women divorce to escape abuse, but unemployment and cheating the system are also involved. The increase has been noted by case workers, and several men have complained that ACCESS is causing divorces.

The workers in the centers are eager to work within the Arab social systems and are not always trying to substitute new dependencies on the welfare state, which has problems of its own. Of the factors that contribute to ACCESS's success, the centrality of the bilingual staff is crucial.

### Comparisons of Life Here and in Yemen

"Life is freer here, we don't ever have to wear the veil. At home, we had to wear it to go to town." Women made such remarks with a sense of relief. In the same breath, they mentioned that they long for their homes in the cool tall buildings of Yemen. They miss the mountains and fresh air and do not like the pollution of Dearborn and the cold, grey winters. Some stated that there is less housework here, but others said it is about the same, indicating that it used to be harder in Yemen. They felt inadequate not knowing English and had trouble with their children in school. They said they felt more controlled by the society in Yemen, but they miss the supportive aspects of kinship and family too. In the end, about half said they liked it better here and half liked it better in Yemen.

### LEBANESE WOMEN
#### Migration

The Lebanese interviewed in this study are representative of different migration patterns than the Yemen. They arrived during the period from 1948 to 1977. The most recent migration occurred after the Lebanese Civil War began in 1975. They originate from Shiᶜa villages in South Lebanon and from Sunni villages in the Bekaᶜa Valley. Those who migrated earlier had fewer relatives here in a smaller Arab community. Those who have come recently have numerous relatives and migrate into village communities, some of which have their own coffee clubs, their particular religious congregations, and a special living area as well as a developed political and social network.

The Lebanese also had more varied backgrounds at home; some have a considerable amount of education, and others have little or none at all. Some women had work experience as teachers or with relatives in stores. But another had little education and was brought here as a second wife for a widower thirty years her senior who already had eight children. Overall, 60 percent of the sample had had no education at all, and all wanted more. Thirty percent are currently employed in such jobs as janitors in schools and hospitals, aids at ACCESS, cooks, babysitters, and teachers. Thus, their job skills vary considerably. A woman in her forties with children and little English has a more difficult time than those who came as adolescents and finished their schooling here, for example. Many who had no education have several children in college. Some have put their children in Catholic schools for what they perceive to be a better education, as well as for their more restrictive social environment. As with other immigrants, many of the women have done hard work and scraped to get their children educated. Also there seems to be an equal emphasis upon college education for girls as well as boys.

It is important to note that the recent group are really refugees and thus have had some fearful and stressful experiences in their villages and in Beirut. They have suffered psychologically and have often had to interrupt both their own education and their children's.

### Role of Women and Relationships in the Home

About half of the Lebanese are married to cousins on their father's side, but only 20 percent said they had arranged marriages, compared to 75 percent of the Yemeni. The majority do the housework with husbands helping out, while some indicated that their husbands regularly do the dishes and cook. Seventy percent said they spend most of their time at home and visiting, but those who were employed said they had little time for visiting. Similarily, they spend time watching television and videos and shopping. Since they have relatives here, there is more emphasis upon visiting them with their husbands than there is among the Yemeni women, who visit more with their women friends. Also, in contrast to the Yemeni, they frequently shop outside the community, and many drive. They will often run errands for each other and sometimes for Yemeni women.

The majority said that they jointly control the money with their husbands, and half indicated they went to the bank. However, like the Yemeni, all the Lebanese husbands handled the budget. Ninety percent said that both husband and wife were involved in decision-making, but none claimed she made major decisions, except for ones relating to the children. All of these patterns indicate that Lebanese women have more economic power in the home than Yemeni women as a result of their greater knowledge of English, their jobs, their higher education, and their kin networks, all of which also lead to an increasing participation in American society.

Polygyny was felt to be unfair and was disliked by 80 percent but only 20 percent were threatened with. Like the Yemeni, none felt it was permissible to beat wives, but 20 percent felt it was permissible to hit children. The majority went to relatives for assistance with marriage problems. Seventy percent felt a woman could get a divorce if she is beaten. A high 80 percent felt women should get custody of the children until they are adults and that the laws are much fairer in the United States than in Lebanon on this issue. As has been noted, the divorce rate appears to be increasing among Lebanese. Both the number of divorces and the increase may be related to bringing relatives here through the green card remarriage offers, to the increased economic pressures caused by unemployment, and to increased stress and abuse and the inability to return to the war-torn country, where children might otherwise have been sent.

The problems of teenagers are more evident among the Lebanese, who may have come with older children. Not only is it more difficult for the parents to assimilate, but migrating in later life means that they have left much behind. The concern about children assimilating and rebelling is immediately evident, but having relatives and a strong community to buttress them makes it easier. The largest concern is for those left behind; there is much everyday stress in trying to get news about relatives or to get visas to allow their reunion. Although the second and third generations provide aid in assimilation, some of the new immigrants see patterns they disapprove of, such as outmarriage, wearing shorts, dating, and the employment of women. There have been numerous disputes between the American-born Arab-Americans and the new immigrants. Some boys fight over girls attire and behavior. Girls of the second generation who once wore shorts often do not now. Fears about intermarriage may cause stress, as parents see it as a loss of the cultural heritage in the next generation. This concern is particularly evident among parents who themselves have had to give up their country of origin. In addition, there is also the patrilineal bias against outmarriage for girls.

There are also some cultural reversals in traditional patrilocal patterns when a man is brought to this country to marry a girl, rather than the girl being sent home to Lebanon to marry. The woman may be more assimilated than her husband and have more kin here, which increases her power in the relationship. Mirdal also notes this in Denmark.

### Women in Islam and in Public

Half of the Lebanese described themselves as very religious and half as somewhat, while none said not at all. Because Lebanese kin groups are active in religious and political societies, women are drawn into them. That revivalism of Islam is found among the Lebanese is largely the result of events in Lebanon and the revivalism among the oppressed Shiʿa there. It is also a reaction to the Anti-Arab and Anti-Islamic attitudes in the United States and in the local community. This religious politicization is more evident in Lebanon than in Yemen currently. It is also the Lebanese who are more organized in combating the conscious and unconscious anti-Arabism in the schools. Many members of the active civic organizations are second-generation Lebanese, and they give guidance to the new immigrants. There is a prominent second and third generation among them that has combined Lebanese and American forms of women's groups. Early Lebanese immigrant women were active in establishing the first mosque in the community in the 1920s and in maintaining it before it came under more conservative and predominantly Yemeni control in the late 1970s. Members of the former Sunni mosque are relocating their congregation. Women in the Shiʿa mosque have also been very active in religious organizations. Lebanese women joined other Arab women in Arab political and charitable groups.

Some of the recent immigrants bring their political attitudes with them, particularly if they are educated. Their public participation varies according to such factors as their experiences in Lebanon, how long they have been in the United States, whether they drive, whether they are employed, and their level of education, but the existence of an established community greatly aids their participation.

By contrast the Yemeni are religious but not yet as integrated as the Lebanese; the Yemeni see their mosque more as a refuge than as a political organization to combat American antagonism. The lack of an as-

similated Yemeni class also isolates them somewhat from understanding some levels of discrimination felt by those who are more assimilated or who have relatives who are.

Eighty percent of the Lebanese would give their children Muslim
names, 90 percent would not allow daughters to date, and 60 percent
would not allow sons to do so; half the women pray, a third go to the
mosque, two-thirds read the Qu'ran, and the majority approve of modest religious dress. Ninety percent would stop their child from marrying outside of Islam, but a third said it is permissible if the spouse converts. Fifty percent said it is permissible to marry into another Islamic
sect. None would directly arrange their children's marriages, and half
want them to marry Lebanese Muslims. As with the Yemeni, there was
more leniency towards males than females in marriage patterns.

The majority claimed that their degree of religiosity has increased
because of events in Lebanon. Half have had relatives killed in the civil
war, and all have been involved in some local activity related to the war
such as meetings or fund raisers. In contrast to Yemeni women, Lebanese women think women should be active in Arab and non-Arab affairs, and 70 percent said they have been.

### Outside Employment

While only a third of the women were employed part time, when they
were asked whether women should work outside the home, 90 percent
responded in the affirmative, and 80 percent expressed a desire to do
so. When they were asked whether their husbands would be opposed,
20 percent said they would be strongly opposed, 35 percent said "Yes,
but not strongly," 20 percent said "Maybe," and 25 percent said "Not
at all." As with the Yemeni, many of those in the last category had been
or were on welfare. All indicated that it would be permissible for their
daughter to work. Again most felt they would rather their daughter
would work in a store or a traditional female job, but 20 percent said
an unskilled factory job was acceptable. I know of only a few second
generation girls who do in fact work as laborers in factories.

### Health and Assistance: Views of Life Here and in Lebanon

In the area of health, Lebanese villagers had similar problems to the
Yemeni; however, more have had experiences with hospitals, and they

had more criticisms of them. Also a number of those who had lived in Beirut or had higher education had more knowledge of illnesses and hospitals. Half had health insurance, 20 percent had none, and 30 percent are on medicare.

Many of the problems of the Lebanese relate to the civil war. Ninety percent expressed strong anxiety about Lebanon, giving it the top point on a scale of 1 to 10 in terms of the distress it has caused them. Eighty percent said they would still rather live in Lebanon if it were not for the war. The recent refugees seem to nurture the hope that they will return, but they wonder how it will be possible with the danger and the ruined economy.

Their major problems, of course, vary; however, the majority of the complaints centered on unemployment and raising children among American students and on the problems of keeping their values. They frequent the Family Counseling Center of ACCESS more than Yemeni women; many are asking for immigration information in order to bring their families, but many also bring family problems. There is more familiarity with medicare assistance, and requesting family assistance seems easier for them.

## SUMMARY AND DISCUSSION

Migration has caused disruptions in Muslim immigrant families and thereby affected the role of women, but the nature of the disruption and the accompanying problems, opportunities, and adaptations vary according to migration conditions, the stage of the family cycle, and the characteristics of the host environment.

All the women in this survey were hindered in gaining employment in the United States and thus control over resources by a number of factors. First, the male-dominated auto industry is distinct from other immigrant occupations, such as small store ownership in which Middle Eastern women have a tradition of participation, from the situation in countries like Germany where women are guest workers, and from other cases in the United States where women are employed in industry. Secondly, the rich-peasant mentality of the husbands encourages women to stay home as a status symbol and leads to sexual segregation and increased dependency upon the breadwinner. Thirdly, entrance into an alien culture increases the emphasis upon Islamic modesty and segregation, particularly since the host culture encourages dating for

mate selection, and, in recent times, sexual intercourse in the host culture has also become more frequent before marriage. Traditional Arab
concerns with virginity have sometimes led to violence and often to
early marriages, which retard the education of girls and place further
limitations on their education and employment opportunities and
emancipation.

Although men have more economic power, women are still responsible for the upbringing of children, and blame for their misbehavior
(*'ayb*) is placed on them. Thus many of the women's stress-related
problems have to do with their control over their children and fear of
their children's misbehavior. They want their daughters to get educated but fear for their daughters' and their own reputations. In addition, children often acculturate faster than parents, causing problematic role reversals. There were discussions of some wife-beating and
also mistreatment by brothers and children.

Unemployment, welfare, and rules involving child custody that favor mothers in divorce cases are factors affecting women's thinking, especially since the devastating unemployment crisis in the 1980s. The
fact that, until recently, there has not been the dramatic change
Browner and Lewin found among the Hispanic migrants in divorce
and mother-headed families is related, in my opinion, to traditional
patrilineal rules controling custody and divorce patterns, whereby children remain in the patrilineage. But these are beginning to break down
increasingly as unemployment becomes greater, as women learn their
rights, and as migration conditions change. For the Yemeni women
divorce is not as great a stigma, with marriages frequently, and remarriages sometimes, being related to immigration factors primarily determined by male members of the patriline. For the Lebanese in particular, marriages, divorces, and remarriages are also related to the critical
need to assist relatives. In addition, returning to Lebanon is no longer
a way out of marital and economic problems. Thus, there appears to be
an increase in separations and divorces, often with women keeping
some of the children. Fathers usually try to retain daughters to protect
their reputations. These changes have brought increased stress to men
as well as to women and children.

There are differences among the women. We find from other studies
that the earliest Lebanese came without extended families, and many
had worked double jobs in stores and at home. They pushed their chil-

dren to assimilate and get educated. They encouraged their daughters to get an education and many second-generation girls worked, but not in factories with men. Eventually large kin groups resulted, and these groups helped in raising the children, in getting jobs for men, and in forming social, political, and religious associations. They put pressure on local schools, were active in negotiating and even confronting city policies, took part in groups concerned about foreign politics, worked with non-Arab groups, and most recently assisted second generation Lebanese women in their candidacy for political positions in Dearborn.

But as the kin groups and the size of the local community expanded, these units also became important cultural pressure groups and in some ways limited individualism. Although a woman's brother might help her with her husband, he is also watching her behavior. Her mother and sister are here to help her, but her mother-in-law is also here to control her. The attacks on the Arab community in the United States and Dearborn have produced a sense of defensive unity or revitalism in regard to ethnic and religious traditions.

The recent immigrants also bring diverse ideologies, often including increased religiosity and reformism. There has been considerable intergenerational conflict because many Lebanese have teenagers, and there has also been conflict between the more assimilated second- and third-generation youngsters and newly arrived teenagers. There are also conflicts between various ideological groups, primarily between the religious and secular groups, and Lebanese women became involved in these political groups.

The Yemeni women, on the other hand, are in some ways similar to the early Lebanese women since they are forming nuclear families, are not forced to share the running of their home with a mother-in-law, and are freer from the responsibility for caring for their elders. But they also miss the assistance of their kin. While none are employed outside the home and they have few marketable skills they have a sense of independence. The vast majority have a member of their patriline here, a father or brother, who represents their interests in relation to their husbands as well as watches and controls their behavior.

In contrast to the early Lebanese, Yemeni women have an Arabic and Islamic community to support them. Consequently, they face fewer pressures to assimilate and are more isolated from American society. On the other hand, the Yemeni women have also developed important neighborhood networks, and they are not isolated from each other. Thus, they do not resemble many American nuclear families that have no such strong neighborhood supports.

For their part, Yemeni men had not been integrated into many institutions of the community because they had no families with them. Now they are being forced to look at educational and other institutions. Yemeni women are not politically involved in the community and are not involved with mosque organizations to any degree. They have also not joined other women's groups, partly because of their lack of experience and a lack of a second generation to help them organize and partly because of their restricted mobility, much of which is forced on them by their husbands. Village dress and lack of education has also caused discrimination, thus furthering their seclusion.

It is important to remind ourselves, that, for the individuals discussed, the family and ethnic community have been restrictive in many ways, but they have provided protection for the individual not found in some other similar income neighborhoods where poverty and crime against individuals is great. In the Southend, people share information, money, and protection. There is less of the alcoholism, drug use, assault, rape, or murder that terrifies nearby communities. The ethic of family honor and shame, 'ayb', limits misbehavior.

Thus, the experiences of the Muslim women in this study are affected by conditions in their homelands, the particular nature of migration, their life-cycle stage, employment conditions, the existence of alternative resources and laws such as welfare and custody, and the specific nature of the local community into which they migrate, as well as the national policies and climates of the host country.

*Notes*

This study was conducted in 1983/84 with the assistance of a sabbatical leave from Wayne State University and a contract with the Arabic Community Center for Economic and Social Services (ACCESS), Dearborn. The author would like to thank various persons for their support and discussions, including Anisa Nasar, Zahour Anouti, Nancy Addadow Gray, Faye Awada, Ismael Ahmed, Ellen Rumman, Helen Atwell and Katherine Amen, as well as, of course, the interviewees.

1. This represents approximately 9 percent of the Arab immigrant families in the Southend community of Dearborn.
2. Since these interviews were given, the Lebanese community has grown significantly due to the wars in Lebanon and its center is now along Warren Avenue, north of the Southend. There are a total of 18,000 Arabs in Dearborn.

# Palestinian-American Muslim Women: Living on the Margins of Two Worlds

## Louise Cainkar

◆    ◆    ◆    ◆

This paper provides a portrait of the life experiences of Palestinian Muslim women born or raised in Chicago.[1] It is based on participant observation and life histories recounted to the researcher between 1982 and 1985. The portrait begins with childhood and proceeds through adolescence to adulthood. As in all life histories, data based on recollections of the past are selective since only those events and feelings that remain prominent are recalled. The fact that the experiences described by respondents were remarkably similar, despite variations in economic status and the fact that respondents grew up in relative isolation from each other, attests to the validity and significance of these recollections. The paper also accounts for variations where they occurred and presents respondents' own evaluations of these experiences.

The women described in this paper are the daughters of what may be called the first wave of Palestinian Muslim immigrants to Chicago, a wave defined broadly to include all those who left Palestine prior to 1967. It is distinguishable from the post-1967 immigration wave in that it was much smaller in size, even though it spanned some sixty years, and the immigrants were a fairly homogeneous group. The vast majority were villagers from the Jerusalem-Ramallah area. They were of similar socio-economic background (modest local landholdings),

had little formal education, and came to the United States for economic reasons. According to Al-Tahir's (1952) study, before 1945 the
community was almost totally male. The men lived in boarding houses
on the near-south side of Chicago and were peddlers or merchants by
occupation. Palestinian Muslim families became evident in Chicago after World War II, when trans-Atlantic travel was once again possible
and political strife characterized the homeland. When the men brought
their wives and children to Chicago, they moved into residential communities. However, because they preferred to live near their places of
business, Palestinian Muslim families did not settle in a concentrated
geographic area but were scattered, mostly throughout the south side
of Chicago.[2]

The 1950s and 1960s witnessed a slow but steady chain migration
of the immediate families and relatives of the earliest immigrants. This
migration did not change the parameters of the Chicago Muslim Palestinian community substantially. It became somewhat larger, and the
newer immigrants had more formal education than earlier ones, but for
the most part they were from the same families, pursued the same occupations, and continued the same residential patterns. Palestinians
immigrating to the United States after the Israeli occupation of the
West Bank and Gaza in 1967 represent a broader range of Palestinians—economically, occupationally, educationally, and regionally—and
their numbers have increased steadily. Nonetheless, most of those in
Chicago hail from the West Bank, as a result of chain migrations and
the fact that Palestinians from the West Bank have passports (Jordanian). Few Palestinian immigrants to the U.S. are from the poorest
segments of Palestinian society.[3] In contrast to the earlier arrivals, the
post-1967 immigrants have tended to settle in concentrated communities. Because they left home for political-economic reasons, their presence has politicized the Palestinian community in Chicago.

The findings presented here are based on participant observation, informal interviews, and formal open-ended life history interviews with
twenty-two Palestinian-American women born between 1943 and
1961. Most of the interviewees were born in the United States; some
were born in Palestine and immigrated to the United States at an early
age.[4] In all but one case, both parents were Muslim Palestinian and
foreign-born. These women were between twenty-six and forty-four
years of age where interviewed. Although their parents were originally

from similar backgrounds, respondents grew up in different socio-economic classes as a result of their parents' different economic experiences in the United States. It is important to remember that because of the scattered residential patterns of the early community, these women were raised in relative isolation from other Muslim Palestinians. While many had relatives in Chicago, they did not live near or with them and usually saw them only on Sunday visits. The women were raised in nuclear family settings in white American Christian neighborhoods. Yet, despite tremendous changes in the size, diversity, and residential patterns of the Palestinian community in Chicago, much of what is recounted below appears to remain valid for Palestinian females currently growing up in Chicago.[5]

## GROWING UP DISCOVERING DIFFERENCES

The most prominent childhood memory of the respondents was the gradual discovery that they were different from other children. This awareness was not something they learned at home or felt inside; it was imposed upon them from outside. They felt they were just like the other children with whom they shared playtime activities. They thought the same way and liked to do the same things, but they were aware that there was something different about their families. There was a language difference between the home and the world outside. In most cases, their mothers spoke only Arabic, while their fathers spoke English as well. English was the language of business; Arabic, the language of the home. They were also aware that they ate different foods. Sometimes they were even embarassed to bring their friends home, for fear that these differences might arouse undue attention. Yet, their perception was that these differences were not important—they were really no different from anyone else, even if their parents were.

Religion had little impact on their early lives; no one recalled that being Muslim was something to hide or that it was a source of distinction or ridicule in their dominantly Christian neighborhoods. Perhaps language and food were visible distinctions, but Islam as a religious ideology was not. As children, they did not attend mosques or Islamic "sunday schools" (which for the most part did not exist), and Islamic rules that would make them different had not yet touched their lives.

Nonetheless, slowly but surely they learned that they were children with a "strange" ancestry. They were Arabs in the American sense—

displaced camel jockeys and tent dwellers who did not belong in the United States. Though they felt a part of the neighborhood, many others did not feel the same way about them. Some respondents remembered neighborhood adults telling them as children "go back where you came from." Many times their names drew sneers and laughter from other children.

> I wish that as an American-Palestinian child growing up people could have seen me for who I was and not just for my name. We did not live in an area of immigrants and we were teased about our names.

Most difficult to endure were the ethnic slurs, which were usually made by other children and became more common when they entered elementary school. Usually they took the form of jokes, such as: "where is your camel?" or "where is your veil?" Though the aim of these jokes was to point out that the child was different, the result in all cases was a desire on the part of the Arab children to prove that they were just the same.

> You wanted to hide the fact that you were different, that your family did things in a different way. The jokes made you want to prove how much like the other kids you really were.

During their childhood years Palestinian-American children concentrated on having fun and downplayed the differences that others wanted to emphasize.

As they proceeded through elementary school, these Palestinian-American girls discovered another source of distinction. This time it had little to do with ethnicity. They became aware of gender, that girls and boys had different rights and responsibilities and that, as girls, they were the unlucky ones. When they became old enough to perform domestic chores, young girls were given responsibility for washing dishes, ironing clothes, cleaning the home, and watching over younger siblings. Their work lessened the load on their mothers, who, in the absence of female kin, bore the entire domestic workload. These responsibilities curtailed the freedom of their early years, reducing their playtime after school and keeping them in the house much more than their brothers. This situation, however, was readily understood by their girl friends, who had more or less similar responsibilities. Girls were expected to help with the housework, no matter what their ethnic background. Initially, ethnic differences were mitigated by the uniformities of gender.

Their brothers were generally spared household responsibilities and had more freedom. But these inequities did not arouse a sense of inequality in the girls as much as they did a feeling that the boys were treated as though they were special. Most respondents believed that their brothers received more attention than they did, particularly from their mothers. In some families, the girls felt as though they were placed in a servile relationship to their brothers.

> They were raised like typical Arab males. We cooked for them, washed their clothes, ironed their shirts, and cleaned up after them. They were more privileged than we and they knew it.

> My brothers were catered to and pampered. They got so much special attention and my sisters and I always lamented over this.

In urban Chicago, there was no economic or domestic role for the young boys, so they were able to pass through their pre-adolescent and adolescent years relatively free from family responsibility, a situation less likely to occur in the differently structured social systems and economies of the Middle East. While the household as a unit of production and consumption is a universal and the need for internal labor a constant, the existence and nature of work outside the home varies by context. In the Palestinian town or village the labor of young boys was put to use very early. In the Western industrial city, where by social custom male labor is considered appropriate only in the extra domestic sphere, their labor loses its viability. The family unit does not work the land, and children are legally prohibited from engaging in paid or unpaid extra domestic labor. Only within the home is unpaid and child labor permissible, and these activities are almost routinely assigned to females. At most, boys might run errands for their mothers, since relations with the outside world have been considered the province of males.

## THE TEENAGE YEARS: ISOLATION & MARGINALITY

If the childhood and pre-adolescent years described above were characterized by discovering ethnic and gender differences, the teenage years for Palestinian-American Muslim girls were marked by the discovery that they were different from *everybody*. During these years they had their most difficult experiences. For most, it was a period of conflict, for some a period of anger and the wish to rebel. In addition to other possible adolescent traumas, Palestinian Muslim girls found out that they had to bear the burden of maintaining the family's honor. Life outside the home became restricted to attendence at school. After school the girls were expected to come home immediately and stay there. Extracurricular activities, school clubs and sports events, dances and dating were forbidden. Many parents forced their daughters to sever their close friendships with American girls because Americans were considered a bad influence. American girls had different morals, and Americans in general did not understand the Muslim or Arab way of life, so they claimed.

This way of life differed in numerous ways from dominant American patterns. But the key differences that led to severe restrictions on the freedom of movement of teenage Palestinian Muslim girls revolved around ideas about acceptable patterns of male-female relations. The idea that unrelated teenage males and females may develop intimate relationships with each other has long been commonly accepted in American society. Only the level of intimacy allowed and character of the partner deemed acceptable has varied, depending upon the time period, social class, and ethnicity of the American reference group. Similarly, individual choice of marital spouse has been fairly broadly accepted among Americans. Neither of these patterns was acceptable to the majority of Palestinian Muslims, and parents of daughters raised in the United States tried to shield them from these possibilities. Their response was to minimize the girls' relations with Americans, while the boys were still allowed their freedom.

For these Palestinian-American girls, adjustment to the life they were now expected to lead was quite difficult, though the level of difficulty experienced varied. Sheer loss of freedom was the main source of discontent, but there were a number of exacerbating factors. The new rules seemed to have been applied suddenly and for reasons that were not clear to them. They had not been prepared for the new restrictions. In most cases, their parents had not stressed from early childhood that they were different from other children and that the rules and values of American society were not to be their rules and values. In Palestinian society, the familial inculcation of religious and cultural values is buttressed by the society outside the home. A young girl can observe her fate by looking around her. In the United States this is not so. As children they had little education in the Arab/Islamic way of life, and it was certainly not visible in the world outside the home.

Thus, the conflicts of the teenage years resulted in part from the lack of conflict between family rules and American social life during the earliest years. Had their families kept them isolated from Americans from the start, perhaps they would not have expected to lead normal American teenage lives. Their childhood had allowed them to fit into American society and assimilate many of its values. Feeling as though they were like other American children, and many times being pushed to prove it, they were distressed by the change to a new set of criteria. When they asked their parents why these restrictions were being placed upon them, the answers they were given did not help much.

When I was in high school I couldn't do anything. No extracurricular activities—and I was a straight A student. I couldn't even have American friends. Why? I was told that this was because I was an Arab.

If I wanted to do anything after school, my brother had to go with me. My parents said this was the Moslem way.

Sometimes the explanation was expressed in terms of being Arab, sometimes Muslim. (Rarely was the term Palestinian used.) Either way it made little sense to these girls, for both concepts were remote from their understanding of their lives. Comparing the reactions to this period of the few Palestinian-American girls whose parents had explained to them at a young age that they were "different" and should expect a life different from their American peers with those of girls whose parents had not prepared them reveals that adjustment to the new rules was much more difficult for the latter.

The restrictions caused further problems. They created distance between the Palestinian-Americans and their American girl friends, especially in cases where the girls were forced to cut all ties with them. Many were allowed to keep their American friends but could not participate in activities with them outside of school.

I began to feel different. My American friends looked at me as if I was strange because I was American in one way but Arab in another.

Whereas as children the Palestinian-American girls could assert to their peers that they were not in fact different, doing so now became nearly impossible because the parameters of their lives proved that they were indeed "different." There was no way around the restrictions; the family was asserting its authority, and nothing short of rebellion could affect it. Rebellion would have entailed great risks, particularly for a daughter. The authority and honor of the family would have been at stake and disciplinary action would certainly follow. For a teenager, dependent upon the family for support, there was really nowhere else to turn.

Adjustment meant coming to terms with being a person on the margins, a person who "stands on the borders or margins of two cultural worlds but is fully a member of neither" (Gordon, 1964:56). Discussions of the classical sociological concept of the "marginal man" (*sic*) typically describe it as a result of volitional behavior on the part of the actor, the actor always being male. The marginal man wishes to be part of a world that is at variance with the world in which he was raised. As the case of these Palestinian females reveals, one can also be forced into marginality by being required to live in a world for which one is unprepared.

The problems of friendship and marginality were clearly increased by the fact that these girls grew up in relative isolation from other Palestinian Muslim girls. There was no one with whom they could share their predicament, no one who could understand; there was no support structure for them. Only if they had sisters did they have someone who could understand what they were going through. The reference group they had grown up with, other American girls, was not applicable anymore. Where did they fit in?

If they turned to their brothers, they found little comprehension. Their brothers followed the same trajectory they had since birth. Their male status overruled all other possible statuses: Arab, Muslim, or Palestinian. Palestinian Muslim boys were allowed to maintain their friendships with Americans and, as seen from the perspective of their sisters, go wherever they wanted, whenever they wanted. They were allowed to play sports, join clubs, go to dances and date. If the girls were restricted on the basis of Islamic or Arab cultural principles, these principles were not applied to the boys. It is not that the boys were encouraged to follow the American pattern, they just were not actively discouraged if they chose to do so.

The unrestricted freedom of the boys greatly increased girls' resentment of the system. Depending upon how the brothers responded to this situation of inequality, they either helped or hindered their sisters' adjustment to it. Some brothers flaunted their privileged status and so added to the girls' resentment. Others empathized with their sisters and took on the responsibility of accompanying them to places they wanted to go in order to increase their mobility. But even in such cases the sense of inequity prevailed, for often the brothers were nearly the same age or even younger than the girls. The girls learned that the scope of their lives was in large part contingent upon the goodwill gestures of their male "guardians."

This liberal policy with regard to Palestinian-American boys seems to have been based on the notion that boys cannot or should not be controlled or restricted. At least, this is the reasoning currently being used by immigrant Palestinian mothers who have teenage sons. During interviews with such women, each conceded that their sons were allowed to have American friends, go to parties, and date, while their daughters were not. They justified this double standard by saying:

You can't tell boys what to do, they do what they want.

You can't force sons to not take their freedom, they just take it.

I discourage my sons from dating, but I let them do it. I don't let them bring their girl friends home. I don't want my daughter to feel bad.

No doubt the context of the United States, where male-female interactions have been fairly standard in the general culture, made it difficult to enforce ideas about the wrongfulness of premarital social and sexual relations between unrelated males and females. But context alone does not explain the patterns found; the temptations and difficulties would have been equal for male and female children. The explanation that boys are given freedom because they cannot be controlled reduces cultural patterns that support male privilege to a biological explanation.

## DISCUSSION

It is clear that gender is an important variable in the immigrant/ethnic experience. During the process of growing up, Palestinian-American females and males had significantly different relationships with the American society they lived in. Their lives were so different that the girls found it extremely difficult to relate to their brothers; each lived in a different world. These differences are not reduceable to biological explanations, nor are cultural or religious explanations sufficient.

This outcome results from an interaction between gender, culture/ religion, and context. The American context actually *exacerbates* the gender disparities which exist in the ethnic cultural and religious systems. This finding conflicts with statements found in the (limited) literature on female immigrants in the United States. For example:

> [Migration is a] liberating process and results in a modicum of sexual equality, causing the rural cognitive modes about women's place no longer to be operative. (Whiteford, 1978)

> [Migration is a] rejection, conscious or unconscious of traditional female roles. (Seller, 1981)

These statements are based on a number of inaccurate assumptions, including the notion that developed or Western countries are "modern" environments which are *by definition* liberating or at least less oppressive for females than developing or third world countries.[6] Recent European studies, however, have shown that migration from the Third World to Western countries may actually result in losses of status and personal freedom for women (for example, Morokvasic, 1984; Phizacklea, 1983; Alund, 1978). In a study of Turkish villagers in the Netherlands, Brouwer and Priester found that Turkish women depended greatly upon the friendship and support of each other because they had few other social contacts:

> This is partly due to the husband's fear of contamination by the "European dissolute way of life" which offends his entire value system and often results in a severe overprotection of women to

prevent the undermining of this value system. Compared to life in Arpa (Turkey) it means in practice a reduced freedom of movement for women. (1983:124)

The interaction of ethnic culture and traditional values, gender, and context can work against female autonomy and mobility, especially where "contamination" from the core culture, perceived as morally bankrupt, is feared.[7]

Gender-based differences in life experiences are not unique to Arabs or Muslims; indeed, every society exhibits such differences. Further, as anthropologists Margaret Mead (1935), Ernestine Friedl (1975), Michelle Rosaldo, and countless others have observed in comparative studies of cultures, "an asymmetry in the cultural evaluations of male and female, in the importance assigned to women and men, appears to be universal" (Rosaldo, 1974:19). Nonetheless, there are qualitative and quantitative differences between societies on this score, and justifications for these differences are usually coded in rationales with culturally specific meaning.

The disparate patterns by gender described above evolved in part from the immigrant parents' application of traditional Arab cultural values, concerns, and role-socialization practices in raising their male and female children. These include greater maternal indulgence of boys in the interest of maintaining the loyalty and affection of sons, whose support and care the mother will someday require, and greater familial control of girls in order to to maintain the reputation and virginity of unmarried daughters and maintain control over a daughter's marital choice. Socialization for gender roles requires teaching daughters domestic skills and self-denial and teaching sons extra-domestic skills— survival in the world outside the home and independence—and self-actualization. But what becomes particularly clear when this traditional social system is transplanted to Western soil is that Arab males and females are raised to participate in two distinct territorial worlds, the male world being much larger, more heterogeneous, and completely surrounding the female.

This implicitly understood but not consciously recognized principle of territorial asymmetry requires that females always stay within the bounds defined by the cultural/religious system, which is there to protect, support and control them. Males, however, may operate both within and outside of the traditional system—they may cross its borders and permeate other territories if they choose to do so, so long as when they are physically within the system they respect its rules. The cultural mandate that females stay within certain clearly marked boundaries which related males are able to traverse freely, but which outside males may never permeate, is a commonly observed pattern of patriarchal systems. Each society bears its own historical form of this pattern, which tends to be reproduced almost unconsciously, irrespective of time and context.[8]

Maintaining the viability and integrity of the patriarchal family and reproducing a patriarchal social structure requires strict female acceptance of and adherence to the rules of the game. The system is not threatened when males go outside its bounds; it is only threatened by female noncompliance. Anthropologist Sherry Ortner has suggested that it is woman's role as the bearer and socializer of children that requires her to be more ideologically and physically controlled if she is expected to reproduce a system which objectively subordinates her:

> Any culture's continued viability depends upon properly socialized individuals who will see the world in that culture's terms and adhere more or less unquestioningly to its moral precepts. Insofar as woman is universally the primary agent of early socialization she will tend to come under the heavier restrictions and circumscriptions. In virtually every culture her permissible sexual activities are more closely circumscribed than man's, she is offered a much smaller range of role choices, and she is afforded direct access to a more limited range of its social institutions. (1974:84-85)

It is the combination of dual territoriality and the American context, where the ethnic group is surrounded by a society with vastly different, and more liberal, social and moral codes, that results in males becoming more free and females more rigidly controlled than they would be in their own country. Palestinian males have considerable freedom of action because they are allowed to participate in both cultures, and any contradiction implied by this behavior is simply overlooked. Since Palestinian females may not step outside the boundaries of the ethnic social system, they are more rigidly patrolled in the United States, where outsiders predominate, than in the Middle East.

Overall, the community in Chicago fundamentally accepts this double standard, though many members, especially young females, do not. The implicity understood rule is that male social and sexual freedom is permissible as long as it is exercised with non-Arab females. Since they are "outsiders," they are not perceived as a threat to the traditional Arab way of life. However, should Palestinian females engage in such behavior, it would be viewed as an act of rebellion. "Outside" females cannot threaten the system, but "outside" males can. American born/raised Palestinian Muslim females live on the margins of two societies, while the males traverse them at will.

Among most segments of the Palestinian community in Chicago, the respect of other Palestinians is gained by showing respect for Palestinian culture. This respect is judged on the basis of the behavior of a family's female members, who are the symbols of a family's commitment to its Palestinian identity. They bear the burden of the family's honor in the ethnic community. This pattern of judgment has taken on a life of its own such that even if a girl's parents were willing to relax some rules, concern over the condemnation of others has stopped them.

The assumption by members of the community that this system of double standards actually preserves the integrity of the ethnic culture and social system and fends off the threats posed to it by American culture is probably false. The result of this differential treatment of boys and girls has had many counterproductive results, though their insidious nature has left them so far unrecognized. The following discussion of adulthood and marriage points to some of the problems that have evolved.

## PATHS INTO ADULTHOOD

The tensions and traumas of life as a Palestinian-American Muslim girl peaked for most respondents during the teenage years and gradually began to lessen after they completed high school. The alternatives that then became available to them were college or marriage. Entry into the labor force was not a viable option since their parents were fearful of the effects of interaction with Americans, especially males. Nor was staying home an option for any extended period of time. Family and community members would interpret this behavior as waiting for marriage proposals. If the girl did not become engaged within a reasonable period, questions would be raised and gossip would ensue. The most graceful way to avoid early marriage was to pursue a higher education.[9] Some women, however, did not have this choice; they were forced into arranged marriages before the age of eighteen. Among respondents in this study, none of these marriages lasted.[10]

The practice of forcing teenage daughters into arranged marriages seems to have practically disappeared in the Chicago Palestinian community. In fact, among my respondents, it happened only to those who were born before 1950. Indeed, although childhood and adolescent experiences were essentially the same for all of the women interviewed, despite the fact that they were born during an eighteen-year range (1943 to 1961), their adult experiences cannot be portrayed monolithically. Respondents reached the age of eighteen between 1961 and 1979, a range of years representing a dynamic period in the history of Palestine, Palestinians, and the Palestinian community in Chicago. The community grew tremendously after 1967, and this change had a significant impact on the lives of the community's earliest members. Based on the data collected in this study, adult experiences can only be portrayed accurately when respondents are broken in two cohorts: those born before 1954 (the elder cohort) and those born after (the younger cohort).[11]

Parental desire to arrange marriages for their teenage daughters was common for Palestinian-American women born before 1954 (age eighteen before 1972). All of the women interviewed were approached with the idea, and all of them were totally opposed to it. Having been raised in a culture in which romantic ideas about love were prized, they did not want to marry someone they did not care for and, in some cases, did not even know. They also felt that they were too young to get married. Alongside these concerns, they wanted to continue their education and knew marriage would make it impossible.

Nonetheless, a few members of this elder cohort were forced to accepted arranged marriages, usually with first cousins. Two were pulled out of high school for such marriages. Their parents feared that they would lose control over their daughters (and their honor) should they attend college or take on employment. Rather than have the girl sit "idly" in the home, it was better to find a marriage partner for her. Each of these girls tried to turn to teachers or brothers for help in escaping their fate but found none. As noted earlier, these arranged marriages did not last, though there are other cases in the community where they have. As a result of these marriages, the female participants were forced to accept their identity as Palestinian-Arabs. The feelings generated by accepting this identity, however, were not positive. They felt that they had been "sacrificial lambs" for the honor of the family. They also saw that their brothers were allowed to pursue their own interests and that their husbands had married them regardless of their wishes. This experience crystallized the unfairness they had felt most of their lives.

None of the respondents in the younger cohort experienced a forced marriage. Although the idea of an arranged marriage had been suggested to them when they completed high school, they were allowed to reject it. Only one respondent in the younger cohort reported having a severe conflict with her family after high school, but it was not over marriage *per se*. She had been a straight-A student in high school and had been granted a number of scholarships, but her father prevented her from attending college. Determined to fulfill her dream, she ran away from home. This was an extremely bold move, and for a number of years she was hunted and threatened by male family members, and eventually she was forbidden to ever return home or to establish contact with family members. Exiled from her family, she finished college, got a good job, rooted herself in a wholly American identity, and married an American man.

Most respondents were allowed and many were encouraged by their families to continue their education after high school. Though the majority attended college, some went to trade schools (for example, beautician's school), and these options were perceived as acceptable when the school was in the Chicago area and the girl lived at home. As students in a postsecondary school these women gained more freedom of movement than they had had during the high school years. But the most important process that occurred as part of the college experience was coming to terms with their identity, primarily as a result of their growing personal maturity and increased knowledge about their ethnic cultural roots. Though they had grown up as entrenched members of an ethnic group, they knew almost nothing about its history and little of the culture. What they had experienced was only part of the culture, and it was mostly the restrictive features. Lacking were the strong extended family and community bonds, the music, the land, the celebration of feasts, and a comprehensive understanding of the cultural whole. Encouraged by the environment of learning, each of these girls began to read about Islam, Arab culture and society, and Palestine.

Their American elementary and secondary school educations had left them with little knowledge of the Arab world or Islam. The great contributions of Islamic/Arab civilization to science and humanity were ignored in text books, which categorized this historical period as the "Dark Ages." The world outside the school had been no better. With the passage of time, the hostility of the American media and the American government to Arabs and Palestinians increased. Many Americans, absorbing this information, developed increasingly anti-Arab attitudes. With all these obstacles before them, yet with a clear recognition that they were Arabs, Muslims, and Palestinians, these women gained new knowledge that helped to round out their understanding of their life experiences and to develop a sense of ethnic pride. In a sense, they had no other choice but to accept their connection to the Arab world, Islam, and Palestine. To reject it resulted in too much personal, interpersonal, and familial conflict.

The ways in which these women gained this knowledge varied by cohort. Members of the elder cohort had to research their history on their own because there were few other Palestinians in school with them. Members of the younger cohort had a significantly different experience. By the time they were in college, the early 1970s and thereafter, the Palestinian community in Chicago had grown tremendously, and it was more diverse. Clear neighborhood clusters of Palestinians were established, large numbers of single males came seeking education, and for the first time, a distinct Palestinian community was forming. The new arrivals had different ideas, for Palestine itself had changed considerably.

Palestinian organizations were formed on college campuses, and for those who sought them, they provided sources of information and opportunities to meet other Palestinians. They encouraged Palestinian identity and pride. Negative feelings about being Arab, carried over from the difficult high school years, were replaced by pride in being Palestinian.

I knew that my family was from Palestine but it seemed that no one had ever heard of it, so I used to say that I was Arab. At one point I hated Arabs because the Arab way restricted me so much. There's no doubt that I am an Arab. But now I have learned a lot and I am proud to be a Palestinian.

I really didn't know what Palestine was. I only knew that I was an Arab because my parents always told me so. But when I went to college I began to learn about Palestine. We Palestinians have come a long way. We still have a long way to go. But I am very proud to be a Palestinian.

Members of the younger cohort benefited in another way from the existence of Palestinian organizations. Since they brought together Palestinians who might otherwise be isolated, their events gave young Palestinian-American women a chance to meet each other. Now, finally, they found compatible peer groups, persons who could understand how they grew up and who shared similar feelings about it. While these friendship groups provided comfort and support, they did not necessarily reduce the marginality of the Palestinian-American woman. As the Palestinian Muslim community grew in size, the foreign-born part of it became much larger than the American-born; the community in Chicago became, once again, essentially an immigrant community. Many Palestinian-American women came to perceive that, as in the case of the larger American society, they did not fit into this community either.

I try to uphold the traditions of the Middle East while living in the U.S. It makes you feel slightly schizophrenic; sometimes you don't feel like a part of either society. I can sit in Arab circles and not feel part of them even though I am familiar with the customs and language. I am not totally accepted there and I am not totally accepted by Americans either.

I know many Americans and Palestinians and I am not totally accepted in either group.

There are certain aspects of the American culture that are part of me. I am a Palestinian but I am also American.

I feel Palestinian, but I also feel somewhat removed from the Palestinian community.

Alternately, for some other Palestinian-American women, organizational involvement produced an alienation from American society and fostered the development of a predominantly Palestinian identity. These women participated in a community organization that espoused as part of its political philosophy ideologically progressive views about women. They felt comfortable with this group because it seemed to have less traditional views about female behavior and allowed them to be active in the community. Political action and community service helped to replace a confused identity. The majority of the people they worked with were foreign-born/raised and new immigrants, and this was the group they came to identify with.

> I don't feel American anymore. Their blind support for Zionism makes them discriminate against Arabs. They don't even know why. If I am American then I am killing my own people.

> The amount of racism against Arabs in this country, and American foreign policy, have pushed me to drop the feeling of being American.

Though they rejected their American identity, these Palestinian-American women also developed their closest friendships with other such women. This generation had grown up straddling two cultures; by adulthood it was just too difficult to excise the difference this created in them.

It is interesting to note that among American-born/raised Palestinians, the females are most active in community organizations; males are not likely to participate in them at all. This pattern is easily explained. Culturally, the males have been allowed to be American, and they have tended to blend into American society. Since they have been less likely to develop the pressing need to come to terms with a mixed identity or a feeling of marginality, they have not sought out Palestinian organizations.

## ABOUT MARRIAGE

Despite the positive developments of young adulthood for the Palestinian-American women who remained single—improved self-image, an understanding of their ethnic roots, partial resolution of identity conflicts, and establishing compatible friendship groups—marriage has been and remains problematic for them. This difficulty is due in part to the attitudes of Palestinian-American women regarding the traditional process of courtship and marriage and in part to real limitations on the pool of potential spouses. A marriage totally instigated and arranged by parents is not acceptable to the American-raised Palestinian Muslim woman. At a minimum, she wants to become familiar with a man prior to marriage, to share expectations of marital life, and to develop a feeling of intimacy. This desire is found among many Middle Eastern-raised Palestinian women as well. The possibility of this kind of "courtship" occurring, while greater now than in the past, has been subject to numerous constraints and limitations.

The Palestinian Muslim woman in the United States is usually held to the cultural and religious mandate that she marry a Muslim man. It is even better if he is Palestinian and from the same village or town as her parents, but given the relative scarcity of Muslims in the United States, these nationality and locale preferences have been relaxed. Palestinian American women have been willing to marry Muslim men provided that the courtship procedures described above could occur and that the men concerned did not subscribe to ideas about male domination and female subservience. Given the experiences of their upbringing, these women were not willing to submit voluntarily to a recreation of their powerlessness.

## THE ELDER COHORT (WOMEN WHO REACHED ADULTHOOD IN THE 1960S)

Once again, time is important in describing the context for courtship and marriage among Palestinians in Chicago. For members of the elder cohort marriage proposals came in the traditional way. They were usually from cousins, who may have been living anywhere: in Chicago, Palestine, or South America. Each of the respondents who were allowed to reject such proposals did. Maybe they did not like the idea of marrying a cousin or were reticent about marrying an Arab man, maybe they did not like the particular man, or perhaps they simply were not ready for marriage, but in any case, they knew they would be prevented from becoming well acquainted with the man before making a decision.

The parents of these women left Palestine when ideas about appropriate courtship behavior were more conservative and the educational level of Palestinians as a whole was much lower than now. Yet, even if certain parents had been willing, in principle, to allow their daughter to see a suitor alone a number of times before she reached a decision, many other factors held them back. Should their daughter be seen in public with an eligible man, a scandal would ensue. Had they allowed her to see a suitor and then she decided against marrying him, they would have to be concerned over what the man would say to others (remember, he was usually a relative and usually the woman is blamed). The process could not be repeated with another man without it appearing that the parents approved of dating. Concern about gossip, reputation, and honor holds many people to traditional ways, even if they personally do not agree with them. In the end, the man approaching the Palestinian-American woman in the traditional way was rejected as much because of the courtship method and what it symbolized as for himself.

The courtship method was not the only obstacle to marriage. In the opinion of these Palestinian-American women the marriage proposals came too early; they were teenagers and wanted to attend college. The men, foreign-born and without a college education, were not interested in marrying a college-educated woman. In Palestinian village society of the 1950s and 1960s this preference was not at all unusual.

After she finished college, the Palestinian-American woman of this cohort was too educated for most of the Palestinian men she would meet through family and community ties. In a way, her education drove her out of the potential marriage market. Later, in the 1970s when college-educated Palestinian males could be found in Chicago, these women were in their mid-twenties to thirties and were seen as "too old" for marriage, given the cultural preference for young brides. The following vignette provides some perspective on the thinking of a Palestinian-American woman from this cohort (now turning forty):

After college I would have considered the proposal of a stranger. When I was in high school a cousin came to ask for my hand in marriage but I was really more interested in my education. I wanted to go to college and I didn't want to marry. My uncles came and told me what a nice young man he was. But I just wasn't interested in marriage. My father accepted that. Then I had another proposal for marriage and I refused that one also. This cousin was in the U.S. I knew that if I was married we'd start a family and I would have to split myself between home and school. My father broke with family tradition at that time and gave me his blessings to attend college. He was not overly hung-up about securing my honor and virginity, which is why fathers like to see their daughters married early. He trusted me.

I knew that this method of proposal was the way it was done. That's how it was done with my sister and my cousins. I knew that was the way it should be. I just wasn't ready for marriage. I knew from what I saw around me that arranged marriages could be happy. I didn't see the high divorce rate I saw among American families. I felt there was something to it. At that time it was just not something for me.

For Palestinian-American women like her, there were at the time few other ways to meet Palestinian Muslim men, or any other Muslim man. The few community or religious organizations that did exist were small, and they were the creation and domain of foreign-born males. Further, the custom that the female must be passive in courtship procedures added another barrier to finding a mate. If there were logistical and compatibility problems in the way of marrying a foreign-born/raised Palestinian Muslim male, what about marrying one raised in the United States?

Such men might seem more suitable partners for Palestinian-American Muslim women, given their familiarity with American customs and ways of thinking. However, most American-born/raised Palestinian Muslim males married American Christian women. This was a natural outcome of their being able to date American females and to be part of American society with impunity. They grew up socializing mostly with Americans, and like other Americans, they dated and married women they fell in love with. It was not that these men necessarily preferred non-Palestinian women; rather, they had no real access to Palestinian women because of familial restrictions on them and the nature of community sentiments. Like the women, they wanted to marry someone they knew and had feelings for. It was simply easier to gain this familiarity and develop intimacy with American Christian women. Consequently, for Palestinian-American Muslim women, most Palestinian-American Muslim men were also excluded from the pool of potential spouses. The outcome for the majority of this group of Palestinian-American women has been that they have remained single into their late thirties and forties. A few did marry but are now divorced. One woman married an American Jew and her family tried to support her choice, but her relatives and the community never accepted it.

## THE YOUNGER COHORT (WOMEN WHO REACHED ADULTHOOD IN THE 1970S)

Palestinian-American women born since the mid-1950s reached adulthood in the 1970s and 1980s, when the community had increased tremendously in size, was more diverse, and included large numbers of single Palestinian men, either attached to immigrating families or alone pursuing a college education. Through school and Palestinian organizational activities, now geared to many sectors of the community, Palestinian-American women of the younger cohort were able to meet Palestinian men, almost all of whom were foreign-born/raised, and their large numbers greatly improved the potential marriage market for Palestinian-American Muslim women.

Despite a large pool of potential spouses, there are still obstacles in the way of marriage for these women. Though they are no longer more educated than the available men, and the attitude that women in their twenties are "too old" for marriage is not as commonly held, the attitudes of foreign-born Palestinian men towards Palestinian women who are a product of American society provide a new barrier.

A large proportion of the foreign-born men do not want to marry Palestinian-American women; they see them as undesirable marriage partners. These women are perceived as having an inadequate Palestinian cultural background, while Palestinian political ideology stresses the importance of maintaining and reproducing the culture to offset the destructive effects of nationlessness, foreign occupation, and exile. This idea has been widely impressed on the consciousness of the generation of Palestinians who grew up under occupation or in exile in an Arab country. From this perspective Palestinian-American women are found lacking: their Arabic is poor, and they are seen as not being able to create a Palestinian home environment or to raise children who will be able to reproduce Palestinian language and culture.

Further, many foreign-born Palestinian men fear that Palestinian-American women might be too assertive and self-determined. They fear that the women may not be as selfless as their Middle-Eastern-raised counterparts, and that, consequently, as men, they may not be as pampered as they are used to and that too many demands may be made upon them. In sum, Palestinian-American women are seen as "too American." This view is most likely to be held by those men who prefer to hold women to traditional roles. But it is not exclusive to conservative men. Many men who are quite liberal in their view of women's roles feel that given the trouble, expense, and risk involved in marrying a Palestinian-American woman, it is preferable to marry either a "real" Palestinian from overseas or an American.

The Palestinian-American woman who has reached adulthood since the 1970s finds herself in the vacuum created by her family's wish to marry her in the traditional way and the Palestinian man's view that she is not a traditional Palestinian woman. Should a Palestinian man consider marrying a Palestinian-American woman, he would want to become familiar with her before asking for her hand, given his reservations about her knowledge of the culture and her attitudes; the woman's family would insist that this behavior was not proper. The Palestinian man would be expected to have sufficient money for a dowry (Palestinian men claim that Palestinians in Chicago request a large amount for their daughters), and, if he were not established with a good income and his family were overseas, getting familial support for the wedding would be more difficult than if he married someone with whom his family could negotiate.

Moreover, Palestinian men can date and develop premarital intimacy with American women. Should a Palestinian man decide to marry an American, he would have an idea of the woman he is marrying, and he need not be concerned with dowry and wedding expenses. Again, Palestinian American women lose out because foreign-born men see them as American but their families see them as Palestinian.

Despite these attitudes and constraints, Palestinian American women who reached adulthood in the 1970s and 1980s in Chicago seem to have fared better overall than the elder cohort. Forced early arranged marriages lost support among Palestinians in the community, some families have modified traditional courtship procedures to fit the exigencies of the context, and organizational contacts between Palestinian-American women and foreign-born Palestinian men have enabled some to gain enough familiarity to choose each other.

Some respondents married foreign-born Palestinian men through a modification of the traditional method. The man and the woman, in many cases almost strangers, were allowed a brief courtship period before the engagement. This period occurred after the woman's family approved of the man and the man and woman involved felt there might be marriage potential. The courtship was usually brief and occurred under restricted parameters; time and place were limited, and sometimes a family escort would join them. Other respondents married men they had met and become acquainted with through organizational activities, particularly those who participated in organizations encouraging the involvement of Palestinian-American women. As part of their political identity, these women have sought to improve their Arabic skills and speak Arabic to their children, even though they may have disliked the effects these ethnic "differences" had on their own lives when they were growing up. Now these actions have political meaning to them. Further, there is now an ethnic community to which their children can belong.

Still, the maintenance of traditional ideas and cultural expectations that the women be the passive recipients of marriage proposals, in combination with the relative freedom accorded to males, leaves many Palestinian-American Muslim women stranded. Many single women are not permitted by their families to participate in organized activities, so they remain relatively unknown to the community. If many of their relatives live in Chicago, the situation is better. Growing up as marginal members of two cultures, one of which they cannot marry into while the other sees them as deficient, Palestinian-American women continue to have difficulties finding an appropriate spouse.

## CONCLUSION

Alongside the political alienation felt by Palestinians in the United

States, the enormous struggle required to assert the validity of their political claims, and racial hostilities, Palestinian-American Muslim women bear an additional burden. The Palestinian cultural and political preferences for marrying within the group have not been adjusted to come to terms with the unique problems and biases faced by Palestinian Muslim women raised in Western countries. The asymmetry between men and women is probably unparalleled in the Arab/Islamic world. Palestinian females are expected to be morally better and psychologically stronger than Palestinian males. While Palestinian men dominate religion and politics, religious ideas about appropriate behavior and political ideas about the importance of maintaining a Palestinian identity are imposed to a far greater extent on the women. The situation of Palestinian-American women can only be improved by strategies that reduce the level of inequality between genders within the family and the society.

This portrait of the lives of Palestinian American women reveals that the dynamics of immigrant/ethnic communities cannot be understood without looking at the lives of both male and female participants. Data based on the experiences of males only cannot be generalized to describe a community, although this has been the historical trend. Studies of immigrant communities have pointed universally to the fundamental importance of the family in maintaining and reproducing ethnic culture. Many studies of Muslim and Arab communities in North America have pointed to the maintenance of the patriarchal family structure as one major component of the expression of traditional culture. Precisely why and in what ways the family is so crucial for ethnic identity has never been adequately addressed. Family, in part, seems to be shorthand for the work of women and the lives of girls in reproducing ethnic culture. This study also shows that ethnic communities are not static entities; as the community changes, so do the lives of the people within it.

### Notes

1. This paper is part of a larger study of the Palestinian Muslim community in Chicago, with a special focus on the lives of its female members. The re-

search was conducted between 1982 and 1985; in 1983 I spent two months in Palestine and Jordan. The results of this study are presented in detail in my doctoral dissertation, "Coping with Tradition, Change and Alienation: Palestinian Women in the United States," Department of Sociology, Northwestern University. I want to thank Professors Janet Abu-Lughod and Arlene Kaplan Daniels, and my colleague Sandra Schroeder for their assistance. I am deeply grateful to the Palestinian community in Chicago for accepting me openly into their community, homes and lives.

I chose to focus on Muslim Palestinians, although there is a significant Christian Palestinian community in Chicago, in order to reduce the number of variables which entered into the study. Studies of Christian Palestinian communities in the United States and my own observations have led me to conclude that the portrait presented in this paper has much validity for them, although there are certain differences because they share a religious affiliation with the core American society. Since we are just beginning to *describe* ethnic Arab/Muslim communities, it is my belief that analytical comparisons would be premature.

2. The characteristic dependence upon kin for economic support and shelter was common upon initial immigration, but independence, as soon as it was economically possible, was the preferred state. Usually, a man would not marry or bring his wife and children over until he could establish a separate home for them. Al-Tahir (1952) noted that Palestinian Muslims, at this time, preferred to live near their businesses. Palestinian Muslim families were therefore scattered throughout the south side of Chicago, mostly in communities that bordered on the black belt, where most conducted their business.

3. For a detailed history of Palestinian immigration to the United States and the Palestinian community in Chicago, see my doctoral dissertation.

4. Palestinian women born/raised in the United States are defined as those who were born in the United States or who immigrated to the United States before the age of thirteen. This categorization is based on my research findings. That is, in general, Palestinian women who immigrated before age thirteen tend to have attitudes, orientations, and experiences similar to American born Palestinian women, while those who immigrated in their teens tend to have more Middle Eastern orientations. This difference can only be explained hypothetically at this point. Because of the sample size, this cutoff point is not intended to be generalizable; it merely establishes categories for meaningful discussion.

5. This statement is based on the responses of female Palestinian teenagers to this paper when it was presented at the Arab community center in Chicago and to an Arab-American youth group.

6. These assumptions require full discussion since they are based on a number of false premises and selective data. This discussion can be found in my doctoral dissertation.

7. I have found this to be true for immigrant Palestinian women within cer-

tain sectors of the Palestinian community in Chicago, although it is not true for all of them. Certain variables seem to influence this outcome, including socio-economic status, male's occupation, and subgroup "membership."

8. The historical forms of this dual territoriality in Arab society are discussed more fully in my dissertation. One example from Islam is the rule that Muslim females must marry Muslim males but that Muslim males may marry from among Muslims, Christians, and Jews. Outside females can be brought in, but inside females may not leave. The assumption underlying this dictate is that a non-Muslim female may become a member of a Muslim family since it is expected that her former ways will be replaced by those of the male and his family. But if a Muslim female marries a male of another religion, she, according to patriarchal principles, will take on the religion of her husband. Thus, she will be lost to the system and so will her children.

9. For the most part, this is still true among Palestinians in Chicago.

10. A few of my interviewees had a relative or older sister who accepted an early arranged marriage that has lasted. None of these women reside in Chicago. They married cousins and moved to Palestine upon marriage.

11. Though 1954 as a cut-off year is valid for this sample, given the methodology and sample size this specific year cannot be assumed to have generalizable validity. It does seem accurate to say that since the Palestinian community in Chicago changed in size and character after 1967, the lives of its earlier members also began to change sometime after 1967.

# Reflections on Islamic Tradition, Women, and Family

## Marilyn Robinson Waldman

◆　　◆　　◆　　◆

N orth America is undergoing a transition. While the Americas still tend to be viewed as essentially part of the Atlantic community, an extension of European history, increasingly they can be viewed as a collection of unique societies with their own dynamics and distinctive population mix. Within this setting, scholars are gradually becoming aware that the religious profile of North America has shifted, that the number of North American Muslims is growing and, on several fronts, that Islam is an "American religion," not a foreign one. In fact, in the original Nation of Islam, the United States has had a unique form of indigenous Islam not practiced anywhere else in the world. Given the expansion of immigration and the proportion of Afro-Asian emigrés, the numbers of Muslims in North America are expanding rapidly. Both Canada and the United States have long been nations of immigrants, but their distinctive compositions are changing; the dominance of European immigrants is being seriously challenged.[1] Situated as it is within this transition, the study of Muslim women in North America must also consider Muslim women worldwide as well as other North American immigrant groups with whose experiences those of Muslim women might usefully be compared.

These various contexts supply different kinds of questions. How important a factor is Islam in comparison to other variables such as class, education, occupation, ethnicity or minority status? What is the relationship between subjective and objective measures of the saliency of Islam? How valuable is the distinction many Muslims are making between Muslim and Islamic?[2] When applied to women, such a distinction separates women who happen to be Muslim from those who self-consciously aim to live according to their accepted normative definition of Islam. If we do make that distinction, does the relationship between American Muslims and Muslims living in predominantly Muslim societies become more important for the purposes of analysis?

How special is the North American context for Muslim women? And how special are *Muslim* women in the North American context? The mixture of different types of Muslim women is perhaps unparalleled: students and wives of students, some visiting, some permanent, some responding largely to the local context, some more to the global one; academics and other professionals; employed and non-employed suburban wives of affluent professionals; non-employed and, less frequently, employed wives of factory workers and of artisans and shopkeepers; Islamic feminists; anti-Islamic feminists; Afro-American women, some heirs to the original Nation of Islam, some to its transformation, the American Muslim Mission in the West. Furthermore, nowhere else is one likely to find public forums for interaction and debate between Muslim men and Muslim women, as well as with non-Muslims, so available.

To what extent will the "Muslim" family be distinctive in the North American context? How are we to understand the stress on family that is so important among many American Muslims? Has immigration to North America accentuated the concept of the Muslim family or of other "Islamic" practices, such as Islamic dress? Has it made being Muslim a more salient characteristic for women than it was in the old country? Has stress in the Afro-American family accentuated it for Afro-American Muslims?[3] Will Muslim women have to be analyzed in the context of family and male roles to an extent that American feminist critics have generally resisted? Or can Muslim women be viewed largely from the perspective of *women's* studies?

Will Islam become a more salient characteristic, especially for those who want to use it as the source of a critique of North American society? Will those persons tend to stress aspects of Islam not always stressed in the old country?[4] Can such persons be viewed as the Islamic equivalent of the Amish or the Mennonites?

What will be the fate of the "private" power of immigrant Muslim women in a society where public power is so much stressed, especially by the women's movement, and where sustained sex segregation is generally infeasible.

How much can we learn about immigrant Muslims and their off-spring by studying the generational experiences of previous immigrant communities? Will resistance to assimilation be strongest where "old country" family mores are associated with piety? Will imported Muslim institutions, like the mosque, adopt American forms that affect the role of women in community life? Questions like these encourage us to set the study of Muslim women in North America in as many contexts as possible. For example, we would also do well to remember that persons of faith all struggle with modern society; sometimes the tension is a source of conflict for them, sometimes an opportunity.

Our answers to such questions will also be more meaningful if they can be informed by both statistical and historical perspectives.[5] Muslims in the Western hemisphere are ethnically diverse; they represent about sixty nations. Muslim organizations estimate a population of at least two to three million in the United States; that figure includes American and foreign-born citizens as well as resident aliens and about 750,000 international students, many of whom may become citizens. Arab Muslims number 100,000 (there are nine times as many Arab-American Christians); Iranians, 90,000, a figure that is presumably growing; and Turks, 85,000. Canada is thought to have about 100,000 Muslims, of whom 20,000 belong to Nizari Ismaili communities.

Muslims have constructed two hundred mosques or Islamic centers in more than half of the American states, and there is at least one mosque in each Canadian province. Most imams, however, are foreign-born and foreign-trained; there are no major Muslim educational institutions in North America. Except for the Nation of Islam, national Muslim organizations emerged only in the 1950s.

Historical perspectives add another dimension to statistics. African Muslims may have arrived in the Western hemisphere before Christopher Columbus did, but they were definitely present in Spanish America by 1550. Although an estimated 14 to 20 percent of the slaves brought to the Americas from Africa may have been Muslim, less Muslim culture appears to have survived among African-Americans in North American than in South American and Caribbean locales such as Surinam, Guyana, Trinidad, and Tobago. The community in Guyana was swelled by turn-of-the-century British importation of Urdu-speaking Muslims from India, but they did not unite with "African-Muslims." The Guyana community came to be split between a conservative segment, which practices, for example, *purdah* and arranged marriages, and a reformed group, which, for example, engages in selling goods ordinarily prohibited to observant Muslims in India itself. The experience of South American Muslims raises a number of important questions for the future of Muslims in North America, and especially for women and family.

How much will Muslim identity transcend ethnic identities? For example, will African-American Muslims identify more than they presently do with other American-born Muslims and with immigrants? Unlike emigration from Europe, emigration from Asia and Africa has not yet peaked, so we can probably assume that heavy emigration from predominantly Muslim areas is only just beginning; meanwhile, African-American Muslims seem to be moving closer to the Islam of the immigrants. America's indigenous form of Islam may well provide more and more of a host environment for immigrant Islam. As the numbers of American-born Muslims grow, will we see the emergence of a "reformed," cultural Islam comparable to Reformed Judaism? North America may provide the environment for a reformed Islam that Germany did for Reformed Judaism. Will the forms of Islam that emerge in North America have the socio-economic dimensions associated with the three major forms of Judaism?

Muslim families in North America are often put in a social situation for which their tradition has not prepared them. Islam, like Christianity and unlike Judaism, has historically been hegemonic, not minoritarian; Islam has not primarily existed in pluralistic environments, like Lebanon and India, where it is not hegemonic. Even in Andalusia (Islamic Spain) where Muslims probably never became a majority, they were still hegemonic. Minorities usually adjust in some way to hegemonic social and cultural forms; non-Muslims have historically done so in Muslim societies, and some American Muslim institutions seem to be moving in the same direction. Witness, for example, the pressure on some Islamic centers or mosques to structure themselves like Christian and Jewish congregations, organized around membership lists, funded by dues, and led by "cleric-like" *imams* with pastoral functions that require a kind of training not hitherto provided in the world's leading Muslim institutions of higher learning. Counseling in matters of marriage, parenting, family, and divorce has become important for Christian and Jewish congregational leaders. If Muslim religious leaders come to be expected to perform such tasks, they will of necessity have a new impact on women and the family. If the model of the congregation becomes more influential, the role of women in the life of the mosque will probably expand into new opportunities for social and political experience.

As their incorporation into North American life intensifies, Muslims will have to learn to deal with plurality, just as their presence, and the presence of other religious groups not historically viewed as "American," will enable, indeed require, an enlargement in American concepts of pluralism. In North America, Muslim children grow up knowing more about Jews and Christians than vice versa, and accept their faiths, at least on a certain level. Muslims have in their tradition the premodern world's most explicit recognitions and systematizations of religious plurality, but prescriptions for living in non-hegemonic situations are much less well developed. Moreover, pre-modern Muslim societies had no notion of one law before which all are equal. Muslim inclinations to sacralize the mundane could mesh with an increasing North American concern with values; suggest alternatives to dichotomies like church and state, religion and politics, or religious and secular; and challenge traditional consensuses on key issues of foreign policy.

Should Muslims really begin to play such roles in the United States, they may heighten the already visible tensions in the way the First Amendment addresses religious matters. In the words of one author who has skillfully analyzed the tensions:

[The First Amendment] proscribes governmental actions and initiatives which adversely implicate the ability of the American to exercise his religious beliefs freely. Less well known and seemingly less well appreciated is the fact that the Amendment also proscribes governmental actions and initiatives which aid or establish religious beliefs and practices.

In the pertinent part, the First Amendment provides that

"Congress shall make no law respecting an establishment of religion, or prohibiting the free exercise therefore. . . . " There are, therefore, two operative clauses on the subject of religion in this amendment—the establishment clause and the free-exercise clause. The command at first glance is rather clear and simple. The Congress (i.e. the government) may not impede the religious beliefs of the American, and it may not aid them . . .

But are the necessary lines so easily drawn? Do they so readily admit of the requisite precision? . . . When the state exempts the church from its duty to pay taxes, does such an action not aid the church and hence implicate the establishment clause? But would not compelling the payment of taxes by the church violate the command of the free exercise clause?[6]

Further complexities result from the fact that the free-exercise clause has been interpreted to distinguish belief, freedom of which is absolutely guaranteed, from action, which may be regulated when the "imperatives" of the social order demand, as in the case of military service.

A Christmas 1987 controversy in Columbus, Ohio, provides a good illustration. Every year a large Christmas tree is erected on the Statehouse lawn. In 1987, a small group of Jews received permission from the city to erect a large *menorah* alongside. They were quickly asked, largely on the basis of protest from the public and the American Civil Liberties Union, to take it down because, as a religious symbol displayed on public property, it violated the "establishment" clause. The Christmas tree did not, it was explained, because it has been designated by the courts as a non-religious symbol of a holiday season that belongs to all faiths.

The paradoxes in the First Amendment may have seemed less acute in the past because only two religious groups, one a small minority, have had to be taken seriously. Even so, awkwardness often results; and what will happen to such already shaky arrangements when they must accommodate a significant number of Americans who adhere to other faiths? Are Lois al-Faruqi's proposals for laws that favor the extended family "religious" in nature, in terms of what religion means in a "secular" state?[7] Will the right to corporal discipline or arranged marriages or restriction of movement that Muslim heads of households can claim constitute the free exercise of religion as does refusal of medical treatment on the part of some Christians? Or will the distinction between belief and action be brought to bear?

Analyses of the Muslim family and Muslim women must take into account not only Muslims worldwide, Muslims in North American societies, and other pertinent American sub-group affiliations, but also the context of these large societal and historical issues. If we want to speak intelligently and productively about Muslim women worldwide, we must begin by resisting two natural tendencies: the tendency to equate modernization with secularization and the tendency to overgeneralize and oversimplify.[8] Persons who live in societies that have undergone a process of European-generated modernization, or wish to, tend to assume automatically that the attributes of that type of modernization will of necessity emerge in any society that is modernizing or will modernize in the future and that they will automatically appeal to any group immigrating into such a society. Secularization, widely assumed to be an important marker of modernity, involves the weakening or elimination of traditional faiths as sources of public as well as private values and institutions.

Often, this suspicion of tradition extends beyond religious tradition, and among overly enthusiastic modernists, "militant" modernists, if you will, it leads to a naive understanding of the role of tradition in human societies and to a dichotomous view of tradition and modernity that makes the former antithetical to the latter. In short, a strongly anti-traditional bias and mentality takes over.

Yet most Muslims live in societies in which the force of tradition is very strong and in which modernization has also penetrated more or less deeply. In many closely knit immigrant Muslim communities in North America, tradition, including religious tradition, is being drawn upon more and more as a source of change, social reform, modernization, or even as a critique of modernity, just as it has been among Afro-American Muslims. Consequently, the Western equation of modernization and secularization is beginning to be severely tested and even undermined. In fact, any historian of religion could point out that religious traditions have always had it within them to be not only forces for intense conservation but also vehicles for radical protest against the status quo and for equally radical social and political change.

The "Islamic world," if such a vast entity can be said to exist meaningfully on any level at all, is so diverse as almost to defy description.

The world's approximately eight hundred million Muslims occupy a long and broad, multicultural, multinational stretch of land centered on the Afro-Eurasian landmass but trailing off to the Americas in one direction and to the Pacific islands on the other. Lifestyles vary dramatically. Because of such diversity, any overall analysis of the place of women in Muslim societies would have to be based, at least at first, on culture-specific observations.

Furthermore, we can never assume that Islam as a normative spiritual and ideological tradition plays *the* critical role in determining the status and role of women, or a woman's self-conscious identity, or that there is any one way in which it can provide that identity. Despite the cliché that Islam is an all-pervasive "way of life," it may not play such a role at all in some societies or among some individuals or groups, or it may play its roles in a much more qualified, complicated manner. Like any other systematic source of ideology and values, Islam has always been forced to relate to and compete with others for what we might call the "mental space" of its adherents and simultaneously to define its stance towards pre-existing and coexisting extra-Islamic cultural attributes.

Its own legal system, especially with regard to key family matters such as marriage, inheritance, divorce, and the regulation of sexuality, incorporated into its new moral context much of pre-Islamic West Asian practice. Furthermore, in the application of Islamic law, cultural variation is always possible—through reinforcement of extra-Islamic custom, through direct subversion by an essentially male judiciary, or by recourse to alternate systems.

Another source of variability is "normative Islam" itself. Like all members of great historical religious traditions, Muslims have not agreed on how to define or interpret their own normative sources. For most Muslims throughout history, normative Islam has somehow or other meant the concrete and discrete Islam of two major texts, the Qur'an, the revelations of God through Muhammad, and the *hadith*, recognizably authoritative collections of reliable reports about Muhammad's *sunna*, his exemplary speech, action, and tacit approval. Through *fiqh*, a particular process of study and inquiry, Muslims produced a written and unwritten corpus known as *Shariᶜa*. Yet, not all Muslims have included the hadith as normative; some of the most radical reformers have sought, by limiting themselves to the Qur'an, to circumvent the accumulation of *traditional* interpretation represented by the hadith and the Shariᶜa. And even those who have accepted both have not always agreed on how to interpret either or on what to include among the reliable hadith.

Such debates have special importance for the lives of Muslim women, since much of what normative Islam has to say about them is derived from the hadith and developed in the Shariᶜa. The not-so-widespread practice of "veiling" or, more properly, of *hijab*, various sorts of special modest dress for public wear, is a good example. The Qur'an enjoins men and women to dress modestly in the name of the dignity and propriety of the human individual and to preserve moral standards and social stability. The hadith at their most extreme extend that injunction to the covering of all but hands and face, though the face-covering practice of Muhammad's wives is used to justify the ultraconcealing hijab worn by a small number of Muslim women, except on *hajj*, when it is prohibited to them. The more concealing types of hijab, apparently already a custom among many pre-Islamic West Asian peoples, persisted and took on an Islamic justification, partly because it was neither banned by normative sources nor inconsistent with them. Modernist Muslims can also use normative sources to justify a rejection of veiling as well as of the seclusion and sex segregation that sometimes accompanies it, especially if they can argue that veiling and seclusion are inconsistent with the Qur'an's emphasis on human dignity and individual worth in the sight of God. Thus, both the normative sources of Islam and the traditions that have developed in conjunction with them can be used as a basis for change or for adapting to new circumstances and but also as a way of resisting it.

It would be safe to say that Muslim women have rarely been the submissive, passive, retiring, powerless species of popular Western imagination. The very forms of public clothing that outsiders see as the ultimate symbol of weakness are not only atypical, but, where they do occur, they are representative of a much more mixed and complex reality. At the same time, it is important to point out, especially for the many Muslim societies that have favored some degree or form of sex segregation, that the power and roles of women have been much more private and indirect than in modern Western industrial nations and therefore, much less accessible to the awareness of outsiders. Often living within societies that differentiate sharply between the public and private spheres and situate women in the latter, Muslim women have exercised an unusual degree and type of power and influence. In fact, the existence of two essentially separate societies has often enhanced certain types of female traits and powers and continues to do so even within the process of modernization.

Such social structures arose out of a coherent and not so unfamiliar understanding of human behavior and sexuality, and of family and gender relations and requirements. A primary assumption of that understanding was that if two marriageable adults are left alone together, it is natural to expect that sexual relations will take place. Since marriage was seen primarily as bringing two families rather than two individuals together, the simplest way to prevent disaster or an interruption of marriage arranging practice was to make inappropriate consorting and parenting impossible. The result of more or less rigid separation of marriageable males and females was to provide for women within their own society an almost unfettered occupancy of a limited amount of "social space." Not only did running the household and rearing the children fall to women, but they came to possess critical pieces of information necessary to the happiness and social success of males but inaccessible to them directly. The information about eligible women that is needed to make marriage contracts is one such type of information.

Islamic law tended, if applied with integrity, to enhance this freedom of action in one important area, the inheritance and manipulation of property and other forms of wealth. Where women were actually allowed to hold property in their own name, as the Shariᶜa guaranteed, they could easily become wealthier than the husbands who dominated them in other ways. Nor should we dismiss the managerial skills necessary to run a well-to-do pre-modern household, with its large numbers of domestic servants and relatives for whom provisioning had to be arranged. How often the reality met the ideal we cannnot say, but the ideal could be idealized in the extreme. A medieval Muslim sage was once asked, "Are women equal to men?" He replied, "No, but neither are men equal to women. How can you compare the smell of a rose to the smell of jasmine?"

The separate-but-equal philosophy surfaces frequently in the writings of Muslim men and women in North America, with varying degrees of sincerity and, one would presume, from varying motivations.

But even in the face of the most cynical reaction to such a stance, one will recognize that certain possibilities are lost to Muslim women in ostensibly sex-integrated societies like the United States and Canada. For example, it is estimated that 40 percent of Saudi Arabia's *personal* wealth is in the hands of women, who in select areas have their "women's" banks to go to for financial advice and socializing.[9]

The public power of Muslim women in sex-segregated societies has been severely restricted, but the cultivation of private and indirect influence has been potentially limitless. In North America, proponents of women's colleges have often argued that they allow women to assume all necessary roles and activities freely and that they promote female solidarity and mutual respect. There is some evidence that a sex-segregated society can do the same. Larger percentages of women enter the professions in some Muslim societies, Egypt, for example, than in the United States. There they are aided in child care by the extended family, as al-Faruqi points out.[10]

The North American context demands a multivariate and nuanced analysis. A brief account of some ways in which accommodation to life in America has occurred illustrates its variability. The first example involves a heavy, though small, concentration of Muslims in one neighborhood, the southeastern section of Dearborn, where one or two ethnic groups predominate.[11] In this case, there has been a high degree of cultural reproduction of "old country" forms (even ones not actually used in the particular old country) and of isolationism from the surrounding non-Muslim society. Ethnic differences, exacerbated by socio-economic cleavages, seem to have kept Islam from becoming a predominant and shared source of identity.

The second example involves a prosperous international community in Tempe, Arizona, closely associated with a university. Here, Muslims have put innovative technologies to the service of updated traditional institutions: a "mosque-complex" that combines prayer, commerce, student residence, and outreach to the non-Muslim communities. A similar development is occurring within the highly international Muslim student community at Ohio University in Athens, Ohio.

The third example involves a major urban area, greater Toledo, where Muslims are more international and less concentrated than in Dearborn. In its Islamic Center, located in a field in Perrysburg, Ohio, the "old country" functions of the mosque have of necessity expanded to include a mortuary and plans for youth and senior centers. The imam has also become active in social service and public policy work for Muslims and non-Muslims alike. Women's presence in the *salat* (prayer) is encouraged, as the equally inviting *wudu'* (washing) facilities for men and women attest.

In example four, a particular ethnic group, in this case Turks, responds in different ways to different circumstances but maintains a high degree of ethnic identity. In some urban areas first- and second-generation professionals and their American-born offspring, scattered in affluent suburbs, adhere to the basic beliefs of Islam but are not very observant, distinguishing ethnic-Islamic customs from ritual observance and stressing the "Turko-Islamic" cultural heritage. Rochester, New York contains a cluster of artisans and shopkeepers from one area of Turkey, the southeast, who stress both heritages, Turkish and Islamic, have their own Turkish mosque, observe the dietary laws and Ramadan, and try to make the hajj. Windsor, Ontario, provides yet another pattern in its Turkish community, which is composed largely of the families of skilled laborers, who associate restrictive social rules for young people with being Muslim (those from eastern Turkey are more socially conservative than those from western Turkey). They share a mosque with other ethnic groups and use it mostly for marriage ceremonies; they celebrate major Muslim holidays at home.

Just as some Muslim women in North American contexts lead a very restricted life, perhaps more restricted than in the old country, others are very outspoken and aggressive. The writings of American Muslim women use Islam as a basis for criticizing American society, including its women's movement. They often stress a distinction between "Muslim" and "Islamic." According to them, the fault is with Muslims, not with Islam, as thinkers like Jamaluddin al-Afghani (1739-1897), Muhammad Abduh (1849-1905), and Muhammad Iqbal (1877-1938) argued two or three generations ago. Like those men, many female American Muslim writers and speakers have adopted a type of modernist analysis. For example, they frequently argue that what American feminists have recently "discovered" to be desirable was really discovered in the seventh century, as illustrated by Qur'anic quotations, and then forgotten by Muslim, not Islamic, men and women.

For example, in the October 1985 issue of *Islamic Horizons*, Karima Omar criticized the well-known Moroccan feminist Fatima Mernissi for attributing the oppression of women to Islam. According to Omar, wherever and whenever Muslims oppress women, they are exhibiting unacceptable innovation in what is truly the Islamic ideal, brought on partly by their own regressiveness and partly by a distortion of Islam brought on by European colonialism.

> She [Mernissi] has fallen into the trap which so many non-Muslims slip into—that of confusing Islam with the actions of Muslims. . . . Unfortunately, Ms. Mernissi probably wasn't exaggerating when she spoke of the rampant misog[y]ny in her homeland [and] the Arab world as a whole. The pre-Islamic Arabs were notorious woman-haters. . . . The sexism and double standards which exist today are throwbacks to this earlier time, regressions of some Muslims to the ways of their ancestors—not products of Islam. Occupying forces have also left their stamps on many Muslim countries, confounding the problems.[12]

Zarina Awad, in a presentation to the Islamic Society of North America in August of 1985, went even further: the feminism of true Islam is better than American feminism.

> Sisterhood is powerful—but not powerful enough to demand more than watered-down feminism: not powerful enough to resist the subtle extortion which society is inflicting on the women's movement, the notion that women must be identical to men if they wish to be equal, that they must suffer for their suffrage. Yeah, you can have equal pay for equal work, women are told; you can be sled dog drivers or longshoremen, but there's a price. And that price is emotional and psychological well-being. Women feel compelled to make this sacrifice, to accept this incomplete feminism—after all, half a loaf is better than none, so let's just settle for our physical rights—let's not ask the impossible.
>
> But why not? For 14 centuries ago, a truly radical feminist ideology was born. Radical for its age as well as ours; radical not only in its letter but its spirit. For it provided not only for women's—for humanity's—social, economic, and legal rights, but emotional and spiritual rights as well.[13]

Thus, the North American setting is promoting both anti-Islamic feminism and an intra-Muslim debate about its desirability. It is even allowing Muslim professional women to debate in print with male Muslim scholars. The January 1979 *al-Ittihad* (a publication of the Muslim Students Association of the United States and Canada) contained an illustrative exchange of letters between Amina Abdullah CNM, R.N., and Mahmoud Abu Saud. In a previous issue, Saud had written an essay entitled "Sex Roles—A Muslim Point of View," in which he argued that marriage and thus, woman's traditional marital roles are dictated by nature. Amina Abdullah's critique centers on Saud's alleged purveying of scientific, particularly biological, misinformation. She argues that Saud has used this inaccurate information to justify positions that demean women. Her reply puts Awad's and Omar's theoretical arguments into practice:

> Finally, I myself as a woman and as an intelligent human being resent what the brother was trying to do in his theme. I consider it an insult to Muslim womankind. We have intelligence and God given talents. We have the right to use them *outside* as well as inside the home!
>
> I will not accept the supremacy perpetuated by Br. Saud to the point where he advocates man's rights over women's rights. Islam does not contain such teachings.
>
> Finally, in the future, whether you like it or not you will see Muslim women the world over stand up for their rights. I will be helping Insha'Allah to make that happen![14]

In his reply, Brother Saud first argues that Sister Abdullah has misunderstood and misrepresented his article, but his non-technical remarks are of more interest here:

> Sr. Amina 'resents' what I established in my paper and considers it an insult!! She was carried adrift by her 'feminine' emotionality and narcissism, and alluded that I denied intelligence to women. That is completely untrue, as nowhere in my paper I belittled women's intelligence; though for sure, there are some women more intelligent than others . . . I hope. Sr. Amina owes it to her 'womankind' to admit that.
>
> As to the use of 'intelligence, and God-given talents,' I believe the correct answer is what God has ordained in this respect. A woman—as well as a man—has 'the right' to use God-given intelligence and talents the way she or he likes. Yet, there is no *absolute*

right, and every Muslim and Muslimah is supposed to accept the laws of existence made by God and the injunctions of Islam. And that is exactly what I tried to illustrate in my paper; but it seems that this demonstration was not clear enough to gain the approval of our sister.

Sr. Amina Abdullah described herself as a specialist in 'gynocology [*sic*] and obstetrics and . . . a scholar in women's affairs in Islam.' However, she did not refer to a verse from the Qur'an or to a Hadith in her indignant comments. She has simply adopted a 'Quixotic' attitude and admonished the writer 'whether you like it or not' that women 'will stand up for their rights,' and of course she will be 'helping to make that happen.'

I wish Sr. Amina had given the Islamic proof of a mistake I committed or the Islamic ruling I omitted. I sincerely wish that Sr. Amina would spend some more time studying Islam.[15]

Although Saud's last remark is probably not a sincere invitation, he can rest assured Amina Abdullah and others have already risen to the challenge. Still other Muslim women will find their way in North America by avoiding or rejecting Islam. And yet others, perhaps the majority, will use the old and the new in various subtle combinations to fashion viable day-to-day strategies for living.

Who will guide the study of Muslim women in North America? Islamicists, who will want to evaluate them according to "universal" Muslim norms and compare them with their sisters in predominantly Muslim cultures? Women's studies scholars, for whom being Muslim and, indeed, American is incidental to being female? Students of American history and society, who focus on the dynamics of transplantation, assimilation, ethnicity, and minority status? Or scholars of American religion, for whom Islam is one of many religions, heretofore not viewed as fully "American"? None of these groups has yet appropriated the study of Muslim women in North America, an "interstitial" subject that does not fit comfortably within their conventional intellectual parameters and that is therefore well placed to challenge them all.

## Notes

1. Charles H. Long has frequently argued, orally and in writing, that American studies and the study of American religion have not yet come to grips with the African presence and with America as an entity separate from its European "past." *Significations: Signs, Symbols, and Images in the Interpretation of Religion* (Philadelphia: Fortress Press, 1986), especially chapter nine, "Interpretations of Black Religion: Visible People and Visible Religion," pp. 148-55.

2. See, for example, Lois Ibsen al-Faruqi, "An Extended Family Model from Islamic Culture," *Journal of Comparative Family Studies*, Vol. 9, no. 2 (Summer 1978), pp. 243-56. See also Karima Omar, "Dissenting Initiative: A Response to Fatima Mernissi," *Islamic Horizons* (October 1985), p. 14. See also Fazlur Rahman's discussion of "normative" versus lived Islam, "Approaches to Islam in Religious Studies: Review Essay," in (ed.), *Approaches to Islam in Religious Studies*, Richard C. Martin (Tucson: University of Arizona Press, 1985), pp. 195-96. It might be interesting to compare Marshall Hodgson's well-known distinction between "Islamic" and "Islamicate," *The Venture of Islam: Conscience and History in a World Civilization* (Chicago: University of Chicago Press, 1974), 1:57-60.

3. See, for example, in this volume, Na'im Akbar, "Family Stability among African-American Muslims."

4. See, for example, in this volume, Barbara Aswad, "Yemeni and Lebanese Muslim Immigrant Women in Southeast Dearborn, Michigan." There Aswad carefully details how forms of dress can be adopted that were not worn at home and how important visitation can become when the extended family is no longer present. Even in a student-oriented suburban shopping center near The Ohio State University, I myself recently observed a female driver wearing modest dress that included white cotton gloves and a veil for the lower face. These observations remind us always to ask whether we should think of Islam in America as an extension of Islam in predominantly Muslim countries of origin or as a potentially new form of Islam in a novel environment. For Islam as a basis of critiques of North American society, see, Akbar, "Family Stability"; al-Faruqi, "Extended Family Model"; and Omar, "Dissenting Initiative."

5. Much of what follows has been taken from Barbara J. Bilgé, "Islam in the Americas," *Encyclopedia of Religion*, Vol. 7. Edited by Mircea Eliade (New York: MacMillan Publishing Co., 1987), pp. 425-31.

6. Isaac James Mowoe, "The Church, the State, and the First Amendment: Permeable Walls and Constitutional Doctrines," *Papers in Comparative Studies* 3 (1982), pp. 99, 100.

7. See al-Faruqi, "Extended Family Model," pp. 9-10.

8. What follows is an abridgment and adaptation of material that appears in Marilyn R. Waldman, "Women in the Islamic World," in *Women in Development, Seminar Proceedings, Spring 1982*, Erika Bourguiqnon and Francille H. Firebaugh, eds. (Columbus: Ohio State University Depart-

ment of Home Management and Housing, College of Home Economics, 1982), pp. 17-28. See also two other articles by the same author: "Tradition as a Modality of Change: Islamic Examples," *History of Religions* 25, no. 4 (1986), pp. 318-40; and "Islamic Resurgence in Context," *The Contemporary Mediterranean World*, Carl Pinkele and Adamantia Pollis, eds. (New York: Praeger, 1984), pp. 98-123.

9. Martin Douglas, "Saudi Banks for Women Thriving," *New York Times*, January 27, 1982, Section 4, pp. 1 and 33.
10. See al-Faruqi, "Extended Family Model," pp. 4-5, and passim.
11. For a fuller treatment, see Bilgé, "Islam in theAmericas," and Barbara Aswad, "Yemeni and Lebanese Women."
12. See Omar, "Dissenting Initiative," p. 14.
13. Zarina Awad, "The Qur'an and Family Life: Women's Emotional Rights in Islam" (paper presented to the Islamic Society of North America, 31 August, 1985), p. 1.
14. "Spectrum," *al-Ittihad* 16 nos. 1-2 (1979), 71.
15. Ibid., p. 72.

# Part Five

## Epilogue: Prospects and Assessments

◆　◆　◆　◆

◆  ◆  ◆  ◆

The expanding Muslim immigration to North America and Islam's global geo-political visibility have generated increased scholarly interest in the study of Islam and Muslim peoples. The family, that most intimate of societal institutions, provides an important medium for interpreting the impact, meaning, and transmission of Islam and its relation to the adaptation and integration of ethno-cultural groups.

In North America, Muslim families find themselves in a minoritarian position. They must chart their way through a somewhat ambivalent world where the religion of their ancestors is often treated with open hostility and animosity. Their children are raised in a pluralistic setting, not only exposed to other religions but often faced with the portrayal of Christianity as normative, and Islam as alien. Muslim families live with the knowledge that they have little control over such twisted imagery. These images and their antecedents have implications for perpetuation of tradition: the retention and transmission of religion, the development of family identification and family esteem, and the nature of the continually evolving paradigm of family values.

The articles in this collection illustrate the diversity among Muslim families in North America and show that while these families can be pivotal as repositories of religious values, inculcators of belief and practice, and exemplars of the religion to non-believers, there is no *one* single family form on the North American continent. However, the common practices, ideological justifications, and spiritual tenor associated with being Muslim do help to shape and pattern similarities. A variety of factors (e.g., origin, nativity, occupation) operate to introduce differences, but the resulting diversity is reflected not only in comparisons between families but, as well, in comparisons *within* Muslim families.

How does Islam translate into the interpersonal experiences of the *variety* of family members? The contributors suggest that there may be differences between younger and older siblings in their views on assimilation and religio-ethnic identification; between male and female family members regarding obligatory codes of moral conduct; and between parents and children about mate selection. Hence, variations in age, gender, marital, parental, and generational views and roles are all

329

analytically important in the study of Muslim families. This book suggests critical priorities for new research extending out from the central adult frame of the family in two directions: toward socialization and the study of the pre-adult family component and toward aging and the eldest generation. For social and cultural reasons, information on children and youth is less easily obtained. At the other end of the family continuum, research on the aged presents difficulties related to cultural and linguistic accessibility. Nevertheless, there is need for more work that reflects the diversity of voices across age and generation within and between Muslim families. The need to give more extensive consideration to issues of gender is related to this, given that age (and/or generation) and gender have an interactive relationship. While survey and sampling techniques applied to the Muslim separation of male and female gender domains clearly reveal the family as the domain of women, complementary, parallel research done by male and female scholars may enrich future perspectives—here too, an individually experienced reality needs to be made part of explicitly formulated research design and methodology. The materials call for comparisons between Muslim and other North American groups on the relationships between religion, day-to-day kin intimacy, and interaction with the larger society.

It has been the intent of this volume that it should generate authentic information on a subject of acknowledged topicality. We have tried to include the voices of the community itself, both of its scholars and of lay informants. The ethnographic component of this volume is predicated upon a relationship of equivalence between researchers and human subjects as collaborators. As such, both parties share a bond that (ideally) negates vestiges of traditional or neo-colonial subject-object research orientations. The cooperation between researchers and subjects is characteristic of a rapidly expanding research orientation that arises in this instance from the reality of multi-ethnic societies in which scholars and their "subject" communities live within a larger polity. Increasingly, differences between them may be blurred, as is evidenced, for example, by the expanding number of scholars studying their own communities. Given this reality, analytic, if not social, distancing emerges as a research goal, especially where the topic is likely chosen by and access granted to a researcher with some form of community membership—as is the case with a substantial number of contributors in this volume. This factor, then, raises questions concerning the researchers' identification with the group and feelings of accountability toward it. The issue of research from the inside, together with the familiar problems of research from the outside, suggest that there may well be merit in future *triangulations* of research methods and researchers themselves. Clearly, no single approach has a monopoly on appropriating authenticity.

The multidisciplinary perspectives in this volume provide an empirical focus on the history, evolution, and adaptive experience of Muslim families. Analytical studies and typological approaches that may encourage further theoretical development have been more recent additions. The on-going public, media, and governmental preoccupation with the reputed weakening of the North American family and its possible connection to a range of social ills suggest the utility of testing assumptions by studying Muslim families as examples of conservative family alternatives on this continent. The continuities and changes in adaptive experiences of Muslim families are of analytical import, but so are the longer-range issues of the potential impact of Muslim families on the larger socio-familial climate of North America itself. The increasing presence of Muslim families promises to add a new dimension of social and ethical criticism.

The volume shows clearly not only the importance of Islam to Muslim families in North America but also the essentially indirect, culturally and socially enmeshed, way this importance manifests itself. The religious factor can be elusive and multi-faceted. Thus, it is argued that it is best seen within a socio-cultural frame of reference which avoids religious determinism and is sensitive to the diversity as well as the commonality between the range of Muslim families and family groups in a new setting: a North America made up of *three* major world religious traditions.

Finally, the volume demonstrates the need for respect across religious and cultural boundaries, suggesting that expanded disciplinal frontiers are necessary to assess the nature and impact of Muslim families. It is our hope that this collection will generate further research and help to enrich our understanding of religion and family life in North America.

# Bibliography

◆ ◆ ◆ ◆

Abadan-Unat, Nermin. "Implications of Migration on Emancipation and Pseudo-emancipation of Turkish Women." *International Migration Review*, 2, no. 1 (Spring 1977): 31-57.

Abdal-Ati, Hammudah. *The Family Structure in Islam*. Plainfield, Ind.: American Trust Publications, 1977.

——. "Women in Islam." Unpublished paper, 1975.

——. "Modern Problems, Classical Solutions: An Islamic Perspective on the Family." *Journal of Comparative Family Studies* 5, no. 2 (1974):37-54.

Abdel-Malek, Anwar. "L'Orientalisme en Crise." *Diogenes* 44 (Winter 1963):109-142.

Abraham, Nabeel. "The Yemeni Immigrant Community of Detroit: Background, Emigration and Community Life." In *Arabs in the New World: Studies on Arab-American Communities*. Edited by Sameer Y. Abraham and Nabeel Abraham, pp. 109-34. Detroit: Wayne State University Press, 1983.

Abraham, Sameer Y., Nabeel Abraham, and Barbara C. Aswad. "The Southend: An Arab Muslim Working-Class Community." In *Arabs in the New World: Studies on Arab-American Communities*. Edited by Sameer Y. Abraham and Nabeel Abraham, pp. 163-84. Detroit: Wayne State University Press, 1983.

Abu-Laban, Baha. *An Olive Branch on the Family Tree: The Arabs in Canada*. Toronto: McClelland and Stewart, 1980.

——. "The Canadian Muslim Community: The Need for a New Survival Strategy." In *The Muslim Community in North America*. Edited by E. Waugh, B. Abu-Laban, and R. Qureshi, pp. 75-92. Edmonton: University of Alberta Press, 1983.

—— and Sharon McIrvin Abu-Laban. "Educational Development." In *The Arab World from Nationalism to Revolution*. Edited by A.

Jabara and J. Terry, pp. 32-54. Wilmette, Ill.: Medina University Press, 1971.

——, eds. *The Arab World: Dynamics of Development*. Leiden: E.J. Brill, 1986.

Abu-Laban, Sharon McIrvin. "Stereotypes of Middle East Peoples: An Analysis of Church School Curricula." In *Arabs in America: Myths and Realities*. Edited by Baha Abu-Laban and F. Zeadey, pp. 149-70. Wilmette, Ill.: Medina University Press, 1975.

——. "Arab-Canadian Family Life." *Arab Studies Quarterly*, vol. 1, no. 2 (Spring 1979): 135-56.

Abu-Laban, Sharon McIrvin. "The Co-existence of Cohorts: Identity and Adaptation among Arab-American Muslims." *Arab Studies Quarterly* 11, nos. 2 & 3 (1989):45-63.

Abu-Lughod, Janet. "Migration Adjustment to City Life: The Egyptian Case." *American Journal of Sociology* 67, no. 1 (July 1961): 22-32.

Adams, Bert N. *The American Family: A Sociological Interpretation*. Chicago: Markham, 1971.

Ahmad, Khurshid. *Family Life in Islam*. Leicester: Islamic Foundation, 1974.

Akbar, M.M.U. *The Orations of Muhammad*. 2nd ed. New Delhi: Kitab Bhavan, 1981.

Akbar, Muhammad. "Muslims in the United States: An Overview of Organizations, Doctrines and Problems." In *The Islamic Impact*. Edited by Y. Haddad, B. Haines, and E. Findly, pp. 195-217. Syracuse: Syracuse University Press, 1984.

Akbar, N. "The Restitution of Family as Natural Order." In *The Family and the Unification Church*. Edited by G. James. New York: Rose of Sharon Press, 1983.

Alba, Richard, and Reid Golden. "Patterns of Ethnic Marriage in the United States." *Social Forces* 65 (September 1986): 202-23.

Al-Faruqi, Isma'il. "Islamic Ideals in North America." In *The Muslim Community in North America*. Edited by Earle Waugh, Baha Abu-Laban, and Regula Qureshi, pp. 259-70. Edmonton: University of Alberta Press, 1983.

——. *New Directions for the Muslim Intellectual in North America*. Presidential Address, First Annual Conference, The Association of Muslim Social Scientists, 1972.

Al-Faruqi, Lois Ibsen. "An Extended Family Model from Islamic Culture." *Journal of Comparative Family Studies* 9, no. 2 (Summer 1978):243-56.

Ali, Ahmed, trans. *Al-Quran*. Karachi: Akrash Publishing, 1984.

Ali, Maulana Muhammad. *A Manual of Hadith*. Lahore: Ahmadiyya Anjuman Isha'at Islam, 1951.

——. *The Holy Qur'an, Arabic Text, Translation and Commentary*. 4th rev. ed. Lahore: Ahmadiyyah Anjuman Isha'at Islam, 1951.

Al-Quazzaz, Ayad. "Images of the Arab in American Social Science Textbooks." In *Arabs in America: Myths and Realities*. Edited by B. Abu-Laban and F. Zeadey, pp. 113-32. Wilmette, Ill.: Medina University Press, 1975.

Al-Tahir, Abdul Jalil. "The Arab Community in the Chicago Area: A Comparative Study of the Christian Syrians and the Muslim Palestinians". Ph.D. diss., University of Chicago, 1952.

Altorki, Soraya. "Family Organization and Women's Power in Urban Saudi Arabian Society." *Journal of Anthropological Research* 33 (1977):257-77.

Alund, A. *The Immigrant Women: Emancipation via Consumption*. Ekot Fran Gardagen. University of Umea, Sweden, Department of Sociology Research Report, 1978.

Alvirez, D., F. Dean, and D. Williams. "The Mexican American Family." In *Ethnic Families in America*. Edited by C. Mindel and R. Habenstein, pp. 269-92. 2nd ed. New Holland, N.Y.: Elsevier, 1983.

American-Arab Anti-Discrimination Committee. *Activity Report 1986-89*. Washington, D.C.: American-Arab Anti-Discrimination Committee, 1989.

Anderson, Alan B., and James S. Frideres. *Ethnicity in Canada: Theoretical Perspectives*. Toronto: Butterworths, 1981.

Anderson, J.N.D. "The Eclipse of the Patriarchal Family in Contemporary Islamic Law." In *Family Law in Asia and Africa*. Edited by J.N.D. Anderson, pp. 1-15. New York: Praeger, 1967, 1968.

——. "The Islamic Law of Marriage and Divorce." In *Readings in Arab*

*Middle Eastern Societies and Cultures*. Edited by Abdulla M. Lutfiyya and Charles W. Churchill, pp. 492-504. The Hague: Mouton, 1970.

Anshen, Ruth Nanda. "The Family in Transition." In *The Family: Its Function and Destiny*. Edited by Ruth Nanda Anshen, pp. 3-19. New York: Harper and Row, 1959.

Anwar, Muhammad. *The Myth of Return: Pakistanis in Britain*. London: Heinemann, 1979.

Aramco Magazine. *The Arab Immigrant* (September/October 1986), pp. 16-33.

Armstrong, Frederick H. "Ethnicity in the Formation of the Family Compact: A Case Study in the Growth of the Canadian Establishment." In *Ethnicity, Power and Politics in Canada*. Edited by Jorgen Dahlie and Tissa Fernando, pp. 22-37. Canadian Ethnic Studies Association. Toronto: Methuen, 1981.

Aronson, Don R. "Ethnicity as a Cultural System: An Introductory Essay." *Ethnicity in the Americas*. Edited by Frances Henry, pp. 9-19. The Hague: Mouton, 1976.

Aswad, Barbara C. "The Southeast Dearborn Arab Community Struggles for Survival against Urban 'Renewal'." In *Arabic-Speaking Communities in American Cities*. Edited by B.C. Aswad, pp. 53-83. New York: Center for Migration Studies, 1974(a).

——. "Visiting Patterns among Women of the Elite in a Small Turkish City." *Anthropological Quarterly* 47 (Jan. 1974b): 9-27.

——. "Rural Family Size and Economic Change: A Middle Eastern Case." In *And the Poor Get Children: Radical Perspectives on Population Dynamics*. Edited by Karen Michaelson, pp. 163-84. New York: Monthly Review Press, 1981

——. "Profile of Family Counseling Community Mental Health Services Contacts." Mimeo. Family Counseling Program. Dearborn: ACCESS, 1987.

——. "The Lebanese Muslim Community in Dearborn, Michigan." In *The History of Lebanese Migration*. Edited by N. Shehadi, in press. London: Tauris Press.

—— and Nancy Gray. "Challenges to the Arab Family and ACCESS, a Local Community Centre." Unpublished paper, 1990.

Atwood, Margaret. *Surfacing*, Toronto: McClelland and Stewart, 1972.

Austin, Allan D. *African Muslims in Antebellum America: A Sourcebook.* New York: Garland, 1984.

Awad, Zarina. "The Qur'an and Family Life: Women's Emotional Rights in Islam." Paper presented to the Islamic Society of North America, New York, 31 August, 1985.

Awan, Sadiq. *The People of Pakistani Origin in Canada.* Ottawa-Hull: Canada Pakistan Association, 1976.

Axelson, Leland J. "The Marital Adjustment and Marital Role Definitions of Husbands of Working and Nonworking Wives." *Marriage and Family Living* 2 (May 1963): 189-95.

Badawi, Gamal A. "Woman in Islam." In *Islam: Its Meaning and Message.* Edited by Khurshid Ahmad. London: Islamic Council of Europe, 1975.

Barazangi, Nimatz Hafez. "Arab Muslim Identity Transmission: Parents and Youth." In *Arab Studies Quarterly* 11, no. 2 & 3 (1989):65-82.

——. "Perception of the Islamic Belief System: The Muslims in North America." Ph.D. dissertation, Cornell University, 1988.

Barclay, Harold. "The Perpetuation of Muslim Tradition in the Canadian North." *Muslim World* 59, no. 1 (January 1969): 64-73.

——. "The Muslim Experience in Canada." In *Religion and Ethnicity.* Edited by Harold Coward and Leslie Kawamura, pp. 101-14. Waterloo: Wilfrid Laurier University Press, 1978.

Barkley, Murray. "The Loyalist Tradition in New Brunswick: The Growth and Evolution of an Historical Myth, 1825-1914." *Acadiensis* 4, no. 2 (1975):3-45.

Barron, Milton. *American Minorities: A Textbook of Readings in Intergroup Relations.* New York: Knopf, 1957.

Ba-Yunas, Ilyas. *Muslims in North America: Problems and Prospects.* Plainfield, Ind.: American Trust Publications, 1975.

Bean, Lee L., and Mohammad Afzal. "Informal Values in a Muslim Society: A Study of the Timing of Muslim Marriages." *Journal of Marriage and the Family* 3 (August 1969): 583-88.

Beck, Lois. "The Religious Lives of Muslim Women." In *Women in Contemporary Muslim Societies.* Edited by Jane L. Smith. London: Associated University Press, 1980.

Bell, Richard. *The Origins of Islam in Its Christian Environment.* London: Edinburgh University Press, 1926.

Bellah, Robert N., et al. *Habits of the Heart: Individualism and Commitment in American Life*. Berkeley and Los Angeles: University of California Press, 1985.

Besanceney, Paul. *Inter-Faith Marriages*. New Haven: College and University Press, 1970.

Bilgé, Barbara J. "Islam in the Americas." *Encyclopedia of Religion*, Vol. VII. Edited by Mircea Eliade, pp. 425-31. New York: MacMillan Publishing Co., 1987.

Billingsley, Andrew. *Black Families in White America*. Englewood Cliffs, N.J.: Prentice Hall, 1968.

Blitsten, Dorothy R. *The World of the Family*. New York: Random House, 1963.

Bochner, Stephen, ed. *Cultures in Contact: Studies in Cross-Cultural Interaction*. International Series in Experimental Social Psychology, Vol. 1. Oxford: Pergamon Press, 1983.

Bourguignon, Erika, and Francille H. Firebaugh, eds. *Women in Development. Seminar Proceedings, Spring 1982*. Columbus: State University Department of Home Management and Housing, College of Home Economics, 1982.

Bowker, Joan. "Health and Social Service Needs Assessment Survey." University of Michigan, Dearborn, 1979. Mimeo.

Broderick, Carlfred B. *Marriage and Family*. 3rd ed. Englewood Cliffs, N.J.: Prentice Hall, 1988.

Brouwer, Lenie, and Marijke Priester. "Living in Between: Turkish Women in Their Homeland and in the Netherlands." In *One Way Ticket: Migration and Female Labour*. Edited by Annie Phizacklea. London: Routledge and Kegan Paul, 1983.

Browner, Carole, and Ellen Lewin. "Female Altruism Reconsidered: The Virgin Mary as Economic Woman." *American Ethnologist* 9, no. 1 (February 1982): 61-75.

Cainkar, Louise. "Life Experiences of Palestinian Women in the United States." Paper presented at Middle East Studies Association, New Orleans, 1985.

——. "Coping With Tradition, Change and Alienation: Palestinian Women in the United States." Ph.D. dissertation, Northwestern University, 1988.

Canada. Department of Manpower and Immigration. *A Report on the Canadian Immigration and Population Study Immigration Pro-*

*gram.* Green Paper on Immigration. Ottawa: Information Canada, 1974.

*Canadian Institute of Public Opinion.* Ottawa, 1974.

Clifford, James and George E. Marcus. *Writing Culture: The Poetics and Politics of Ethnography.* Berkeley, California: University of California Press, 1986.

Confrey, J. "Conceptual Change, Number Concepts and the Introduction to Calculus." Ph.D. dissertation, Cornell University, 1980.

Coulson, N.J. *A History of Islamic Law.* Edinburgh University Press, 1978.

Cox, D.R. *Religion and Welfare: A Study of the Role of Religion in the Provision of Welfare Services to Selected Groups of Immigrants in Melbourne, Australia.* Melbourne: Department of Social Studies, University of Melbourne, 1982.

Cuber, John F. "Alternate Models from the Perspective of Sociology." In *The Family in Search of a Future: Alternate Models for Moderns.* Edited by Herbert A. Otto, pp. 11-23. New York: Appleton-Century-Crofts, 1970.

Cumming, Elaine. "Further Thoughts on the Theory of Disengagement." In *Aging in America: Readings in Social Gerontology,* Edited by C. Kart and B. Manard, pp. 19-24. Port Washington, N.Y.: Alfred, 1976.

Cumming, Elaine, and William F. Henry. *Growing Old: The Process of Disengagement.* New York: Basic Books, 1961.

Davie, Maurice R. "American Immigration and Its European Sources and Patterns." In *American Minorities: A Textbook of Readings in Intergroup Relations.* Edited by Milton Barron, pp. 229-38. New York: Knopf, 1957.

D'Antonio, William V., et al. "Religion and Family Life: How Social Scientists View the Relationship." *Journal for the Scientific Study of Religion* 21, no. 3 (September 1982): 218-25.

D'Antonio, William V. "The Family and Religion: Exploring a Changing Relationship." *Journal for the Scientific Study of Religion* 19, no. 2. (June 1980): 89-104.

—— and Joan Aldous. *Families and Religions: Conflict and Change in Modern Society.* Beverly Hills: Sage, 1983.

Demerath, N.J., and V. Theissen. "On Spitting against the Wind: Organizational Precariousness and American Irreligion." In *The Sociology of Organizations: Basic Studies*. Edited by Oscar Grunsky and George A. Miller, pp. 240-47. New York: Free Press, 1970.

Desseaux, Jacques E. *Twenty Centuries of Ecumenism*. Trans. M.J. O'Connell. New York: Paulist Press, 1984.

de Vaus, David, and Ian McAllister. "Gender Differences in Religion: A Test of the Structural Location Theory." *American Sociological Review* 52, no. 4 (1987):472-81.

Dorsky, Susan. *Women of 'Amran*. Salt Lake City: University of Utah Press, 1980.

Douglas, Martin. "Saudi Banks for Women Thriving," *New York Times*, January 27, 1982, Section 4, pp. 1 and 33.

DuBois, W.E.B. *The Negro American Family*. Atlanta: Atlanta University, 1909.

Dwyer, Daisy Hilse. "Ideologies of Sexual Inequality and Strategies for Change in Male-Female Relations." *American Ethnologist*. 5, no. 2 (1978):227-40.

Edwards, Harry. "Black Muslim and Negro Christian Relationships." *Journal of Marriage and the Family* 20, no. 4 (November 1968):604-11.

El-Amin, M. "Family Life." *Muslim Journal* 10, no. 35 (June 28, 1985):9.

———. "Family Life." *Muslim Journal* 10, no. 50 (Oct. 11, 1985):9.

———. "Family Life." *Muslim Journal* 11, no. 1 (Nov. 2, 1985):9.

———. "Family Life." *Muslim Journal* 10, no. 47 (Sept. 20, 1985):9.

———. "Family Life." *Muslim Journal* 11, no. 5 (Nov. 29, 1985):9.

El-Amin, Nafissa Ahmad. "Sudan: Education and Family." In *Change and the Muslim World*. Edited by Phillip Stoddard, D. Cuthell, and M. Sullivan, pp. 87-94.

El-Awa, Mohamed S. *Punishment in Islamic Law: A Comparative Study*. Indianapolis: American Trust Publications, 1982.

Elkholy, Abdo. *The Arab Moslems in the United States: Religion and Assimilation*. New Haven: College and University Press, 1966.

———. "The Arab Americans: Nationalism and Tradition Preservations." In *The Arab Americans*. Edited by Elaine C. Hagopian and Ann Paden, pp. 3-36. Wilmette, Ill.: Medina University Press, 1969.

——. "Evolution of the Moslem Family in North America." Paper presented at the Dimensions of Islam in North America, Symposium, Edmonton, University of Alberta, 29-31 May 1980.

Elkin, Frederick. "The English-Canadian Family." In *The Family in Various Cultures*. Edited by S. Queen, R. Habenstein and J. Quadagno, pp. 335-45. New York: Harper and Row, 1985.

*Encyclopedia of the American Religious Experience: Studies of Traditions and Movements*. Edited by Charles H. Lippy and Peter W. Williams. New York: Scribner, 1988.

*Encyclopedia of Islam Hadith*. Houtsma, M. Th. et al. Vol. 4. Leiden: E.J. Brill, 1913-38.

*Encyclopedia of Islam*. New Edition. Vols. 2 and 3. Leiden: E.J. Brill, 1971.

Esposito, John L. "Law in Islam." In *The Islamic Impact*. Edited by Y. Haddad, B. Haines, and E. Findly, pp. 68-69. Syracuse: Syracuse University Press, 1984.

——. "Muslim Family Law in Egypt and Pakistan: A Critical Analysis of Legal Reform, Its Sources and Methodological Problems." Ph.D. dissertation, Temple University, 1974.

Essien-Udom, E.U. *Black Nationalism: A Search for Identity in America*. Chicago: University of Chicago Press, 1962.

Fakhouri, Hani. *Kafr El-Elow: An Egyptian Village in Transition*. New York: Holt, Rinehart and Winston, 1972.

Fardan, Dorothy B. *Understanding Self and Society: An Islamic Perspective*. New York: Philosophical Library, 1981.

Farghani, Iman Fakhruddin Hasson Bin Mansur al-Uzjandi, commonly known as Kazee Khan. Trans. M.M.Y.K. Bahadur. M.W. Hussain Publishing Co., Lahore, Pakistan, 1977. References in text as Fatawa.

Faris, Hani A. "Heritage and Ideologies in Contemporary Arab Thought: Contrasting Views of Change and Development." In *The Arab World: Dynamics of Development*. Edited by B. Abu-Laban and S.M. Abu-Laban, pp. 89-103. Leiden: E.J. Brill, 1986.

Farsoun, Samih. "Family Structure and Society in Modern Lebanon." In *Peoples and Cultures of the Middle East*. Edited by L. Sweet. Garden City, N.Y.: Natural History Press, 1973.

Frazier, Edward F. *The Negro Family in Chicago*. Chicago: The University of Chicago Press, 1934.

———. *The Negro Family in the United States*. Chicago: The University of Chicago Press, 1939.

Friedl, Ernestine. *Women and Men: An Anthropologist's View*. New York: Holt, Rinehart and Winston, 1975.

Fuller, Anne H. *Buarij: Portrait of a Lebanese Muslim Village*. Cambridge, Mass.: Harvard University Press, 1961.

———. "The World of Kin." In *Readings in Arab Middle Eastern Societies and Cultures*. Edited by Abdulla M. Lutfiyya and Charles W. Churchill, pp. 526-34. The Hague: Mouton, 1970.

Fyzee, Asaf A.A. *Outlines of Mahammedan Law*. New Delhi: Oxford University Press, 1949. Reprint 1974.

Gee, Ellen M. Thomas. "Comment on: 'An Extended Family Model from Islamic Culture.'" *Journal of Comparative Family Studies* 2, no. 2 (Spring 1980): 265-67.

Geertz, Clifford. *The Interpretation of Cultures*. New York: Basic Books, 1973.

Ghalem, Ali. *A Wife for My Son*. Trans. G. Kaziolas. Chicago: Banner Press, 1984.

Ghayur, M. Arif. "Muslims in the United States: Settlers and Visitors." *Annals of the American Academy of Political and Social Science* 454 (March 1981): 150-63.

———. "Estimating Muslim Population in North America." Paper presented in the 9th Annual Conference of Association of Muslim Social Scientists, Indianapolis, 1981.

Gibb, H.A.R. *Modern Trends in Islam*. Chicago: University of Chicago Press, 1947.

Glasser, Paul H., and Lois N. Glasser, eds. *Families in Crisis*. New York: Harper and Row, 1970.

Glazer, Nathan, ed. *Clamor at the Gates: The New American Immigration*. San Francisco: ICS Press, 1985.

Glazer, Nathan, and Daniel R. Moynihan. *Beyond the Melting Pot: The Negroes, Puerto Ricans, Jews, Italians and Irish of New York City*. Cambridge: Mass.: MIT Press, 1970.

Goiten, Solomon D. *Jews and Arabs: Their Contacts through the Ages*. New York: Schocken, 1955.

Gold, G.L. "Some Comments on Ethnicity in Canada." In *Ethnicity in the Americas.* Edited by Frances Henry. pp. 408-12. The Hague: Mouton, 1976.

Gonzales, Nancie. "Family Organization in Five Types of Migratory Wage Labor." *American Anthropologist* 63 (1961):1264-80.

Goode, William J. *The Family.* New York: Free Press, 1963.

Gordon, Milton. *Assimilation in American Life: The Role of Race, Religion and National Origins.* New York: Oxford University Press, 1970.

Haddad, Safia. "The Woman's Role in Socialization of Syrian-Americans in Chicago." In *Arab-Americans: Studies in Assimilation.* Edited by Elaine C. Hagopian and Ann Paden. pp. 84-101. Wilmette, Ill.: Medina University Press, 1969.

Haddad, Yvonne Yazbeck. "The Muslim Experience in the United States." *The Link* 2, no. 4 (November 1979):1-3.

——. "Muslims in Canada: A Preliminary Study." In *Religion and Ethnicity.* Edited by Harold Coward and Leslie Kawamura, pp.71-100. Waterloo: Wilfrid Laurier University Press, 1978.

——. "Arab Muslims and Islamic Institutions in America: Adaption and Reform." In *Arabs in the New World: Studies on Arab-American Communities.* Edited by Sameer Abraham and Nabeel Abraham, pp. 64-81. Detroit: Wayne State University, Center for Urban Studies 1983.

——. "Islam, Women and Revolution in Twentieth-Century Arab Thought." In *Women, Religion and Social Change.* Edited by Yvonne Haddad and Ellison Findly, pp. 275-306. Albany: State University of New York, 1985.

——, Byron Haines and Ellison Findly, eds. *The Islamic Impact.* Syracuse: Syracuse University Press, 1984.

Haddad, Yvonne Yazbeck and Adair T. Lummis. *Islamic Values in the United States*, New York: Oxford University Press, 1987.

Haley, Alex. *Roots.* Garden City, N.Y.: Doubleday, 1976.

Hannerz, Ulf. "Some Comments on the Anthropology of Ethnicity in the United States." In *Ethnicity in the Americas.* Edited by F. Henry, pp. 433-36. The Hague: Mouton, 1976.

Hansen, Marcus Lee. "The Third Generation in America." *Commentary* 14 (November 1952):492-500.

Hargrove, Barbara. *Reformation of the Holy: A Sociology of Religion.* Philadelphia: F.A. Davis, 1971.

——. *The Sociology of Religion: Classical and Contemporary Approaches.* Arlington Heights, Ill.: AHM Publishing Corporation, 1979.

——. *Family in the White American Protestant Experience.* In *Families and Religions: Conflict and Change in Modern Society.* Edited by William V. D'Antonio and Joan Aldous, pp. 113-40. Beverly Hills: Sage, 1983.

Harrison, Algea, Felicisma Serafice, and Harriet McAdoo. "Ethnic Families of Color." *Review of Child Development Research* 7 (1984):329-71.

*Harvard Encyclopedia of American Ethnic Groups.* Edited by Stephen Thernstrom. Cambridge, Mass.: Belknap, 1980.

Havighurst, R.J. "Successful Aging." In *Process of Aging.* Edited by R. Williams, C. Tibbitts, and W. Donahue. New York: Atherton Press, 1963.

Haykal, Muhammad Husayn. *The Life of Muhammad.* Trans. by Ismail R.A. al-Faruqi. Plainfield, Ind.: American Trust Publications, 1976.

Heaton, Tim B., and Kirsten L. Goodman. "Religion and Family Formation." *Review of Religious Research* 26, no. 4 (June 1985): 343-59.

Helm, Hugh, and Joseph Novak, eds. *Proceedings of the International Seminar: Misconceptions in Science and Mathematics.* Ithaca: Cornell University Press, 1983.

Herberg, Will. *Protestant, Catholic Jew: An Essay In American Religious Sociology.* Garden City, N.Y.: Doubleday, 1955.

Hewson, P.W. "A Conceptual Change Approach to Learning Science. *European Journal of Science Education,* 3, No. 4 (1982):383-96.

Higham, John. "Current Trends in the Study of Ethnicity in the United States." In *Le facteur ethnique aux Etats-Unis et au Canada.* Edited by Monique Lecombe and Claudine Thomas, pp. 17-25. Lille: PUL, 1983.

Hill, Robert B. *The Strength of Black Families.* New York: Emerson Hall, 1971.

Hodgson, Marshall. *The Venture of Islam: Consciences and History in a World Civilization.* Chicago: University of Chicago Press, 1974, 1:57-60.

Hudson, Michael C. "The Ethnoreligious Dimension of the Lebanese

Civil War." *Journal of South Asian and Middle Eastern Studies* 1, no. 3 (1978): pp. 39-45.

Humphrey, Hubert H., Jr. "The Stranger at Our Gate." In *American Minorities: A Textbook of Readings in Intergroup Relations.* Edited by Milton L. Barron, pp. 240-60. New York: Knopf, 1957.

Hunt, Richard, and Morton B. King. "Religiosity and Marriage." *Journal for the Scientific Study of Religion* 17, no. 4 (December 1978): 399-406.

Iqbal, Sir Muhammad. *The Reconstruction of Religious Thought in Islam.* Lahore, India: Muhammad Ashraf Publishers, reprinted 1962.

Isajiw, Wsevolod. "The Process of Maintenance of Ethnic Identity: The Canadian Context." In *Sounds Canadian: Languages and Cultures in Multi-Ethnic Society.* Edited by Paul Migus, pp. 22-30. Toronto: Peter Martin Associates, 1975.

———. "Definitions of Ethnicity." *Ethnicity* 1, no. 1 (1974):1-12. Reprinted in *Ethnicity and Ethnic Relations in Canada: A Book of Readings.* Edited by Rita M. Bienvenue and Jay E. Goldstein, pp. 5-17, 2d ed. Toronto: Butterworths, 1985.

Islam, Anwar. "The Family: An Islamic Perspective." In *The Guidance*, M.C.A./M.S.A. Newsletter. Edmonton: Muslim Students' Association, 1984.

Jackson, Jacquelyne Johnson. "Contemporary Relationships between Black Families and Black Churches in the United States: A Speculative Inquiry." In *Families and Religions: Conflict and Change in Modern Society.* Edited by William V. D'Antonio and Joan Aldous, pp. 191-220. Beverly Hills: Sage, 1983.

Jeffery, Arthur. "The Family in Islam." *The Family: Its Function and Destiny.* Edited by Ruth Nanda Anshen, pp. 201-38. New York: Harper and Row, 1959.

Jones, Donald G. "Civil and Public Religion." *The Encyclopedia of Religious Experience in America.* Edited by Charles H. Lippy and Peter W. Williams, pp. 1393-1408. New York: Scribner, 1987.

Joseph, Suad. "Women in the Neighborhood Street in Borj Hammound, Lebanon." In *Women in the Muslim World.* Edited by L. Beck and N. Keddie, pp. 541-57. Cambridge, Mass.: Harvard University Press, 1978.

Kalbach, Warren E. *The Impact of Immigration on Canada's Population.* Ottawa: Dominion Bureau of Statistics, 1970.

Kenkel, William F., Joyce Himmler, and Leonard Cole. "Religious Socialization, Present Devoutness and Willingness to Enter a Mixed Religious Marriage." *Sociological Analysis* 26, no. 1 (Spring 1965): 30-37.

Kenny, L.M. "The Middle East in Canadian Social Science Textbooks." In *Arabs in America: Myths and Realties.* Edited by B. Abu-Laban and F. Zeadey, pp. 133-48. Wilmette, Ill.: Medina University Press, 1975.

Khafagy, Fatma. "Women and Labor Migration: One Village in Egypt." *MERIP Reports No. 124* 14, no. 5 (June 1984): 17-21.

Khalidi, Omar. "Urdu Language and the Future of Muslim Identity in India." *Journal: Institute of Muslim Minority Affairs* 7, no. 2 (July 1986): 395-403.

Khan, Verity Saifullah, ed. *Minority Families in Britain: Support and Stress.* London: Macmillan, 1979.

Kiefer, Christie W. *Changing Cultures, Changing Lives: An Ethnographic Study of Three Generations of Japanese Americans.* San Francisco: Jossey-Bass, 1974.

Kiray, Mubeccel. "The Family of the Immigrant Worker." In *Turkish Workers in Europe, 1960-1975: A Socio-economic Reappraisal.* Edited by N. Abadan-Unat, et al. Leiden: E.J. Brill, 1976.

Kirk, Dubley. "Factors Affecting Muslim Natality." In *Family Planning and Population Programs: A Review of World Developments.* Edited by B. Berelson *et al.*, pp. 561-579. Chicago: University of Chicago Press, 1966.

Kokosalakis, N. *Ethnic Identity and Religion.* Washington, D.C.: University Press of America, 1982.

Korson, J. Henry. "Student Attitudes toward Mate Selection in a Muslim Society: Pakistan." *Journal of Marriage and the Family* 1 (February 1969): 153-65.

Kosack, Godula. "Migrant Women: The Move to Western Europe—A Step towards Emancipation?" *Race and Class* 17, no. 4 (Spring 1976): 369-79.

Kudat, Ayse. "Structural Change in the Migrant Turkish Family." In *Manpower Mobility across Cultural Boundaries: Social, Economic and Legal Aspects: The Case of Turkey and West Germany.* Edited by R.E. Krane, Leiden: E.J. Brill, 1975.

Kuhn, T. *The Structure of Scientific Revolutions.* Chicago, Illinois: University of Chicago Press, 1970.

Ladner, Joyce A. *Tomorrow's Tomorrow: The Black Woman.* Garden City, N.Y.: Doubleday, 1971.

Landis, Judson T., and Mary G. Landis. *Building a Successful Marriage.* 4th ed. Englewood Cliffs, N.J.: Prentice-Hall, 1963.

Lanfry, Jacques. "Islamic-Christian Dialogue: Approaches to the Obstacles." In *Christianity and Islam: The Struggling Dialogue.* Edited by Richard W. Rousseau, pp. 15-32. Scranton: Ridge Row, 1985.

Larsen, Lyle. and Walter Goltz. "Religious Participation and Marital Commitment." Unpublished paper, Edmonton: Department of Sociology, University of Alberta, 1987.

Lazar, P. "Asian Family and Society." In *The Family in Asia.* London: Allen and Unwin, 1979.

Lemon, B., V. Bengtson, and J. Peterson. "An Exploration of the Activity Theory of Aging: Activity Types and Life Satisfaction among In-Movers to a Retirement Community." In *Aging in America: Readings in Social Gerontology.* Edited by C.S. Kart and B.B. Manard, pp. 61-86. Port Washington, N.Y.: Alfred, 1976.

Lenski, Gerhard E. *The Religious Factor: A Sociological Study of Religion's Impact on Politics, Economics and Family Life.* Garden City, N.Y.: Doubleday, 1963.

Levy, Reuben. *The Social Structure of Islam.* Cambridge: Cambridge University Press, 1962.

Lin, Yih-Chyi Nina. "Educational Needs in Intergenerational Conflict: A Study of Immigrant Families in New York Chinatown." Ph.D. dissertation, Cornell University, 1978.

Lincoln, C. Eric. *The Black Muslims in America.* Rev. ed. Boston: Beacon Press, 1968.

Lipsky, George A. *Saudi Arabia: Its People, Its Society, Its Culture.* New Haven: Hraf Press, 1961.

Long, Charles H. *Significations: Signs, Symbols, and Images in the Interpretation of Religion.* Philadelphia: Fortress Press, 1986.

Lovell, Emily Kalled. "Islam in the United States: Past and Present." In *The Muslim Community in North America*. Edited by E. Waugh, B. Abu-Laban, and R. Qureshi, pp. 93-110. Edmonton: University of Alberta Press, 1983.

Luo, Wen H., and Yung-Mei Tsai. "Social Networking, Hardiness and Immigrant's Mental Health." *Journal of Health and Social Behavior* 27, no. 2 (June 1986): 133-49.

Lutfiyya, Abdulla M. *Baytin, A Jordanian Village: A Study of Social Institutions and Social Change in a Folk Community*. The Hague: Mouton, 1966.

Makdisi, Nadim. "The Moslems of America." *Christian Century* (26 August, 1959): 969-71.

Makhlouf, C. "Changing Veils: Women and Modernization." In *North Yemen*. Austin: University of Texas Press, 1978.

Mamiya, Lawrence H. "Minister Louis Farrakhan and the Final Call: Schism in the Muslim Movement." In *The Muslim Community in North America*. Edited by E. Waugh, B. Abu-Laban, and R. Qureshi, pp. 234-55. Edmonton: University of Alberta Press, 1983.

Mandel, Eli. "The Border League: American 'West' and Canadian 'Region'." In *Crossing Frontiers*. Edited by Dick Harrison, pp. 105-21.

Marciano, Teresa Donti. "Families and Religions." In *Handbook of Marriage and the Family*. Edited by Marvin B. Sussman and Suzanne K. Steinmetz, pp. 285-315. New York: Plenum, 1987.

Marsh, Clifton E. *From Black Muslims to Muslims: The Transition from Separatism to Islam, 1930-1980*. Metuchen, N.J.: Scarecrow Press, 1984.

Martin, Richard C. "Symbol, Ritual, and Community: An Approach to Islam." In *Islam in the Modern World*, pp. 41-57. Edited by Jill Raitt. Columbia, Mo.: St. Louis University, Department of Religious Studies, 1983.

Maududi, Abul Ala. *Understanding Islam*. Lahore: Ashraf, 1970.

McAdoo, Harriette, ed. *Black Families*. Beverly Hills: Sage, 1981.

McCubbin, Hamilton I. "Integrating Coping Behavior in Family Stress Theory." *Journal of Marriage and the Family* 41, no. 2 (May 1979): 237-44.

McGoldrick, Monica. "Ethnicity and Family Therapy: An Overview." In *Ethnicity and Family Therapy*. Edited by M. McGoldrick, J. Pearce, and J. Giordano, pp. 5-20. New York: Guilford Press, 1982.

McVey, Wayne W., Jr. "Population Dynamics." In *An Introduction to Sociology*. New York: Guilford Press.

Mead, Margaret. *Sex and Temperament in Three Primitive Societies*. New York: Morrow, 1935.

Mernissi, Fatima. *Beyond the Veil: Male-Female Dynamics in a Modern Muslim Society*. New York: Schenkman, 1975.

Mindel, Charles H., and Robert W. Habenstein, eds. *Ethnic Families in America: Patterns and Variations*. 4th ed. North Holland, N.Y.: Elsevier, 1983.

Mirdal, Gretty M. "Stress and Distress in Migration: Problems and Resources of Turkish Women in Denmark." *International Migration Review* 18, no. 4 (Winter 1984): 984-1003.

*Mishkat al Masabih*. Trans. Dr. James Robson, Vol. 1. Lahore: Ashraf, 1975. Reprinted 1981.

Moore, R. Laurence. *Religious Outsiders and the Making of Americans*. New York: Oxford University Press, 1986.

Morokvasic, Mirjana. "Birds of Passage Are Also Women...." *International Migration Review* 18, no. 4 (Winter 1984): 886-907.

Mowoe, Isaac James. "The Church, the State, and the First Amendment: Permeable Walls and Constitutional Doctrines." *Papers in Comparative Studies* 3 (1982): pp. 99, 100.

Moynihan, D.P. *The Negro Family: The Case for National Action*. Washington, D.C.: U.S. Department of Labor Office of Planning and Research, March 1965.

Muhamad, Akbar. "Muslims in the United States: An Overview of Organizations, Doctrines and Problems." In *The Islamic Impact*. Edited by Y. Haddad, B. Haines, and E. Findly, pp. 210-40. Syracuse: Syracuse University Press, 1984.

Muhammad, Elijah. *Message to the Black Man*. Chicago: Muhammad's Mosque of Islam No. 2, 1965.

Muhammad, Nuri. "The Muslim Woman's Dress." *Muslim Journal* 11, no. 17 (Feb. 21, 1986):6.

—. "Polygamy: An Islamic Perspective." *Muslim Journal* 11, no. 20 (1986):6-7.

Muhammad, W.D. "Responsibilities of the Muslim Male." *Muslim Journal*, 11, no. 11 (Jan. 10, 1986).

Mullins, Mark R. "The Organizational Dilemmas of Ethnic Churches: A Case-Study of Japanese Buddhism in Canada." Paper given at the Learned Societies, McMaster University, Hamilton, Ontario, June 1987.

Munscher, Alice. "The Working Routine of Turkish Women in the Federal Republic of Germany: Results of a Pilot Survey." *International Migration Review* 18, no. 4 (Winter 1984): 1230-46.

Murdock, George P. *Social Structure*. New York: Macmillan 1949.

Murphy, Robert, and L. Kasdan. "The Structure of Parallel Cousin Marriage." *American Anthropologist* 61 (1959): 17-29.

Myntti, Cynthia. "Yemeni Workers Abroad: The Impact on Women." *MERIP Reports 124* 14, no. 5 (June 1984): 11-16.

Nadui, Abul Hasan Ali. *The Musalman: Social Life, Beliefs and Customs of the Indian Muslims*. Lucknow: Academy of Islamic Research and Publications, 1972.

Naff, Alixa. *Becoming American: The Early Arab Immigrant Experience*. Carbondale: Southern Illinois University Press, 1985.

Nanji, Azim. "The Nizari Ismaili Muslim Community in North America Background and Development." In *The Muslim Community in North America*. Edited by E. Waugh, B. Abu-Laban, and R. Qureshi, pp. 149-64. Edmonton: University of Alberta Press, 1983.

——. "The Ismaili Muslim Identity and Changing Contexts." In *Identity Issues and World Religions*. Edited by V. Hayes. pp. 119-24. Adelaide: Australian Association for the Study of Religions, 1986.

Nassal, Laila. "The Role of Shame in Societal Transformation among Palestinian Women on the West Bank." Ph.D. disseration, University of Pennsylvania, 1984.

Nelson, Cynthia. "Changing Roles of Men and Women: Illustrations from Egypt." *Anthropological Quarterly* 41, no. 2 (April 1968): 57-77.

——. "Public and Private Politics: Women in the Middle Eastern World." *American Ethnologist* 1 (1974):551-63.

Nimkoff, Meyer, ed. *Comparative Family Systems*. Boston: Houghton Mifflin, 1965

Nobles, Wade W. "Africanity: Its Role in Black Families." *The Black Scholar* 5, no. 9 (June 1974): 10-17.

——. *A Formulative and Empirical Study of Black Families*. Washington, D.C.: U.S. Department of Health, Education and Welfare, 1976.

——. "African Philosophy: Foundations for Black Psychology." In *Black Psychology*. Edited by Reginald Jones. New York: Harper and Row, 1972.

Noldeke. *Geschichte des Quran*. Vol. 2. 2d ed. Leipzig: Dieterich, 1909.

Nyang, Syleman S. "Muslims in North American A Historical Analy sis." Paper presented to the first Hijra Seminar, Plainfield, Indiana, 1983.

Nye, F. Ivan, and Felix M. Berardo. *The Family: Its Structure and Interaction*. New York: Macmillan, 1973.

Omar, Karima. "Dissenting Initiative: A Response to Fatima Mernissi," *Islamic Horizons* (October 1985), p. 14.

Omar, K. "Condemnation of Muslim Feminist." *Muslim Journal* 11, no. 16 (1986):13.

Ortner, Sherry. "Is Female to Male as Nature Is to Culture?" In *Woman, Culture and Society*. Edited by Michelle Rosaldo and Louise Lamphere. pp. 67-87, Stanford: Stanford University Press, 1974.

Osako, Masako M., and W.T. Lee "Intergenerational Relations and the Aged among Japanese Americans." *Research on Aging* 8, no. 1 (March 1986): 128-55.

Palmer, Howard, and Tamara Palmer. *Peoples of Alberta: Portraits of Diversity*. Saskatoon: Western Producer Prairie Books, 1985.

Papanek, Hanna. "Purdah in Pakistan: Seclusion and Modern Occupations for Women." *Journal of Marriage and the Family* 3 (August 1971): 517-30.

——. "Purdah: Separate Worlds and Symbolic Shelter." *Comparative Studies in Society and History* 15, no. 3 (June 1973): 289-325.

Parsons, Talcott. "The Kinship System of the Contemporary United States." *American Anthropologist* 45, no. 1 (January-March 1943): 22-38.

——. "The Normal American Family." *Man and Civilization: The Fam-

*ily's Search for Survival*. Edited by Seymour M. Farber, Piero Mustacchi, and Roger H.L. Wilson. New York: McGraw-Hill, 1965.

Patai, Raphael. *Golden River to Golden Road: Society, Culture and Change in the Middle East*. Philadelphia: University of Pennsylvania, 1962, 1969.

Pelikan, Jaroslav. *The Vindication of Tradition*. New Haven: Yale University Press, 1984.

Phizacklea, Annie, ed. *One Way Ticket: Migration and Female Labour*. London: Routledge and Kegan Paul, 1983.

Picard, Elizabeth. "Political Identities and Communal Identities: Shifting Mobilization among the Lebanese Shiʿa through Ten Years of War, 1975-1985." In *Ethnicity, Politics and Development*. Edited by Dennis L. Thompson and Dov Ronen, pp. 159-78. Boulder, Colo.: L. Rienner, 1986.

Pickthall, Marmaduke. *The Glorious Quran, Text and Explanatory Translation*. New Delhi: Taj Company, 1983. Reprint.

Pinkele, Carl, and Adamantia Pollis, eds. *The Contemporary Mediterranean World*. New York: Praeger. 1984.

Piscatori, James P. *Islam in a World of Nation-States*. New York: Cambridge University Press, 1986.

Posner, Geroge J. "A Model of Conceptual Change." *Proceedings of the International Seminar on Misconceptions in Science and Mathematics*. Edited by H. Helm and J. Novak. Ithaca, New York: Department of Education, Cornell University, 1983.

Prothro, Edwin T., and Lutfy N. Diab. *Changing Family Patterns in the Arab East*. Beirut: American University, 1974.

Queen, Stuart A., R.W. Habenstein, and J.S. Quadagno, eds. *The Family in Various Cultures*. 5th ed. New York: Harper and Row, 1985.

Rack, P. *Race, Culture and Mental Disorder*. London: Tavistock, 1982.

Rahman, Fazlur. "A Survey of Modernization of Muslim Family Law." *International Journal of Middle East Studies* 11, no. 4 (1980):451-65.

——. "Approaches to Islam in Religious Studies: Review Essay," in *Approaches to Islam in Religious Studies*, Richard C. Martin (ed.) Tucson: University of Arizona Press, 1986.

Rashid, A. *The Muslim Canadians, A Profile*. Ottawa: Statistics Canada, 1985.

Rassam, Amal. "Towards a Theoretical Framework for the Study of Women in the Arab World." *Cultures* 8, no. 3 (1982): 121-37.

Reiss, Paul J. "The Extended Kinship System: Correlates of and Attitudes on Frequency of Interaction." *Marriage and Family Living* 4 (November 1962): 333-39.

Rey, B. "Activity and Disengagement: Theoretical Orientations in Social Gerontology and Minority Aging." In *Minority Aging: Sociological and Social Psychological Issues*. Edited by Ron C. Manuel, pp. 191-94. Westport, Conn.: Greenwood Press, 1982.

Riesman, David. *Individualism Reconsidered*. Glencoe, Illinois: Free Press, 1954.

Roberts, Robert. *The Social Laws of the Quran*. London: Curzon Press, 1925. New edition, 1971.

Robertson-Smith, W. *Kinship and Marriage in Early Arabia*. Boston: Beacon Press. First pub. A & C Black, 1903.

Rodinson, Maxime. *Mohammed*. Trans. Anned Carter. London: Penguin, 1983.

Rosaldo, Michelle. "Woman, Culture, and Society: A Theoretical Overview." In *Woman, Culture and Society*. Edited by Louise Lamphere and Michelle Rosaldo. Stanford: Stanford University Press, 1974.

Rose, Peter I. "Asian Americans: From Pariahs to Paragons." In *Clamor at the Gates: The New American Immigration*. Edited by Nathan Glazer. San Francisco: ICS Press, 1985.

Ross-Sheriff, F. "Cultural Conflicts Experienced by Indo-Pakistani Muslim Youth in North America." Paper presented at the annual meeting of the Asian American Psychological Association, Los Angeles, California. August, 1985.

Runciman, Steven. *A History of the Crusades*. 3 vols. Cambridge: Cambridge University Press, 1951-54.

Rutledge, Paul. *The Role of Religion in Ethnic Self-Identity: A Vietnamese Community*. New York: University Press of America, 1985.

Saadawi, El-Nawal. *The Hidden Face of Eve: Women in the Arab World*. Boston: Beacon Press, 1980.

Sachedina, Abdul-aziz. *Islamic Messianism: The Idea of Mahdi in Twelver Shi'ism.* Albany: State University of New York, 1981.

*Sahih al-Bukhari.* Trans. M.M. Khan. 5th rev. ed. New Delhi: Kitah Bhana, 1984.

*Sahih al-Bukhari.* Vol. 3. Trans. M.M. Khan. 5th rev. ed. New Delhi: Kitab Bhavan 1984.

*Sahih Muslim.* Trans. Abdul Hamid Siddiqi. New Delhi: Kitab Bhavan, 1984.

Said, Edward W. *Orientalism.* New York: Pantheon, 1978.

——. *Covering Islam: How the Media and the Experts Determine How We See the Rest of the World.* New York: Pantheon, 1981.

Saleh, Saneya. "Women in Islam: Their Status in Religious and Traditional Culture." *International Journal of Sociology of the Family* 2, no. 1 (March 1972): 35-42.

Schacht, Joseph. *An Introduction to Islamic Law.* Oxford: Clarendon, 1964.

Schelsky, Helmut. "The Family in Germany." *Marriage and Family Living* 4 (November 1954): 331-35.

Scott, F.R. *Selected Poems.* Toronto: Oxford University Press, 1966.

Seller, Maxine Schwartz, ed. *Immigrant Women.* Philadelphia: Temple University Press, 1981.

Shabazz, A. "Women Have a Right to Attend the Masjid." *Muslim Journal* 10, no. 42 (1985):7.

Shils, Edward. *Tradition.* Chicago: University of Chicago Press, 1981.

Shukri, Ahmad. *Muhammedan Law of Marriage and Divorce.* New York: AMS Press, 1966. First published 1917.

Sigelman, Lee. "Review of the Polls: Multi-Nation Surveys of Religious Beliefs." *Journal for the Scientific Study of Religion* 16, no. 3 (September 1977): 289-94.

Simpson, George E., and J. Milton Yinger. *Racial and Cultural Minorities: An Analysis of Prejudice and Discrimination.* 4th ed. New York: Harper and Row, 1972.

Smith, Jane I. "The Experience of Muslim Women: Considerations of Power and Authority." In *The Islamic Impact.* Edited by Y. Haddad, B. Haines, and E. Findly, pp. 89-112. Syracuse: Syracuse University Press, 1984.

Smith, Wilfred Cantwell. *The Meaning and End of Religion.* New York: New American Library, 1963.

——. *Islam in Modern History*. Princeton: Princeton University Press, 1957.

——. *Modern Islam in India, a Social Analysis*. London, Lahore: Sh. Muhammad Ashraf Kashmiri Bezar, 1946.

Sorokin, Pitirim A. *Social and Cultural Dynamics*. New York: American Book Company, 1941.

*Spectrum al-Ittihad* 16, nos. 1-2, 1979, p. 71.

Staples, Robert. *The Black Woman in America: Sex, Marriage and the Family*. Chicago: Nelson-Hall, 1973.

Statistics Canada. *Population-Ethnic Origin*. Catalogue 92-912, Vol. 1. Ottawa, 1981.

——. *Population-Religion*. Catalogue 92-912, Vol. 1, Ottawa, 1981

——. *Population-Language, Ethnic Origin, Religion, Place of Birth*. Catalogue 93-933, Vol. 2, Ottawa, 1981.

Stinnett, Nick, G. Sanders, J. DeFrain, and A. Pankhurst. "A Nationwide Study of Families Who Perceive Themselves as Strong." *Family Perspective* 16 (1982): 15-22.

Suleiman, Michael W. "The New Arab-American Community." In *The Arab-Americans: Studies in Assimilation*. Edited by Elaine C. Hagopian and Ann Paden, pp. 37-49. Wilmette, Ill.: Medina University Press, 1969.

——. "Perceptions of the Middle East in American Newsmagazines." In *Arabs in America: Myths and Realities*. Edited by B. Abu-Laban and F. Zeadey, pp. 28-44. Wilmette: Medina University Press, 1975.

Sussman, Marvin B. "The Isolated Nuclear Family: Fact or Fiction?" *Social Problems* 6, no. 4 (Spring 1959): 333-40.

Sussman, Marvin B. and Suzanne K. Steinmetz (eds.) *Handbook of Marriage and the Family*. New York: Plenum, 1987.

Swanson, Jon. *Emigration and Economic Development: The Case of the Yemen Arab Republic*. Boulder, Colo.: Westview Press, 1979.

Swierenga, Robert P. "Ethnicity in Historical Perspective." *Social Science*, 52, no. 1 (Winter 1977): 31-44.

Taylor, Elizabeth. "Egyptian Migration and Peasant Wives." *MERIP Reports 124* 14, no. 5 (June 1984): 3-10.

Thanwi, Maulana Ashraf Ali. *Heavenly Ornament (Bahishti Zewar)*. Trans. M.M.K. Saroha. Lahore: Ashraf, 1981, pp. 278-88.

Tomasi, Silvano. *Piety and Power: The Role of the Italian Parishes in the*

*New York Metropolitan Area.* Staten Island: Center for Migration Studies, 1975.

Toth, Anthony B. "On Arabs and Islam." *Washington Report on Middle Eastern Affairs* 5, no.7 (1986):15.

Tucker, Judith. *Women In Nineteenth Century Egypt.* Cambridge: Cambridge University Press, 1985.

Turner, Victor W. *Dramas, Fields and Metaphors: Symbolic Action in Human Society.* Ithaca: Cornell University Press, 1974.

——. *From Ritual to Theater: The Human Seriousness of Play.* New York: Performing Arts Journal Publications, 1982.

Van Sertima, Ivan. *They Came before Columbus: The African Presence in Ancient America.* New York: Random House, 1976.

Waldman, Marilyn R. "Women in the Islamic World." In *Women in Development. Seminar Proceedings, Spring 1982.* Edited by Erika Bourguignon and Francille H. Firebaugh, pp. 17-28. Columbus: Ohio State University, Department of Home Management and Housing, College of Home Economics, 1982.

——. "Islamic Resurgence in Context" in *The Contemporary Mediterranean World.* Edited by Carl Pinkele and Adamantia Pollis, pp. 98-123. New York: Praeger, 1984.

——. "Tradition as a Modality of Change: Islamic Examples" *History of Religions* 25, no. 4 (1986):318-40.

Wallerstein, Immanuel. "Social Conflict in Post-Independence Black Africa: The Concepts of Race and Status-Group Reconsidered." In *Racial Tensions and Natural Identity.* Edited by Ernest Q. Campbell. Nashville: 1972.

Wasfi, Atif A. *An Islamic-Lebanese Community in the U.S.A.: A Study in Cultural Anthropology.* Beirut: Beirut Arab University, 1971.

Watson, James L., ed. *Between Two Cultures: Migrants and Minorities in Britain.* Oxford: Blackwell, 1977.

Watt, W. Montgomery. *Muhammad at Medina.* Oxford: Clarendon Press, 1956.

Waugh, Earle H., B. Abu-Laban, and R. Qureshi (eds.), *The Muslim Community in North America.* Edmonton: University of Alberta Press, 1983.

Weeks, John R. *Population: An Introduction to Concepts and Issues.* Belmont, California: Wadsworth, 1987.

Weiner, Leo. *Africa and the Discovery of America*. 3 Vols. Philadelphia: Innes and Sons, 1922.

Weinfeld, Morton. "Myth and Reality in the Canadian Mosaic: 'Affective Ethnicity'." *Canadian Ethnic Studies* 13, no. 3 (1981): 80-100.

Whiteford, Michael B. "Women, Migration and Social Change: A Columbian Case Study." *International Migration Review* 12, no. 2 (Summer 1978): 236-47.

Wilson, John. *Religion in American Society: The Effective Presence*. Englewood Cliffs, N.J.: Prentice-Hall, 1978.

Winks, Robin W. *The Myth of the American Frontier: Its Relevance to America, Canada, and Australia*. Leicester: Leicester University Press, 1971.

Woodward, Kenneth L., and Phyllis Malamud. "The Parent Gap." *Newsweek*, 1975.

*World Almanac and Book of Facts*. New York: Newspaper Enterprise Association, 1984.

Yeo, Margaret E. The Living Landscape: Nature Imagery in the Poetry of Margaret Atwood and Other Canadian Lyric Poets. M.A. thesis, Carleton University, 1969.

Zimmerman, Carle C. *Family and Civilization*. New York: Harper and Row, 1947.

# Index

◆   ◆   ◆   ◆

A